D1617233

Exploring the Decolonial Imaginary

Four Transnational Lives

Patricia A. Schechter

First published in 2012 by
PALGRAVE MACMILLAN®
in the United States—a division of St. Martin's Press LLC,
175 Fifth Avenue, New York, NY 10010.

Where this book is distributed in the UK, Europe and the rest of the world,
this is by Palgrave Macmillan, a division of Macmillan Publishers Limited,
registered in England, company number 785998, of Houndmills, Basingstoke,
Hampshire RG21 6XS.

Palgrave Macmillan is the global academic imprint of the above companies
and has companies and representatives throughout the world.

Palgrave® and Macmillan® are registered trademarks in the United States,
the United Kingdom, Europe and other countries.

ISBN: 978–0–230–33877–7

Library of Congress Cataloging-in-Publication Datais available from the
Library of Congress.

A catalogue record of the book is available from the British Library.

Design by Newgen Imaging Systems (P) Ltd., Chennai, India.

First edition: January 2012

10 9 8 7 6 5 4 3 2 1

Printed in the United States of America.

This book is dedicated to three brainy, restless, and inspiring women:
Maria del Carmen Gomez Becerra, my mother
Filomena Perugia Scardaccione, my grandmother
Hinda Schechter, my great-grandmother

Contents

List of Previous Publications

Remembering the Power of Words: The Life of an Oregon Activist, Legislator and Community Leader, 2011. With Avel Louise Gordly.
Ida B. Wells-Barnett and American Reform, 1880–1930, 2001.

List of Previous Publications

Illustrations

Foreword

What does it mean to be a transnational person? The Palgrave Macmillan Transnational History Series has already published *Transnational Lives* (2009), containing sketches of 21 individuals whose lives spanned from the eighteenth century to the present and covered many parts of the globe. In this volume, the transnational lives, activities (in different parts of the world), and thoughts of four American women from the late nineteenth century to the first decades of the twentieth are examined in great detail and contribute enormously to examining the question.

All four women were transnational in the existential sense in that they refused to be identified by their nationality alone, but insisted on adding several other identities: race, gender, class, religion, and geography. These multiple identities informed their careers and their attitudes toward the nation and the world. "Transnational lives" is the most appropriate framework in which to understand these women's lives.

They were also individuals living in a world that was fast transnationalizing itself. The late nineteenth century and the early twentieth century were a period of rapid economic globalization and technological innovations, bringing all corners of the globe into closer contact. At the same time, as other volumes in the series have noted, the world had never been so rigidly divided—between colonizer and colonized, capital and labor, the white and other races, the West and the non-West, and not to mention the "great powers" and weaker states. The transnational transformation, then, took two forms, one tending toward the interconnectedness and unity of humankind, and the other toward separation and diversity. History, in a way, went on at two levels, creating cross-national networks of people, goods, and ideas while perpetuating national as well as non-national identities such as races, religions, and civilizations. This dual phenomenon is often understood in terms of the dichotomy between nationalism and internationalism. But neither term accommodates the infinite number of identities and entities that were not identifiable with nations. For this reason, historians, including the editors of this series as well as its contributors, have preferred to speak of transnational phenomena and themes as crucial developments in modern and contemporary history. To describe a world that was becoming at once more unified and more divided, we may speak of transnational unity and transnational diversity.

Whether these two dimensions of transnationalism would come together, or, on the contrary, remain separated was a key question of transnational history in the nineteenth and twentieth centuries. However we understand and examine the question, it is abundantly clear that a nation-centric study of the subject is entirely inadequate. Among the great merits of this book is that it shows how transnational individuals lived in a transnational world with all its promises and contradictions. They were all Americans, but their lives can only be understood in such a broad framework.

Having defined themselves as transnational, the four women, as the author notes, sought to transcend all boundaries, not just national but non-national as well. Sometimes they succeeded, and at other times they did less well. Theirs were lives in which given identities made much less sense than new ones that would be created, but in the process the new identities would encounter obstacles, coming not simply from narrow-minded nationalists but also from others who espoused a different sort of transnationalism. All in all, this is an extremely innovative, insightful study that enriches our understanding of one of the key developments in modern world history.

Akira Iriye
Rana Mitter

Acknowledgments

I incurred many debts during the decade that I spent researching and writing this book. It is with deepest appreciation that I thank the people and institutions that supported me along the way. I salute the group of amazing women historians who have shared their keen minds and good company with me for the past three years. Thanks, first and foremost, to Allison Sneider, and to Kim Brodkin, Jan Dilg, Jackie Dirks, Ivette M. Rivera-Giusti, Rachel Graham, Reiko Hillyer, Beth Hutchison, Jane Hunter, Kim Jensen, Maureen Reed, and Carmen Thompson. Next is my wonderful history department at Portland State University, especially chairs Linda Walton and Tom Luckett, who did everything they could to support my work. Several grants from PSU underwrote research and travel expenses. The excellent assistance of Lisa Donnelly over the last six months of work on this book was a lifesaver. Thank you!

Scholarship is built on the inspiration of example and in the generative energy of dialogue. I have been graced with both of these elements. My earliest draft chapters on Smith and Silva de Cintrón benefitted greatly from feedback at conference seminars: Trends in Transnational Feminism sponsored by the University of California at San Diego's Institute for Feminism and Democracy in 2002 and Latinas in the Americas at the Berkshire Conference of Women Historians in 2008. I am grateful for the comments I received from Breny Mendoza and especially Virginia Sánchez Korrol at those meetings. Claude Clegg's brilliant work on Liberia is foundational in the field, and his warm encouragement of my work has made all the difference in this phase of my career. Ian Tyrrell's guidance and affirmation at a key moment near the end of this project turned out to be a game changer. His invitation to the Rothermere American Institute's American Anti-Imperialism since 1776 conference at Oxford University in 2011 greatly sharpened my thinking, with additional thanks to participants Julian Go, Amy Kaplan, and Jay Sexton. Susan Wladaver-Morgan mentored me along the way, as did Annelise Orleck. Thomas Bender's very generous reading of a draft of the entire manuscript was a precious gift as were the careful appraisals of chapter 4 by Kevin Gaines and Yevette Richards Jordan. Thank you from the bottom of my heart! Sian Hunter believed in this book when it was just a glimmer in my eye. Absolutely everything connected with Palgrave Macmillan has been professional, friendly, and constructive. Thank you, thank you Chris Chappell, Sarah Whalen, my anonymous reviewers, and the production staff for the care and energy you poured into this book. I feel honored that Professor Aikra Iriye and Professor Rana Miller accepted this book for the Transnational History series.

It took a whole lot of library to cover the people and places described in the chapters of this book. I was consistently amazed at the cheerful responsiveness of librarians and archivists everywhere I went. Sherry Buchanan and Min Cedillo at PSU Interlibrary Loan were practically magicians. This project would have been impossible without them. For a book produced during a great recession, the library professionals who enabled long-distance research deserve very special appreciation: Christopher Harter of the Amistad Research Center, Patrizia Scione of the Kheel Center, David Easterbrook at the Herskovitz Library, Pedro Juan Hernandez at The Center for Puerto Rican Studies, and the experts at the National Archives and Records Administration, especially Katherine Vollen, who helped me with passports. It was a boon to meet Cheryl Beredo while trolling Record Group 350. I am thankful for the research assistance she provided, and I look forward to her new work on archives in the Philippines. Diana Carey at the Schlesinger Library and Graham Sherriff at the Beinecke Library were also extremely helpful with my on-site and long-distance research. So was Nicholas Siekerski at the Hoover Institute. It was a pleasure to travel to Indiana University to work in the Liberia Collection and meet Verlon Stone, who has done so much to make Liberia vital and visible in historical studies. I must thank the anonymous traveler who took pity on me when I got off the airplane in Bloomington, Illinois, and let me have her rental car—the last one to be had in that little airport on a Sunday night—so I could drive to the other Bloomington six hours away and salvage my research trip. The view of the cornfields was quite spectacular. Thank you to the New York Public Library, the Frances Willard House in Evanston, *Publisher's Weekly*, and the Library of Congress for help with images for this book, especially Stephan Saks at the NYPL. Special thanks to Mr. Vercelle King at the New York City Board of Elections Archive: someday we will find that voter registration book for the 17th Assembly District in Manhattan from 1936! Without the trust and enthusiasm of Vivian Taylor, telling the story of her grandmother Josefina Silva de Cintrón would have been greatly impoverished. Deep thanks to her and her father, Mr. Roberto Cintrón. Karen Blair of Eastern Washington University helped that connection happen, and I remain very much obliged. Lori Van Deman-Iseri did an excellent job on the index and proofreading.

Two people whose scholarship I admired from afar became warm friends during this project: Elizabeth S. Pryor and Magali Roy-Féquière. Their most excellent minds and most mischievous laughter kept me and this project going at key points. Eileen Boris and Lisa Materson published articles that made a light click on in unlit corners of my brain. I was very lucky to receive encouraging emails from Maria Damon and Priscilla Wald during my wrestling with Gertrude Stein. Priya Kandaswamy was always wonderful intellectual company and turned me on to the fabulous novel *The Book of Salt*. Thomas Dublin and Barbara Welter have been trusted mentors over many years and many miles. Thank you so much for your example, friendship, and professional support.

In and away from Oregon, friends and family cheered me on to get to the end of this project. Amy Lonetree was my favorite office mate and remains a dear friend and inspiration. The dazzling Kathy Moon fed, sheltered, and kept me grounded when I was in New England, as did my brother-in-law, Ham Fish, in New York City. Ted and Vicki Leavitt made me feel at home in their London flat. Mary Ann Fish kept her guest room ready for me for this round of research through Washington, DC, and area archives, just like she did for my dissertation and first book. Thank you! Christina Heuer took tender care of my children when I was away. So did Emma Nollette, who blesses me with her wisdom and friendship. Heather Thompson keeps my spirit stoked and my heart hopeful. Avel Gordly made me her sister and reminded me to breathe. *Gratitude! Gratitude!* And hear this Nick, Maria, Chapin, Alan, Karen, Alana, Kenneth, Jeffrey, and Joy: I was able to write this book because I love you and you love me.

Portland, Oregon
June 2011

Introduction

What Comes Transnationally

"There is no racial hatred," wrote José Martí in 1891, "because there are no races."[1] This study explores four women's resistance to racism and racialization in a nascent global anti-imperial field, a field that Martí helped to write into existence as he pondered the impact of that "formidable neighbor," the United States, on an ideal he called "*Nuestra America.*"[2] The chapters in this book map a related set of critiques of race and empire in Liberian missions, anglophone "new woman" literature, Pan-American feminism, and African labor organizing. Like Martí, my chosen representatives of these movements—Amanda Berry Smith, Gertrude Stein, Josefina Silva de Cintrón, and Maida Springer—worked against essentialist notions of race and were transnational figures who crossed the Caribbean and the Atlantic with crucial stops in New York City. Central to my analysis is their refusal to abide by the rules of racial boundary keeping alluded to in Martí's epigram, rules shaped by ideologies of "civilization" and "race advancement" that were current in his lifetime through World War II. Each woman in this study refused to elaborate or extend racial scripts in their lives and work, a refusal that compromised their ability to earn money, social status, or political currency in their own time and that has left them mostly obscured in our own.

This relative obscurity reflects the ways in which women have historically been most visible in the work of the modern nation: by elaborating the rules of race. From the laws and customs of marriage over which women had little direct control to their activities in missions, temperance, medicine, education, club work, and trade unionism, scholars have documented these undertakings to have been overwhelmingly segregated by skin color in the period 1865 to 1965.[3] The dismantling of the intellectual architecture of race in the United States is usually credited to mid-twentieth-century intellectuals like Boas, Mead, and Myrdal.[4] This study documents such efforts outside of academia or the law and in a transnational frame. I suggest that critiques not just of white supremacy but of race identity "itself" come most clearly into focus when placed in the context of US empire, the shadow of the "seven league giant!" that Martí agonized about. I argue in the following pages that when women refused to make race in their transnational missionary work, novel writing, feminist arts advocacy, or labor organizing, they met with obstacles that highlight how ideologies of nation and empire work together. In other words, the women in this study all challenged the alignment of race and nation in their lives, and their successes and shortfalls help us rethink boundaries often presumed stable, namely, where nations begin and end.

For some years now, historians of diverse interests have used the word "transnational" to track ideas and activities not strictly beholden to the nation-state for their logic, substance, and purpose. Given the strong traditions of statist and exceptionalist historiography in the United States, a transnational approach can put into relief the partial, negotiated, and, above all, contested nature of US cultural modernity and political economy.[5] In seeking out such contested domains, this study follows women writers and activists across national boundaries, tracing the currents of solidarity and attachment that their work fostered. That I describe mostly thwarted circuitries, unhearing audiences, and strangled affiliations makes their efforts no less revealing and instructive. Yet my point is not simply to rescue these figures from the margins of nationalistic domains of power or to point up margins qua margins. Rather, I try to make visible the connection between margins and centers—and the national and the transnational—and attend to this connection as a site of historic possibility and struggle. Each case study discloses a consistent pattern: women's refusal to perform racial boundary keeping (sometimes expressly designated "women's work") broke with the dominant idiom of the political within the nation, and such breaks created intense pressure for them to move.

Thus, the overarching theme of this transnational study is women's critical engagement with racialized categories and practices of national belonging, and how that engagement resulted in geographical and ideological repositioning in their lives. To give shape and meaning to their choices and movement, they reached for terms like "saint," "goddess," and "mother," archetypes whose power transcended nation and race.[6] The first pair of protagonists, Smith and Stein, were the most engrained in US Protestant culture, individualism, and patriotism. The Civil War and Reconstruction framed their personal sense of the nation, though the idea of legal citizenship so central to that era left them a bit underwhelmed. Instead, saint, virgin-mother, and goddess imagery opened more generative space for their talents and restlessness during a long nineteenth century in which marriage and reproduction were the paramount social roles for women. In the center pair of Stein and Silva de Cintrón, art figures as a liberatory practice whose power cannot be contained to the nation. For them, art and creativity addressed a range of social opportunities and exclusions via participatory performance, sales, general appreciation, its effect on "strangers" (as Stein put it), or by sewing and waving a flag like *La Bandera de la Raza* (in Silva de Cintrón's case) and seeing who notices, tears up, cheers, or starts marching. In the final pair of Silva de Cintrón and Springer, who both hailed from around the Caribbean, a warm child- and family-centered sensibility connects each woman to Pan-American feminism, whose signature maternalism struck a dominant note for the entire hemisphere during the first half of the twentieth century. I suggest that the word "transnational" better expresses these women's intellectual and social trajectories than words like "exile," "hybrid," or "expatriate" that are sometimes applied to them or their work.[7] I read their autobiographies, letters, speeches, novels, plays, banners, magazines, interviews, and social organizing as transnational signs of struggle under modes of rule that lead away from—though sometimes also toward—the nation-state. In so doing, fresh horizons for comparison around the politics of race are made visible across seemingly divergent domains of activity, linked by empire.

Reading for the transnational puts into relief the ideological work of the nation with its intensely racializing, subordinating, and hierarchizing pressures, pressures that often put women's bodies and behaviors on the line.[8] As the work of Ann McClintock and Ann Laura Stoler has vividly demonstrated, matters of race and sex have been "the boundary markers of empire," and their theorizations have enabled an explosion of scholarship sensitive to women, the body, affect, and sexuality—withal, the domain of the "intimate"—as important sites of imperial rule.[9] The anthology *Haunted by Empire: Geographies of Intimacy in North America* (2006) stands out in this literature. These essays interpret technologies of empire—like plantation manuals, the census, prostitution reform, labor contracts, child rescue and adoption, health regimes, and intelligence quotient (IQ) testing—as methods for producing, regulating, and deploying bodies in the far-flung yet intimate work of empire. A notable feature of this book, Linda Gordon notes, is its relative "silence" around issues of women and gender. Gender "hides itself so easily, standing so often behind racial and national and class conflicts," she observes, "allowing those more assertive squabblers the spotlight."[10] To redress such shortcomings, Laura Briggs has encouraged historians of women to at least try to "do something more, to trace the processes of subalternization," for example, "and ask how they have eviscerated the conditions of possibility in which certain subjectivities could be legible."[11] This study offers a contribution to such efforts. I give sustained attention to criticism of race, nation, and empire—however oblique—by women who were neither citizen-colonizers, nor, exactly, subalterns. Using the approaches of intellectual and social history, I respond to the need to situate women more precisely in global imperial and anti-imperial fields, as well as answer the recent call for "a fuller transnational history of ideas, one that deals with the lived experience of those ideas and also transcends the elite–subaltern divide."[12]

A transnational approach works for figures whose lives unsettle and exceed the usual categories historians use to capture women's tense relationship to empire and state. For example, the idea of "everyday resistance" or "weapons of the weak" used to characterize the oppositional practices of enslaved or subaltern women come up short where the literary, staged, or institutionalized activities like the ones I take up are concerned.[13] Older words from immigration studies like "assimilation" or "accommodation" have trouble capturing activities either carried out in intense solitude or projected onto sweeping hemispheric or transoceanic geographies. Nor are any of the women I examine fairly understood as a "native helper," figures who assisted, redirected, or reinterpreted colonial institutions like missions, schools, and hospitals in their own and their community's interest.[14] As readerly, creative types, they don't appear in the politically focused scholarship on women, citizenship, and empire, whose findings strike a dominant chord of feminist imperialism with a minor grace note of feminist anti-imperialism.[15] Yet, Stoler's concept of the "the intimate" doesn't quite catch their work either, as they made commitments, however fraught, to the public sphere and to naming the troubles— and maybe making a few of their own—at its sometimes fuzzy borders.

Within a transnational frame, then, what can be said about such efforts by women to mark and reconfigure the boundaries between race, nation, and empire? That is, what kind of politic can be found in the spaces and domains in which they worked? As Briggs has noted: "The 'post-colonial' is weird in the context of the Americas."[16] Historians still debate Martí's politics, given how his most famous, culminating essay cited above teeters, unresolved, between a confident hope in a new "natural man" in the hemisphere born to a special, unifying destiny and his fear of "the octopus" to the north that threatened fresh visions and identifications.[17] Following Briggs's encouragement and the lead of feminist theorist Emma Pérez, I describe the politic and sensibility I discovered in my research as "decolonial." Pérez defines the decolonial as comprising "different, fragmented, imagined, non-linear, non-teleological" domains outside the structuring orders of the state and its subordinating entailments. She labels as "decolonial" that which disrupts the dominant ordering schemas of modern society, especially the binaries of colonizer/subaltern and citizen/alien, identity pairings that usually map on to a white-black (or white/nonwhite) racialized social imaginary in the United States. In this theorizing, Pérez recuperates a "Third Space Feminism" pertinent to her writing of Chicana history.[18] Extending her paradigm, it seems to me that the decolonial can name resistance to racialized categories of state and empire for Smith, Stein, Silva de Cintrón, and Springer, women who never signed on to conventionally political anti-imperialist movements, but whose ideological stance and accomplishments only become fully visible in the context of US imperialism. As Pérez suggests, the decolonial can gather up evidence that does not share the provenance of either the "colonial" or the "post-colonial." The decolonial can specify a particular though by no means predictable politic mobilized in the spaces and flows of transnational social and intellectual formations, formations energized if not completely engineered by empire. The idea of the decolonial also helps reframe a lopsided and polarized historical landscape of invading—some ambivalently, some stridently—feminist imperialists and resistant nascent (counter)nationalists. It also enriches appraisals of the US intellectual milieu in which imperial categories remain muffled in the din of individualistic rights discourses and an engulfing idiom of republicanism, liberty, and freedom.

Though the word "decolonial" does not yet officially exist in the English language, feminist scholars, including Pérez, cite philosopher Gayatri Spivak when they use it.[19] Of Spivak's many generative insights, among the most widely cited concern the "othering" suppositions of the European episteme. "The question is how to keep the ethnocentric Subject from establishing itself by selectively defining the Other," she wrote in her highly influential article "Can the Subaltern Speak?" Spivak pointed the way for a generation of feminist scholars to identify this structuring reflex in the past as well as the present and thereby intervene in colonial knowledge formations.[20] Such critical approaches have helped recast patterns of historicization in scholarship toward a wider engagement with questions of empire and its many meanings for women, especially around issues of race and racism. As Marilyn Lake notes, the modern practice of academic history has been largely "the record of men's public work of nation-building," and she credits the "post-colonial critique of empire" with having "done much to break down the border controls of national historiographies."[21] As this book's title suggests, my search for the decolonial remains an exploration. In scouring state bureaucratic records for another fugitive domain, "the homosexual," Margaret Canaday notes: "Inchoate things can still be studied, however."[22] Like "the intimate"—or the subaltern, for that matter—the decolonial is not easily tracked, contained, or even identified. I saw no archival boxes marked "decolonial" in my research, nor did I expect to. Stoler's warning that "colonialism is not *a* story" also bears mentioning here as does the challenge of straying too far from state-centered concerns with citizenship. The stakes are high for breaking the "narrative contract" between modern history writing and the nation-state, a move that Thomas Bender likens to "sawing off the branch upon which we [historians] are sitting."[23]

In this scenario, a biographical focus can provide analytical and narrative traction for activities that are either more sweeping or more interstitial than the nation. I offer detailed and highly personal accounts of activities—like Amanda Smith's adoption of Liberian children or how members of the *Unión de Mujeres Americanas* baked, decorated, and served a cake at meetings emblazoned with their insignia *La Bandera de la Raza*—that constitute iconic yet everyday gestures by women working at the juncture of public and private life. I explore ideas as they are staged, enacted, and read in a range of public and semipublic settings, from world's fairs and parades to prayer meetings and literary salons. These scenarios provide a view into ideas-in-action and suggest something of the circulation and purchase of ideas in an array of transnational publics and reading markets. I offer portraits that can begin to be correlated to Amy Kaplan's brilliant mapping of the "colonial imaginary" in US law and letters.[24] My essays present episodic, slow pans across a number of transnational intellectual and social landscapes through the lens of the decolonial, less a "history" than a reading strategy. Amid complaints about "over worlding" and pressures to "explain everything," these life-scale studies humanize an agenda that threatens at moments to swamp the transnational project in scholarship.[25] And while challenging the national frame is a premise of this study, I also carefully document the ways in which national authorities enforced various borders and boundaries, archetypically in the case of passports. Much of the action in this book takes place outside the "lower 48" states of the United States, the conventional map of modern nationalist history, but many of the structuring incentives and potential audiences I describe inhabit national and quasi-national markets, namely, the anglophone Atlantic and the Spanish-speaking segments of the Americas. "Lives elude national boundaries," a new anthology on transnational biography reminds readers, and "to capture these fluid and contingent histories requires a more flexible scholarship."[26] A little mixing and matching, movement and stretching, is ahead for readers.

Chapter 1 focuses on the missionary tour of Amanda Berry Smith (1837–1915) in Liberia, Africa, in the 1880s. Born a slave in Maryland, her family bought their freedom and, shaped by the Protestant revivals of the 1840s and the later, post–Civil War decades, Smith embarked on a long career in evangelical Methodism. Through her letters and autobiography, I map the contours of her universalist worldview and the battering it took abroad. As part of a pietistic movement within Methodism called sanctification, Smith's identity as a "saint" was a kind of decolonial space that allowed her to follow God's calling to preach among "blacks" *and* "whites," a call that led her to four continents and an international renown largely forgotten today. That career ended in a crisis, I argue, with Smith pressured to admit that the "racial" identity of missionaries in Africa mattered more than the transcendent power of God or any "saint." She returned to the United States around 1890 and endorsed, under duress, the idea that white missionaries were better suited to the task of Christianizing Africa than black ones. To put in relief the import of Smith's ministry in Liberia—a persistently overlooked sphere of the US empire—the chapter pairs her with Edward Wilmot Blyden (1832–1912). Born in Danish St. Thomas and trained for the ministry as a Presbyterian, Blyden was one of the founders of Pan-Africanism and a leading figure in Liberia, where he moved in the 1850s. A prolific and forceful writer, Blyden advocated conservative "racial" nationalism, and he and Smith spent the 1880s talking past each other in very revealing ways. Despite their ideological disconnect, Smith and Blyden addressed kindred audiences in the United States, many of whom saw in Liberia an important test case for the so-called Negro question of the post-Reconstruction period. That both Smith and Blyden had their hearts broken in Liberia anticipates some of the experiences of both political Pan-Africanists (anticolonialist nationalists who supported political structures for continental unity) as well as poetic pan-Africanists in the diaspora, who nourished ties of memory, heritage, and mythic identification with the continent.[27] Though Christian missionaries generated important and enabling forms of colonial knowledge in the nineteenth century, this chapter suggests why and how Smith's writing about Africa became marginal in those discourses at the turn of the twentieth century.

That the former slave Amanda Smith was nicknamed "The Fifteenth Amendment" (establishing "black" suffrage) on the Methodist preaching circuit in the 1870s may not shock readers of this book. That the granddaughter of German Jewish immigrants, Gertrude Stein (b. 1874), wrote an opera about the Fourteenth Amendment (establishing citizenship as "male") just might. The Civil War and Reconstruction are underappreciated contexts for the affections and disaffections that led Stein to a life of writing in Paris, France, from 1903 until her death in 1946. In addition to holding a salon in the *atelier* made famous by her and her brother Leo's art collection, Stein was a serious Civil War buff steeped in Lincoln's and especially Grant's prose. In order to appreciate Stein's epic late-career re-examination of Reconstruction, I establish the context for her break with the missionizing and assimilative impulses that structured Smith's career in the preceding generation and, of course, fostered the careers of so many high-achieving women in Stein's own, like that of Jane Addams. I reframe Stein's medical school years and the women's club milieu of 1890s Baltimore via her engagement with Charlotte Perkin Gilman's *Women and Economics* (1898), a text that served as a kind of upper-class white women's guide to race advancement and personal achievement. I argue that Stein's rejection of feminism was inseparable from her critique of its white supremacist underpinnings. Then, through a reading of her "new woman" novels, *Fernhurst* (1900) and *The Making of Americans* (1911), I show how Stein struggled to create a viable standpoint outside of whiteness, and how her first publisher, John Lane of London's Bodley Head, acted as a harsh gatekeeper. By way of conclusion, I suggest that Stein saw World War II as a frightening but also liberating crisis of white supremacy, one with both national and transnational urgency. Such was the context for turning her keen eye on race and sex through the opera about Reconstruction, called *The Mother of Us All* (1946), and starring a character called Susan B. Anthony. This opera, I argue, vindicates the childless, never-married woman as the "mother" of the nation, and in so doing, acutely problematizes the tie of racial reproduction to citizenship status. The chapter closes with some reflections on other roads beyond racialization tested but not fully taken by Stein in her long career, especially the shimmering image of a new world venus that peeks out from some her key texts, including *The Mother of Us All*.

Like Gertrude Stein, Josefina Silva de Cintrón (1884–1988) was an arts impresario who viewed aesthetics and creativity as rich domains for expressing deep human meaning. She migrated from Puerto Rico to Manhattan in 1927 and worked in a dynamic community-based context, though like Stein she also conducted a salon. Silva de Cintrón and her neighbors and colleagues of the migrant Spanish-speaking community in New York City embraced a lively Pan-American *feminismo* that came into its own between the world wars. *Feminismo* focused on political rights, world peace, and pride in motherhood and found expression in social organizing, public debate, and artistic performance. The main record of these activities is the monthly magazine *Artes y Letras,* an internationally circulated journal of opinion, which Silva de Cintrón published between 1933 and 1939. Working in much tighter quarters with the categories of scientific racism than either Smith or Stein, however, Silva de Cintrón and her peers embraced the oppositional standpoint of *la raza* to contest white supremacy in the US. Under this flag—literally, *La Bandera de La Raza*—Silva de Cintrón gathered a diverse group of Spanish-speaking women in a transnational organization called La Unión de Mujeres Americanas (UMA), which had branches in Mexico, Columbia, and Peru. By framing an inclusive and nondiscriminatory notion of "race," *La Bandera* evoked a kind of decolonized space apart from the scientific and legal definitions of race so potent in the interwar years. In an echo of Martí, *la raza* was a "race" that refused to discriminate. Silva de Cintrón's efforts peaked—and crashed—at the New York World's Fair of 1939 when UMA's status ran highest, yet met its sternest opposition by both the New York–based Fair corporation and the established male political leadership from San Juan. These officials held tight control over the representation of Puerto Rico and Puerto Rican women at "The World of Tomorrow," an exposition structured by militarism, eugenic white supremacy, and the commodification of sex and whose gatekeepers enacted an occlusion precisely feared by Martí more than a generation earlier.

Maida Springer (1907–2005) migrated with her mother from Panama to New York a decade before Silva de Cintrón and lived nearby in upper Manhattan.

Their trajectories did not intersect, however. Springer lost her Spanish early, and affiliated, through Garveyism, with working-class black militancy in the 1920s. Employed as a dressmaker after the Depression hit, the talented and capable Springer moved into a highly visible role with the International Ladies' Garment Workers' Union (ILG)—at precisely the moment that Puerto Rican women sought their own language-based local with the ILG and were rebuffed by a union leadership newly intent on "Americanizing" immigrants. Nevertheless, Springer's affiliation with anglophone Caribbean-born activists like Charlotte Adelmond, Una Marson, and especially George Padmore helped orient her toward international labor organizing and African nationalism, both of which spiked after World War II. I argue that Springer's attachment to a gendered language of family in both the union and pan-African realms was an essential and striking ingredient in her long transnational career. The idiom of family and fictive kin helped her mediate between the racialism of the Garvey era and the pluralist, unevenly "color-blind" Americanism of the ILG, characteristic of postwar racial liberalism. It also helped her move transnationally. By becoming "Mama Maida" to labor colleagues and allies in Africa, Springer asserted both agency and control in politics, straining as US laborites and civil rights leaders did under the heavy anticommunist directives emanating from the State Department in the 1950s. While this third space of gendered language in pan-Africanism drew energy from the family culture and "social unionism" of the ILG, it unfortunately had limited power against the chauvinisms of US policy on the African continent. Springer's posture toward Africa also stands out in important ways from that of her mentor George Padmore (b. Trinidad, 1903; d. Ghana, 1959), architect of postwar political Pan-Africanism and heir to Edward Blyden. The promise and limitations of Springer's work found tragic expression in Liberia in 1965. There she ended her second labor movement career with the American Federation of Labor and Congress of Industrial Organizations (AFL-CIO)'s International Affairs Department, and one of her union "brothers" ended up in jail, and another was shot to death on the picket line for protesting conditions at the Firestone rubber plantation, a dominant factor in the country's economy since the 1920s.

Liberia provides the bookends for my series of paired biographical narratives. Nearly a century apart in time, Amanda Smith and Maida Springer each had pivotal, career-altering experiences in that country. For almost 200 years, people, ideas, and materials have circulated through Liberia, mediating between Africa and the United States, and among a range of other global actors as well. Not unlike Puerto Rico, which inhabited the legal paradox of being "foreign in a domestic sense," Liberia was something of a contradiction: "an independent colony" of the United States. In the *Journal of Race Development* in 1911, Tuskegee Institute administrator Emmet J. Scott posed the question "Is Liberia Worth Saving?" and, after visiting there, he answered: "I believe that it is." Yet, his description of the country's population as a "queer aggregation of humanity" suggests the inbetweenness of Liberia as a mixed heritage, transnational setting in an ideological context in which "race" and nationhood were ideally and presumptively aligned. Puerto Rico provides something of a foil for Liberia in this study. In the same issue of the journal, lawyer Luis Muñoz Morales pointedly complained of Puerto Rico's status as a "strange entity...vested with purely imaginary citizenship" under the Organic Act of 1900, the law that established its connection to the United States as an unincorporated territory, one not tracked for statehood.[28]

With the dynamics of racialization and the workings of empire as its touchstones, this book about women contributes to recent scholarship on Liberia and Puerto Rico as sites of both decolonial striving and ongoing colonial ignorance for a range of historical actors. Colonial ignorance refers to the flip side of what Edward Said so powerfully theorized and labeled "colonial knowledge," that is, the ways in which information, laws, and policy involving empire are obscured and reformulated as, for example, spreading Christianity, democracy, or prosperity.[29] Thus, an important thread in the chapters that follow is the production of colonial ignorance that I highlight in the realms of Protestant missions, "new woman" anglophone literature, Pan-Americanism, and the "melting pot" family ideology of the ILG. As neocolonial domains, Liberia and Puerto Rico both use US currency (though Liberia has its own dollar as well), play host to US military and diplomatic interests, and serve as points of origin for migrants with a significant presence on the US mainland (especially in New York City and its environs). By treating Liberia as a major destination for African American missionaries, a launch point for US military and corporate ambition, a focus for nationalist aspiration in the African diaspora, and a difficult setting for women's voices to be heard, I hope to make especially vivid this sector of human history touching the United States.

Though three of the four figures examined here are the subject of biographies (in Stein's case, many) few students of US history know of their work; even one of my readers for this publication "had not heard" of them at all (again, except for Stein).[30] I first encountered Smith in my earlier work on Ida B. Wells-Barnett. Wells-Barnett and her husband helped raised money for the orphanage Smith ran just outside Chicago after she returned from Africa. Smith's stature was such that Wells-Barnett thought to treat the Amanda Smith Home in her own autobiography, though she did not live to complete that project.[31] To approach Smith's story, I had to make Africa an intellectual priority, a decision given urgency and support by the second edition of Rosalyn Terborg-Penn's *Women and Africa and the African Diaspora* (1996) and the *Journal of American History's* special issue on transnationalism (1999). I also started reading widely on Puerto Rico to address my own colonial ignorance. Virginia Sánchez Korrol's pioneering study *From Colonia to Community: The History of Puerto Ricans in New York City* (1994) contained an intriguing description of *Artes y Letras*. Since I felt practiced in reading women's journalism and community newspapers, I tackled that primary source next and discovered Silva de Cintrón's story. Reading about—and teaching courses on—Spanish colonialism brought me, in a roundabout way to Stein. For years I cherished her writings on Picasso, especially her musings about how Spain and America had "something in common" in the modern arts.[32] A closer look at these mid-career pieces pointed me back to her formative, new woman writings, confronting me with the transnational dimensions of that fin de siècle literary gambit. The career of Maida Springer combined the threads of colonialism, New York intellectual ferment, and African legacies in the Americas into a ready-made transnational topic. Her postwar activism also afforded me a way into the exciting historical literature on "Cold War civil rights" that took off a decade ago.[33] The lens of the decolonial helps bring these significant if isolated figures into dialogue with the rich transnational and imperial turns in current scholarship, especially concerning ideas about race, and allows them to be, however gingerly, compared with one another.

These women—naturalized, natal, or colonial citizens of the United States—made major marks in the world mostly outside the boundaries of any of its states. Among their key interlocutors were highly interesting and influential men—Blyden, Lane, Martí, and Padmore—who were not US citizens and lived outside its national boundaries (though Martí and Padmore stayed quite a while). Conservative by temperament, these women's relative distance from matters of suffrage and partisanship makes them hard to place in conventional historical narratives, typically tied to the periodizations and rituals of national citizenship politics. Nonetheless, a transnational perspective casts their spiritual, intellectual, and creative choices in a political light. The involvement of Smith, Stein, Silva de Cintrón, and Springer with issues of national belonging, border crossing, and personal identity was never fully separable from state-centered issues and concerns, notably empire and citizenship. Their experiences and choice making elaborate Thomas Bender's contention that transnational approaches to US history do not "subvert the nation" so much as help us "rethink its nature and its relations to alternative solidarities and social connections."[34] All of these dynamics offer rich provocations for how historians might come to define "American" women's history. They reveal transnational trajectories of engagement and creativity—as well as frustration, even danger—left for too long in the shadows of what historians think they know about where nations begin and end.

1
A Kind of Privileged Character

Amanda Berry Smith and Race in Liberian Missions

In 1887, Amanda Berry Smith had a short dialogue with some recently arrived African American women migrants in Cape Palmas, Liberia. A welcome meeting had been planned for the group by resident Americo-Liberians at a local school. "When I heard of it I said I would go," recalled Smith in her autobiography. "But I was told, a little while after, that no women were to go; it was only for men. Then I was more anxious than ever; and, womanlike, I became suspicious, as well as curious." Claiming a kind of parity of citizenship, she reasoned to herself: "Why can't I go? These emigrants are from my country, and I have a right to go, and I will." Smith reported that the excluded wives groused about their husbands' opposition and the lack of proper accommodations for them at the meeting. She then countered that she had no husband to obey and could easily bring along her own chair. Smith further mused: "They all knew I was a kind of privileged character anyhow, and generally carried out what I undertook." Upon her arrival at the meeting, Smith planted her chair "in the middle of the aisle," symbolizing her excluded status and her protest of it to the assembled. She went on in her narrative to chide the conveners of the welcome meeting, pointing to their "talk enough to have built a tower, if there had been anything in it" as well as their puffed-up assertions about Liberia being a "country where they could be *men*."[1] By dramatizing her out-of-placeness at the meeting, Smith silently yet emphatically challenged male exclusionism. By recentering herself in a gathering that tried to ignore her but at which she pointedly said nothing, she affirmed, in still feminine terms, the idea that Liberia's future was the concern of both men and women, though her slight condescension toward the emigrants' wives also deserves note. Smith's gesture, this chapter will argue, was one among many in a life that sought out space, like the middle of the aisle, beyond the binaries of male-female and black-white and citizen-alien that so deeply structured her world. Amanda Smith's eight-year ministry in Liberia has much to tell us about transnational possibilities in an era in which "racial" binaries hardened in US society as well as in nascent African nationalism on the continent.[2]

Smith's self-identification as "a kind of privileged character"—a sanctified Christian, a widow, and an independent evangelist—locates her beyond or at least to the side of racialized citizenship categories circulating in the US and Liberia in the late nineteenth century. This chapter explores these spaces as well as the deeper contexts, costs, and effects of Smith's work in Africa. It argues that her ministry represents an important moment of potential in Liberia, a moment overshadowed by the work of the leading Liberian nationalist of the day, Edward Wilmot Blyden. This chapter also highlights the quiet yet clear stands that Smith took on key issues in Methodist missions in Africa, especially the place of race and sex in church building and leadership. As the welcome-meeting scenario suggests, the Americo-Liberian context accented men's roles in the public sphere, particularly when compared to the post-Reconstruction United States, where African American women's public social betterment work held much more firm, if variable, status.[3] Finally, my exploration puts Smith's writing about Africa in the context of US Protestant clergy's discussions of Liberia. Her sensitive appraisals of native people cut against nefarious "dark continent" stereotypes that abounded in the missionary literature of the period. But Smith's own careful and caring writings about Liberia went largely unacknowledged, while other, more imperialistic voices informed colonial knowledge about Africa and turned a profit to boot.

Smith in Historiography

Since her death in 1915, Smith has been celebrated by Protestant church and missionary advocates as a heroine and only glanced over by more secular-minded scholars.[4] She figures only cursorily in recent history textbooks and anthologies with a black feminist focus.[5] Treatments of religious life in the United States give her some attention, as she was a recognized preaching woman within the oldest and most prominent of the African American denominations, the African Methodist Episcopal (AME).[6] For historians interested in paths to the mid-twentieth century's civil rights movements, Smith had little direct involvement with organized responses to racism. That many of her accomplishments took place outside of the United States accounts for both her mystique and obscurity within the country. Hallie Quinn Brown celebrated Smith in her volume *Homespun Heroines* published in 1926, calling her "one of the most remarkable preachers of any race and of any age."[7] Beyond this early praise, Smith's legacy has only begun to be assessed, thanks to Adrienne Israel's biography published in 1998.[8]

Smith eluded easy categorization during her lifetime, as did a number of "improbable black women" of the nineteenth century, in Mia Bay's suggestive phrase.[9] Like Sojourner Truth, to whom some compared her, Amanda Smith earned much of her reputation in predominantly white Christian circles, for which she faced some criticism. "But my people often called me 'White folks' nigger,' anyhow. So I am in for it, and I don't care," Smith noted in her autobiography. "All I care to do is to keep in favor with God and man as much as lieth in me" (453). This posture reflects Smith's holiness faith, a popular but controversial minority-held doctrine based on the teaching of Methodist founder John Wesley. Holiness, sometimes called "Higher Life Christianity," expressed its perfectionism in a two-step conversion process, first from sin to salvation, then from salvation to sanctification—or, from pardon to purity. The second blessing of heart purity liberated the believer from flaws in his or her moral nature, and it enabled him or her to live as a saint in the world, proof positive of the perfecting power of God's grace and Jesus's love.[10] Some 40 years older than Smith, Sojourner Truth moved within an earlier, related strand of millenarianism in the 1840s. Truth sought direct social engagement with the antislavery and woman's rights movements before, during, and after the Civil War, but Smith spent Reconstruction on the holiness and Methodist revival camp circuits in the northeast and steered clear of state-focused, rights-based activism. And while Israel's biography affirms that Smith "maintained the quest for justice and equality against formidable odds" after she returned from Africa, this conclusion remains more asserted than shown, at least in the conventionally political sense of justice.[11]

Smith's pietism and direct service provision as an evangelist left a distinct, slightly obscured historical record of her work, even though the body of her writing far exceeds the number of texts scholars can attribute to Sojourner Truth. Smith's lengthy and detailed autobiography was published in 1893, and she wrote scores of letters in missionary and Methodist newspapers, especially the holiness organ The *Christian Standard* published in Cincinnati, Ohio. As Nell Irvin Painter has vividly recounted, Truth created a photographic record of herself, engaged the legal system multiple times, and allied, however tensely, with woman's rights advocates who in turn circulated her image and story in venues that academia recognizes as "the" historical record.[12] Like Truth, Smith adopted Quaker dress, but she mostly held herself apart from legal and activist modes of engagement in the 1860s and the 1870s. Then, in 1878 she left the country for over a decade and returned to a ferociously racist US context in which asserting racial equality was to take one's life in one's hands. (Truth died in 1883.) Smith was also distinctly known for her beautiful and powerful singing voice. Had technology permitted its recording at the time, we might today have a very different record and appreciation of her life that was, in large part, a ministry of song in live performance.

Amanda Berry Smith had a regal bearing, striking features, and a special gift for singing. "I had a good voice, and could sing very loud," she noted in her narrative (174). "In those [camp meeting] days I used to sing a great deal, and somehow the Lord always seemed to bless my singing" (194). The transformational energy of group singing was very real, and Smith's ability to sing at the spirit's prompting gave her an important role in worship settings. In 1872, she reportedly upstaged the Fisk Jubilee Singers during the AME Church General Conference in Nashville. "Such a burst of enthusiasm it created," Smith recalled; the audience was "surprised and astonished." Smith suggested that her voice and presence on stage created an important symbol that day, "especially as the question of ordination of women never was mooted in the Conference" (203–204). African American women's contributions to community life generated

1.1   Amanda Smith, ca. 1870.
Photo credit: Frances E. Willard Memorial Archives and Library

high hopes as well as conflict in the denomination, but Smith refrained from taking a position on ordination.[13] In her narrative, she noted only "how they have advanced since then." The AME church voted down female ordination during the 1880s, when Smith was at the height of her powers and renown— and out of the country.[14] Holiness piety and her conservative temperament shaped her reaction to this situation: "I am satisfied with the ordination that the Lord has given me. Praise His name!" (204). The special ordination of sanctification and her gift of song did not translate as easily to the African context, though it primed her to hear God's voice asking her to try.

Sanctification was controversial precisely because it could elevate the saints potentially above—or at least get them around—the clergy and related church hierarchy. Scholars of Protestant missions and the holiness movement argue that African American women, including Smith, transgressed gender norms by remaining at the edges of church life as independent missionaries or as unpaid (if licensed) exhorters. Of Smith and women like Julia Foote (b. 1823) and Zilpha Elaw (b. ca. 1790), historian James Campbell writes: "None of them evinced interest in organized feminism, which they regarded as one more form of worldliness."[15] Nonetheless, these women did encounter and sometimes confront gender inequity. In addition, the gender dimensions of Smith's ministry shaped and was shaped by long-standing currents of female authority in black religious life, streams nourished by African tradition. Historian Cheryl Townsend Gilkes suggests that black women's participation in the Pentacostal and holiness sects of Methodism are marked by this legacy. "Church mothers" and "spirit-filled" women could hold "considerable power within nearly autonomous and well-organized parallel women's worlds," in what Gilkes identifies as a religious "dual-sex system" with roots in Africa.[16]

Also vitally important to Smith's Liberia story is evangelical Protestantism's global vision. Like her peers, Smith viewed Christian faith as transnational, even if they did not use the word. The doctrine of sanctification and its central tenet of self-sacrifice to God enabled Smith to be both morally ambitious and culturally feminine, capacities denied to black women by US society. Holiness also promised a kind of freedom that may have especially resonated for Smith as a former slave. For example, she frequently described taking the pulpit with the Holy Spirit upon her as being at "great liberty" or experiencing "perfect freedom."[17] And, alongside the saints' reputation for being above material, political, and other worldly matters, Smith insisted, "Holiness is a power, not only of and with God, but a power with men that must prevail, amen."[18] That is, spiritual truths connected directly to social relations and the creation of a better world through the community of saints, potentially on a global scale. One of Smith's signature hymns, "All I want, All I want, All I want, Is a little more faith in Jesus," neatly captures the core tension in holiness between worldly renunciation and this-world self-affirmation and engagement.[19] What Christian could be so craven as to deny Smith a "little more faith in Jesus"? Who could have stopped her if they tried?

Sanctification and the Theology of "Whiteness"

As a spiritual autobiography, Smith's narrative focuses on God's leadings and the Devil's mischief, leaving in shadow the broader political context of her choices in the 1870s and 1880s. For example, when Smith noted being called "the Fifteenth Amendment" by New Englanders at a revival meeting near Boston, it was the "first time" she had ever heard of "that bill" (187). Nonetheless, Smith's spiritual path is inextricable from its social context, especially the deteriorating status of free African Americans in the north in the decade before the Civil War. Indeed, her distance from the Fifteenth Amendment alludes to the difficult conditions facing the Berry family after the father, Samuel Berry, purchased their freedom around 1840 in Maryland.[20]

The Fugitive Slave Law in 1850 greatly empowered whites over black people, who were restricted from testifying on their own behalf in court if charged as runaways. The Dred Scott decision of 1857 made free African Americans all but bereft of defensible citizenship rights. Smith's struggle for spiritual "light and peace" (44) in the 1850s and the 1860s helped her get her bearings in an increasingly hostile and polarized society, even in the free state of Pennsylvania where Smith moved in 1845.

As a freedwoman working in domestic service in York County, Smith found salvation in the spring of 1856, at work not at church. That Easter season, Smith battled a desire for an Easter suit, especially a new bonnet, as well as her attraction/revulsion toward a shouting Baptist church in the neighborhood, where worshippers made "a great noise." Participation in such behavior could jeopardize her standing as a "first-class servant girl" who served only "first-class families" (43). Thus, Smith framed her conversion as a classic holiness battle with worldliness, one fraught with gendered and class tensions and one with economic repercussions as well. Desperate to win from God the ability to let go of the desire for the bonnet and her fear of shouting in church, she risked her job to do it, resolving that the family should get their own "bread and butter" for the table upstairs while she went to the cellar to pray. God touched her in prayer that day, and in professing her faith, Smith recounted how "peace and joy" now "flooded [her] soul":

> Praise the Lord! There seemed to be a halo of light all over me; the change was so real and so thorough that I have often said that if I had been as black as ink or as green as grass or as white as snow, I would not have been frightened. I went into the dining room; we had a large mirror that went from the floor to the ceiling, and I went and looked in it to see if anything had transpired in my color, because there was something wonderful had taken place inside of me, and it really seemed to me it was outside too, and as I looked in the glass I cried out, "Hallelujah, I have got religion; glory to God, I have got religion!" I was wild with delight and joy; it seemed to me as if I would split! (47)

The poignant description of being nearly "split" and the tension between her soul's condition and her skin color anticipates something of W. E. B. Du Bois's notion of "two-ness." Salvation both named and potentially resolved the contradictions that threatened to "split" her. While Smith identified with the household as part of a plural "we," she also had needs that diverged from those of her employer. Smith's ability to negotiate this dynamic was essential to her survival and well-being within white majority settings.

Around 1865, she moved to New York City with her second husband, James, who did hotel work while she took in laundry. There, sanctification helped work out the mounting tensions between spiritual and embodied existence. In late 1868, Smith sought out the preaching of Reverend John Inskip, known for his preaching on holiness, and her autobiography recounts her sanctification under his preaching with riveting detail. Inskip visited the Green Street Methodist Church in lower Manhattan, near the Smiths' apartment, a neighborhood derisively known as "Little Africa."[21] He addressed a pressing matter for the saints that Sunday: keeping the spirit of sanctification once attained. Though Smith's seat in church was partially obscured by a post—she bravely sat in the main hall downstairs rather than up in the segregated balcony—Inskip "seemed to look around there," signaling the rightness of her chosen place beyond the color line. The minister drew a parallel between God's ability to live in the saint with the body's ability to breathe all night without being reminded or willed to do so, an analogy here set alongside an image of the body tired out from working all day. Smith's mind jumped "in a moment" to her "washing and ironing all night." "Get God in you in all His fullness," preached Inskip, "and he will live Himself." Upon hearing these words, Smith described a kind of vertigo: "I seemed to sink down out of sight of myself and then rise, all in a moment I seemed to go two ways at once, down and up." Smith "wanted to shout Glory to Jesus!" but she held her tongue from shouting. "Look, look at the white people, mind, they will put you out," warned the Devil. "O, I was so weak. My head seemed a river of waters and my eyes a fountain of tears" (78). Smith prayed for strength to stand up to leave with her dignity intact. As she rose, the last verse of the last hymn of the service was sung out with the words, "Whose blood now cleanseth." Smith was again swept by grace, and she shouted: "Glory to Jesus." Inskip answered: "Amen, Glory to God." In this affirmation, Smith was released from torment. "I don't know just how I looked, but I felt so wonderfully strange, yet I felt glorious." Upon departing the church, she seemed to "feel a hand, the touch of which I cannot describe." This touch on the top of her head made "something part and roll down and cover me like a great cloak!" leaving a "mighty peace and power" in her possession (79).

The narrative describes sanctification as allowing Smith to conquer a whole litany of fears about her place in the world. On the street after the service, she met some "old leading sisters" from the "colored churches," and while the Devil jeers in her ear that she was too weak to confess to them her sanctification, Smith now discovered a "special power in my right arm and I was swinging it around, like the boys do sometimes!" She was now not weak but jaunty and playful, claiming the gendered freedom that boys have in the street; and, of course, at the "right hand" of God was Jesus himself. This new "special power" allowed Smith to answer the sisters' "How are you?" with a simple "God has sanctified my soul" and then to pass blithely on. "I suppose the people thought I was wild, and I was, for God had set me on fire!" In the next paragraph, Smith describes overcoming her intimidation by white people. Her fear was not of them "doing me harm" per se, she wrote, "but a kind of fear because they were white, and were there, and I was black and was here!" alluding to a kind of existential dread. "But now the Holy Ghost had made it clear to me," she affirmed. "And as I looked at white people that I had always seemed to be afraid of, now they looked so small. The great mountain had become a mole-hill" (80).

But brave is not the same as prosperous. Historians of African American religion have been quick to point to Smith's upward mobility through holiness preaching, but she actually continued to work in service and laundering for another decade after sanctification. As a preaching woman, she sustained herself solely via donations, not by a regular salary.[22] Later, when Amanda Smith left domestic work as a sacrifice to God, she took a very real gamble on economic security. As part of her self-authorization as a humble saint, she sometimes referred to herself as a "poor, dark washwoman" who leaned only on Jesus.[23] In the retellings of Smith's sanctification in the evangelical literature, most writers describe Smith's dramatic walk to the front of Inskip's church and the placement of her "wash tub and scrubbing brush" in front of the pulpit.[24] In the choreography of revivals, converts were expected to come to the front of the congregation and, at least metaphorically, "put all on the altar."[25] This detail's absence in Smith's own telling subtly points to how she could not give up her domestic tools and skills and realistically expect to survive. Such skills underwrote her mobility out of New York, in fact, since she hired herself out to wash at the revival campgrounds along the Jersey shore during the summer. In these settings, segregation was generally practiced, with special services for "colored people" usually at the end of the day, when local residents—including those, like Smith, who were employed in camp—were finished attending to whites. Thus, part of Smith's entree to evangelism involved the caretaking of white people on the circuit—even in Africa, as we shall see.[26] For all her mobility and renown, white Methodists never criticized Smith for unsexing herself or neglecting her family out of unseemly ambition or self-seeking; indeed, they easily dissociated her from any personal life at all, as it aided their own comfort and enjoyment to do so.

Though some scholars of holiness note the potential for transgressing hierarchies of race, class, and gender amid the leveling enthusiasms of revivalist subcultures, I see little evidence of this potential as either available or even attractive to Smith, who faced exclusionism and prejudice in evangelical circles throughout her life.[27] Smith was regularly called "Auntie" by white strangers in Christian settings, and she was sometimes scorned, as in when one woman scowled that she "did not come to hear a negro ditty" at services (79, 166, 223). The pressure of living in a color-obsessed culture seeped into the camp and revival circuits of Methodism in the 1870s, where white parishioners would ask Smith to her face if she would not, in fact, "rather be white than black?" Smith described her weary dismay at this kind of ordeal—"What now?" she would think silently to herself as the gawkers approached—and the narrative recounts her patient response, the sarcasm of which is lost on one questioner." 'No, no,' I said, 'as the Lord lives, I would rather be black and fully saved than to be white and not saved; I was bad enough, black as I am, and I would have been ten times worse if I had been white.' How she [the questioner] roared laughing" (118). Religion hardly protected Smith from prejudice, but the doctrine of holiness held antiracist potential by holding white people to a shared Christian standard of "perfect love," one perhaps especially welcome during the highly uncertain years between the Dred Scott decision and the last of the Reconstruction Amendments.

Indeed, that very decade faced Amanda Smith with her most difficult trials: poverty, the end of two marriages, and the deaths of four of her five children; only her first daughter, Maizie, survived to adulthood. The Civil War took away her first husband, Calvin Devine, who "enlisted, went South with the army," and "never returned" (57). Smith had a free-born sister who was remanded to slavery during the war and had to be "redeemed" (50–56). James was a difficult husband, and Smith described herself as "greatly crushed" in her "homelife" (143). For Amanda Smith, the pain of marriage and the cold uncertainties of legal freedom stood in sharp relief to the warmth and optimism of evangelicalism, whose ambition was grand, even global, yet very much scaled to individual agency. Faith worked on a personal basis, even allowing Smith to see Jesus (143–144).

In her narrative, Smith described a series of dreams and signs from God leading her to preach, including one in which a "cold white cross" pressed heavily on her chest, and another in which a strong, white-feathered right arm reached down from the sky toward her during a church event, when Smith felt shunned by brethren and sisters. According to Smith, these signs contained a message: "I soon found out that it was not the will of the Lord for me to confine myself as a servant in any family, but to go and work in His vineyard as the Spirit directed me" (149). The color white in these dreams is striking, but holiness theology held such images out as a space of purity beyond the body and polity to the universals of the spirit. Despite its varied impact on her experience of racism, sanctification allowed Amanda Berry Smith fend off doubt over her soul—perhaps the one thing she could be sure of—and potentially project herself into a world beyond the washtub and domestic strife.

In terms of race relations, Smith's narrative stresses that given their advantages, white people had no excuse not to live righteously under God. She sometimes glossed tense moments of stereotyping and antagonism in her narrative with a flourish of holiness theology: "It's the blood that makes whiteness. Hallelujah!" (118). The idea of Jesus's sacrificial blood as a "whitening" ingredient on the road to perfection captures the radical conservatism of holiness: anyone could be "white" as in "saved," regardless of skin color; being "white" in this sense meant being righteous not "European."[28] Less generous Christians in Liberia made contemptuous play out of categories that in Smith's handling were fluid and hopeful. "I have a boy and girl in my family, natives, and I'm training them to be white," chirped a missionary wife in 1875. "They think they'll be white when they learn to read."[29] For Smith, sanctification propounded a promising contradiction: a third space that might be colloquially called "white" but really transcended color: the means to make one's life a "living sacrifice, good, acceptable, perfect, to Him."[30] "No, we who are the royal black are very well satisfied with His gift to us in this substantial color," Smith affirmed, even though "[s]ome people don't get enough of the blessing to take prejudice out of them, even after they are sanctified" (117, 226). When skeptics second-guessed Smith's spiritual gifts along the lines of skin color and sex prejudice, holiness doctrine countered with the idea, deeply held by Smith, that "human nature is the same in black and white folks" (146). This faith would be sorely tested in her Liberia mission.

Though Smith's narrative attributes much agency to the spirit, her biographer suggests that she found support within the Methodist National Holiness Association (established 1867) and the Woman's Christian Temperance Union (WCTU, founded 1874) for a few key reasons. First, many AME clergy opposed

holiness, notably one Reverend Nelson H. Turpin, minister of Smith's membership church, Sullivan Street AME in New York, where she lived in the 1860s.
Second, Israel suggests that Smith moved away from African American church
work because she rejected the pressure to fund-raise for and in the black community in order to build up local institutions, but this view seems based more
on church leaders' perspective than on Smith's. Finally, Israel conjectures
that Smith "enjoyed associating with wealthy, influential whites" because it
was more lucrative and high-profile work than domestic service, her primary
means of support since leaving slavery.[31] These dynamics are misconstrued
as causal for Smith's holiness ministry, and they hardly point her to Africa.
A more nuanced reckoning with Smith's reception as a preaching woman and
with the dynamics of Methodists missionary ambition makes better sense of
her transnational trajectory after sanctification.

Smith did not abandon black audiences for white, but she did find acceptance, support, and fellowship more consistently with two groups of Christians
in the 1860s and the 1870s: everyday black parishioners rather than clergy
and elites, who viewed her as a rival or oddity, and reform-minded upper-class
white women, who embraced her out of their antiracist and nascent feminist
proclivities. As the end of Reconstruction dimmed prospects for full equality in US society, both of these groups turned internationally. As Nell Irvin
Painter has shown, grassroots "Liberia Fever" caught on among rural black
southerners, and African emigration emerged as a hot topic in the nation-
ally networked black press—with established political and clerical elites very
much in opposition.[32] In New York, Smith may have caught an address at the
Abyssinian Baptist church in by Mary Jane Richards, who celebrated Liberian
progress.[33] At the same time, ambitious white women Methodists, particularly in the temperance realm, set their sights internationally, as they too
were blocked for power within church structures. White Protestant church-
women and, by 1880, their seminary-educated daughters embraced mission
work both at home and abroad, especially in China.[34] Reform-minded white
Methodists, many still proud of their antislavery heritage, welcomed Smith
as a former slave. Smith was neither passive nor opportunistic with regard to
these white women. Rather, in accepting an invitation to preach on temperance at the Keswick Convention in England in 1878, she quietly took a position in the debates of her day in favor of foreign missions, moral reform, the
doctrine of holiness, and women's expanded authority in all these realms.
Moreover, she could draw on the example of African American leaders who
connected with transnational religious and reform efforts in the nineteenth
century, from antislavery greats to postwar figures like Philadelphians Fannie
Jackson Coppin, wife of AME Bishop Levy Coppin, and Frances E. W. Harper,
both of whom worked closely with the WCTU in this period. The Coppins
were also Africa-minded: Fannie Coppin represented the AME church's
Women's Home and Foreign Missionary Society at the centenary conference
on the Protestant Missions of the World in London in 1888; the couple eventually spent a year in South Africa in 1901.[35] The World Woman's Christian
Temperance Union (WWCTU), founded in 1883, sponsored women workers
all over the world, and these networks helped Smith get to India and, eventually, Liberia.

Race and Gender in Liberian Missions

The literature on US missions to Liberia in the nineteenth century conveys a striking consensus. Generally, the mainline Protestant denominations favored white-led missionary efforts, and only included African Americans in their work for one of several backhanded reasons: to preserve the health of white missionaries, to save money (by paying black missionaries less than white), or to uphold racial segregation within national church life and structures, funneling ambitious clergy, teachers, and evangelists abroad rather than moving them up the US-based hierarchy.[36] Initially, the most prominent rationale for African American missionary placements was the belief, firmly in place by the 1840s, that western Africa was a "white man's grave." During the nineteenth century, about 50 African American Protestant missionaries reached Liberia; scholars have documented the severe underfinancing and general lack of confidence in black missionaries on the part of the sponsoring churches.[37] When the US Civil War redirected resources away from foreign fields, Liberian missions suffered accordingly. Then, as northern whites tired of Reconstruction, Protestant churches reemphasized itinerancy and "self support" for already underfunded and undersupported black missionaries, who now found themselves doubly tested abroad. As one Liberia observer noted: "The Boards in America seem to think that *black missionaries* in Africa do not need to eat and drink and have clothing like other missionaries in all other parts of the world."[38] The third area of consensus in this literature is that African American missionaries to Liberia had limited success with either native conversions or church building, hardly surprising given their treatment by their sponsors and mission boards.[39]

In this generally stacked deck, dynamics did vary across denominations. The Episcopalians offered—and then withdrew—a regular bishopric and diocese for Liberian churches planted by African American missionaries. This prospect appealed deeply to a number of leading clergy, notably Alexander Crummell, who envisioned a "National Church" for Liberia and nearly realized it in the 1870s.[40] The Methodist establishment came to insist on itinerancy and the founding of "native" churches as true test of missionary mettle. They took a position of compromise on church structure and created a "missionary bishopric," the authority of which was limited to Africa; their first appointee to Liberia was AME Bishop Francis Burns in 1858, the second was the AME's John Roberts.[41] Ironically, perhaps, southern-based Presbyterians supported most the equitably structured African American missions to the African interior, in the Congo. Though fewer than a dozen African Americans served the Presbyterian Church in Africa between 1890 and 1941, notable accomplishments were achieved by Rev. William Sheppard, who ran a successful mission station at Luebo in the Kasai Valley of the Congo and by Maria Fearing, who ran a school, the Pantops Home for Girls, in the same region for nearly 20 years.[42] Fearing retired quietly to Mississippi in 1915, but Sheppard achieved international renown when he exposed the forced labor practices, torture, and mutilation of native people conscripted into Belgium's rubber industry in the Congo, and then faced a widely publicized libel case filed against him by King Leopold in 1909.[43]

Few white missionaries succeeded, or even survived, in Liberia without the aid of black "assistants" from the United States or "native helpers" from Africa. Nonetheless, the major Protestant churches upheld racial segregation and inequity in mission resources, organization, and the distribution of authority. By 1900, the general goal of self-supporting churches of and for native Christians in Liberia receded from the agenda of evangelizing Africa. A sharper, racist accent on trusteeship dried up support for potentially autonomous black missionaries coming out of the United States. By the end of World War I, "the idea of using black missionaries in Africa was all but dead in white American religious communities," writes historian Sylvia M. Jacobs. As US Protestants turned away from the continent and the European "scramble for Africa" hit its stride, historian Walter Williams notes that a more "mature mission ideology" among African American Christians came into its own.[44] By the 1920s, influenced by growing working-class black nationalism, African American leaders became much more invested in an independent, black-controlled Liberia as a major placement for African American missionaries, who were generally excluded from other world locations.[45]

Along the way, however, there was considerable debate, especially in Methodism. Historian Eunjin Park contends that the "bi-racial era" in Liberian missions was over by 1875, essentially coterminous with the end of Reconstruction, but the career of the third missionary bishop for Africa, a white man named William Taylor, tells a different, more contentious story.[46] His appointment came in 1884 because the general board had backed itself into a corner: whites would die in Africa, so they must, then, appoint blacks to oversee African missionary work. After John Roberts's term ended, another "colored man" was brought forward in 1880, but did "not have the suffrages," and the post went unfilled; in 1884, *two* black men were nominated, and when faced with this prospect the board looked to Taylor, resolving to "turn him loose in Africa" rather than institutionalize African American leadership. Taylor, a former circuit rider from gold-rush California and a seasoned international missionary (Australia, Angola, South Africa, and India were a few of his posts in the 1870s) was, according to one account, "[w]ithin twenty-four hours...nominated, elected, and ordained a bishop in the Methodist Episcopal Church for Africa against the previously declared wisdom of that body, expressed after one of the most thorough canvassings that any subject ever had at the hands of a like body."[47] This way, the general board kept up with the competitive and high-profile "around the world" evangelism projects of the period without making a commitment to supporting black leadership abroad. Taylor was thus named missionary bishop for Africa in 1884.

As already noted, the historic African American denominations were generally cool to foreign missions and African emigration in the nineteenth century, with notable exceptions like Daniel Coker before the Civil War and, later, Henry McNeal Turner in the 1890s. The *Christian Recorder*, organ of the AME church published in Philadelphia, came out strongly against Liberian emigration in the 1870s, some clergy calling it "suicide in the extreme."[48] Nonetheless, a distinction should be made between repatriation and missions. The AME leadership established "correspondence" with the Methodist

Episcopal denomination in Liberia as early as 1855.[49] And while the earliest AME congregation established there was quickly absorbed by the (white majority) ME by 1830, a grassroots "Liberia Mission Church" emerged in South Carolina after Reconstruction. This church grew out of an AME congregation, Morris Brown Church in Charleston, and was organized with the intent to emigrate. The church founded the Liberian Exodus Company, and embarked on its own ship, the *Azore,* in 1878. In the Liberian capital of Monrovia, an AME church was implanted by Reverend Samuel F. Flegler (a protégé of Henry Turner) and S. J. Campbell, it numbered some 135 communicants in 1880, and was still extant in 1891 in Monrovia, when Turner established an official AME Conference in Liberia.[50] In between Flegler and Turner's efforts, opinion softened about Liberia in the pages of the *Recorder;* AME leaders called William Taylor's 1887 Cavalla River missionary expedition "significant" and a "wonderful and daring adventure" though without mentioning a key participant, Amanda Berry Smith.[51] By 1922, church historian Charles S. Smith, who visited Liberia and taught courses at Wilberforce in Ohio, admitted a lost opportunity for the AME church in Liberia back in the nineteenth century. If not for the church's neglect, he lamented, the country "to-day might be occupying a commanding position among the smaller nations of the earth; and there would have been less force to the slogan of Marcus Garvey, 'Back to Africa,' led by secular forces." For this neglect, C. S. Smith blamed the church's "condemnators and opposers," who resented the racism of Liberia's founding agency, the American Colonization Society (ACS).[52]

Threaded throughout Liberian missions in the nineteenth century was the sometimes parallel, sometimes intersecting work of the ACS. The US-based ACS was primarily responsible for founding of the colony (1822), and later the country of Liberia (1847). By 1900, the ACS had assisted the resettlement of more than 15,000 African Americans from the United States to the west African republic. ACS also took credit for the disruption of the market in forced labor in the region, and the reintegration of individuals recaptured from the illegal slave trade, people sometimes referred to as "Congoes," back into Africa. Founded in 1812, the ACS was always controversial. Highly elitist and paternalistic—wealthy southern slaveholders and rich northern philanthropists were among its founders—it was criticized throughout its 80-year existence as a proslavery, white supremacist project, lambasted by Frederick Douglass, Martin Delany, and William Lloyd Garrison.[53]

Run by wealthy, powerful white men and abetted by funding from both state legislatures and the US government, the ACS maintained a shaping hand in Liberia throughout the century. The organization raised money, brokered prestige, and managed political access, like US ambassadorships, even in decades of relatively light emigration. Through its New York and Boston boards especially, ACS raised direct dollars for projects like Liberia College in Monrovia and funneled philanthropy, like bequests, to the country through its accounts. In addition to being a major supplier of food, supplies, and building material to migrants, the ACS distributed land titles via a highly paternalistic policy that anticipated the allotment system of the Dawes Act for Native Americans in the 1880s.[54] Reports and correspondence from paid agents and officers in Monrovia, like Charles T. O. King, allowed the ACS to keep tabs on politics and affairs of state, news of which circulated through its organ, *The African Repository and Colonial Journal*, published in Washington, DC.

All of these activities rolled into an agenda of Liberian nation building in a civilizationist framework, that is, a project that linked Christianity, English-language literacy, monogamy, and the related cultural forms and technologies dominant in the world's rapidly industrializing countries.[55] According to the *Repository*, Liberia represented "the success of a combined Christianity and Republicanism *upheld by Africans on Africa's own shores*"—though defining exactly who was an "African" proved tricky from the start.[56] Neither whites nor natives could be citizens under the founding Liberian constitution. Over time, however, the work of nation building shifted from being the unique, God-given responsibility of both the "Anglo- and African-American" to a more strictly racialized project, a kind of test case for "the Negro" on a world stage.[57] In the 1880s, the *Repository* began to accent "scientific" thinking about race, supplanting beliefs about universal brotherhood and the shared destiny of the worlds' peoples around a singular biblico-historical trajectory. This shift prompted a retraction of "white" investment in Africa and a provocative corollary: only "genuine" or "unadulterated Negroes" from within the diaspora could properly understand or carry out the work of nation building and Christianization in Africa. "Mulattos" or those people "denationalized by a duplicate or triplicate genealogy" could claim neither legitimate leadership of US-based African Americans from a "racial standpoint" nor any genealogical "heirship" to Africa, since such "half breeds" held "rather imperfect title."[58]

Generally, African American writers about race did not completely sever science and scripture in this period; as late as 1897, W. E. B. Du Bois invoked, in aptly mixed metaphors, the "whole scientific doctrine of Human Brotherhood" in his case for the "The Conservation of Races."[59] Similarly, the Princeton-educated T. McCants Stewart, who spent four months in Liberia in 1886 and came out in opposition to emigration, affirmed: "God not we 'divided the nations their inheritance' and 'separated the sons of Adam.' The Negro has for his portion Central-Tropical Africa, and no one race will supplant or permanently rule on that soil."[60] The correspondence between God's will and Nature's work in (re)connecting peoples to lands bore directly on ACS policy for emigration and nation building. The ACS held no strict "racial" criteria in its migration policy, and referred only to "negroes," a designation that Du Bois described—with a capital "N"—as "the most indefinite of all" terms.[61]

Race and Sex in Liberian Nationalism

Thus, just as Amanda Smith arrived in Liberia, her cherished beliefs in the essential unity of humanity and in the universal thrust of Christian salvation were under vigorous debate, even assault. "Whiteness" took on stronger biological grounding, eroding its power as a metaphor for spiritual attainment. In addition, Liberia's government was in a state of "chronic embarrassment" with the Christianization of the native population stalled.[62] This combination of factors alarmed idealistic missionaries like Smith, who wanted Liberia to become a properly settled Christian society, rather than a secular (or pagan) trade-oriented entity in which natives were either ignored or exploited. At the same time, a number of prominent African American leaders turned their attention to Liberia and allied themselves with the ACS out of their own evangelical-cum-nationalist visions. Among the most important were US-born clergyman Henry Highland Garnet (AME), who served briefly as US ambassador, Henry McNeal Turner (AME), and Caribbean-born scholar and statesman Edward Wilmot Blyden (Presbyterian). They held a redemptionist view of Liberia, reworking race via science into God's plans for the universe: "God has established Liberia to furnish for the African work protection, racial adaptation, and political and ecclesiastical independence," Blyden wrote in 1888.[63]

1.2 Edward Wilmot Blyden, ca. 1860.

Photo credit: Library of Congress Prints and Photographs Division

Initially, Blyden believed that "civilized" people of African descent had a special role in uplifting Africa, and that Liberia, in turn, had a special destiny on the continent as a whole. Having migrated in 1853, Blyden served in a number of critical capacities in Liberia, including secretary of state (1860–64), president of Liberia College, located in the capital, Monrovia (1880–84), and minister to England. As a vice president of the ACS in the 1880s and a major contributor to the *Repository*, Blyden also had the ear of New York leadership and a prominent platform for articulating Liberian nationalism in this period.[64]

Amanda Smith shared these leading clergymen's general redemptionist framework.[65] "My heart yearns for that dark land," she wrote in 1881. "Africa must be redeemed back to God."[66] For Blyden and ACS officers, however, Liberian colonization entailed a complex set of spiritual, scientific, and political imperatives bound up with policing the nation's geographic, theological, and reproductive boundaries. Initially, at least, Blyden's redemptionism was centered in the Hebrew Bible. Like many, he took inspiration from the line in the Psalms "Ethiopia shall soon stretch forth her hands unto God," and he also relied on models from Exodus and Deuteronomy for building what he called a special "Negro nationality."[67] His vision was elitist, stridently nationalistic, racist, ambitious, and seemed to find affinity among the more upper-class Presbyterians and Episcopalians who wanted Liberia to take its place in the world alongside other modern nations.

By contrast, Smith embraced more Methodist- and Baptist-friendly leveling beliefs rooted in the equality of souls before God and the essential sameness of human nature. In Liberia, Smith's ministry concerned simple, homely truths for everyday people; Blyden embraced grand theory and addressed the world. He touted moral basics for Liberian nationhood, like the Fifth Commandment—honor thy father and mother—and endorsed specific rules for tribal integrity outlined in Deuteronomy 23: 2 and 8 in order to get the nation built. In so doing, Blyden took to logical extreme ACS's premise of repairing the dislocations of slavery by restoring Africa-descended people to their native lands, social policy writ large as prelapsarian conceit. "The restoration of the Negro to the land of his fathers will be the restoration of the race to its original integrity, to itself," effused Blyden.[68] In the 1860s and the 1870s, he had hoped that African Americans and Africans would blend easily, "flow together as readily and as naturally as two drops of water" as they had been separated by "accidental and temporary circumstance" but were "in reality *one people*—one in race, and one in destiny."[69] Liberia observer T. McCants Stewart also promoted "FUSION WITH THE NATIVES" (emphasis in original) for US migrants. But over time, new and harder-edged scientific notions of race convinced Blyden that mixed-heritage individuals from the diaspora—those he called mulattoes or "mongrels"—were impure, inferior, and weak physical types, doomed for extinction and inappropriate for building up Liberia.

According to Blyden, mixed-heritage people from the United States, usually the children of "white" fathers and "black" mothers conceived via coerced sex, were unable to live by the Fifth Commandment. They could neither honor fathers who were "scoundrels" nor mothers who were at best, victims or, at worst, despised social outcasts. People unable to honor the most basic moral principles were unfit for nation-building work in Liberia.[70] Blyden self-identified as a "pure Negro," and regarded mixed-ancestry African Americans as "legal as well as racial bastards," doubly impugning their moral worth and suitableness for Liberia, with its large and putatively unmixed native population.[71]

Reproductive politics and issues like bastardy and monogamy were key in Liberia, a settler, frontier society in which enforcing US style-laws and Anglo-American Christian norms of marriage proved difficult. In Monrovia, ACS agent C. T. O. King tried to institute a system of "oaths" to be sworn by male newcomers as a bulwark against "immigrants repudiating their wives after being sometime in the country on the ground that they were not legally married in America (the 'broomstick' custom prevailing in the South in the days of slavery...)."[72] In the 1850s, migration critic William Nesbitt mocked moral standards in Liberia by way of discrediting the pretensions of the ACS, noting, "Colonist women have been reduced to the extremity of marrying or taking up with naked native men, and are living with them in shameless cohabitation."[73] Skin-color prejudice also interfered with enforcing Christian rectitude and family boundaries. Blyden complained of the difficulty in prosecuting cases of fornication or seduction by missionaries, with light-skinned men escaping without censure and darker men facing harsh penalties by mission boards.[74] The indiscreet behavior of high-profile African Americans, including US ambassadors J. M. Turner and C. H. J. Taylor discouraged prospects for a wholesome fusion of peoples across the Atlantic.[75] White missionaries in Liberia exhibited racial prejudice, especially where sexual morality was concerned.[76] At the Episcopal Mission at Cape Mount, white Americans trained but did not have full confidence in native converts.[77] "The Cape Mt. Episcopal mission has been a moral stench since it passed into the hands of the Colored," commented the prickly Mary L. Sharpe to ACS officials. "And as far as my observation goes the number of illegitimate births exceed the legitimate."[78]

The sexual double standard exhibited by racist whites and the sexual privilege assumed by some African American men in Liberia played right into Blyden's reading of Deuteronomy. According to this text, a child who was the product of a "forbidden marriage" was prohibited from "entering the house of the Lord" unto the tenth generation. This was a definition of bastardy distinct from the modern legal one, tied to tribal *cum* "racial" boundaries rather than to the technicalities of legal marriage; a paper contract could not fix reproductive transgression, only time could.[79] Blyden read these biblical prohibitions as consonant with the laws of nature and as a perfect expression of divine plans for humanity: God created groups of people in particular places, with unique features and gifts, and with specific destinies. When Man interfered with these, only doom and failure could result. "The mongrel is not a natural man, is not in accord with nature," asserted Blyden, "He dreads Nature for he knows that she is everywhere working for his extinction, especially in Africa." Blyden further cited race in his perception of higher mortality rates in Africa among "white" and mixed-heritage people compared to "black." To be sure, Blyden's ideas were controversial on both sides of the Atlantic: the *Christian Recorder* noted that Blyden's "theory of the races is the theory of our bitterest enemies."[80] Yet, there may have been a kind of popular version of racialist nationalism circulating in Liberia during Amanda Smith's time there. For example, Benjamin Anderson, secretary of state, observed in the 1880s: "I am glad to see white people themselves impressed with the fact that *miscegenation* is a *gross impiety* and an undoing of the Creator's own works."[81]

As in Amanda Smith's commitment to an inclusive doctrine of "perfect love" under Christianity, Blyden's insistence that powerful whites abide by separatist precepts offered a fulcrum of power in neocolonial contexts like Liberia: a chance to keep whites on their side of the color line, and thus enable self-determination for Liberia and all black people. Blyden deserves neither credit nor blame for these ideas; they had been circulating in the "American School" of ethnology since the 1840s. Such thinking was reemphasized in the 1880s by deportation-minded white supremacists in the United States and made their way, Eric Love has argued, into anti-imperialist arguments against the incorporation of non-Europeans outside of North America into the US body politic.[82] Blyden's policy stance reflected a strain of this sort of anticolonial sentiment.[83] The major focus of Blyden's criticism in these years was the ACS itself, for abetting settlement in Liberia among supposedly deracinated African Americans. Mulattoes really could not be blamed for their tainted natures and were doomed to die out anyway, according to Blyden, but the ACS's colonization policy contradicted its own premises for nation building. "We have had all kinds of mixed blooded imparted among us, in various degrees—of Indian, Mongolian, and Caucasian; and these have largely been in the lead. Yet we have been expected to solve the Negro problem," complained Blyden, adding bitterly: "This looks like making fun."[84] He bemoaned the power imbalance across the color line: "Why is the Negro so unfortunate that he can have even in his own country, no hand in the deciding matters upon which his future and the future of his people depend?"[85] "What you can not do in America without homogeneousness you cannot do in Africa without homogeneousness," he lectured ACS official William Coppinger. "The attempt to construct a mongrel nation on this coast will happily be only an attempt—for you can neither lead or cajole Nature. But the attempt to do this is not doing unto others as you would have others do unto you," he intoned.[86] The disconnect was even deeper. Coppinger's 1883 pamphlet "Winning an Empire" ignored the practical and political matters of statecraft that Blyden shouldered. Instead, he approvingly tallied facts and figures (converts, dollars) across the African continent all to the credit of Christianity and even included "the colored people in the United States" as part of this empire and rightfully subject to colonial tutelage.[87]

Smith embraced African redemptionism, but from her holiness standpoint. Holiness figures sometimes placed themselves outside the body politic, and many missionaries on the ground in Africa preferred to step around the inner workings of nation building, empire, and sexual politics whenever possible. Methodists and Baptists tended to be tenacious and hardworking, but also more modest, gauging success on a smaller scale by looking to simple self-support of individual congregations rather than in frank competitiveness with Islam or other colonizing nation-states from Europe addressed frontally by Blyden. When articulated at all—William Taylor's voice is strongest on this point—missionaries identified their goal as "one Christian nationality," a rather ethereal, if encompassing, concept.[88] Or, as Smith put it: "May God hasten the time when this kingdom will be taken from them [the natives] and given to the King of kings [Jesus]."[89] Blyden would have found such formulations useless, even infuriating by the 1880s, much as Smith would have scratched her head at his touting of "rights for races" or his denigration of US Protestantism as "mongrel Christianity."[90] Holiness doctrine focused on the soul, not the body, and emphasized moral and behavioral piety rather than biological or genealogical purity. Ironically, the strongest African nationalists, like Blyden and eventually W. E. B. Du Bois, believed that Africa's gifts to the world of nations would be along moral, spiritual, and psychological, lines; for Edward Blyden, Africa's destiny was to serve, suffer, and redeem the world, like Christ, rather than to control and consume like white modernizers; Africa conserved, Europe destroyed.[91] Yet, a viable modern nation-state demanded power, money, and guns to defend both national and reproductive boundaries, thereby preserving Africa's very survival. Blyden's 1908 declaration that Liberia was "racially an unconstitutional State in Africa" is a distressing verdict indeed.[92]

Given the insistent construction of Africa by Blyden and his peers as a "*Fatherland*," gender and sexual politics deserve further comment.[93] Nation building meant family formation, and educating only native men in the ways of Christianity, industry, and republicanism would only accomplish half of this work.[94] African women and girls needed the gospel; they also had to be elevated as fitting spouses for new Liberian men. "Help the black girl if you want black men for Africa and patriotic mothers for the future children of Liberia," Blyden affirmed.[95] For decades, Christianized, English-speaking African men were paired with Christian, English-speaking Americo-Liberian women, who exhibited, as far as he was concerned, all the physical maladies and divided loyalties of the mulatto group. Blyden complained bitterly that ACS resources went to educate the daughters of the elite migrants in Monrovia, much to the neglect of those he regarded as pure or purifying Negroes: rural migrants from the US south and native west African girls. ACS policy thus extended the population and power of "mixed" families rather than worked toward a purification of the Liberian body politic Blyden sought under Deuteronomy 23.

Blyden described himself as personally suffering from this situation: "I myself was forced to marry a mixed woman or not marry at all."[96] His wife Sarah was from a well-to-do migrant family and, according to him, she was unable to endorse his vision and work. Blyden referred to his marriage as an "uncongenial relationship"; Sarah left Africa for the United States in 1887, apparently to her husband's relief.[97] African American missionary Jennie Davis hinted to an ACS officer confidentially about Blyden's "unpleasant family relation," and a quiet rumor about a disabled child born to the couple casts another shadow on their Liberian life.[98] Pushed to the breaking point, Blyden gave in to woman-blaming. "The moment the Negro young man takes to his bosom a mulatto or quadroon girl, he is, as a rule, compromised for his race," he asserted. "You see great black men earnest in their way and you wonder why they do not give their life to Africa—follow them home and you will see the cause."[99] Blyden faced public fallout for his beliefs in the Liberian context. He tried to teach young people to choose proper mates for the new nation, but he was criticized publicly for "raising the caste question." As a teacher at Alexander High School and at Liberia College, Blyden reported: "I felt this. The classes generally contained a majority of mixed boys and it was impossible to give the Negro youth lessons on the importance of race integrity without giving offence throughout the community and making bitter enemies which unfortunately I sometimes did." Blyden's efforts in teaching "race duty and responsibility" proved a lonely task.[100]

From the record, it is not clear how Smith approached matters of sex and sexuality in Liberia. She noted lapses in family and marital Christian norms there, but did so in moral not racial terms. In order to trade, Americo-Liberians could be drawn into the countryside for months, even years, and they sometimes married or purchased a native "country wife" in addition to keeping a "town wife," polygamy being normative in west Africa. Smith understood these as lapses as falling into the "customs and habits of the heathen," noting a bit sensationally: "This is not an uncommon occurrence!" (347–348). Indeed, such had taken place since earliest settlement times, and the Liberian government accommodated the practice, passing a statute in the early 1880s that allowed for the legal recognition of children born outside of wedlock and leaving the practice of polygamy intact.[101] Smith poked gentle fun at a newly arrived white missionary man from Sweden, who asked for her opinion about marrying a "nice colored woman" to help his career in Liberia. "Mr. Johnson seemed to think if he only married a colored girl, he being a white man... it would be such a strong proof to the colored people that he really loved them, that they would take him right into their arms..." (425). Smith's racial categories (i.e., "colored") would have rankled Blyden, who spoke in white and black. Smith offered neither Johnson nor anyone else any homily on nature, sex, or nation, insisting only on deep faith in God to discern the right.

Holiness promised to transcend "black" and "white," but Smith's Liberian ministry forced her to take policy positions on "race" in missions. The autobiography framed her Liberia years as a kind of referendum. As soon as Smith's vessel reached African shores (from India), the color issue immediately arose. Docked briefly at Sierra Leone, the curious Smith inquired about the state of the church of a white minister who boarded ship to greet passengers. He disparaged the limited success of "colored missionaries," at which comment Smith "felt quite indignant" (332). "But after I had been there awhile, and got to understand things better, I quite agreed with what the missionary told me on my first arrival to those shores." Rather than see this response as her buckling to prejudice, however, I view Smith's comment as a rejection of racialist thinking—that is, that "race" did not determine success with the gospel in Africa or anywhere else; "black" missionaries could fail just like "white" ones, despite the rhetorical insistence of an Edward Blyden.

In the uneasy, close-quartered social environment of Monrovia—a community of a little over a thousand people—one might expect Smith to be viewed as suspect, perhaps especially by Blyden. She was not properly tied to a husband and family, she assumed public authority as a preaching woman, and she was an African American sojourner, a foreign, potentially meddling individual whom he was inclined to view with suspicion. However, an editorial from February, 1882, in the Monrovia *Observer* newspaper, possibly written by Blyden or the US-born A. B. King, was "very pleased" with her presence, and the author, having "frequently heard" her speak, opined: "She is doing a more important work than she is perhaps aware."[102] Here, Blyden-style bias may have worked in Smith's favor, for as condemning as he was of "half-educated mongrels" from northern cities in the United States, he celebrated the "hardworking mechanics and farmers of the South."[103] As a self-educated "popular preacher," a former slave of southern heritage, and someone with an unpretentious and cheery disposition, the *Observer* placed Smith on the credit side of the ledger for Liberia. Indeed, Smith's independence from a sponsoring church made her politically safe as well. Liberian President H. R. J. Johnson bitterly pointed out the divisive presence of well-funded (white) missionaries who could outspend local elites as dispensers of financial largesse; during the colonial phase, the "agent of the church wielded a money patronage five times as great as that of the government."[104] As an itinerant, Smith had no money, and she impressed the editor not as a leader of a potentially disruptive movement of women (or of anyone else), but as a more limited exemplar of female "intellectual capacity," who expressed herself "well and forcibly" but "without any undue strong-mindedness." The editor judged Smith's "words and actions... [to be] essentially womanly" without any "undue assumption of the masculine character." Her work and example gave "new impetus" to the need for higher education of women in the young nation.[105] On this issue, Smith and Blyden would have most certainly agreed. "There is so little attention paid to the education of girls; not a single high school for girls [exists] in the whole republic of Liberia," she noted, a lack she dubbed "a great shame and a disgrace to the government" (342).

Smith's Ministry in Liberia: Gospel Temperance

Scholars acknowledge Blyden as a brilliant and passionate architect of African nationalism whose career was undermined by forces outside of his control. Smith's work in Liberia, by contrast, was an all-but-forgotten success. In his various roles as teacher, scholar, diplomat, and advisor in Liberia, Blyden struggled to resolve Liberia's northwest boundary dispute with Great Britain, prevent Liberia College from sinking, and institute workable migration policy and marriage norms for the country. For his trouble, he nearly lost his life in an assassination attempt in 1885 when his name was floated as presidential nominee for the Whig party. By contrast, Amanda Smith was credited in her day with almost single-handedly raising the issue of temperance to success in the Liberian legislature. William Taylor thought liquor imports in Liberia to be down three-fourths by 1888. "Why the change?" he asked a New York audience. "Well, I think it is owing mainly to the agency of Amanda Smith. She went there and throttled the thing—took the lion by his beard in his own den, and on the line of holiness and temperance brought about this wonderful change."[106] While certainly Smith provided Taylor with a useful object lesson for his own missionary balance sheet, he felt strongly enough about her accomplishments to cite her in his report to the General Conference of

Methodists in 1888 and praise her elsewhere in print as "one of the prophetesses spoken of by Joel."[107] Other observers in Monrovia agreed: "The evangelist, true to her work and calling, has lectured again and again in nearly every hamlet and every pulpit, her voice has been raised and the cause of temperance vindicated."[108] C. T. O. King reported to New York that Smith's labors "intensified" existing opposition to alcohol and helped form temperance bands "throughout the county," whose purpose was to rid Liberia of the "use, sale and manufacture of ardent spirits."[109] Smith did this work while Blyden sought safety in nearby Sierra Leone, where he stewed over his own and Liberia's misery, and tried to keep his spirits up by writing and research. King noted in the summer of 1885 that when a local military official held a wedding for his daughter in Monrovia, Smith was among the guests but not Blyden or himself, hinting at her cache among Americo-Liberians compared to these two men, both born in the Caribbean.[110]

Yet, in her prolific writings on Liberia, Smith herself did not draw attention to her social success or to the temperance legislation that passed during her tenure in country, referring to the 1884 tariff law only in passing in her narrative and not at all in her letters back to *The Standard*.[111] Smith's basic message in Liberia was "gospel temperance," in which swearing off alcohol was yoked to confession of sin and acceptance of Jesus as savior, a revival method well honed in WCTU circles and camp meetings. Smith spread this message in both town and rural settings, where alcohol use was entrenched in trade relations with native populations. She met a pressing need. President Johnson advocated that "care should be taken to guard the aborigines against the introduction of those pernicious influences which have proven so detrimental to aboriginal races elsewhere," he told the Legislature in 1883. "Ardent spirits and all intoxicating liquors should be entirely suppressed, or admitted under severe restrictions."[112]

In the Liberian capital and the more sophisticated northern towns, Smith encountered populations familiar with US–style temperance traditions.[113] In Monrovia, this context made her work easier, but elsewhere it actually made her redundant. Baptists at Arthington put her off entirely: "I was never asked in a Baptist church to take a service, while I was there [at Arthington]; only to address a Sabbath school" (413). Clay-Ashland was ready for the "higher life" of sanctification, and Smith established a "Holiness Association" there in 1888 (381). The temperance message was well taken in Monrovia, but the city held special challenges. Native youth were very vulnerable, especially the boys who sought work or schooling in town. "Here the courts are held, the Legislature meets; the stores are here, rum shops are here and it is impossible to keep the boys from coming into constant contact with sinister influences," explained C.T.O. King.[114] Smith noted the challenges facing native youth employed in Monrovian households who, when not at work, were left to shift for themselves, unshepherded to church or school. "I was a little surprised that there were no native Churches, or schools of any kind in Monrovia for the natives, but there is none."[115] She was fairly dismissive of nearby Liberia College, the pet project of the ACS and the focus of Edward Blyden's dreams. "Yes, they boast of a college," she sniffed in her narrative. "I often told them that it did not come up to a good high school in this country, not in any sense" (453).

Smith missed—and misjudged—some potential allies in the capital. She initially made a sour appraisal of President Johnson. During his independence day address in 1882, Smith noted that Johnson railed against "the foreign church" with its "'isms' and 'schisms' and doctrines and disputes and contentions" that came to Africa wrapped in assumptions about the "inferiority of the negro" (335). Smith took his words seriously—quoting a passage from the printed speech in her narrative—but the construction she put on his argument is unfortunate, as she defensively personalized a position she could have used to her advantage. Johnson underlined the need for "independence in religion" for Liberia based on his well-founded anger at manipulative US church officials, who resisted authorizing independent conferences and bishoprics abroad, keeping missionaries under their own control and practically starving out black workers. This was the crucial context of Johnson's complaint about "foreign churches."[116] Smith's holiness orientation kept her away from official politics, but in judging Johnson to be close-minded, she perhaps missed a promising source of support and encouragement, as the editorial in the *Observer* highlighted. This situation was doubly regrettable since Bishop Samuel Ferguson of the local Episcopal Church had so coolly received her. Ferguson rejected Smith's offer to preach in a "great, lengthy epistle," pointing to "a clause in our Methodist discipline"—whether against women preaching or holiness is not clear from Smith's discussion (438). Smith was stung by this rejection on account of Ferguson "being a black Bishop," but the situation was further proof to her that "human nature is the same in black men, even in Africa, as in white men in America" (438). Given these difficulties, Smith kept a low profile, and sought quietly to improve things on her own through her message of holiness and love.[117]

After adjusting to the climate during the winter and spring of 1882, Smith opened a Sabbath school for native boys in Monrovia in the rooms of an old Episcopal seminary building, and organized local women into a praying "Band of Hope" with her hostess, Sister Patsey Payne, at its head (336–338). Under Smith's guidance, Payne eventually became sanctified, and the Payne household was Smith's home base in her Liberia years. She also had the support of a native convert named Brother Charles Pitman in town, a "prince of Israel," who also received sanctification and was "quite American in his ideas" having lived for some years in the United States. "He received me as [would] a Christian brother," explained Smith, "and stood by me in all the work of the church" (432). However, in early summer of 1883, Smith removed herself from the native school, temperance band, and a third project, care of a Bassa girl she adopted named Frances, leaving all of these in Patsey's hands. Smith described herself as eager to get out of Monrovia and into the hinterlands. When Bishop Taylor arrived tending south toward Cape Palmas, she made a great effort to catch up with his ministry and stayed away from Monrovia for over two years.

Smith's attraction to Taylor's ministry is understandable given his personal charisma and international renown in Methodist circles. Taylor was, in Smith's words, a "grand old man" around whom the missionaries "gather[ed]...like a lot of birds with mouths and ears open to catch every word."[118] This esteem was shared even by secular figures in Monrovia who complained of the "slowness and slovenliness of matters in Church and School and State" in the country, and expressed the "hope that the new Methodist Bishop Taylor will resuscitate things."[119] Taylor was slow to take Smith on, but in the end, they each proved critical to one another as they sought entree into the interior.

Heading south to Sinoe County, Smith began enthusiastically, with a mind "to help everybody I could, in every way I could" with practical Christian service, especially visiting the sick, ministering to the dying, and assisting with the spiritual wants of anyone who asked, black or white (437). She tried to lead with what she called her "mother heart" (60, 319) and taught on temperance and sanctification directly from scripture or occasionally from little books, like the "Believer's Hand-book of Holiness." Smith also stressed the power of personal testimony to stir the power of the Holy Ghost, which she found so lacking among Americo-Liberian congregations. As in Monrovia, Smith started her ministry unobtrusively, with youth, in places like Lexington and Greenville. She began with "the Gospel Temperance work among the young people and children" and, when later "asked for co-operation and help," made the bridge to adults, often assisted by youthful preachers and testimony from within her classes and prayer groups. Smith's ambition to help "everybody" included native Africans, though due to language, health, and mobility barriers, much of her time was spent among English-speaking settlers. Smith made her way more or less alone in 1883 and 1884 through Sinoe and Bassa counties, where she was repeatedly struck by the "spiritual indifference" of the people, giving her ample opportunity for outreach (342).

Smith's letters to the *Christian Standard* in 1883–84 convey more travelogue than social and political context in Liberia. By contrast, the autobiography contains sharp details, especially of the planting of "Band of Hope Gospel Temperance Societies," which frequently centered on youth and women. She also documents organized resistance to her presence. In small towns like Hartford and Fortsville, she found male church leadership opposed to temperance: "Preachers and laymen all thinking there is nothing they can do but trade" (347) in alcohol in order to survive and cope with the surrounding native population. She established Bands of Hope and Temperance Societies in Greenville and Lexington only after wading through two years of "trials," "deception," and plans "to overthrow the work" by opponents (349). "The darkness of mind here among the people is very great," she wrote in the *Standard*. "Through ignorance there is much opposition to the temperance work" (352). By "ignorance" Smith seems to mean illiteracy and isolation, profiteering on alcohol sales to natives, and the attitudes of those who held a "great deal of prejudice against women preaching" (354). In the Greenville area, she felt that "the needs of the people here are great in every way" and that the town had a deservedly "low" reputation because "ignorance and superstition are fearful."[120] Sometimes, she encountered "old societies" like the Good Templars and Daughters of Temperance that had "once flourished"—probably in the early years after migration from the United States—but these had "well nigh died out" (355). "So to show them that I was with them in anything that was for the well-being of the people, I joined them, and helped what I could," she recalled. "But, Oh, how hollow, and empty, and unreal" (355).

Back in Monrovia in early 1885, Smith finally met up with Bishop Taylor, and she attended the Methodist Conference, one of the quarterly meetings of the denomination. She expressed a desire to accompany him to more interior areas, but Taylor declined as she lacked the necessary language skills for effective work among the native populations.[121] However, her reputation for hard work and concrete temperance success seems to have made an impression on him. In addition, Smith knew how to make herself useful. Taylor was scheduled to reappear in church to the south at Edina and then, Smith anticipated, move on to Cape Palmas, long a desired destination of hers, perhaps because she knew that AME Zion missionaries made a strong showing in that town in the early 1880s.[122] She managed to team up with Taylor, sure that she could "be of some service to look after the Bishop a little, and do all I could ....I was quite sure I would be of service" (376). During their subsequent travels, she prepared his morning tea and other meals and also acted as mediator with nervous Americo-Liberian hosts who put up the famous Bishop in their simple, often rustic homes. Smith reasoned that since Taylor had come to Africa "to help my people by establishing missions and schools, I felt it was my duty to do all I could to help" (384). Smith also acknowledged the limitations of itinerant work and likely sought reinforcement and support from Taylor. Revivals, conversions, and pledges could sometimes feel superficial, with leaders always only beginning a work rather than maturing the commitment into something lasting.[123] As she ultimately admitted of her Liberia years: "There were possibilities, but not many probabilities" (417).

Rewriting Africa

One of the possibilities taken up by Smith was the chance to engage with African people. Writing about her tender and caring ministry helped her refute negative stereotypes of Africans, especially in her autobiography. Smith's work is striking compared to the Liberia writings by male clergy in this period. This literature was an important exercise in self-definition in which national and transnational identifications were weighed and measured.[124] Works by Henry M. Turner, William Nesbitt, and Martin Delany were the result of visits to Liberia that lasted weeks or sometimes months. These writers mostly appraised the land and people as promising for settlement and development but found the lack of infrastructure strongly prohibitive to migration. Amanda Smith's discussions of Liberia's peoples and customs fall in a different register, almost anthropological and highly sympathetic, like those produced by William Shepard or T. McCants Stewart.[125] Her autobiography contains especially moving accounts of her interactions with and observations of Grebo, Vei, and Kru peoples. Like Sheppard, Stewart, and, later, Henry Turner, Smith's appraisals strongly rebutted contemporary racist presumptions about African inferiority. And while her descriptions sometimes turned on "civilizationist" assumptions, they also evinced deep appreciation for African family life and parenting, for native skills in pottery and weaving, the physical beauty and dignity of the people, and, most surprisingly, respect and accommodation for native customs and cosmologies.

Like the redemption-minded clergy, Smith regarded Africa and Africans as having an equal claim and rightful place in world history. However, unlike would-be patriarchs who spoke in the language of race, science, and nationalism, Smith tried to lead with what she termed a "mother's pity in my heart" (374). Blyden, at points, argued that the "people must be forced—flogged—to their duty" to Liberian nationalism as he saw it.[126] He wrote from a place of deep pain and struggle for belonging; his ire was overwhelmingly directed at his political competitors among the Americo-Liberians rather than natives. "*I am not at home in Monrovia*" he declared to the ACS. [127] With a return to the United States likely and her well-developed apolitical identity as a "saint," Smith moved more easily than Blyden did toward nurturance and fellowship. Granted, she was more modest in her ambitions and did not come with an expectation to recreate nation, race, or even home in Liberia, but to extend God's kingdom. One thing Blyden and Smith shared, however, was an optimistic and generous view of the native population.

Some of Smith's reporting on cannibalism, slavery, and polygamy reflected "dark continent" stereotypes of the Victorian era. "The poor women of Africa," she noted, "as a rule, they have all the hard work to do" (389). This was a standard identification of the native woman as a downtrodden drudge, in need of uplifting by Christianity. But Smith had "tears in her eyes" for native people not because she was revolted by their culture or ashamed of their habits but because she was moved by their beauty, especially of the women and children. Bishop Taylor dismissed Cavalla River people in Liberia with a wave; they were "as destitute of clothing and the knowledge of God as the tribes I met on the Congo"; African American migrant Samuel Williams thought the most pressing legislation for Liberia in the 1850s should be to "outlaw nakedness" in Monrovia.[128] Smith was more open-minded. "Some of the women were very good looking; good features and beautifully formed, as are also their children," wrote Smith. "Oh, how my heart longed after them for Jesus" (379). When a chief invited her to drink wine with him in a celebration, she, of course, declined but also offered to fix him some cocoa to share so that the two might become "friends" (389).

Christian missionaries frequently described native belief systems as "devil worship," and Smith also used this language in her assessment of African religion. But where white missionaries literally kicked over, swiped at, or mocked sacred objects and practices—William Taylor recounted how a white missionary literally beat with a stick a so-called devil doctor, driving him out of a Kru village—Smith instead asked questions, as best she could.[129] For example, native women usually burned fires inside their huts for cooking and left rice and other offerings outside for the "devil." Smith longed to cook outside on an open hearth, but after taking her query to the local king, she reported that: "I just did what I was told, and did my own cooking in my own native house."[130] Similarly, when Smith was disturbed by parenting practices—like the apparent force-feeding of an infant with boiled rice or the custom of rubbing a baby, even its eyes, with pepper to ward off disease—Smith engaged the mothers and came away appreciative. "Well, it is wonderful," notes Smith, "there is a pretty good logic in it" (407). Sensationalist tales of missionary child saving—several west African groups believed twins to be of the devil and such infants were left in designated areas—were stock and trade of triumphalist missionary lore but earned only restrained acknowledgment from Smith. Stories of twin sacrifice struck her as "sad, and yet interesting" rather than outrageous and beyond the pale (408). Christianization entailed domestic reform and bodily discipline around child rearing, sexual comportment, and foodways that frequently lead to struggle and negative moral judgments of natives by Euro-Americans. Yet Smith affirmed: "Really I never saw a dirty native baby" (406). She also praised native peoples' skills with pottery and especially cloth, calling them "great geniuses" in such work (410–412; 385). These descriptions firmly intervened in judgmental missionary discourses that viewed Africans as physically, intellectually, and morally inferior, permanently stagnated compared to so-called advanced Europeans.[131]

Amanda Smith did, however, embrace two key missionary tropes of her day, Christianity as key to the "elevation of woman" and the mercy of child rescue. Both figured in her critique of marriage and of what she perceived to be bride "selling." As in other foreign settings, white missionaries from the United States devised a range of strategies to intervene in native marriage systems: wardship, apprenticing, and adoption among them. In Liberia, a system of indenture evolved that created a pathway to citizenship from which natives were otherwise constitutionally excluded. By indenturing a native child, especially girls who were generally less mobile than boys, settlers and missionaries believed they could "save these educated girls to Christian civilization and the Church."[132] For once a husband had paid his dowry, according to Smith, his authority over a wife was absolute. "The laws in this are very strict. A man's wife is his wife, and no one dare interfere" (390). For Smith, this scenario was symptomatic of the social system in which the "moment a girl child is born, she belongs to somebody," usually the future husband. "Poor things, they are not consulted; they have no choice in the matter."[133]

Smith's solution to this injustice was highly interventionist. She offered no extended critique of polygamy or the dowry system, but affirmed simply: "It is so much better for the missionary to buy the girls." "If a girl has been bought by a missionary," Smith continued, without irony, "she is free as long as she lives." By contrast, "Boys are [already] free; no dowry for them. They can go and live with missionaries, marry and settle, just as they like" (392). According to Smith, native families profited from daughters through the dowry system. Missionaries lost money on girls, who would be reclaimed by families after a little schooling to earn them a higher bride price. Boys were the wild card. Native families could either relieve themselves of care for sons by letting them "walk about"—a traditional rite of passage by which young men proved their survival skills—or encourage them to get a foreign education, especially in language, so that they could secure a better livelihood in commerce with Europeans. Native girls "cost" missionaries capital whereas boys "added." Girls had to be paid for, schooled in domesticity and dependency, and then married off to Christianized native men. Boys came for free and could be hired, often cheaply, to work and add value to missionary and other settler enterprises.[134] This pattern extends into the present, with Liberian sons usually laying primary claim to a family's resources because they cannot "spoil themselves [sic]" with early pregnancies like a daughter.[135]

In adopting two native children, Smith bobbled these difficult dynamics. Placing girl children usually entailed exacting negotiations between natives and missionaries, but little Frances, the Bassa girl referred to earlier, was apparently gifted to Smith by her father, after having first bound her to a Mr. and Mrs. Brown of Monrovia as a servant. The girl's father seems to have not been able to meet Smith's price for her return. Smith later explained that Frances's "mother died, and I told Mr. Brown [her master, that] if her people wanted her [back], they must pay me two bullocks; for it had cost me that with the care and trouble I had had with her" (392). The adoption of a boy named "Little Bob" was, by contrast, painstaking and involved repeated petitions by his parents for "mammy" (Smith) to take this "pick'n," so that "he can sabe God proper," and weeks of prayerful soul searching on Smith's part. Ultimately, a contract was signed in February, 1888 (and reprinted in the autobiography's text) with Bishop Taylor himself as one of the witnesses (395–397). Smith's poor health, her preference for a number of other boy children in town, and his young age—Little Bob was perhaps three years old, Frances was closer to six or seven—account for some of her hesitancy in parenting the child. Yet, the structure of the narrative also suggests issues of value and gender. Both children were to be missionary object lessons: Frances was to be a missionary, Bob a missionary doctor. Though Smith once called Frances "my little treasure" in a letter to the *Standard*, she is scarcely mentioned in the text of the autobiography.[136] She was frequently in the care of the Payne family and remained behind in Liberia when Smith left. By contrast, Little Bob's adoption, education, conversion, and removal to England takes up more than a whole chapter and is rendered with literary flare and riveting detail. The reader learns of Smith's "mother's heart" in action with Little Bob, as they pray together, work through learning English (she threatens but refrains from switching him for resisting his lessons), and she coaches him through dealing with racist taunts on the streets of London. By contrast, almost nothing about Frances is offered. The girl is described as a something of a drain and burden, in the end too sick to leave the country at all; the boy is held up as a success story and an object lesson against racism. "Now when all is considered, I don't believe that there is a child in this country born of Christian parents, that would have shown a capability beyond that child's," Smith bragged of Little Bob. "It is nonsense to say that a native African is not capable of learning" (399). Later readers of Smith's newsletter, *The Helper*, would hear regularly about Bob's life and Christian progress.[137]

The adoption passages direct attention back to the dynamics of hierarchy and paternalism in Liberian missions, evident in language and forms of address as they moved across the Atlantic. Especially striking in Smith's adoption passages is the slang from US slavery: the appellation "mammy" for adult women and mothers and the nicknames "pick'n" and "little darky" for African children—Smith even refers to Little Bob by such monikers (398, 407). In addition, the official documents of Liberia—contracts, treaties, agreements, maps—make use of this slang, place names like "Piquinny Cess" and the designation of native peoples as "cuffee" or "Black so and so" by Americo-Liberians.[138] Worse, the sympathetic T. McCants Stewart encountered natives renamed "Jack Savage," "Slow Coach," "Poor Fellow," and a father and son pair called "Big Potato" and "Little Potato." Appalled by this "barbarous" mockery of natives, he renamed two young men he met "Toussaint L'Overture" and "Hanibal," adopting the men into a grand history of military achievement.[139] "[A]ll foreigners and Liberians are called 'Mammy' and 'Daddy,'" explained Smith, "but when the natives use it, it is as we would use 'Mr.' and 'Mrs.'" (394). This passage suggests that the use of slang by native people toward migrants and colonizers was somewhat less insulting than the other way around.[140] The legacy of US slavery and racism in the lives of native African Liberians took many forms; that Smith advocated buying African girls to protect them from their own society and that she called her own adoptive son a "darky" makes final assessment of her posture difficult.

More wholesome bonds of identification obtained among nonnative Christians, especially among the sanctified, in Smith's telling. Americo-Liberians were indispensable to Smith's well-being in Africa. At the top of the list was the Payne family, including Sister Patsey Payne, sister-in-law of former Liberian president Daniel Spriggs Payne. Smith also referred to Sister Payne's son, B. Y. Payne, as a "son."[141] J. S. Pratt, a native helper, dedicated convert, and friend of the Methodists called Smith "Ma" (396). She referred to senior women Christian workers, like "Ma Harmon" and "Mother Goldie," in respectful terms; these women were fluent in native languages and were important models and allies for Smith. Another important group of Christian fictive kin lived at Clay-Ashland, including the Baptist Ricks family, especially Martha Ricks with whom Smith made a prayerful pact to uphold each other in the paths of holiness. The Paynes, the Ricks family, and Mother Harmon and even a few white women missionaries played roles of praying sister, nurse, traveling companion, and interpreter during Smith's Liberian ministry. Perhaps not surprisingly, Bishop Taylor referred to Smith as "Amanda" in direct speech as recorded by her, though generally he used "Mrs. Amanda Smith" in published materials; she exclusively used "Bishop" when referring to him in all of her writings and in the rendering of their dialogues in her narrative.

Outside of religious circles, Smith's identification with Liberian natives and Americo-Liberian emigrants remained ambivalent. She referred to Africans as "my people" (384, 425) while projecting a more active connection to those she called "home folks" or "my own country people" (425), meaning migrants and other Americo-Liberians. By referring to Africa as the land of her "forefathers" and later lavishing the spotlight on Little Bob, Smith expressed and reinforced the patriarchal tone of everyday social discourse and practice in Liberia, which affirmed the primacy of men and fathers.[142] Female support and solidarity with Smith was evident in the domestic sphere and the quasi-private sphere of prayer meetings and friendly visiting. To move between towns and institutions, Amanda Smith had to negotiate with or around powerful men. In the end, Smith fell back on nativity if not legalistic concepts of citizenship as a touchstone for identity and belonging. The group that earned her most despairing appraisal was the recent US migrants from the south, three parties of whom arrived during Smith's Liberia years. "They are real American citizens," argued Smith and should remain in the United States. "Like many of the foreigners that come, they are not all industrious; and to be poor, and ignorant, and lazy is bad enough at home. But to be seven thousand miles away in a heathen country is ten times worse" (452). Indeed, in anticipation of her adoption of Little Bob, settlers in Monrovia "wanted [that she] should take a Liberian," that is, an Americo-Liberian (393), presumably to keep her sympathies and resources on their side of the cultural boundary line where, in fact, Smith herself mostly remained.

Racism and Colonialism in Liberian Missions

Smith began her Liberian work among the coastal English-speaking population and ended it evangelizing those living inland as an assistant to William Taylor in 1886–87. This episode functions as the culmination of her autobiography, taking up the final third of the story, and it was the work that made her "famous." "Of course, such a thing was never heard of on the west coast of Africa," she noted, "—a woman preacher, and a black woman at that. Such a novelty!"[143] Her alliance with Taylor also seems to have eased the personal loneliness and isolation that Smith's holiness standpoint—"alone, yet not alone"—sometimes fostered.[144] "I never saw a man that could so smile darkness away as Bishop Taylor can," wrote Smith in a letter to the *Standard*. "Clouds and darkness seems to be ashamed to be around where he is."[145] Smith was sure that she could be of help to him in his planned Cavalla River trip in southern Liberia. Since "the grand old hero with his band of self sacrificing missionaries are here in Africa for my people's sake," she wrote to the *Standard*, "I feel I ought to stay as long as I possibly can, and so I will. God help me."[146] Liberia was a near-final stop for Taylor's "Round the World for Jesus" missionary tour, and Smith accompanied him for the opening of 16 mission stations in the southern region. Although the trip elevated her status, it also effectively ended her Liberian ministry. It ended in part due to health issues but more importantly because the expedition brought to a head simmering issues touching race and colonialism in missionary work.

Given that the ME General Conference "turned him loose" in Africa, Taylor's narrative of the Cavalla River trip has something of a last hurrah about it. But it actually both expressed and provoked a crisis because it highlighted native Africans' own critique of Blyden-style nationalism in Liberia and their struggles with colonialist pressure on their land and way of life. Not only did chiefs request their "own" missionaries as a hedge against encroachments by secular or other competing European forces, but they also specifically requested white men. Both Taylor and Smith recorded this emphatic request. "'No want black man; no want a Liberian'" (meaning Americo-Liberian).[147] "The natives almost without exception have asked that white teachers be sent them," noted Smith.[148] Of the demand that "white men be sent to them," Taylor sniffed: "Such is the effect of the 'Caucasian civilization' of this coast, of which we expect so much." Taylor blamed an imported racism for the situation, when in fact the chiefs were on to what Hillary Johnson well knew: alliances with people attached to resources made a huge difference in the balance of power in this minimally developed society. The chiefs wanted not people with white skin, but access to resources, diplomatic prestige, and trustworthy allies. Taylor analogized this sour situation to that existing between "our American traders and the Indians," but he really did not think too hard about the chiefs' position as beset by a range of contending foreign forces.[149] For her part, Smith was taken aback by natives' neediness. She described how, upon their arrival in a Cavalla River village, "the old women would get down and take hold of the Bishop's feet, and then they would turn to Pratt, and say; 'Oh! Daddy, you mouth no lie this time. You mouth no lie. You got true mouth.'" "My heart ached when I saw their kindness, and I wept," she continued. "Poor things!"[150] Edward Blyden even asked the ACS for white leadership in despair.[151] Blyden was provoked to even more cynicism when Taylor "proclaimed that colored men are *not* wanted even by the natives," and imagined a foolish "rush of such persons" from the United States determined to prove Taylor wrong.[152]

Blyden was right that Taylor behaved and thought about Liberia superficially and with detachment. Initially the Bishop's vision of self-supporting mission stations involved, in his words, *"native Christian missionaries"* who he thought would work much more cheaply and efficiently than people from the United States and who could compete more effectively with "Mohammedan missionaries," who seemed to "go everywhere without money or food."[153] Given the chiefs' desire for "white men" and the difficulty of obtaining them, however, Taylor initially sought something of a compromise, to recruit those he called "educated 'negroes'" from the United States, a group some Africans actually regarded as "white."[154] Taylor arranged for a pamphlet and lecture series about Amanda Smith's work to drum up support. Money and interest raised from the pamphlet's sales were supposed to "raise recruits" from African American communities in the United States. The project's failure is a telling index to the shifting racial politics within Methodist missions and the liabilities of Smith's "privileged" status as in but not of church politics and structures, "black" or "white," US or Liberian.

The up-front costs to publish and distribute the pamphlet were primarily raised among unnamed "colored friends" of the mission cause. The document was grandly titled *The Life, Travels, Labors, and Helpers of Mrs. Amanda Smith, The Famous Negro Missionary Evangelist.*[155] The text held Smith up "especially to women" as "not only the greatest Negro woman, but the greatest of the race in these times," comparing her favorably to poet Phillis Wheatley, preacher Sojourner Truth, and educator Frances E. W. Harper. "As an enlightened, thoroughly consecrated Christian evangelist, among Negro women, Mrs. Amanda Smith takes the first place in American history."[156] Taylor failed at both the work of enrollment and financial management. In addition, controversy over the pamphlet's publication fund and its profits prompted AME Church commentators to dub it a piece of "ill-fated propaganda" and castigate its authors for presuming to anoint the "greatest of the race."[157] Smith herself complained in print from abroad. "Many of my friends have been misled in regard to the little book," for they understood that the profits from sales were to benefit her directly since she was an unpaid missionary dependent on donations for survival. With so much suspicion surrounding where the profits, if any, went, the project resulted in little of substance and with hard feelings and poor publicity all around.[158]

Such misfirings characterized much of the Cavalla River trip. Taylor emphasized the Methodist goal of self-supporting native churches. Self-support took important cues from the industrial school movement in the United States at this time and strongly echoed its focus on physical labor and market productivity for natives and converts. Methodists regarded Africa as "one of the earth's noblest seats for future empire," and while they might have meant this "empire" in a spiritual sense (as Smith surely did), as a practical matter Taylor's time in Liberia was substantially taken up by mediating disputes over land deals and trading rights, normative imperial concerns.[159] Indeed, when Taylor's band ventured into much disputed territory in the southern coast, they broached an area where the Liberian government had sent troops beginning in January, 1887, and which had been a long-standing locus of struggle for control. The Grebos attacked and then banished some Christian converts in an attempt to stop land cessions that were tied to missionary activities backed by the government.[160] The situation greatly alarmed Amanda Smith, who recalled being stopped by the natives in an armed "siege" upon arrival. To the Grebo, "It meant war; that these white missionaries were only coming to take the country away from them." "Oh! It was terrible," Smith recalled. It took weeks to regroup and relaunch on the river from Cape Palmas (457). This situation at least qualifies William Coppinger's assertion earlier in the decade: "The natives of the interior of the [Liberian] Republic are anxious for the planting of civilized settlements" in their midst, unless anxious meant anxious and not, conventionally, "eager."[161]

Smith endorsed the idea of self-supporting missions as early as 1883, calling it the "only hope" for success. She had seen first hand the demoralization of undersupported foreign missionaries in Liberia, who turned to either corrupt worldly interests like the liquor trade to make ends meet or who would simply "give up and die" for lack of purposeful, sustainable living in Africa (414). Blyden also worried about liquor. "Isolated missionaries are followed by the rum-sellers; and they are helpless to check its increase more and more. Until the drink manufacture is suppressed in Christian lands," he warned with no little sarcasm, "the liquor traffic will be one of the difficulties which will confront Bishop Taylor in his wonderful enterprise."[162] Liquor was only one of many challenges. Smith concluded at the end of the Cavalla trip: "Unless the Lord shall baptize and send help from America, or somewhere else, from a human standpoint we shall expect failure" in Liberia.[163]

Smith wanted missions to succeed because she did not want "beautiful Africa" to be "given up for lost."[164] Like Blyden, she believed that Africa was wrongly perceived by outsiders as "backward." Africans had never had a fair chance, having been interfered with for centuries by the slave trade and other foreign incursions. "These poor people have longed for the gospel—they have not rejected it, for no one carried it to them," she insisted.[165] Some African American Christians believed that African missions were a way to heal the wounds of slavery on the continent as well as among the "exiles" in America: "It would be poetic justice to see a Negro-American civilization redeeming Africa," observed R. T. Greener of Howard University.[166] Blyden, of course, thought such "cross-racial" endeavors worse than foolhardy, but doomed: "The Bishop [Taylor], you see, thinks that colored men are of course an 'indigenous agency' on the vicious theory that all men of African blood are Africans..."[167] While planting missions in west Africa, Taylor described traveling literally along the "caravan trails of the ages" of the slave traders. He movingly—or sensationally—claimed to "hear the dead speaking" to him along the way of his travels, chastising him for not having come "before we died" under the ravages of the trade.[168]

Despite the mixed motives and confused tactics of Taylor's Cavalla River trip, Smith's proven record of effectiveness made her a key member of the missionary band. The group made a year-long journey, primarily by boat. Taylor was the only white westerner in the group; his main assistants were Smith and Pratt. The party also included another native convert and translator, Tom Nimly, "a man over six feet in height with proportions massive and symmetrical and a native born orator"; Lace, a young boy of the coastal Kru people (who were expert navigators and sailors); Thomas, described as a "bush boy"; a carpenter, a boat captain, and two stevedores who carried supplies and, not infrequently, the missionaries themselves. Taylor and Smith were sometimes carried in hammocks over rivers and up and down treacherous stony hills during the journey by these men. The boatmen pushed against the current to travel upriver, moving Taylor to comment on the "heroic pluck of our Kroo boys" that "brought tears to my eyes."[169] The irony of the natives carrying, steering, and essentially saving the missionaries was lost in the correspondence generated and sent home by the "Taylor Band," including Smith, on this historic journey to "win Africa for Christ."[170]

Initially, Taylor envisioned the veterans Smith and Pratt as staying on after the establishment of the mission stations, thinking they could "receive and settle our [new] missionaries for this coast next December and January."[171] For several years, already, Pratt had run a supply station on the Cavalla. Smith seriously contemplated staying on herself, as she had "been here quite a while and [knew] many of the people."[172] She felt it a "great privilege" to be "present at the opening of all the stations," but in the end, the work left her "so thoroughly broke down" that she had to leave Africa.[173] Trekking and canoeing during the rainy season took a severe toll on mind and body, and she described parts of the trip as "so sad" that at points she could scarcely get out of the boat and walk (395). At the end of one particularly miserable day, she cried "for two or three hours" out of exhaustion and frustration when put up for the night in a smokey "native home" that lacked a chimney.[174] Smith may not have been alone in this anguish as she noted in another letter that after the hard physical trials of the journey, "Tears would come in spite of ourselves. Then we would after an hour or two have the headache after the tears dry up."[175]

The work was not just physically debilitating but politically daunting. Mission establishment involved negotiations with chiefs over treaty and land rights, and the Grebo people needed extensive assurances about land and power, pressured as they were by the French and the English to the north and the east. Taylor hoped to exploit the weaknesses of secular treaties in Liberia, in which he felt various European groups had "failed entirely" to fulfill their promises to build schools for the native tribes in exchange for trading rights and other privileges. Coastal tribes requested their own foreign missionary, not wanting to be slighted or disadvantaged compared to any other band or village. But Taylor drove a hard bargain, demanding not just prime land for "mission farms" and schools but extracting the promise of free labor for the construction of buildings and homes along western lines. This required harvesting and hauling timber lumber from great distances for major construction efforts. Taylor engaged in supreme understatement when he reported mildly in the *Christian Standard* that these negotiations frequently got "stuck on the land question."[176]

Like the pamphlet fiasco, Smith's experience along the Cavalla showcased her talents, but it left her drained and without clear direction. She mused in the end, "Perhaps, I did a little." She was forced to admit that despite Taylor's credentials and sincerity, there was "not that deep Christian sympathy for him and this work, even among his own people at home and also in *Africa—I mean Liberia*."[177] The best Taylor could muster was: "Liberia, with all its faults and mishaps, is not a failure."[178] Well before Taylor's arrival, however, Smith acknowledged the uphill nature of missionary work. "There is so much to do here, and one can see it all around, and can only do a little and up to a certain point and then one must stop," she admitted in 1885, adding, "This often pains me."[179] She placed part of the blame on a want of true holiness: "So many try to do this work unconsecrated and unbaptized and fail. Then it is hard to get others to take hold."[180]

Smith's assessment of the dilemmas of mission work circled around but did not—perhaps could not—resolve a key problem. Superficially, "white" missionaries seemed more successful than "colored." She noted the "low" state of Liberian counties where "they have never had a white missionary...The difference is so very prominent one cannot help comparing."[181] Yet, there was not much real sympathy or enthusiasm for white people—even Bishop Taylor—among the natives or the migrants. For their part, African American Liberia watchers wanted an independent black republic, not a stepchild tutored by whites. Blyden was, on this point, emphatic: "Bishop Taylor is doing a work which cannot benefit Africa."[182] He continued: "And if the [AC] Society is not able to control the racial character of their emigrants, Bishop Taylor's work, if it succeeds will only, in less than twenty years, make Liberia a scene of sanguinary strife."[183] What then to do? While in Africa, Smith tried to take a nonracial position: "The work is great; no time to stand on color lines. What is needed is men and women: black, white, English, American, Scotch, Swiss, Irish or German" who were fully consecrated to God.[184]

By the end of the decade, Edward Blyden moved away from redemptionist politics in favor of authentically native Christianity and social organization (and increasingly, toward Islam), but Smith remained committed to Protestant religious practice and US cultural norms.[185] Since her daughter Maizie declined to take up African missions herself, Smith considered staying on another year. But by late summer 1887, she determined to follow the advice of doctors, who said she "must leave the country" for health reasons.[186] It took about a year to regain her health, raise money, and find transportation. While Taylor bragged about her and the trip abroad in print, C. T. O. King opined to New York: "...I think the Bp. is rather sanguine as to the impression he has made upon the heathen and the permanency of his establishments among them."[187] Smith may well have been dispirited by reports from Cape Palmas about how her holiness band of converts was "greatly persecuted" in her absence and about Brother Pratt's trouble in extracting labor from tribes without bartering tobacco—the new substitute for alcohol—even as the new white missionaries installed by Taylor preached against tobacco use. One white Cavalla missionary's gloss on this troubled situation—"If we have to starve, amen!"–points up a dogmatic attitude, especially since foreign missionaries could leave the country, a coping strategy unavailable to most native converts.[188]

Amanda Berry Smith steadfastly believed in evangelizing Africa, but her ministry in Africa made her an opponent of colonization. Though in her narrative she wrote: "God Bless the Colonization Society" for launching mission work, by the end of her years in Liberia, she believed the ACS had done what it could. "From the standpoint I look at it, I would move its disbandment forthwith." She explained: "[L]et the white people who want the Negro to emigrate to Africa so as to make room for the great flood of foreigners who come to our shore, know that there is a place in the U.S. for the Negro" (452). This was a strong argument for African American claims on the US nation-state and something of a contraction of her earlier vision. She eventually deemed emigration to be "an enterprise so detrimental in every possible way to our people," and declared that her "heart ache[d]" for "our people who are so hard-headed" as to leave the United States for Liberia.[189]

The mobility and latitude offered by Amanda Smith's status as a "privileged character" under holiness had its limitations over the long term for Christianizing Africa, and the last chapters of her autobiography explore the weaknesses of missionaries on both sides of the color line. She deeply lamented the presence of white missionaries abroad "who were just as full of prejudice against black people as they are in this country," who "did act mean and [did] mean things" (424). She also decried "all raking of white people!" by African Americans who went to Liberia to escape the torment of US racism. Antiwhite sentiment distracted people from the hard work of making missions; further, they ran counter to the ideal of "perfect love" fostered by true consecration to God. "It is the wrong spirit to be cherished and cultivated and perpetuated," she maintained. "I have never seen any good from it." She suspected the motives of the African American migrants who vented "hard things" against white people because such views were "very much admired by the Liberians and is a mark of real race loyalty" (416). Antiwhite sentiment may have very well been one of the few unifying elements among a growing transnational population of peoples from various corners of the African diaspora, separated as many of them were by lines of religion, class, and culture, as well as by temperament and ideological commitment.

Smith felt pressured to take a stand on the question of race and missions, and she staged her response in a dramatic climax to her autobiography. According to Smith, in proportion to the number of whites that died, withdrew, or limited their activities in Liberia, the work of schools and missions overall "declined." She admitted that white missionaries frequently developed "good native teachers and preachers, who are loyal and faithful and true," even indispensable to the cause. Nonetheless, when "the whole work is left to [native converts], the interest seems to flag...which the teacher feels, but cannot help." She also noted that black missionaries suffered from underpayment and overwork and that this was a "great mistake" leading to superexploitation and unending self-sacrifice, even unto death. Like Edward Blyden, her imagined questioners posed the mission issue in "black" or "white," and Smith answered with a scathing flourish:

> "Then you think, Mrs. Smith, it is better that white missionaries should to go Africa."
> Yes, if they are the right kind. If they are thoroughly converted and fully consecrated and wholly sanctified to God, so that all their prejudices are completely killed out, and their hearts are full of love and sympathy, and they have firmness of character and good, broad, level-headed common sense, and are possessed of great patience, and strong, persistent, persevering faith, and then keep up the spirit of earnest prayer to Almighty God, day and night. I do not say that it is necessary to be under a dead strain all the time; not at all; but my own personal experience is that the more one prays and trusts in God, the better he can get on, especially in Africa. (423)

This statement is hardly a ringing endorsement of white missionaries over black and is more evidence of a polarized debate. On the one hand, Smith's position explains her distance from revived efforts within the AME Church for to Christianize the continent, a race advancement project lead by Henry Turner in the 1890s, as well as the silence around her work in the church's official history.[190] But on the other hand, it also held out the prospect of an inclusive rather than exclusive approach.

Indeed, her last word on the subject in the narrative was a moving closing passage citing the work of an African American missionary, Miss Susan Collins, a graduate of a training school in Chicago whom she met in Africa in 1887. "I perceived in Susie Collins timber that meant something," wrote Smith. "She was a woman who had been well raised and well trained; she had good, broad, common sense, and knew how to do a little of about everything; she was patient, and of a happy, genial disposition, of high moral character and sturdy piety." The narrative ends with advice, prayer, and praise for the next generation of black woman missionaries: "These are the qualifications that will generally stand the heavy pull in Africa. May God bless her, and continue to make her a blessing" (465). Even though "race" had nothing essentially to do with one's potential to do God's work, Smith endorsed the idea that African American women might provide a special and especially successful model for Africa and the world.

Conclusion

Amanda Berry Smith's African mission points up the power of transnational thinking in Protestantism in the late nineteenth century. For white Protestants, this thinking was in terms of empire; for Smith, the idea of the decolonial better describes the kind of liberty and forthrightness she craved in the world. Amanda Smith drew little security or inspiration from the rights-centered citizenship project of Reconstruction unfolding in the United States, nor did the patriarchal, racialist nation-building plans of Blyden (or President Johnson) in Liberia garner her commitment. Faced with corruption and disaffection at many mission stations, notably around the alcohol trade, Smith applied herself to the duty nearest at hand, offering practical and spiritual help to those open and able to accept it. When her alliance with William Taylor tilted her engagement with Africans toward colonial practice, she recoiled with fear and doubt. As a writer, Smith's tender and respectful appraisal of African people was a nonstarter in the US debates of Liberia and African empire, since those discussions were about "progress" and resolutely economic in focus. Smith cannot be charged, as some black and white missionaries were charged, with leaving their natal land in the hopes of raising their status by acquiring riches, servants, or property in Liberia—ironically, one of Smith's great supporters, Ida B. Wells-Barnett, advocated that African Americans do just that.[191] By leading with her "mother's heart," Smith made bonds with Americo-Liberian Christian women and a few men, too, bonds that bolstered her faith and steadied her hand as an evangelist. The toll on her health proved more than she could bear.

The contrast between US missionaries in Liberia and China is telling at this point. Jane Hunter has argued that turn-of-the-century white women missionaries realized extended gendered power in China. They experienced "fulfillment" and "satisfaction," which fostered their physical health and emotional happiness as they built up schools and related institutions, often in partnership with their husbands.[192] Structurally deprived of the domesticity and materialism that constituted white women's "empire" overseas, Smith experienced continuity of self-sacrifice and deprivation as an African missionary, rather than expanded gendered power. Her ministry comprised direct service provision and caretaking rather than household management or institution building, as in the case of her adoption of Little Bob and Frances. Holiness and perfectionism rejected the lavish materialism of Chinese mission homes documented by Hunter. As an unsalaried evangelist reliant on donations, Smith cultivated a persona of upright abstemiousness known by her "big poke Quaker bonnet," simple and unadorned.[193] "The life of an African missionary is not the same as in India or China," lamented a writer in *The Africa News* in 1889. "Poor Africa! Poor Africa! Millions of souls and a handful of missionaries who suffer more than you know of."[194]

Nor did Smith become, as did white veteran missionaries who took up the cause of "poor China," an authority or advocate for "poor Africa." Her efforts were devalued by Liberia watchers like the AME Church's C. S. Smith who dismissed the efforts of "'faith' missionaries" in favor of efforts toward "organized government" and the "extension of commerce" in Africa.[195] William Taylor, by contrast, did not miss a beat. Not only did the *Christian Standard* publicize its appeals for Africa funds under his rather than Smith's name—he was, after all missionary bishop of all of Africa—but he launched his own moneymaking enterprises based on his years of foreign travel. Taylor took extensive personal photographs on his long journeys abroad and founded a journal, *Illustrated Africa,* in which to circulate them. He also published a thick autobiography and a lavish, display-worthy edition of his Africa materials with copious plates, heavy leather binding, and gilt edging.[196] When Smith returned to the Methodist circuit in 1892–93, she did not focus on issues of race or Africa. She preached on holiness, touching back on the days of John Inskip, who had since died and was now lionized in Methodist circles.[197] She steered clear of worldly affairs like Taylor's publishing ventures, and stood apart, it seems, from the "excellent" Liberia exhibit at the World's Columbian Exposition and the World's Congress of Representative Women that met in Chicago, where she settled upon her return from Africa.[198]

As the burden of building a better world in Christ divided rather than united people across the "color line" at the turn of the twentieth century, Smith turned her attention to African American children in the United States. She founded the Amanda Smith Home in Harvey, Illinois, in 1899. The WCTU's *Union Signal* noted of Smith: "Her great heart is stirred to its depths by the needs of her people and if the children are trained to be intelligent workers many of the phases of the Negro problem will be solved."[199] By refraining from explicit agitation around racism and demurring to advocate for female ordination in AME circles, Smith remained a bold yet conservative figure, and her "peculiar tact" won her praise from white Methodists. [200] Even so, her work fits more rather than less in line with the grassroots agenda of her peers in the National Association of Colored Women at the time, an organization that worked to protect people, especially women and children, from the harshness and deprivations of racism.[201] Blyden, pressed beyond the limits of "tact" in dealing with the ACS, opted for biblio-scientific "racial" solidarity in opposition to white supremacy and imperialism. His insistence on an authentic Liberian nationalism—"as little as possible americanized"—resurfaced in the concept of "the African personality" animating nationalist thinking in the post–World War II era.[202] Later Pan-Africanists invoked Blyden, but they actually used ideas—like raceless human universality or cultural tolerance—that had at least as much in common with Smith's vision and practice. Like AME church fathers in the 1880s and 1890s, Amanda Smith herself was basically agnostic about formal empire building by nation-states.[203] If imperialism was not quite visible to Amanda Berry Smith in her Liberia years, the dire situation facing African Americans when she returned home certainly was. "The [civil] war is past, there are no more slaves, but, (and we say it carefully) *the Negro is not free!*"[204] Before returning to the Africa case, the next chapter takes on the issues of race and racism in the critical decade of the 1890s in the life of another transnational figure who sometimes identified with saints and other divine women: Gertrude Stein.

2
Unmaking Race

Gertrude Stein, the New Woman, and Susan B. Anthony

"It is queer the use of that word," Gertrude Stein mused in her memoir *Everybody's Autobiography* (1937), "native always means people who belong somewhere else, because they once belonged somewhere." "That shows that the white race does not really think they belong anywhere," she continued, "because they think of everybody else as native."[1] Nativity helped Amanda Smith sort out identity in the transnational, quasi-colonial setting of Liberia, but Stein's view of the word native as "queer" and unstable situates such designations in a highly dynamic grammar of meaning. By detaching "the white race" from any fixed sense of home, place, or belonging, Stein cut the ground out from nativity as an organizing principle for identity and turned to sand any assumption of security or prerogative based on it. The pronoun "they" seems to position the author outside the category "white race." Yet, regardless of what "they" or "everybody else" might feel, claim, or seem to be, all of such designations are ultimately an effect of power, in this case, colonial relations. (Stein's immediate referent was the presence of Moroccan soldiers in France, who were colloquially termed "native troops.") Who gets to be or feel at home or to claim citizenship (or not) is a product of social relationships rather than a natural fact like birth; human identification and attachment can only be apprehended as an unfolding and contingent product of history.

This stance generated a lively, lifelong set of preoccupations about identity and national belonging for Gertrude Stein, one productive of a tremendous oeuvre that was literally never done. As the opening epigram suggests, Stein used word play, dissociation, and teeter-totter syntax to draw attention to the ideological underpinnings of grammar and meaning frequently to the point where her sentences almost cannot be read at all, making our work as readers never done as well. Stein staged her sentences as dramas of human knowing out of the conviction that "a long complicated sentence should force itself upon you, *make you know yourself knowing it...*"[2] Her allusion to violent sexual congress suggests how power and desire suffuse human meaning making, pointing up the gendered prerogatives of enforcing and regulating identification—who gets to name and be named or count and be counted—as part of the family, "race," or nation. These dynamics existed in creative—and sometimes debilitating—tension for Stein as a writer.

This chapter explores how Gertrude resisted social and intellectual pressure to produce certain kinds of fixity and readability in her work around the categories of race, sex, and national belonging. If Amanda Smith claimed a "whiteness" that was not "white," as in race, Stein toyed with other ideas about being/identity, among them, a color that was not a color: transparency. This thinking expressed Stein's decolonial consciousness about identity. Over time, she came to identify the United States as more, rather than less, characteristic of the racist and colonizing forces in the world that so troubled Amanda Smith in Africa. My analysis centers primarily on two texts, Stein's most personally beloved, the novel *The Making of Americans: A History of a Family's Progress* (written 1902–1911; published 1925, hereafter *The Making*), and her still-performed opera *The Mother of Us All* (1946), a tribute to Susan B. Anthony.[3] I place these works in a transnational context, as Stein wrote each one at particularly intense moments of critical reflection on national belonging. The novel is linked to her relocation from the United States to France around 1903, and the opera was written in the immediate aftermath of World War II. My perspective on Stein is also grounded in the transatlantic intellectual ferment of the 1890s, a period in which she tried on other voices, like lady novelist and lady doctor, that were more conventionally feminine than the more playful, philosophical one she evinced in *Everybody's Autobiography*. Stein's writings from the earlier decade grappled with racial degeneration, social uplift, and sex in higher education, topics which intersected in popular and academic discussions about the so-called new woman in England and the United States.

The phrase "new woman" was a media label applied to women who sought higher education, questioned gender norms, and asserted themselves in the public, as opposed to the domestic sphere. Gertrude Stein rejected traditional marriage and motherhood as well as the prospect of being a new or "advanced" woman, committed to feminism, reform, or the uplift of self and others. My treatment of the 1890s suggests that Stein's intellectual coming of age entailed pushing the tensions between these paths to female destiny to the breakpoint. These breakpoints were linguistic and grammatical, sexual and geographical— and they all touched matters of race and national identity. Critics have often characterized the distancing maneuvers of Stein's life as exile, describing her as the quintessential "expatriate" writer who created a language of her own, outside of the United States.[4] Scholars have also pointed to Stein's diffidence about feminism via the statement found in *The Autobiography of Alice B. Toklas* (1933): "Not, as Gertrude Stein explained to [her friend] Marion Walker, that she at all minds the cause of woman or any other cause but it does not happen to be her business."[5] But did "the cause of woman"—or the nation—make it their "business" to include Gertrude Stein? By highlighting texts produced during border crossings, my analysis spotlights passages of inclusion and exclusion that were so troubling and so generative for Stein. Stein never actually expatriated—that is, forfeited her US citizenship—and, as we shall see, she clung tightly to her many US passports at national borders, especially in war-time. By unpacking her critique of the of new woman, exploring her troubles at borders and check points, and examining her vindication of the childless, never-married Susan B. Anthony as a "Mother of Us All"—this chapter investigates in detail how Stein grappled with the politics of sex, race, and nation in the age of Anglo-American empire.

Stein in Historiography

Gertrude Stein did not usually pitch her voice in a register that historians are trained to consider evidentiary, like those found in the typical government document, newspaper editorial, trial transcript, sermon, luncheon club address, or how-to book. In her writings, Stein parodied many of these genres— witness "everybody's" autobiography—and she strikes me as a ventriloquist or mimic, begging the question of whose voice is ever truly authentic. Her best-known voice is the wifey-poo protagonist, Alice Toklas, in the "autobiography" quoted above (quoting Stein), regarding the cause of woman. Notable other voices include the controversial urban black woman Melanchtha Herbert from *Three Lives* (1909), the fly's eyeball view of domesticity of the prose poem *Tender Buttons* (1914), a "genius," and, more privately, "Baby Woojums," a moniker developed in the decades-long correspondence she kept up with New York City art critic Carl Van Vechten, who played "Papa," and Toklas, "Mama."[6] Stein liked to be—and enjoyed others—in costume, and among her favorite analogies to history were "a play" and "a landscape."[7] She punned, goofed, and took risks with language that frequently, perhaps even mostly, failed, provoking frustration and even wrath among readers in her own time and now.[8] It is a cliché but nonetheless true that Gertrude Stein is easy to quote and difficult to read.[9]

She did not start out that way. Stein's first publications were scientific articles appearing in 1896 and 1898 in the *Psychological Review* based on her undergraduate research at Harvard Annex (later, Radcliffe College) and performed under the supervision of William James and his protégé Hugo Münsterberg.[10] Her earliest draft short novels *Q. E. D.* (a women's love triangle) and *Fernhurst* (a campus romance) are conventionally narrated, and her mildly experimental first published fiction, *Three Lives*, received mostly polite and encouraging reviews.[11] Gertrude Stein and her family were prominent art collectors in Paris in the decade before World War I, during which time she sat for a now-famous portrait by Picasso, completed in 1906, and wrote numerous works, almost exclusively at night. My point is that until at least 1925, when *The Making* was published by Contact Editions in Paris, Stein's main accomplishments touched science and art. Women garner the bulk of historians' attention in the US academy as members of religious groupings and families, and as citizens, activists, or workers. Stein's work as a scientist or art collector as well as her later persona as a "genius" are hard to assimilate under these academic rubrics, making her easy to ignore.[12]

Charged with explaining beginnings and endings, causes and effects, historians mostly conclude that Stein inspired other artists and writers but generated no identifiable school of writing of her own. While her influence is acknowledged (on Hemingway, mostly), concrete impacts and legacies are harder to pin down and she slips through historical narratives focused on causation, whether of canon or nation.[13] But she was also pushed out. Cushing Strout, an intellectual historian at Cornell University, showed Stein the door in 1961. Describing her as "most bizarre" notwithstanding her status as one of William James's "most devoted pupils," Gertrude Stein's troubled relation to narrative threatened to give American pragmatism a bad name. Strout named Stein in an essay on James and historical practice, but he did not cite any of her writings, alluding only to her cheeky and well-publicized late-career affection for detective stories. "The historian can exploit [James's] view [about the contingency] of change only by the technique of narrative," concluded Strout, "which runs counter to that modern prejudice against storytelling as an evasion of analysis," assigning some unspecified culpability to Stein.[14] Stein's merciless send-ups of bureaucracy ("organizations being dull") and the professions (which made her "bored"), as well as her big ego, fanciful flights of contradiction, and uber-preciousness have fanned reader hostility for decades. In this vein, "Think of the Bible and Homer think of Shakespeare and think of me" is an especially ripe Steinian sentence, as it will not keep still and mean just one thing.[15] For historians, some especially acute provocations might include:

> I want to write a history of every one. Sometime I want to be right about every one.
>
> (*The Making of Americans*)

> Let me recite what history teaches. History teaches.
>
> ("If I Told Him: A Completed Portrait of Picasso," ca. 1923)

> The only thing that is different from one time to another is what is seen and what is seen depends upon how everybody is doing everything.
>
> ("Composition as Explanation," 1926)

> ...a genius is someone who does not have to remember the two hundred years that everybody else has to remember.
>
> (*Everybody's Autobiography*)

Strout's dismissal reeks of sexism, but Stein's epigrammatic style—poet William H. Gass usefully reminds us that "Gertrude Stein never 'argues' anything"[16]—might be legitimately cited as a barrier to wide circulation of her texts in historical debate.

That Strout and others find no before and after Stein is related to the notion that there is no "before" and "after" *in* Stein—an idea that has quite a bit do with William James. Stein strove to render in language James's notion that the mind apprehended stimuli in a "continuous present," an effect she likened to "a cinema picture made up of succession and each moment having its own emphasis..."[17] Yet, even those commentators who view her as an heir to James's spirit of inquiry and his approach to phenomenology of the mind (she rejected his pragmatism) admit: "The method worked only for her."[18] By writing outside of conventions of time and narrative, then, Stein assured herself a place in history, if an ironic one. Given the difficulty of reading work structured by and expressive of a space outside of time—she called it "the music of the present tense"—Stein remains a monument, an icon, a colorful prop (or a dead end) in the drama of modern art, sometimes admired but just as easily bypassed.[19] Since she eschewed organized feminism and left the United States just as things got interesting for the woman suffrage movement and social reform, she does not figure in those historiographies; her Anthony opera remains an outlier, mostly overlooked, and *The Making* largely unread by historians.

Until recently. Thanks to the work of poet and literary scholar Jennifer Ashton, *The Making* has resurfaced in scholarship as a philosophically ambitious and serious work, up from its status as the first flop of literary modernism. Ashton contends that the novel takes up the question of how to represent wholes and parts in modern (i.e., post-teleological) human existence and how, she goes on to argue, the book failed to deliver. With great brio and erudition, Ashton suggests that Stein eventually used mathematics, namely, the principle of substitutability, following Bertrand Russell and Alfred Whitehead, to solve the representational challenge of wholeness—but much later in her career, as late as the novel *Lucy Church, Amiably* in 1930 (a resolution more lightheartedly evoked by the title *Everybody's Autobiography*).[20] Ashton's exciting work mostly extends the critical consensus about *The Making* as a failed novel or, at best, as a revealing and well-documented crisis of the novel genre because, as she describes it, Stein embedded within it an irresolvable contradiction. *The Making* tried to chart a story of "family progress" through time (say, on an "x" axis) while insisting, simultaneously, on providing a taxonomy of "every one" (say, on a "y" axis). These never-to-cross purposes lead to infinity rather than plot a beginning, middle, and end, and at some point Stein just gave up. In her later essay *The Gradual Making of The Making of Americans*, Stein admitted: "And I went on and on and then one day after I had written a thousand pages, this was in 1908 I just did not go on any more."[21] Ashton makes a functionalist argument, namely, that abstraction worked and while noting the deep importance of James, she credits European thinkers with decisively shaping Stein's mature insights about grammar, logic, and—literally—counting.[22]

In this orientation, Ashton follows Leon Katz, whose pathbreaking work in the early 1960s paved the way for anyone intent on keeping a Gertrude Stein away from the canons of "American" philosophy. In his 1963 dissertation completed at Columbia University, Katz also linked the writing of *The Making* to European thought. Based on a cache of newly discovered early notebooks, he argued that Stein's later claim about organizing *The Making* around a Jamesian "continuous present" had no such basis in either her notes or her early drafts of the book, and that the later assertion was a sort of retrospective fig leaf over the exposed failure of the novel. Instead, Katz contends, Stein was deeply immersed in European thought, old and new, via a reading program of the entirety (!) of English literature from the sixteenth century to the present (essentially a second graduate career undertaken via Mudie's Circulating Library and the British Museum in 1901–02), naturalist fiction (especially Zola), and a pernicious one-off work of "characterology" entitled *Sex and Character: An Investigation of Fundamental Principles* (1903) by German-trained Jewish psychologist/philologist and tragic wunderkind, Otto Weininger.[23]

In contrast to Ashton and Katz, American Studies scholar Priscilla Wald identifies *The Making* as an immigrant novel of loss and displacement that grapples with the assimiliationist pressure and xenophobia rife at the turn of the twentieth century, making Stein kin to Antin and Yezierska.[24] My reading of Stein's notebooks indicates that she read Weininger with a certain reactionary amusement while writing *The Making,* but Wald rather than Katz is on firmer ground in terms of getting at Stein's literary ambition and sensibilities. However, Stein's sights were set not on New York and the range of "Jewish" voices taking shape there but on London, the epicenter of new woman fiction, and in particular on the high modernism of the Bodley Head, her first choice of publisher for *The Making.*[25] Furthermore, Wald's conclusion that Stein was "indeed a white, middle class woman of her times" breaks down in light of Stein's writings on the new woman.[26] Stein positioned herself neither as the radically assimilated immigrant like Mary Antin nor as forever tormented by "two-ness" á la W. E. B. Du Bois. She determined herself to be one, whole, and undivided, not white but transparent, like the "blind glass" metaphor that opens *Tender Buttons*, a graceful vessel that could both hold and shine.[27] My reading further suggests that *The Making* contains a significant breakthrough around the issue of representation and who counts in a key riposte to William James concerning the one and the many.[28] In a kind of decolonizing move, Gertrude Stein stripped the grammar of existence down to "one" via her new woman writings culminating in *The Making.* Then, over time, she re-enfleshed that bare "one" into a female form, the figure of the saint/hero Anthony as a "mother" of us "all" and, in the process, critically renegotiated the connections between race, citizenship, and sex in the opera, her final consideration of "Americanness." This work puts her in the company of other restless, modern women's thinking about gender and race at the turn of the century, like Charlotte Perkins Gilman, Jane Addams, Ida B. Wells-Barnett, and Emma Goldman, who are pillars of academic US feminist historiography, unlike Stein.

The New Woman, Race, and Empire

As Stein encountered it, the new woman was a fundamentally transnational and literary figure of the nervous 1890s.[29] US readers were introduced to the phrase via popular British women fiction writers in the spring of 1894. The term was coined in England by novelist Sarah Grand (1854–1943) in an essay published in the Boston-based *North American Review*. Grand wrote "The New Aspect of the Woman Question" as the wildly successful author of the *The Heavenly Twins*, a novel that criticized legal inequality in marriage and rigid gender socialization of children. Grand's essay remonstrated against a "Howling Brotherhood" of detractors of women in public life and belle letters and criticized their retrenchment agenda of a restricted woman's "sphere." According to Grand, these "Bawling Brothers" failed to keep up with the educated woman's new accomplishments and new demands, preferring instead to exploit the situations of "cow-women" and "scum-women" locked in marriage and prostitution, respectively. Fed up with the sexual double standard and frustrated by gender exclusiveness in the professions, the "new woman is a little above" her male peers, explained Grand, and "...now woman holds out a strong hand to the child-man, and insists...upon helping him up."[30] Two months later, the *Review* printed a lacerating rebuttal to Grand. Marie Louise de la Ramée (1839–1909), who published widely under the name "Ouida," scoffed at Grand's assumption of female moral superiority over men, chided feminists for their supposed humorlessness (and poor fashion sense), excoriated their contradictory demands for chivalric deference *and* conventional political power, and piled on a condemnation of higher education as "hardening and deforming." Decrying the state of motherhood (woman's record there "does not do her much honor," she sniffed) and trumpeting literary women's historic accomplishments attained without "rights," Ouida disqualified the coarse and grasping new women, a "hybrid, self-contained, opponent of men," from any "title or capacity to demand the place or the privilege of man," in any sphere.[31]

The snide tone and ugly metaphors of this exchange, to say nothing of the US media's staging of a transnational catfight to mock and discredit nascent feminism, echoed across the "new woman" debate for more than a generation.[32] From the outset, many viewed the catchphrase "new woman" as a caricature and distraction. "What is a new woman?" bristled social reformer Florence Kelley in *The Outlook*. "It is now sixty years since Lucretia Mott...became an advocate of woman suffrage. Is Mrs. Howe new at ninety?"[33] Nonetheless, the term served as a container for discussions of marriage reform, higher education, and political equality for women in Europe, the United States, and even further abroad, notably in missionary and imperial contexts. Transnational in its first articulations, new woman status indexed the moral and physical health of the body, the psyche, the family, and the nation; as such it became a key marker of "racial" progress and viability within and beyond these intersecting domains.

In the Anglo-American discussion, the new woman's appearance was mainly taken as a sign of physical weakness, loose morals, and racial "degeneration," another imprecise and much decried term that nonetheless worked overtime in the 1890s to name the decade's peculiar uncertainties. An important, indeed symptomatic, link between the new woman and "racial" health was hysteria, and the discourses of "hysteria" and the "new woman" repeatedly converged in the anglophone periodical literature about women at the fin de siècle. The phrase "new woman," according to the London-based *Quarterly Review*, was simply a "grand name for hysteria"; 20 years later, an antifeminist screed in New York's *Harper's Weekly* maintained that the new woman's demand for suffrage was nothing more than "a product of hysteria."[34] In other popular uses hysteria was visible in vaguely hereditary physical signs, from harelip to psychological manias, as evidence—stigmata, even—of "racial" degeneration.[35]

As Laura Briggs suggests for the diagnosis of hysteria in the context of imperial medicine and gynecology, new woman commentators calibrated women's physical and mental health to the viability of missions and expansionist projects across the globe.[36] Most striking, however, is that new woman status in colonial contexts signalled promise and regeneration rather than horror and decline. If medical discourses described white women as hypersensitive, overcivilized, nervous, and nonperforming compared to "savage" women who were more "natural" mothers but were obdurate, insensate, and stuck in a state of arrested "racial" development, the new woman in colonial contexts was the picture of health. Both the missionary and her female converts appeared wholesome, balanced, and aligned with the proper order of things, especially God's order. Religious and secular writers celebrated the "New Women of India," "The New Woman in the Mohammedan World," and "The New Woman in China and Japan" as proof positive of the tonic of modern civilization in these so-called backward environments.[37] If Africa was conspicuous by its absence in these reports, the Philippines boasted "good material here with which to begin," according to G. A. Miller in the *Overland Monthly*. Proffering a variant on the noble savage stereotype, Miller figured Filipinas as "[s]traight-shouldered, clear eyed, frank of face [women], that stand erect and meet the world with honest candor." Given the "low tension" and "relaxed" mode of life in the Pacific archipelago, the Filipina had "less need for bromo seltzer...than some of her whiter sisters of the West." Moreover, the native woman was not deformed or proved selfish by her interest in the modernization of her sex; on the contrary, her embrace of Christianity, higher education, self-supporting employment, and republican forms of government, including the suffrage, was utterly sane and salvific. The adoption of new woman strategies could even neutralize "racial" physiognomy, changing the expression of the "Oriental" woman from a "stupid wooden-faced" visage into "features expressive and refined," in a kind of engulfing colonial makeover.[38]

The helpmeet of the native convert in this triumphalist reportage was none other than US and English women teachers and missionaries. In foreign contexts, missionaries were the advance guard of "the women's movement," because they cultivated "a sense of the value of human personality and a passionate desire for service." At home, the "women's movement" aroused controversy, where it was tainted with irreligiosity and the unseemly pitting of the interests of one sex against the other.[39] Migrating over from the "higher life" of Protestant perfectionism in which Amanda Smith worked, women's cosmopolitan aspirations in the arts were mocked as "Higher Hysterics."[40] But when spreading the Gospel abroad rather than competing with men at home, the new woman as missionary or convert was a source of hope; they "lead the way for the inevitable."[41] This transnational, hysteria-inflicted context of new woman discourse is helpful for understanding why Gertrude Stein eventually chose abstraction—literally the idea of "one" beyond sex, beyond race, beyond nation, beyond contention and partisanship, and perhaps beyond argument at all—as a metaphor for identity.

On the way to "one," however, Stein was terribly hard on the new woman. This figure was a flashpoint for marriage debates in England, but in the United States, the new woman anchored discussions of higher education. University training and school reform entwined with a range of colonizing, uplift, and assimilative projects of the late nineteenth century, from the industrial education movement, to home and foreign missions, to Indian training schools, to the new women's colleges and the coeducation debate. The term "college bred" marks the racialist and hereditarian undertones of that discussion, even as education was held to be a mitigating factor in building the body politic out of a diverse population.[42]

Stein struggled with the racially saturated categories of the Anglo-American colonial imaginary as expressed in higher education. Especially prominent in her assessments were the missionary-heathen dyad with its US variants of white-black, north-south, native-immigrant, and Christian-Jew. In her college notebook from the winter of 1894, Stein portrayed "An Annex Girl" as overworked and physically deformed, even crushed, by her studies:

> There she stood a little body with a very large head. (and loaded) She was loaded down with books and was evidently very dismal. Suddenly there broke forth a torment, "I don't want to be superior" she wailed despairingly, "I am tired to death of standing with my head craned constantly looking upward. I am just longing to meet one simple soul that ((don't)) want to know everything. one weak happy naive consciousness that thinks higher education is (*either rot or has never heard*) of it." She gave a long-drawn (ou) Oh! And (*then collapsed the books*) on top of the miserable little heap.[43]

The Annex girl inhabits an intensely hierarchizing milieu, with her "head craned constantly...upward"; the pressure to "be superior" privileges the mind ("very large head") over body ("little"), entailing a loss of wholeness. Judgments about superiority and inferiority echoed in racial science and popular Anglo-Saxonism as well as in discussions of morality with women sometimes coming out "naturally" superior to men. To get some resistant traction in this situation, Stein reached for simplicity ("naive consciousness"), primitiveness, and self-racialization, though not via Jewishness, per se.[44] Another notebook theme involved a "dark-skinned girl in the (full sensuous development of budding) woman-hood" who complains: "Books books... is there no end to it. Nothing but myself to feed my own eager nature. Nothing given me but musty books."[45] This student departs the library and sets to wandering free and alone outside. In her novella *Q. E. D.*, the Stein-like young protagonist Adele appears "brown and white"—encompassing if not resolving the binary—in the eyes of her more conventionally feminine peers while these three Americans travel together in Europe.[46] Stein's notebooks and unpublished manuscripts record resistance to the pressure to conform, "whiten," and uplift herself. But as she moved into more professional and public settings after college, this effort proved difficult to project and sustain.

The breakdown of this nascent third space is especially visible in two essays Stein wrote around 1900, "The Value of a College Education for Women" (1899) and "Degeneration in American Women" (ca. 1901). In the first piece, written while in medical school at Johns Hopkins University, where she matriculated in 1897, Stein considered the work of Charlotte Perkins Stetson (Gilman). Gilman's widely respected *Women and Economics* (1898) put female aspiration in progressive racialist terms, but the book left Stein cold, sending her backward to romantic and republican frameworks rather than forward into modern biopolitics. In the second piece, Stein assessed medicine's role concerning the low birth rate among US women and judged science inadequate to the task of getting women to embrace reproduction as their proper contribution to the nation's work. Art and inspiration had to play a role. In both pieces, Stein looked askance at the feminist prospect of liberating women from inequality in marriage, and instead she endorsed the intensified disciplining of women's choices toward motherhood and private domesticity. Nonetheless, she rejected this disciplining for herself and was equally unwilling to make her life's work the business of imposing it on others.

Stein thought *Women and Economics* "eminently suggestive" and "worth while considering."[47] Drawing on both Darwinist conceptions of evolution and the productive potential of industrialization, then in full force, Gilman hung women's future on their increased participation in paid/public work outside the home. According to Gilman, the subordination of wives in marriage was a temporary condition that a "race" could modify, outgrow, and even abandon on the way to fulfilling its evolutionary destiny. Grand viewed women to be "ahead" of men, but Gilman projected a more chivalric dynamic in which men would graciously allow women to catch up to them, as it was in their own interest to do so. "Our distinctions of sex are carried to such a degree as to be disadvantageous to our progress as individuals and a race," she argued.[48] *Women and Economics* thus mapped an extended realm of action and increased individualization for women without threatening the basics of conventional gender identity. "So the 'new woman' will be not less female than the 'old woman,' though she has more functions," affirmed Gilman. She will be, "with it all, more feminine," because her mothering, as an expression of and service to race advancement, will be more sophisticated and effective than "our present wasteful and grievous method."[49] Theoretically, any "race" could so develop. Jews were an especially promising group, according to Gilman, Africans almost certainly not. Better for a child to be "left absolutely without mother or family of any sort, in the city of Boston," she declared, "than to be supplied with a large and affectionate family and be planted with them in Darkest Africa."[50]

Having identified herself, at least privately, as "brown" and desiring rather than self-sacrificing or "advanced," Stein's lecture on Gilman struggled to confront this heavily racialized developmental schema. Her 1899 address to a group of Baltimore club women, "The Value of College Education for Women," defended university training for women by drawing on Gilman but fumbled for further integration or fresh synthesis. Written in the middle of her medical school career, this talk was framed provocatively for a southern audience, thick with college alumnae.[51] "You people are wrong" regarding education, Stein announced. "There is nothing more striking" than the "complete differences in the ideals and occupations between the North and the South"—originally typed into the manuscript as "Cambridge" and "Baltimore"—regions she starkly described as home to "two classes of humanity" and clearly aligning herself with the former in this, her parents' hometown.[52] Stein then asserted that "every woman in New England" made her children's education her active "duty," but in the south such was to "a great extent unknown" and school children were "wretchedly housed."[53] She did not itemize (backing off quickly with a dismissive "But enough of this subject...") and only referred to a vague, if negative, appraisal of the "inadequacy of the present system" of preparing women for "demands made upon [them] under present conditions." She did so via an overview of *Women and Economics*, with a barbed comment to her hearers: she declared "it extremely likely that most of you have not read it."

Pitch perfect as the tactless missionary, Stein recapped Gilman's argument that women, especially those of the upper classes, were "over-sexed" because economically dependent marriage confined them to the pleasure and service of one man in a private home. But where Gilman saw female dependency as a holdover from "primitive" conditions that needed updating, Stein saw only a static, unchanging reality. Not only were women "as a rule," supported by "some male relative a husband a father or a brother," but Stein contended that they even failed as deserving dependents: "I'm afraid we must admit that the average woman is not worth her keep economically." Gilman identified the modern economy as pulling women, healthfully, into the public sphere and economic marketplace; Stein emphasized not opportunity but deficit: "the supported women of today... is not to use a slang phrase worth her keep."

In this scenario, college remained important since modern husbands required wives who could "at least read a newspaper and understand a little something of the affairs that are uppermost in men's mind"—if not much else. To be sure, Stein maintained that college far better equipped women for adulthood than did "society." The debutante was unprepared to be a "modern mother" because she lived for years "devoted... to the mysteries of self adornment," leaving her "a little older but not very much wiser." The college woman, by contrast, gained "increased efficiency" and, if not the particular skills of housewifery, at least self-reliance and initiative to seek out up-to-date methods. College actually fostered interest in motherhood by putting women's "sex functions" in proper balance, suggested Stein, curbing allure and freeing up maternal impulses. The debutante was "more apt to lose her maternal sex desire" because her skills in "attraction" were overdeveloped. "[S]o the training in the higher education does not tend to unsex but to rightly sex a woman," concluded Stein, and motherhood remained both a "normal function" and "very strong desire" in college graduates. Moreover, education made "her sex desire... a much purer one [than the debutante's] as it is not marred by being a means of obtaining a livelihood."[54] To put it plainly.

Stein's stand in support of women's higher education, given the public fretting over school's negative impact on a girl's "chances" in the marriage market at this time, deserves credit in this southern social context, though her tin ear regarding local pride in Baltimore's Goucher College for women (opened in 1885) and recent (1898) city-wide school reform spearheaded by the local Women's Civic League also bears mentioning.[55] Compared to Gilman's ethnocentrism, though, Stein's address is hardly a paean to racial civilization. As late as 1937, Stein admitted only: "I was brought up to believe in the North," here recuperating geography as a kind of direction for identity or faith, via the Civil War.[56] But Gilman exulted in "the joy of racial action in full freedom" and relished the prospect of "enormous racial advance" to be released "like a spring" by the liberation of wives from subjection in marriage.[57] A self-described "convert" after reading Gilman, the highly accomplished British writer Vernon Lee (Violet Paget) rang extended praise for

Women and Economics in the *North American Review* in 1902. Lee zeroed in on the text's racial cues and her essay-length review explicitly addressed "my Anglo-Saxon readers." She drew out the vision of gender-inclusive racial power from Gilman into an imperial frame, concluding her piece with an elaborate Orientalist flourish regarding the "Moorish" peoples of Tangiers, unfavorably comparing their oversexed ("veiled and painted") women and their "effeminate," "languid" men to the "sporting," "masculine," and "colonizing" English, female *and* male.[58]

Stein's lecture gestured at a racial grounding for identity in US. society, but it was, vague and backward looking rather than "progressive" and racialist. In delineating precisely what was "extremely inadequate" about higher education, she could only point to the "lower public schools" whose "general scheme of coeducation" did not "accentuate[ ] the sex question but admit[ted] the *inalienable right* of all human beings to have their race considered before their sex" (emphasis added). Echoing Gilman's assumptions (race over sex), Stein hooked into a republican and patriotic idiom rather than science or evolution to attach a racial basis for the founding of the United States and, presumably, its historical fulfilment. While a conservative like Edward Blyden endorsed a related concept of "race rights," Stein's lecture failed to elaborate such an idea or explain exactly how or why such a "right" to be racialized became compromised after grade school, much less what to do about it. She does vaguely self-authorize as "white" via the category "North" (or "Cambridge")—for all the good it would do her in Baltimore. Not only did the Maryland women's club movement have "nothing of the new woman about it," but it eschewed activism altogether. "The reformer, obstinately insisting upon her reforms with no regard to existing local conditions are the ones to be most dreaded," intoned one early officer.[59]

Much of Stein's address, like Gilman's text, concerned the cares and anxieties of mothers and mothering—"the children problem," she called it—and this talk clearly tested out a public voice as a doctor-in-training with a specialty in women's complaints. But Stein's weak framing of Yankee authority did not build to substantial vision of personal status or identity, nor did she effectively combine her scientific training with Gilman's racial-civilizationist feminism into a definite social trajectory. Rather the work remained in a much more republican, even Emersonian register, as in its matter-of-fact closing statement: "Through [the] discipline [of college education] you become a self-respecting human being," outside any gender or race binary. Her final anecdote about how Stein and her friends caught crabs in Chesapeake Bay and then "neatly severed their brains from their spinal columns" before boiling them alive added a gross-out scene to a hectoring discourse that could have hardly won over future patients in town. In a parody, really, of the of decorous women's club lecture (think: H. L. Mencken not M. Carey Thomas), the crab boil scene split and lampooned the difference about whether such behavior was civilized or savage, and I would suggest that the talk builds, if only implicitly, toward a rejection of model minority status held out to Jews at the turn of the century.[60] Historian Beth Wenger points out that Jewish military service in the Spanish American war going on at this same time sealed the assimilation of the earlier Jewish immigrant cohorts into US culture, and that Jewish men's combat service against a European power went a long way toward dissolving their suspiciously foreign ties in the minds of many opinion shapers.[61]

Twenty-five years old in 1899, Stein was pushing the age of marriage, and her speech alluded to personal concerns over calling and vocation. When she described "the ordinary indeterminate worrisome ill adjusted life of the individual who has no definite tasks and whose effective accomplishment is out of all proportion with the nerve force expended," she evoked the nervous, even hysteria-like symptoms familiar to women of her class and well-studied by those with her training in psychology and medicine.[62] Stein was hardly alone in struggling with the college woman's authenticity and social purpose at the turn of the twentieth century. That same year as her cameo on the women's club lecture circuit, Jane Addams penned a very elegant essay in *Atlantic Monthly* entitled "The Subtle Problems of Charity." In it, she described the "young college woman, well-bred and open-minded" as full of promise yet at sea ethically and practically in charity (later, "settlement") work. "She feels the sordidness of constantly being obliged to urge the industrial view of life" on her clients, complained Addams, since such graduates really knew nothing of earning or saving money; "whatever her virtues may be, they are not the industrial virtues." As would expound at length in her autobiography, "Subtle Problems" pointed out that the college graduate's grandmothers were at least not in a situation of hypocrisy, "because [they] *did* have the industrial virtues" as well as other practical "housewifely accomplishments" that could succor a poor neighbor.[63] Stein's narrator in *The Making* would also praise the "good foreign women, the grandmothers we need only to be just remembering," and much of the novel pondered the weakness and mediocrity of their educated American grandchildren, male and female.[64]

Where Gilman and Lee worked aggressively (and Addams, more gently) for race advancement and civilizing missions, Stein's Baltimore talk looked backward, accenting Yankee self-reliance and an implied northern tutelage of an inferior, retrograde south. This stance made for a kind of colonial posture in Baltimore, though one resonant more of Reconstruction than the Spanish American War. North-South patronage waned sharply at the turn of the century, a moment marked by white solidarity across the Mason-Dixon Line. These cultural adjustments were visible in the myriad ways white Americans made sense (news, stories) of imperial war and the colonization of nonwhite peoples in the Caribbean and Pacific, rescuing a fair Cuba from a dark "Spanish tyrant" and recasting of the former Confederacy as a site of colonial nostalgia.[65] Yet, Stein's inability to "see" the Spanish American war at precisely this moment deserves comment. While in medical school at Hopkins, she seems to have barely noticed what at least one historian calls the "frantic" state of Baltimore during the outbreak of war with Spain, a period that included the explosion of mines in the harbor, the rapid construction of batteries, including guns and mortars, and curfews and lights out along the river, all jitteringly reported in the *Sun*.[66] Only after World War II does Stein note a memory of watching soldiers depart San Francisco for the Philippines. In *Wars I have Seen* (1946), she describes them, hauntingly, as being "deported," here analogizing the exercise of state power over its presumably highly valued citizen-soldiers to actions typically directed at more suspect residents: subversives or aliens.[67]

Stein's earlier, exceptionalism-inclined historical consciousness was displayed in her unpublished essay "Degeneration in American Women" (ca. 1901). In this essay, "true American push"—whose assumed destiny it is to triumph over old world decay—is threatened from within by "the characteristic inefficiency" of "the American woman."[68] "Degeneration" responded to an American Medical Association journal article by George Engelmann, MD, entitled "The Increasing Sterility of American Women," and it represents a penultimate effort by Stein to test out a professional medical voice. Engelmann's alarm focused on doctors' inability to get at the "moral causes" of fertility patterns that were not biological but rooted in women's reproductive choices, including "criminal abortion" and "artificial sterility" (i.e., birth control) especially among the upper classes and the college set.[69] With medical authority so compromised and uncertain, Stein's essay—written in the context of her own increasing weariness and "boredom" at Hopkins—worked out a harsh, goading reprimand to future patients rather than parsed statistics or raised research-oriented questions to professional peers in the field.[70]

After summarizing Englemann's figures, Stein's essay strung together a number of sociological observations about the causes of "voluntary sterility" picked up in her clinical work in Baltimore and part of common knowledge of the day.[71] Among the "laboring classes," she explained, the advice of "charity workers" and the "knowledge obtained" from "the use of dispensaries" caused the spread in "methods of prevention." Among elite women and alumnae, Stein decried a "negation of sex," an "abhorrence of virility," and a false "exultation of female ideal of moral and method [sic]," all leading to a "lack of respect for both the matrimonial and maternal ideal." Though previously supportive of higher education, now Stein singled out "the terror to the trained professional mind, the intelligent mother" as a fearful obstacle to medical authority. "When this generation learns over again the truth that the training of children should on the one hand consist of a back ground in the home tradition that stands for honesty and right living and that for the rest it should [leave] in the hands of trained professional," concluded Stein, "the morbid responsibility for the offspring will disappear." This declaration amounts to a revanchist stance á la Ouida: simple virtues and sexual reproduction for the masses, superintendence by the few in an aristocracy of expertise (if not race or class), effectively launching Stein's critique of feminism and the new woman.

Stein concluded "Degeneration" with a sweeping condemnation "of every class of the American population" by referring not to science but to art. She described George de Forest Brush's painting "Mother and Child" (1895), located in the Boston Museum of Art. Of the mother in the portrait, Stein stated: "She is worn and weary but the vigorous struggling baby in her arms transfigures her weariness and changes it from a sacrifice to the purest pride." The painting's radiant, light-skinned and blonde-haired child embraced by darkly clad mother with downcast eyes and drawn cheeks against a classical background points to the ideologically and racially charged task of motherhood at the time: literally holding up the fair-haired ideal.[72] That Stein pointed to art as a guide for gender-role confusion deserves special note. A strong current of transnational opinion blamed art and literature for decay in moral and "racial" life, expounded upon at length in Max Nordau's widely read volume *Degeneration* (1895).[73] In his skewering of literary artists from Ibsen to Tolstoy to Zola, Nordau claimed that the "emotionalism" and "moral insanity" of their novels was evidence of physical and mental "stigmata," markers of "deviation from an original type," a definition of "degeneration" based on ideas from evolutionary theory and early criminology propounded by Cesar Lombroso (to whom the book was dedicated).[74] Nordau was roundly criticized and dismissed in the United States—"a pathological book on a pathological subject," declared the *Psychological Review*—and commentary by William Dean Howells and William James happily pointed up the comparatively fresh and untested potential for American belle letters and "native" genius.[75] In 1902, *Popular Science Monthly* offered a cheery, upbeat answer to the by-then more general question, "Is this a degenerate age?" To those daunted by doings in Europe—either by the current crisis or past accomplishment—the writer offered encouragement: "The Shakespeares and Miltons of our day write in prose."[76]

Gertrude Stein could have used such encouragement that year. Just a few months earlier, one of her graduate instructors suggested that she make "special reference to the literary form" in revising her last scientific article intended for publication: diagrams and discussion of sections of embryo and adult brains.[77] She had performed this research in Dr. Franklin Mall's anatomy lab at Johns Hopkins with a focus on sex differences, investigations that Gilman keenly appreciated. "The brain is not an organ of sex," Gilman could confidently assert in *Women and Economics*. "As well speak of the female liver."[78] But Stein seems to have gotten little comfort from these scientific findings. From the hysteria- and racism-tinged environment of advanced higher education, Stein emerged as a conservative woman rebel, trying to hold her own but uncomfortable with the social meanings of medicine, namely, racial reproduction, uplift, and advancement, either as agent or object. No role or label spoke to her deeply and, as several biographers underscore, Stein's burgeoning romantic and sexual interest in women added complexity to her life around 1900.[79]

In interpreting Stein's shift from medicine to literature, Steven Meyer connects her to earlier intellectual traditions, especially in Emerson, that did not radically oppose science and art.[80] Emerson's claim in his 1841 essay "History" strikingly—almost eerily—anticipates Stein. He wrote: "I can symbolize my thought by using the name of any creature, of any fact, because every creature is man agent or patient." And again: "Yet every history should be written in a wisdom which divined the range of our affinities and looked at facts as symbols."[81] Emerson's standards for Genius or Mind were very stringent, and any mere system—like a "just learned botany" in the hands of a "girl"—would yield only superficial, passing strength, and fleeting, inauthentic vision.[82] Stein seems drawn to the Emerson of the "transparent eyeball" who celebrated acute, transcendent powers of human perception rather than the Emerson of "we, Saxons" recently described by Nell Irvin Painter.[83] Given the challenge for women to lay steady, reliable claim to power over language, and the authority to name in Emerson's day or her own, it is little wonder Stein devised a literary practice that searched out, as she later put it, ways to write "that would not invent names, but mean names without naming them."[84]

But first she turned her hand to conventionally voiced fiction in order to confront the new woman. Around 1900, she drafted a novella entitled *Fernhurst*, a thinly veiled story based on events she heard about through friends at Bryn Mawr College. The plot concerned a love triangle between the dean and two faculty members, one her glowing female protégé and the other a dashing (and married) young male philosopher. In this unpublished campus novel of sexual scandal, some of Stein's most pungent and negative appraisals of feminism can be found.[85] *Fernhurst* roundly condemns several cohorts of the new woman: the senior cadres represented by the school's dean and founding benefactors, the faculty generation, and the current students. The action opens with the "post prandial attention[s]" of a "learned lady" who gushes to her audience: "We college women we are always college girls." The lady is "mocked in undertones" by the narrator, who "read[s] a condemnation in this praise."[86] Then the narrator indicts the whole project: "I wonder will the new woman ever relearn the fundamental facts of sex," she fumes. "Will she not see that college standards are of little worth in actual labor" (4). Here, the narrator elides two orders of knowledge, scientific and social. The "facts of sex" point the reader to the biological, but "actual labor" points more to social arrangements in the world. Rather than pause to clarify, ridicule follows. "What! does a reform start hopeful and glorious with people to remake and all sex to destroy only to end in the same old homes with the same men and women in their very same place?" (7). The narrator's rejection of the "doctrine of the equality of the sexes" avoids deeper reflection on resistant social conditions, and this narrator takes no—well, maybe just a few—prisoners: "In short I would have the few women who must do a piece of the man's work but think that the great mass of the world's women should content themselves with attaining to womanhood" (4–5).

Stein was in good company with the direction, if not conclusion, of such critiques. Addams voiced related concerns about higher education and female potential. Her now-famous question "After college, what?" crystallized the dilemma facing middle-class white women searching for a social purpose outside the narrow confines of private domesticity, and she answered that question with public service in the cause of expanded democracy.[87] Emma Goldman was more than impatient with the turn-of-the-century's "advanced woman" who was as poisoned by philistinism as any other domain of the bourgeoisie. In the "Tragedy of Woman's Emancipation" (1910), Goldman railed at the "narrowness of the existing conception of woman's independence," its remoteness from what she called "woman nature." These "soulless, joyless creature[s]," bargained away the fullness of their humanity, especially sexual expressiveness, for intellectual and economic freedom, a choice she condemned as false.[88] But Addams and Goldman made commitments to social engagement that Stein had little interest in, and the *Fernhurst* narrator instead defended the status quo, admonishing readers that "established virtues and methods are at once more honorable and more efficient" (6) than the pretense and hypocrisy of campus women, who, for all their "genuine belief in liberty and honor and a disinterested devotion for the uplifting of the race" (17–18), in the end, remained "in their very same place" (49).

The *Fernhurst* narrator's contempt for "the uplifting of the race" stands out here. She is unimpressed with the dean's assumption, á la Gilman, that "the future of the race was in the hands of those who trained the generation that followed after" at the college. She dismisses the college's main donor, a "rich spinster of Virginia," who performed her duty to the nation via white supremacist conceit, securing "the future of the race to the extent of five hundred young women every four years" (16–17). Fernhurst College is full of foolish white people—smug Quakers, breathless midwesterners, and corrupt southerners—doomed to stasis amid their prophesying about progress and faith in new worlds. Notable is the new woman protagonist, the educated faculty wife Nancy (Talbot) Redfern, a woman with a physiognomically impossible aspect: a "blonde good-looking face" (12).

In *Fernhurst*, Nancy embodies unexamined assumptions about sex equality. During her undergraduate years at a midwestern college, such assumptions inform campus "self government" and "College Democracy." This "Democracy was too simple and genuine to be discussed" or critically examined, the reader is told, but it can be known by its signal feature: "simple comradeship between the sexes" (24). Stein's handling has shades of Henry Adams about it. He had little positive to say about the new woman and feared that democracy had become just another ideology all too vulnerable to debasement.[89] Nancy's blithe commitment to sexual equality dazzles her beau, the southern gentleman Philip Redfern whose surname is that of a popular brand of corset and who perceives in her "a whole new world" for his conquest and enjoyment. Redfern's "elaborate chivalry" is a rigid script of false deference to women that masks control and subordination, but Philip at least can comfort and justify himself with tradition. Nancy lacks even the patina of dignity and self-possession that long-standing social tradition offers. For all her good looks and book learning (the reader sees her "sitting alone studying a Greek grammar"), her mind remains undiscriminating, useless, doomed to throwing herself against the wall of social convention; she "never learned the rules of the game." After Philip leaves Nancy for the perfected intellect he perceives in the dean's protégé faculty member, Nancy goes to Germany for more classical training, still trying to make herself "worthy of his companionship," deluded to the end (48). Nancy believes that human fulfillment is a prize for doing well at school, and through her foolishness, the narrator mocks this facile popular ideology circulating around American higher education.

It is this failed worldview—the "naïve realism" endlessly debated by faculty in Fernhurst's philosophy department—that the narrator mostly condemns; feminism is just a symptom. It is almost too easy to deride "the doctrine of [sexual] equality with a mental reservation in favor of female superiority," but the problem is deeper. As proof, the students at Fernhurst are "harsh and crude young things" who "laugh and dissect the things their elders dare not see," (35) meant to be typical of callow American youth. Stein's narrator rejects the "narrow new world humanity" of the college scene and the "hasty sandwich" style of interaction that passes for thinking, reflection, and connection. Only the "cultivators of an infinite leisure" have time to feel "the gentle approach, the slow rise, the deep ecstasy and the full flow of joy" of deeper humanity, notes the narrator, here phrased in sensuous—indeed, Goldmanian—terms. "To our new world feeling the sadness of pain has more dignity than the beauty of joy," the narrator complains (38). Pain is quicker and less ambiguous and, of course, gendered: scripted to the feminine vocations of disappointment, suffering, and grieving and at which Nancy Redfern becomes expert.

Stepping outside these terms, the narrator carves out a space of exceptionalism for herself:

> Had I been bred in the last generation full of hope and unattainable desires I too would have declared that men and women are born equal but being of this generation with the college and professions open to me and able to learn that the other man is really stronger I say I will have none of it. And you shall have none of it says my reader tired of this posing I don't say no I can only hope that I am one of those rare women that should since I find in my heart that I needs must. (7–8)

I read this statement as more a rejection of the everyday terms of politics and society than feminism per se. While Stein's narrator is only too happy to point out the sloppy and superficial nature of campus democracy, she has nothing to say about the content of any other form of democracy. Whether it is "Susan B. Anthony clamoring for the increase of the suffrage or John Marshall pleading for its restriction," the narrator remains diffident: "I gaze at them…and realize that they are both eager that the truest justice should be granted to all." Stein's narrator prefers to wave away or simply run away from regular politics (7).

In *Fernhurst*, Stein worked toward a full-blown rejection of both the feminine vocations of moral superiority and uplift as well as disappointment, grieving, and heartbreak—and, implicitly, heterosexual marriage with its burdens of race and nation building.[90] But she was still not done raking the new woman, whose reach was transnational and very much intertwined in politics of everyday life and literature that Stein wanted to avoid. Nancy Redfern reappears as Martha Hersland in *The Making* only to marry Redfern all over again and fail, I will suggest, even more starkly in her living. Then in *Tender Buttons*, her next completed work, Stein took a swipe at Jane Addams and her Hull House. The *Fernhurst* narrator may have shrugged off imperial politics—the finer points of colonial policy within England's "Manchester school" compared to that of "Joseph Chamberlain" trouble her not—but they caught up with Stein abroad, as the questions of nation, sex, and race were deeply entwined in literary London, the epicenter of the new woman novel.

Whether in literature, opinion, or science, discussions of the new woman carried a remarkably consistent gendered premise: "Woman is incapable of grasping an abstract idea."[91] A masculine proclivity toward invention and theorizing and projection was persistently set against a feminine predisposition for the concrete, for repetition, and memory—despite the findings about human brain anatomy in the lab at Johns Hopkins. As Hugo Münsterberg himself put it, "The average female mind is...disinclined to abstract thought."[92] When "Alice" recalls important advice that Stein's teacher William James reportedly gave her in college, she underscored a variant of this point:

> Keep your mind open, he used to say, and when some one objected, but Professor James, this that I say is true. Yes, said James, it is abjectly true.[93]

In other words, some "this that I say" could be true, but since there is only one system of truth, the rest is "abjectly true," positioned outside acceptable norms as degraded, hysterical, unintelligible, other. It is against this consignment to abjection that Stein set her hand in *The Making*, the only way that writing "a history of every one" could make any sense and be worth doing, and the only reason she could remain committed to that book and its purpose for a lifetime.

The Making of Americans

The Making is many things. It is a dual family biography of the Herslands (of the west) and the Dehnings (of the east); it is a long meditation on the meaning of American success; a defense of "singularity" and "queer folk" in the face of the mass-production machine age; it is about the fulfillment of deep human "being," and, as I've already noted, it is a would-be history of "every one." Stein professed a deep personal attachment to the novel. She quoted it at length in her public lectures, interviews, and essays as a kind of proof-text of her writerly status. She also privately called it her "eldest son," her "*ainé*" (first born) or sometimes just "The Family," and scholars have long mined it for snippets of Stein family detail.[94] Indeed, Stein pegged much of the life cycle of this massive, almost unpublished, barely read novel to the narrative arc of what became her most-read, best-selling book *The Autobiography of Alice B. Toklas*, which mentions the book by its title at least 30 times and whose denouement is *The Making*'s translation into French in the year 1932.[95] Most literary scholars assign *The Making* to a discreet epoch in her writing (the early novels) after which she moved on to other genres (portraits, poems, operas, plays, and meditations) and other ideas, as Ashton suggests. That is, most critics agree that Stein discarded, resolved, or "retracked"—to use Leon Katz's exquisite malapropism—the book's central and vaguely historical premise: the idea of being able to describe every person who ever lived.[96] As late as *Everybody's Autobiography*, however, Stein still pressed the novel upon her readers and reidentified herself with its founding project:

> *The Making of Americans* is a very important thing and everyone ought to be reading at it or it and now I am trying to do it again to say everything about everything only then I was wanting to write a history of every individual person who ever is or was or shall be living and I was convinced it could be done as I still am but now individual anything as related to every other individual is to me no longer interesting....It is important yes I think so that it should be looked at by every one.[97]

The bobbling "it" in this paragraph could mean the novel *The Making* that might be "read at" (meaning what?) or read (conventionally), or "looked at" like a piece of art, overall drawing our attention to the politics of reading. The "it" might also mean the idea of making Americans, a project that points outside the text to the reader, society, or nation. *The Making* ends in a very similar place, with the charge to "some" to remember a family's history. "Any family living can be one being existing and some can remember something of some such thing" (925). Maybe.

The Making responds to the problem of the new woman in several ways. Thematically, it revisits the fate of the new woman in the character of Martha Hersland. The entire *Fernhurst* novella is redacted in the middle of the chapter that bears her name; Martha Hersland becomes Mrs. Philip Redfern and fails as a "college-bred" wife all over again. *The Making* is also a new woman novel in a second sense, via its attempt to recuperate a history for women. At several points in the novel's opening chapters, the narrator (who functions more like a character in the book and whom I will identify as The Writer) promises a history of many women. "There are many kinds of women," states The Writer. "This is a history of only a few kinds of them" (166). Of Mrs. Fannie Hersland, "a foreign woman," we learn: "There was nothing in her to connect her with the past the present or the future, there was not any history of her" (100). The reader is additionally promised the stories of other socially marginal women. There will be "much discussing of this spinster nature" (199) and even a "history of servant queerness" (179).[98] Male characters, like Alfred Hersland, have fathers and traditions: "This made a history for him" (123). But for women, "there would be existence, there would be changes, but no history" (102). On an acknowledged if not fully realized level, history might rescue women from abjection, powerlessness, and invisibility. And, in a final, related move, the novel answers the charge of hysteria generally leveled at the new woman, particularly the charge of an inability to be abstract. Stein's notebooks mark her quiet patience with her ambition in the project. "I need not be in a hurry to give birth to my hero because it will be an enormous task to struggle his development. I want to realise [sic] everybody in the book the way I am."[99] No hasty sandwich here. Yet, once the hero, Martha Hersland's brother David, articulates the abstraction of "one," The Writer kills him off.[100] This denouement fulfills Emerson's hypothesis in "Nature": "But perception is not whimsical, but fatal."[101] That is, after one can see/name, seeing ends, and the result is a kind of death of perception.

Over many hundreds of pages, The Writer starts over and over again, struggling to answer the charge of hysteria—that is, unintelligibility or abjection—with the facts of history. The Writer's definition of history is functionalist and almost unrelated to the narrative assemblage of arguments based on verifiable evidence that Cushing Strout defended and that is practiced in today's academy. History in *The Making* starts off as genealogy, as in "a history of a family's progress." By the middle of the book, history operates more like a recognition system for "kinds" and "types" of people. By the final chapter about Martha's brother David, The Writer abandons the schema of kinds and types for an even more abstract rendering of "one," as in "Each one is one" (872). At that point, The Writer as narrator vanishes, and David, the new protagonist, dissolves into nothingness. This idea of "one" pushes back against judgments about who is hysterical (forgettable, powerless, unintelligible) and who is historical, who counts and can be counted in a story of family progress. The sentence "Each one is one" is also perfectly ambiguous, collapsing the poles of meaning that James's pragmatism sought to negotiate: the one and the many. "Each one is one" can be read to express perfect monism—each one is one *with The One*—or radical pluralism—each one is *just a* one—depending on how you read it.[102]

Initially, however, The Writer's invocation of history is expansive and potentially democratic. "Sometime then there will be a history of every one and so then every one will have in them the last touch of being a history of any one can give to them" (180). Precisely at this upbeat, capacious moment, The Writer separates the word "everyone" into "every" and "one" and persists in this usage throughout the text. On p. 179, the compound nouns "everyone" and "anyone" and "someone" become "any one" "some one" and "every one." Once "one" is separated from any qualifier, The Writer is free. There is hint of this theorizing back in Stein's Radcliffe notebooks. A sketch titled "In the Red Deeps" (1894) starts as follows: "The (*more or less*) common-place incidents of the outer world are well enough for those (*poor unfortunates*) who(m) nature has given no inner ((one))" [*sic*].[103] It's tempting to simply read "one" as "soul," but the sentence's marked-up face alerts us to the provisional and what Stein later called the "lively" aspects of her writing.[104] The word "one" is the ultimate unifier and simultaneously the ultimate placeholder, at once full and empty, encompassing and solitary. In Jewish tradition, many of these dimensions inhabit the *Sh'ma*, a traditional prayer and usually a child's first. "Hear O Israel, the Lord is our God, the Lord is One" (*Shema Yisrael Adonai eloheinu Adonai ehad*), with the Hebrew *ehad* sometimes translated as "alone."[105] The splitting off of "one" also points to Stein's "little aunts" in Baltimore who "count one one one," a form of knowledge associated with neither a unifying hierarchical divinity nor a fragmented modernity but with folk wisdom; Stein's little aunts count "like Chinamen."[106] "One" is where math meets metaphor, it simultaneously asks and answers the question of counting, of mattering, of being at all—at least in English.

As readers of *The Making* know, "being living," "living being," even "being being" are among the strongest leitmotifs of the novel. The grandchildren of the immigrant Hersland family—Martha, Alfred, and David—fail at all of these, but the would-be new woman heroine Martha most of all. Nancy Talbot grows up with breezy, unexamined faith in democracy, but Martha is dominated by the old-style law of the father. Martha was "not very interesting ever to her father or ever very interesting really to any one who ever knew her" (409). Her body and desires are regulated, violated, and ignored in turn by the men around her. Understandably drawn out of the house toward the neighbors, Martha is remanded indoors by both Davids, father and brother (421). The elder David Hersland determines, in fits and starts, to "make of her the kind of educated person that it was right he should have for a daughter." This education included "cooking and sewing and feeling like the women he was seeing in the neighborhood in him to him," implying that father and daughter probably see different things in the same neighboring people and, the reader can infer, different things in education as well (422–423). Young Martha desperately needs words and the power they can bring. When her siblings abandon her on a rainy walk home from school, she threatens to "throw her umbrella in the mud" to get attention; even so "no one heard her [threat] as it burst from her," and no restitution is made for the breach of safety or sympathy.[107] Another umbrella/law of the father episode ends her childhood entirely. Martha espies a man beating a woman with an umbrella in public, but the incident is socially normalized; no one actually uses words to name or complain about any of it. Martha is moved, however: "She would go to college, she knew it then" (424). The Writer also describes some kind of transgressive sexual contact between Martha and a boy in the neighborhood, another scenario that eludes a substantive vocabulary and thus fails to join meaningfully to history. "One little boy wanted her to do loving the little boy" (412) we are told, and again, "one little boy as I was saying tried a little in loving, in things they should not be doing and really she was not resisting" (416). Nothing of these strains and violations in Martha's growing up is ever explicitly named much less resolved. The troubled and troubling connection between daughter and father thus endures, though later in the story there is a sort of parricide (489).

Most striking about Martha is neither her inner nature nor her outer actions, it's the membrane between the two: her skin. If Nancy Talbot is a prisoner of her "blonde" face, Martha Hersland is trapped in her skin. Martha's skin receives extended commentary, and she is the only character so treated in the novel. Martha is defined largely by her skin, a surface for others' projections and penetrations. Many of *The Making*'s characters are rendered like lab specimens, and Martha is a "being in solution in a fluid condition" (398). Her skin is especially important, as it "held this one from flowing over everything" (386). Martha's skin is rendered through a series of very oblique descriptions, usually as "a skin" as in, a particular skin, rather than just the organ called "skin" that every human has. "This one was a whole one because this one was held together by a skin, as I was saying" (387). At moments, the narrator implies the more generic form of skin, as in: "…there are always many millions of them living and each one of them is held together as a whole one by the skin of each one" (386). The Writer seems also to be punning on skin/kin, in a kind of chicken and egg conundrum about family formation, race/skin color, and identity. At yet other points, a deeper kind of self-possession is implied by skin: "…this one [Martha] was different from all the others of them for this one *had her own skin* and so was separated from all the others of them that have or had or will have the same kind of being to make them…(387, emphasis added). Sometimes, Martha appears to have integrity in spite of her skin: "…it was not only the skin that kept her apart from other ones, there was actual being actual individual being always in Martha" (398). Indeed, "she would keep together even without the skin of her to hold her" (406). However, in the last rendering of Martha's skin, the narrator tells us that she was "a whole one only ever by the skin of her holding her together" (419). Skin/kin is all she's got.

After this build-up about Martha, the plot line and characters of *Fernhurst*—here called Farnham College—are introduced. The "completely chivalrous"

(442) Philip Redfern appears and falls for Martha at college, (mis)taking her for "the new world" (433). Gone from this version of the story is the drubbing of the "doctrine of the essential sameness of sex" on campus, though it is mentioned. The dean reappears with her female faculty protégé. Unlike the novella, however, the Redfern marriage has arrived on campus already in shambles; the "blond good-looking" Mrs. Redfern is thus even more fated and constrained as her husband falls for the other woman (sic, 432). As in *Fernhurst*, this Mrs. Redfern has "little understanding" despite her efforts to "arrange and explain it by her western morality and her new world humanity" (438). The Nancy Talbot Redfern character from *Fernhurst* is barely sympathetic, but Martha Hersland has been traumatized and the plot line in *The Making* feels unfair and forced.

As in *Fernhurst*, Mrs. Redfern's looks/skin fail to protect her. The rules of the game go totally unnamed, not even blamed on a dogmatic official democracy, sophomoric feminism, or old Virginia white supremacy. As in the novella's denouement, Martha strives "to be pleasing by knowing Greek and naïve realism" (447), and even after the breakup she is "always working at something to have him [Redfern] again" (457). Though Philip does his share of failing in *The Making*'s version of the story, it is Martha who is painted as a disaster, chided repeatedly for having "no understanding in desiring" and being deficient in even basic self-knowledge (462). After her marriage fails, Martha returns to the family home to care for her elderly father. Formerly "very annoying" to the senior David Hersland, she now irritates him daily, as she can't remember how he takes his coffee and always helps him with his coat, which he detests (471). Martha Hersland Redfern neither breaks free of the conventions of femininity nor fulfills them. Trapped in her skin, she remains an odd specimen. Martha and a number of other characters are mildly hysterical, exhibiting tics and repetitive behaviors (standing, sitting, flinging, and jumping); they are more like lab rats trapped in an experiment than characters who develop. But Nancy at least gets a trip to Europe at the end of her marriage; Martha is remanded to her father's house, facing daily failure and shame. If Fernhurst women stay "in the same place," Martha goes positively backward in *The Making*.

Given Martha Hersland's centrality to the story, *The Making* strikes me to be as much as a new woman novel as anything else. With her bleak fate, *The Making* might even be an anti-new woman novel, for which there was also an audience and market.[108] Though the "sale of these books is not a healthy sign," according to at least one worried English critic, new woman fiction was extremely popular and profitable. Sarah Grand's *Heavenly Twins* went into six printings the first year, and sold strongly in the United States, where it was welcomed by reviewers.[109] In a draft letter from ca. 1903, as she was launching into the *The Making* project, Stein noted her intention to begin "devoting my whole energy to meditating on how seven volume novels are written," and the comment, however jeering, puts her squarely in the company of Grand (*The Heavenly Twins* ran to three volumes).[110] Her decision in 1912 to seek out John Lane of the Bodley Head, a leading London publisher of new woman authors, just after completing *The Making*, further points up Stein's interest in critical examination of family norms as well as a search for audiences attentive to avant-garde artistic standards.

Stein got some coaching about how to place the book from Roger Fry, the English critic and painter. He thought that the higher status of "an English publisher" could "give a book more of a reputation" than one in the United States and that the Bodley Head was a superior distributor across the Atlantic.[111] John Lane was experienced in transnational marketing, having published the *Anglo-Saxon Review* with backing from US-born Lady Randolph Churchill (Winston's mother) in 1899–1901.[112] Lane was married to a monied Boston widow, Annie P. King, author of *Kitwyk*. The details of Stein and Lane's interactions are hard to pin down. In *Everybody's Autobiography*, she claimed: "I wanted in England to have the Bodley Head for sentimental reasons." "[A]fter all John Lane was the only real publisher who had really ever thought of publishing a book for me," Stein continued, "and you have to be loyal to every one if you do quarrel with any one."[113] These sentences refer to an absurdly feminine—or outrageously opportunistic—standard of behavior ("loyal to everyone") in a commercial setting stilted by tea-time decorum and "sentimental reasons" (a sly oxymoron). Lane's letters to Stein indicate that her work went out to readers for review and that he also "dipped into it" himself; the *Autobiography* claims that no one except Lane's wife actually read her manuscripts. "He put it into their hands and took it out again and inaudibly he announced that Gertrude Stein was here. Nobody was introduced to anybody," explains "Alice."[114] Lane rejected and returned *The Making* in early 1913, but invited Stein to send another manuscript "if it is not too long." He accepted and printed, in 1915, 300 copies of *Three Lives*.[115] Stein had paid the Grafton Press herself to publish the first edition in the United States and she owned the plates, which Lane insisted upon using. In fact, his edition still had "Grafton Press" stamped on the spine; presumably buyers could not see the more trendy "Bodley Head" imprint in the book unless they opened it. This made the volume a weird kind of a bastard child with the publisher's name on the inside but not the outside.[116] Lane's behavior was doubly insulting. He told Stein that active marketing for her short stories was "a costly luxury," which increased the value of the cover's external markings on the shelf—but then he deigned to so imprint the book.[117] It was a kind of colonial move in which the book was taken but not fully accepted as an equal in the press's offerings.

Possibly lurking and unnamed in this frustrating scenario was homophobia. Stein had been introduced to Lane via letter by US-born portrait artist Myra Edgerly, and she and Toklas stayed with Edgerly and her friends in the winter of 1912–1913. They made a second visit to England in 1914 and met at the Lanes, sometimes for Sunday tea.[118] Stein claimed that she was warned by another American friend Mildred Aldrich (also living in France) to "look out for John Lane, he is a fox…"[119] Lane dropped Oscar Wilde from the Bodley Head immediately after Wilde's arrest in 1895, goaded in part by some of his own authors who were eager to protect their reputations and livelihoods from scandal. "Lane never completely threw it off," according to a former employee, J. Lewis May. "For a long time he was morbidly suspicious and discerned a pervert behind every tree," May claimed. "According to him the number of the tainted ones was legion."[120] Toklas may not have accompanied Stein on at least some of these awkward Sundays at the Lanes or at the press office. Instead, she waited outside. "How well I knew all the things in all the shops near the Bodley Head because while Gertrude Stein was inside with John Lane while nothing happened and then when finally something happened I waited outside and looked at everything."[121] Even if Toklas sat in on some of the conversations, Stein seems to be giving us a message about Lane's unwelcome and duplicity.

Stein never developed an explicit language—what she called in her next book, *Tender Buttons*, a "system to pointing"—to name Lane's mistreatment of her or his homophobia. She did, however, take shot at Jane Addams in this prose poem, her next work, published in 1914. One of Stein's most sensitive interpreters, Marianne DeKoven, puzzles over the line near the end of the "Objects" section of that work that reads: "Excellent, not a hull house."[122] In a 1994 essay, DeKoven drew out the life resonances between Stein and Addams: their strong ambition (and father figures), their deep attraction to art, their med school mishaps (both dropped out), their lifelong partnerships with women, and their restaging of domesticity as a site for their own innovative life work. DeKoven sees a parallel and complementary social function between their "houses."[123] But like so many Stein phrasings, "Excellent, not a hull house" thrusts the reader into an associational mode, and I come up with the cliché, "Anything but a hull house" (which has the same number of syllables and a kindred alliteration). Then what about hot house? Whore house? Fun house? Nut house? My reading of the topsy-turvy domestic inventory of *Tender Buttons*—with its "Objects Food Rooms"—tends toward *anything* but a Hull House, that is, the opposite of a safe, predictable site of assimilation, uplift, and domestication.

Further evidence of Stein's antiassimilationist stance can be found earlier in *Tender Buttons*, in "Rooms." A paragraph that begins "Checking an emigration" (which could mean, at least, ending migration or inspecting migrant bodies) concludes: "Powder, that has no color, if it did have would it be white." At a minimum, this line acknowledges the make-up-ness/made-up-ness of racialized, feminine, and national identities.[124] These lines mark Stein's distance from civilizing missions and uplift expressed in the settlement work of Hull House as well as her rejection of assimilation as a properly feminine literary purpose. Stein's anger with the *Atlantic Monthly*, where Jane Addams and Mary Antin both found favor, is also salient here. Stein traded barely restrained barbs with editor Ellery Sedgwick and his rejection caused her burning resentment.[125] Questions about her writerly voice, literary purpose, and national belonging nagged at Stein abroad. Indeed, *Tender Buttons* makes the feminine norm of being "at home" feel more like "foreign in a domestic sense." This phrase is also the legal principle devised to explain the US relationship to Puerto Rico and one that fairly describes John Lane's brutal treatment of Stein's *Three Lives*, a kind of "foreign" book that he took but did not fully and fairly incorporate. Stein's *atelier* in Paris might be thought of as a kind of "unincorporated territory" of the United States, not exactly part of it but somehow connected.

By the eve of World War I, Gertrude Stein had written hundreds and hundreds and hundreds of pages talking herself out of any patrimonial, assimilated, or state-sponsored identity. Yet, the war put intense pressure precisely on national

2.1   Gertrude Stein, ca. 1913.
Photo credit: Yale Collection of American Literature, Beinecke Rare Book and Manuscript Library

identity and citizenship status. Safe inside, she could play at/with history, but at the borders, Stein had to submit to official regulators. In *The Autobiography*, "Alice" recounts their visit to the US embassy in London in 1914 as they attempted to get back to France after war broke out that summer:

> The embassy was very full of not very american looking citizens waiting their turn. Finally we were ushered in to a very tired looking young american. Gertrude Stein remarked upon the number of not very american looking citizens that were waiting. The young american sighed. They are easier, he said, because they have papers it is only the native born american who has no papers. Well what do you do about them, asked Gertrude Stein. We guess, he said, and we hope we guess right.

And now, said he, will you take the oath. Oh dear, he said, I have said it so often I have forgotten it.[126]

This passage is full of seesawing meanings about "native" identity and how one claims, disclaims, declaims before, or is claimed by a nation-state. Little is clear or consistent in this description—which is the point. The lower-case "a" destabilizes the word America, as in The United States of. Which (part of) "america" is being referred to? The only thing for sure about the phrase "not very american looking" is that it forces the reader to conjure up their own assumptions and possibilities. The sighing and exhausted clerk's identity appears less in question; as an employee of the state, his identity is not at issue in the way the passport applicant's is. Then the telling reversal: the clerk's job is easier with the naturalized citizen because they have authenticating documentation; the "native born American"—the common euphemism for white natal citizen at the time—is the problem here, not the foreigner. A fierce send-up of bureaucratic meaning making is at hand: clerks have to "guess" about identity/truth to serve the state, when the stakes could not be higher: in wartime. Even the solemn oath is, in the end, just words and forgettable. Elsewhere in the text, "Alice" notes Gertrude Stein's "pleasure" in seeing "various French officials" struggle with spelling "Allegheny, Pennsylvania" when filling out forms requiring place of birth, a peep into a bit of passive aggressive hostility indulged in at a clerk's expense and another hint at Stein's discomfort at national borders.[127]

The day that Stein and Toklas applied for their emergency passports—October 6, 1914—was actually a slow one at the US embassy in London. Native born rather than naturalized US citizens predominated among the applicants, and the latter were all of European origins. No applicant was given a passport solely on "personal examination" or interview by the clerk—no guess work that day—but this was not so when war broke out in August. Almost 200 passports per day were issued in that earlier rush to leave the country, with "personal interview" as the main proof of identification. On October 6th, however, only 32 people showed up, and about two-thirds of them applied on the form for "natives." In the "Description of Applicant" section, some 19 of these had their "complexion" noted to be "fair," "light," or "fresh"; the others were "ruddy" or "dark." Alice and Gertrude were "dark." The passport application included racially inflected categories, notably physiognomy ("stature," "forehead," "mouth," "chin," and "hair"), but not any category for "race" per se.[128] The idea that the clerk had to "guess" the identity and nativity of a passport applicant is Stein's way of unsettling the business of knowing who any one is and drawing our attention to the governmental machinery and fallible humanity that can make or remake or unmake or break those identities.[129] Each one is one. Maybe.

Reconstructions

The borders between the United States and England, between Americanness and Englishness, and between US history and British history recur as themes in Stein's writing on war, empire, and national boundaries. After World

War II, her thinking underwent a kind of radical reconstruction. Before then, like most of her literary peers in the United States, Stein's direct comments on imperialism focused negatively on Britain.[130] Her address "What Is English Literature?" (1934) suggested that British writing underwent a "weakening" over time from the seventeenth century forward because it moved away from the "phrases" that stated the plain truths of "island daily living" toward sentences and paragraphs devoted to explaining "owning everything on the outside" of the island, i.e., empire. "But as they owned everything outside, outside and inside had to be told something about all this owning, otherwise they might not remember all this owning and so there was invented explaining and that made nineteenth century English literature what it is," that is, inseparable from the rise of the nation-state and the ideological requirements of imperialism.[131] After the Boer War, Stein quipped, "The writing was not so good." As for the twentieth century, the English "just went back to the nineteenth century and made it a little weaker, and that was because well because they were a little weaker. What else can I say?" Stein projected a bobbling ambivalence about where US literature fit in this historical sequence of nation, empire, and decline:

> And so slowly the paragraph came to be the thing, neither the words of the earlier period, the sentence of the eighteenth century, the phrases of the nineteenth century, but the paragraphs of the twentieth century, and, it is true, the English have not gone on with this thing but we have we in American literature.

The ungrammatical, unpunctuated phrase "but we have we" is the fulcrum of seesawing meaning in this sentence, a question as much as a statement. Stein continued: "It has often been known that American literature in a kind of a way is more connected with English Elizabethan [writing] than with later writing," that is, with Shakespeare's England, a more or less precolonizing England, and, notably, a reign in which England resoundingly defeated Spain (1588). All this functions as a retrospective foreshadowing of the US's defeat of Spain in 1898 and perhaps, too, its assumption of leadership of the arts (eclipsing Picasso?). Yet, Stein's is a very oblique rendering. After listing out the writers Irving, Emerson, Hawthorne, Whitman, and Henry James, she concluded: "This makes what American literature is, something that in its way is quite alone," expressing an exceptionalist or even triumphalist historical sensibility.[132]

Stein (like Jane Addams) primarily attached US national identity to the Civil War and Reconstruction, pointing up a parochial rather than clearly imperial or fully cosmopolitan vision. If anyone "did not know the America that made the Civil War they do not know about America," Stein wrote, "and always sometimes America will be that thing."[133] Addams deeply admired Lincoln; Stein was an enormous fan of U. S. Grant. In her notebooks, she described her early interactions with Alice Toklas as "my attack...like Grant's on Lee...always a forward pressure."[134] In *Four in America* (1933), she wrote: "I was with Grant," such is her imaginative intimacy with his writing and his war.[135] "...I had always known everything about the Civil War," she later insisted: "There never will be anything more interesting in America than that Civil War never."[136] Then "Alice" explains in *The Autobiography*:

> I did not realise [*sic*] then how completely and entirely american was Gertrude Stein. Later I often teased her, calling her a general, a civil war general of either or both sides.[137]

This passage puts into "Alice's" mouth a kind of girlish silliness about war as play and war as confusion. World War II kills off such silliness and demands new clarity. Like the Civil War for Grant, World War II changed everything for Gertrude Stein. She perceived the war as a major crisis of many things, notably of white supremacy, a crisis that had been building since the conventionally imperial wars of the turn of the twentieth century, wars she had trouble naming and identifying (with).[138]

In her World War II memoir, *Wars I Have Seen*, Stein wrote of the Spanish American war: "I did not know anybody who was fighting or any of their relations, but it was the time when anglo-saxonism had come into America to be a very conscious feeling." This Anglo-Saxonism was "disappointing" because "it was something different" from Kipling's romance of empire, "Only we did not know it..."[139] "Of course there were Indian wars," Stein acknowledged, but "they were not real wars, not as real as some English wars in history and certainly not as real as the American civil war. A very real war" (8–9). These sentences suggest the difficulty of making imperial war visible and "real" in a US context and the slippage between "Indian wars" and other contests for control. In the voice of a nervous feminine spectator to war, Stein identified the operation of her own and others' colonial ignorance. "From babyhood to the Boer war there was no war. No war at all," a jittery double negative construction that alludes to the opposite reality (9). "And I was right because the American civil war was the prototype of all the wars the two big wars that I have completely lived. Also the American civil war" (8). Stein played at talking herself into weak-kneed rationalizations about American innocence. During her growing up years in the United States, she noted: "There was no really outside war at least none that I noticed or that anybody around me noticed," an outrageous understatement about political consciousness (10).

World War II in France confronted Gertrude Stein most acutely with the politics of race, national belonging, and state-sponsored identity. "And now in 1943 it is here," she stated in *Wars I Have Seen*: "It is disconcerting to know and it gives you a funny feeling, that any time not only that you can be told to go and you go but also that you can be taken" (50). She recalled the "Oscar Wilde trial" and "the dryfus case and anti-semitism" (51). Then the devastating quip: "Anyway financially there is no sense in anti-semitism" (56). Stein still praised her hero U. S. Grant, but the romance of heroism and sacrifice is completely drained out and replaced by fear. In this new vision, the prisoners at Andersonville, the *reconcentrados* of Cuba, and inmates of World War II concentration camps come into new alignment as Stein reconstructs her exceptionalist view of US history.

"Some one was just telling me that in German universities they had professors who studied characteristics of races," Stein declared. "Quite unnecessary if you went to school with them but naturally the Germans did not know that." "General Grant did." "He had been to school with all the Generals of the civil war so he always knew what they would do" (8). These sentences permit an interpretation of the United States as a diverse, inclusive country freed from a need of racial classification and hierarchy, but in their fuzzy silly-seriousness, they pointedly juxtapose, if not exactly equate, German racism with US racism. Reviewing the Civil War in the light of the excesses of World War II, Lee comes off even worse. "Alice" might be scatty about playing a "civil war general of either or both sides," but in *Wars I Have Seen,* Lee is put in his place. "Lee in the civil war, who was such a typical public servant, and who believes what he was supposed to believe" about slavery and the Confederacy (53). Sides matter. Now in World War II, Stein evoked "the general confusion, the general fear, the general helplessness, the general nervousness," that is, fear *of* as well as fear *among* military leaders (13). No heroes anywhere.

As Jews living in southern France, the state's policing of identity and borders came directly home to Stein and Toklas. *Wars* described an official in the town of Belley as stating: "Tell these ladies they must leave at once for Switzerland, to-morrow if possible otherwise they will be put into a concentration camp" (50). The two were determined to stay in Belley, where they rented a farm house, and *Wars* recounted the daily toll taken on the nerves of everyone living with fear.[140] After the US forces arrive in France, Stein related a bitter anecdote about avoiding identification by the state, any state:

> To-day for the first time since the landing we had some letters from Lyon they came from the Swiss consul who has charge of American interests and they solemnly ask us to make out a paper stating if we wish or do not wish to be repatriated. It is a charming thought, ten days after the landing in France the American authorities seem to be quite certain that as soon as they like they can repatriate all Americans still in France. We giggled we said this is optimism. Naturally American authorities not really realizing what it is to live in an occupied country ask you to put down your religion your property and its value, as if anybody would as long as the Germans are in the country and in a position to take letters and read them if they want to. The American authorities say they are in a hurry for these facts *but I imagine that all Americans will feel the same* better keep quiet until the Germans are gone just naturally play possum just as long as one can. Just that. (200, emphasis added)

This passage suggests both Stein's very real fear of the Germans and her resistance to complying with the bureaucracies that produce certain identities and then can protect or destroy them—and the people attached to them—at will. At first, Stein seems bluff and commonsensical about her a natural (i.e., animal) impulse to duck and hide in response to being threatened, or that Americans will cluck in sympathy at her child's game (playing possum) analogy to avoiding capture—undercut by a sardonic: "Just that." But the word "same" also functions as the seesaw of meaning in the sentence. Maybe it means, actually, that "all Americans" will agree that facts are needed "in a hurry," thereby putting at risk those who are being urged to comply; maybe "all Americans" feel "the same" as the Germans do about Jews, homosexuals, and foreigners. In February, 1944, Stein and Toklas actually did each fill out a *passeport de protection* with the Swiss consul in Lyon, an office acting as "*Chargé des Intérêts des Etats Unis d'Amérique.*" These forms contained even fewer of the physiognomic parameters inventoried by the US passport applications from back in 1914–16, asking only for height, hair, and eye color and any "particular signs" to which *néant* (nothing) was Stein's answer. While the form lists each applicant's nationality as "*Américaine,*" none asks for religion nor does it indicate that any supporting documentation of identity was presented (as Stein did with her 1915 passport application). The *passeport* permitted temporary residence in France through August 1944, perhaps only a small comfort for the risk involved.[141]

None of Stein's extant passport materials identified her religion or her "race" as Jewish.[142] But the politics of race and the state's claim on bodies, especially women's bodies, are central in her next major work, the opera *The Mother of Us All*. The opera is a culminating statement of a number of Stein's mature intellectual preoccupations: the phenomenon of counting and national belonging, the nature of knowing, and the meaning of success; it revisits the new/hysterical woman as well. The central figure of Susan B. Anthony is cast as a "mother" figure. The sage and oracular quality of her speech and her death/nondeath in the drama (she dies but remains on stage to address the players) casts "Susan B." in something of a divine light. A childless, never-married woman, Stein's Anthony has at least nunlike qualities, presumably virginal, possibly saintly.[143] Figuring her as the "mother" of "us all" plays to and undercuts a panoply of clichés about "mothers of," but perhaps especially "of the nation" and "of invention." If some "all" are metaphorical kin of hers, so, too, are we "all" kin to one another, neatly undercutting the lines of race and nation that structured legal marriage and citizenship in Anthony's era. And at a minimum, the nature of the family we "all" belong to is ambiguous, fraught, and even imperiled, not unlike a world shattered by genocide and nuclear bombs.

By making herself and a sprinkling of her personal friends characters in the opera, Stein writes her generation into a historical trajectory that begins with the Civil War/Reconstruction but whose denouement remains open-ended, despite the Allied victory in World War II. The work contains historical figures from Anthony's generation and a handful of allegorical ones, like "Angel More," "Chris the Citizen," "Indiana Elliot," and "Jo the Loiterer." The opera's repeated question "What is marriage?" opens up the relationship between genealogy and national history, between sexual reproduction and citizenship. The libretto explores the Reconstruction Amendments that defined US citizenship as federal and male. In the wake of racialized war, Stein's Anthony ponders the ethics of victory and success for a country stuck on skin/kin/win; she also mulls the distinction between winning and being right. Following the Hersland family's dispersal and failures and Stein's observations in *Wars*, "Although everybody is civilized there is no progress" (62), electoral or military triumph does not guarantee a better tomorrow in the opera. "We cannot retrace our steps," affirms the Anthony character near the end of the opera, and, "going forward may be the same as going backwards."[144]

Family relations and national belonging come immediately into focus in act 1, scene 1, the moment in which the Stein and Anthony characters occupy the same frame of time and space. The prime issue is origins, namely paternity, and the *dramatis personae* initially declare, in unison: "Daniel was my father's name." The Stein character then echoes and revises this statement: "My father's name was Daniel... not Daniel in the lion's den, not Daniel, yes Daniel...." (280), ambivalently identifying both her father (Daniel Stein) and the Israelite Daniel of the Hebrew Bible.[145] The book of Daniel forms the opera's through line via the issue of idol worship, the first test of faith in the biblical story; it also provides a focus for the falling action of the opera's last scene, staged around a statue of US woman suffragists.[146] Initially, the Anthony character states her own name and affirms that "Everything" is in a name (280). She then declares: "I had a father, Daniel was not his name," even though, in fact, her father's name was Daniel, pointing up the barriers to patriarchal inheritance for women. The opera contrasts Anthony's resolution to "fight" for suffrage with the pacifism of her Quaker upbringing; her ardent desire to vote further contrasts with her father's suffrage abstention and tax resistance. Daniel Anthony was a freethinking and supportive father who eventually was read out of meeting by the Society of Friends for his liberal views and breaches of Quaker custom.[147] Daniel Anthony failed in business but succeeded in parenting, the mirror opposite of Daniel Stein, who prospered as a business man but was a difficult, unloving father. The Stein character associates her father with a "beard," "a bear," and then a "black beard," (280) riffing on Daniel Stein as bearded (Jew/foreigner), a bear (i.e., his personality), and just plain bad, like the pirate Blackbeard of legendary greed and malice.[148] As in *The Making*, Stein foregrounds daughters' struggle with fathers, aligning and then distinguishing the Anthony/Stein characters' origins and life trajectories.

Threaded through these opening genealogical statements are the words of another Daniel, Daniel Webster, who declaims about an unnamed man who "digged [a deep pit] for his brother" (280). Intrafamily sabotage stirs a number of associations between family drama and national history: World War II and a divided Europe, Japanese Americans interned in the United States, the biblical rivalry of Cain and Abel, the Stein family's history of tension between brothers Daniel and Solomon (as wells as siblings Gertrude and Leo), and, of course, when placed in the mouth of Daniel Webster, portents of the US Civil War (which on Stein's mother's side, divided the family).[149] The words "I had no father no father," (280) from Indiana Elliot closes the scene on at least an ambiguous note: possibly defiant, possibly wistful (possibly both).

Stein grumbled about the living in "days of the fathers" back in the mid-1930s, when she observed mass deference to patriarchal leaders Hitler, Mussolini, Roosevelt, Stalin, and Franco, whose rise signaled a further eclipse of the individual and "singularity." "Fathers are depressing," she wrote several times in *Everybody's*, glossing her own father's death as a relief to the children: "Then our life without a father began a very pleasant one."[150] A number of "fathers" populate the later opera: John Adams, a founding father, Anthony Comstock, the paternalistic morals enforcer, president Andrew Johnson, and his opponent, Radical Republican Thaddeus Stevens; these latter two figure in a group of three self-identified "V.I.P.s," among whom Webster looms largest. Quite striking in the opera is its criticism of men as a group as much as fathers. *The Making* described an irascible, patriarchal David Hersland, but the later opera adopts a more general stance of complaint against the sex. For example, the Anthony character declares that men are "so conservative, so selfish, so boresome" (287), and again, "men are conservative, dull monotonous, deceived, stupid, unchanging and bullies" (288).

Denunciation was hardly typical of Anthony's stump speeches, which emphasized the structuring power of the law and a spirited yet down to earth vision of the woman citizen.[151] When the Anthony character laments "...there is no humanity there are only laws"(302), Stein puts into her mouth sentiments closer to those held by Lucretia Mott or Emerson or, of course, herself. The opera also cheekily undercuts the notion of the franchise as much of a solution to anything, particularly given general male obtuseness. Since "[m]en can not count" (298), observes Anthony, how can they be trusted to accurately reckon votes, much less women's interests? Yet, the Anthony character speaks men's language: "Now said Susan B., let us not forget that in each place men are the same just the same, they are conservative, they are selfish and they listen to me. Yes they do said Susan B" (287). Men, "poor things," can comprehend her arguments, even if they reject the content. Such is men's dullness, the Anthony character states, "They do not know that two and two make four if women do not tell them so" (298). Here, Stein evokes the Victorian notion that men are what women make them, a view not unpopular with woman suffragists and a late echo of Sarah Grand's notion that the new woman will elevate a backward manhood.

If the Anthony character can stump, she can also philosophize, á la Lincoln: "Men want to be half slave half free. Women want to be all slave or all free, therefore men govern and women know, and yet" (298). Stein's Anthony points out how, ironically, men's divided psychology, their insistence on having it both ways, garners them power while women's consistency gives them greater self-possession but leaves them in a limbo of "and yet." By evoking Abraham Lincoln's house divided speech, an analogy is drawn between the imperatives of the union/antislavery and woman suffrage. In that speech, Lincoln declared that the country "will become all one thing, or all the other" regarding slavery, the logic of which Stein projects on to Anthony's efforts for the vote.[152] Voting will not solve everything—even the "right to sleep is given to no woman" (284)—but the opera assesses the fight as just and necessary, even visionary, as prophesy fulfilled. Much as Jane Addams, for all her later peace activism, regarded the Civil War as successful and held Lincoln's legacy above reproach, the vote is hailed by the opera's characters as almost heavenly—"glorious glorious glorious"—and, implicitly, as a vindication of Lincoln's expanding democratic vision (306).

The opera explores the idea of the Civil War and woman suffrage as winning causes, as necessary and just, maybe even divine, yet also unfinished and ambiguous. "So successful," the Anthony character sighs as the curtain falls on scene 7 of act 1 (306). Stein permits Susan B. Anthony to worry out loud—as she could not during her many campaigns—about whether voting will incite or degrade women, or maybe just have no effect at all. Stein's Anthony is no tinny idealist; she anticipates that with the vote and the entry into competitive politics, women "will become like men, become afraid like men, become like men" (304). Stein highlights the moral ambiguity of vindication and celebrity by asking whether the victory of woman suffrage makes Anthony "right" or merely the winner. The Anthony character certainly garners status and deference—"we are all very grateful to SBA because she was so successful," coo her acolytes—because everyone loves a winner. But Anthony insists that being right "is not very remarkable." In fact, she declares that it is "easy to be right," because winners accrue advantage by mere numbers and crude sociology. "It does do what it does," muses Anthony, noting rather drolly: "really it is useful to be right" (287). The Anthony character then reflects on the limited value of the esteem she enjoys with subtle perceptiveness:

> Yes I know, they love me so, they tell me so and they tell me so, but I, I do not tell them so because I know, they will not do what they could do and I I will be left alone to die but they will not have done what I need to have done to make it right that I live lived my life and fight. (301)

A leader needs followers to follow through and "vote my laws" (301–302) more than faddish celebrity worship; Anthony herself did not live to exercise the franchise (she died in 1905). Stein's Anthony is hardly exultant; she is humble and clear-eyed enough to be daunted by her own accomplishment, keenly aware of her embeddedness in an all-too-human social movement and a shallow and competitive political context. "Winning" the vote, like women's work, is never done.

This psychologically complex Anthony, equally skilled at "counting" and winning, is a far cry from the bland, rigid reformer of negative Victorian stereotype. Anthony as a skilled tactician, a "Napoleon," was made accessible to Stein through the work of feminist activist and writer Rheta Childs Dorr, whose biography of Anthony, written in 1928, Stein characterized as "a passionately interesting life" and which she read in preparation for writing her opera.[153] Determined to inspire a new generation of feminists, Dorr underscored how Anthony's legacy and memory was literally in others' hands, a truth also weighing heavily on Stein in her last years of life. The opera seeks to shape those terms.

By writing herself and Anthony into a canon of US heroes, Stein makes Susan B. Anthony sound more like Gertrude Stein than herself in the opera. While the libretto contains direct quotations from Anthony's writings, Stein also puts two of her favorite sentences into the suffrage leader's mouth. In so doing, she raises her own playful, philosophic, and epigrammatic use of language to the status of both "winning" and "right" and makes her own words the star of the show. The first quotation occurs near the end of act 1, when Anthony declares, while wrangling with a blustery Webster: "I understand you undertake to overthrow my undertaking" (284). Humorous on many levels, this sentence was Stein's favorite cryptogram, and it effectively parries the puffing, posturing Webster.[154] When the Anthony character declares another much-quoted favorite of Stein's, the Victorian sampler line, "When this you see remember me," it creates a startling alignment across time and frame of reference (286). As these womanly or girlish words traverse discursive frames, Stein draws attention to how women's ideas get around, and how they, much as Congressional debate á la Webster and Stevens, form part of the work of national history, memory, and identity. "When this [what?] you see remember me [as a...what?]." Thus, the simplest commonplace embroidered by a girl child evokes the deepest puzzles of perception, memory, and attachment pondered by great men like Emerson and James, confronting us with the politics of reading that is everybody's autobiography/work and also never done.

Like paternity and family, skin color is a deeply animating element in the opera, around which the drama's turning point occurs in act 2, scene 2. Here, Anthony confronts the politics of the Fifteenth Amendment which she opposed in favor of universal suffrage. Anthony mulls the false choice presented by yea or nay to language that she wanted to rewrite altogether: "I must choose colored or white white or colored" (291). As she delivers these lines, she is crowded and menaced by the "all the men." When "Jo" then calls out the playground chant "Fight fight fight between the nigger and the white" (291–292), Stein lays out a central issue in the Reconstruction era and her (and our) own time: anyone even considering interference with normative white male power becomes figuratively darkened ("nigger") and subject to punishment. When "Chris" chimes in "and the women," Stein highlights women's bodies as the terrain of racialized struggles for power. As the confrontation unfolds, the chant recurs as "Fight fight between the nigger and the white and the women" (293). Who, exactly, is who in this tussle? When Andrew Johnson gazes in the mirror, fantasizing, "I often think I am a bigger man than a bigger man," Stein calls up Richard Wright's Bigger Thomas (she well knew and admired *Native Son*) ironizing the alcoholic president as additionally besotted with penis envy and a "white negro" complex. "I often think I am bigger" states Johnson, pausing to admire himself in the middle of the fight in another dizzying, destabilizing "look" at skin/win.

This violent scene is not so much resolved as frozen, triggered by the word "Missouri" in the mouth of the character Virgil T. (Virgil Thompson was the opera's composer and a native of Missouri.) The stage directions at that point are "everybody suddenly stricken dumb", evoking the Missouri Compromise of 1820 that temporarily stayed political conflict over slavery (293). Daniel Webster then introduces "a woman without a last name," Henrietta M., whom he describes as "rare delicious and troubling" as the characters stand around staring. His presentation of Henrietta stops the fight/show, effectively upstaging Anthony. If played like vaudeville or a strip tease, Henrietta M. could be just a distraction, like the ubiquitous World War II pinup. Or, Henrietta could be revealed as kind of an american venus, a new woman come alive as fully adult, beholden to no man. As a woman "without a last name," the character Henrietta M. suggests that when women cease to embody male property interests and racial status, race and sex will become depoliticized. The traffic in women will end. The show will stop. The racist sexual violence will cease. Indeed, race "ends" as a viable metaphor/construct for identity. Stein thus puts into Webster's mouth an answer to the question "what is marriage?": a mechanism for reproducing racial difference, sexual hierarchy, male property rights and, of course, the nation. The objectified and eroticized Henrietta M. reveals Webster to be as creepy as he is correct. For another potential outcome lurks: if women cease to be the marker and means for a husband's or father's dominion, they could then become subject to any or all men's designs, a "troubling" prospect for some, a "delicious" prospect for others.

The frozen quality of the debate over the Reconstruction Amendments is restaged in the very next scene when an unnamed "negro man and negro woman" appear with Anthony in "a snowy landscape." In a few open-ended lines, Anthony and these two characters rehearse the dilemma of the Fourteenth that included the word "male" as a criteria for full citizenship rights. As in actual events during Reconstruction, the voice of the "negro woman" in Stein's opera remains muffled; she uses her voice just once, and then only in unison with the "negro man" character. The two seem to accede to the suffragist's indecisiveness—"might, might, might there be what might be" Anthony whimpers—with the words: "All right Susan B. all right." They submit to her power ("[you have] all [the] right") rather than agreeing with it ("alright"), an interpretation only available in looking at the written text, rather than hearing the spoken words, placing much pressure on the actors' interpretation and delivery. The black characters are frozen out of debate, reduced to "following" Anthony as she sinks into the cold white snow (293). Stein deprives these characters the personal dignity of a name; they remain types not historical or allegorical figures like the others. But maybe that is her point: the sexual and racial economy reduces their humanity to type. The Anthony character then expounds the dimensions of racist psychology, heightened in war time:

> They [men] fear women, they fear each other, they fear their neighbor, they fear other countries and then they hearten themselves in their fear by crowding together and following each other, and when they crowd together and follow each other they are brutes, like animals who stampede, and so they have written in the name male into the United States constitution, because they are afraid of black men because they are afraid of women, because they are afraid afraid. Men are afraid. (304)

If "everything is in a name," what of the artifice of the "name male," despite its conventional association with biological true-ness, now enshrined in the constitution as the standard for full citizenship? Jo the Loiterer asks: "What can I do, if a name is not true, what can I do but do as she tells me." In the end, Anthony rejects celebrity worship and pushes the question of what to do back on her fans, even as the characters attempt to do, stereotypically, what women are supposed to do: mourn and commemorate their fallen heroes.

The opera's last scene is set in Congressional Hall, in front of Adelaide Johnson's statue of suffrage leaders Stanton, Anthony, and Mott. Women activists gifted the statue to the federal government in 1921, but it was quickly removed (closeted? buried?) into the Capitol "crypt," where it remained for 76 years.[155] The scene takes place after Anthony's death (which occurs off stage), but she continues to address the other characters from behind the statue. They are unsure what to make of it, and gather around variously sighing, bowing, frowning, and curtseying. (When this you see...?) One asks: "Does it really mean that women are as white and cold as marble does it really mean that?" (306–307). This question can be read in at least two ways. First, as the typical "anti" position; that political participation will harden women, canceling out their sympathetic, comforting nature/role. Second, the question invokes the exclusionary "whiteness" that attended expanded citizen rights for women in the United States. Neither Reconstruction nor the Anthony Amendment *effectively* enfranchised African Americans, for example. The initial Johnson statue unveiling took place during the National Woman's Party convention in Washington, during which black women activists were pointedly rebuffed by party leadership concerning their limited access to voter registration and the polls.[156] When Andrew Johnson "shuffles in" (drunk again?) and offers the despairing view "I have no hope in black or white...no hope," this limitation is both underscored and ironized, since Johnson supported neither "Negro" nor "Woman" suffrage. It points as well to the limit of laws written in "black and white" in a society whose dominant psychology fosters racial and gender tension and whose most powerful members enforce inequality through violence (307).

The statue's whiteness also has an obscuring, blinding effect, conveyed by yet another character: "I cannot see what is so white" (307). Here "whiteness" is not associated with divine power or universal salvation, as for Amanda Smith, but with blotted out vision and sensory deprivation. For Stein, white is the opposite of transparent, as in clear/understanding. At the end of the opera, the characters encircle the suffrage statue, blinking and unsure. The statue obscures as much as it explains, forgets as much as it memorializes. Indeed, the figures themselves in Johnson's piece are mostly hidden. The sculpture features three busts in a progression, without legs, hips, or hands; they are rendered half people (maybe having clay feet, like the idol in the book of Daniel), and voting is symbolized as only half the victory for women's freedom. No black activists are represented at all, an exclusion remarked upon by the National Political Congress of Black Women in 1997, when the statue was reinstalled in the rotunda, and, too, by First Lady Michelle Obama, when a bust of Sojourner Truth was unveiled in Independence Hall in 2009.[157] From behind the statue, Anthony pronounces a sobering, haunting challenge to the viewers about what they understand from the history, commemoration, and art displayed before their eyes: "Do you know because I tell you so, or do you know do you know?" (310).

As in the denouement of *The Making*, Stein places the burden of remembering and meaning making squarely on her audience. Though her handling of black characters is limited and stereotypic, the overall thrust of the opera is antiracist and antiwhite supremacist: whiteness silences, obscures, and blinds. With *The Mother of Us All*, Stein aligned herself with major and successful, if unfinished, currents of expanding democracy in US history via the franchise. But she also argued against unthinking, reflexive submission to the winners and heroes, whether they are female forms encrusted in marble or military generals on white horses. As a culminating intellectual statement by Stein, the opera situates women's bodies, violence, and marriage at the center of the racist political economy of the modern nation-state, an interpretation

2.2   Marble statue of three suffragists by Adelaide Johnson in the Capitol crypt, Washington, DC.
Photo credit: Library of Congress Prints and Photographs Division

as incisive as anything Ida B. Wells-Barnett produced on this subject in the 1890s. The opera's vague and vaguely pagan title also puts me in an associational mode: "[*White supremacy is*] The Mother [*expletive*] of Us All."

In the opera, Stein found some language to push back against white supremacy and "stupid" men as well. She began serious work on it in October of 1945; *Wars I Have Seen* came out from Random House publishers in March of the same year. Editor Bennett Cerf's recollection of *Wars's* promotion in 1944 provides additional context for the opera's production. Random House parried their competitor Macmillan's sexy-lady-author marketing strategy by printing in *Publisher's Weekly* a picture of Gertrude and Alice over the caption "Shucks, we've got glamour girls too!" The photograph featured Gertrude and Alice wearing heavy jackets and boyish caps while grasping their "Indian fetishes."[158] The pair appear frumpy and masculine or even witch-like; in his memoir, Cerf reprinted the image next to the soft-focus, hetero-sexy Kathleen Winsor, in case his readers missed the point (he also kept a copy of the ad in his personal scrapbook). "Gertrude was just as amused as everyone else was," regaled Cerf about this marketing ploy. "I don't think I've ever met a better sport."[159]

Stein initially exempted Cerf from the censure she directed at "the fathers" in *Everybody's*, indulging him as an inferior on whom she was dependent. "Bennett himself is more a brother and a nephew or a great nephew than a father," she wrote, "that is the reason we like him and like him as a publisher."[160] This she could still say after a rather explosive interaction they had had back in 1934. When Cerf interviewed her on the radio in New York City during her book tour for *The Autobiography*, he goaded Stein on the air about not understanding her writings. In her retort, she called him "nice...but rather stupid." The in-house audience "roared" with laughter and the interview unfolded fine, according to a chastened Cerf, who "didn't kid around" after the upbraiding and was "very respectful." When Stein's friend Miriam Hopkins—whom Cerf dubbed "a devil"—found out that Stein had not been paid for her interview, she was outraged and told her not to do one again unless she received $500 per appearance. Cerf judged this reaction to be unfortunate, because, "we could have gotten her on a lot of shows for nothing and sold a lot more of her books," implying the women had no real business sense, or at least none of the kind that profited him. "That marked the end of her [Stein's] radio career," he sniffed in his memoir *At Random*.[161]

2.3 *Publisher's Weekly* advertisement, from Bennett Cerf's scrapbook.

Photo credit: Bennett Cerf Papers, Rare Book and Manuscript Library, Columbia University

Cerf concluded his memoir's discussion of Stein by stating that he was "deeply touched" by her prefatory "Message" in Carl Van Vechten's anthology of her work (also put out by Random House in 1946). She wrote (as he quoted):

> Then there was my first publisher who was commercial but who said he would print and he would publish even if he did not understand and if he did not make money, it sounds like a fairy tale but it is true, Bennett said, I will print a book of yours a year whatever it is and he has and often I have worried but he always said there was nothing to worry about and there wasn't.[162]

Here, Stein seemingly casts Cerf as the prince in this publishing "fairy tale." At the same time, her words call up the duplicity of John Lane, who "printed" but did not really "publish" *Three Lives*. And, it's entirely possible to read this passage and conclude that Bennett Cerf was, in the end, actually stupid. Either he lacked business sense and published work that "did not make money" or basked uncomprehendingly in reflected light, a mindless celebrity hound. This sentence, as in the opera, *The Making of Americans,* and this chapter's opening epigram, points up the ambiguities and the high stakes for counting, value, naming, and belonging in the canon/nation-making process. Like John Lane, Bennett Cerf crossed the line of fairness and professionalism, but Stein can't quite come out and say so. Upon hearing of Cerf's wife's pregnancy in early 1945, she wrote to him: "I do hope it is a little girl, you would be a really delightful father for a little girl, and even if it isn't [illegible] you should be a father to a little girl, you should."[163] This is a sentence that seems to have some critique of paternalism embedded in it and is pure Stein: colloquial yet stylized, odd, funny, poignant, and almost impossible to read.

Conclusion

Though *The Mother of Us All* is self-serving in its Stein-Anthony parallels, it also marks a significant break with Stein's usual textual strategy of horizontal violence: against campus feminism, lady reformers at Hull House, the persnickety Ellery Sedgwick (who later came around to serialize *The Autobiography*), rumpled clerks in government offices, and the defeated Robert E. Lee. Henrietta M. strikes me as a kind of reimagined new woman, representing hope and untested potential rather than a symbol for "racial" purity or moral innocence—possibilities ahead rather than mission accomplished. Henrietta M. also evokes the Adele character in the novel *Q. E. D.* referred to earlier. When Adele meets up with her friend Helen in Italy, the latter exclaims: "Why Adele where did you come from? You look as brown and white and clean as if you had just sprung out of the sea."[164] Henrietta M. could be played on stage as a kind of new world venus, a surprise appearance who is a little hard to figure, like the central character in Botticelli's lush, enigmatic painting. In the wake of the military victory of World War II, Stein also holds up an iconic/ironic mother figure, the childless, unmarried Anthony, as having a very important lesson to teach "us all" about the political economy of race and sex in the postwar world. These images strike me as decolonial figures that operate in critical tension with patriarchal and racial-nationalist typologies.

The glimmerings of Henrietta W. and Adele are important moments in Stein's oeuvre that also registered its share of folk-racialist sensibility. As she put it in *Everybody's Autobiography*: "Well its name is Negro if it is a Negro and Jew if it is a Jew and both of them are nice strong solid names and so let us keep them."[165] Nonetheless, for a woman highly skeptical of fictions of closure and fixed meanings, she ended her career with an epic work that put down in precise and critical terms how sex and race imbricated with the work of the nation. That is, she keenly dissected the sexual politics of marriage and citizenship as productive of race and racial hierarchy, enforced by state violence. If Stein's last great work declared whiteness a washout, the next chapter will show how, in a related decolonizing move, Josefina Silva de Cintrón and her colleagues essentially concocted a "race" that refused to discriminate.

3

¡Adelante Hermanas de La Raza!

Josefina Silva de Cintrón and Puerto Rican Women's *Feminismo*

Gertrude Stein's last opera featured an iconic virgin "mother" who voiced skepticism about voting as a reliable device for determining what's right—or anyone's rights. In similar spirit, Puerto Rican feminists in New York City endorsed equal political rights for women but also critiqued the trappings and rituals of liberal citizenship. The monthly magazine *Artes y Letras*, published in Spanish between 1933 and 1939 by Josefina Silva de Cintrón (1884–1988), conveys the rich landscape of their thinking and activism.[1] In Stein's opera, "mother" was literally a fabulous metaphor. So, too, was *Artes y Letras* rife with maternal iconography, though the journal also documented the everyday loves and labors of living mothers with very real children. Its editors focused on flags rather than statuary. As Stein so keenly grasped, the expression of modern nationalism involved public performances and stagings in which control over images is essential. *Artes y Letras* focused on just such fields of activity, placed Puerto Rican women's mothering at the center of its perspective, and labeled it all *feminismo*.

Silva de Cintrón and her colleagues defined *feminismo* as a cluster of rights that drew on their identifications as mothers, cultural cosmopolitans, Puerto Ricans, and US citizens. In their activities, they exercised their citizenship rights alongside a more expansive concept of rights, one "delinked," as Walter Mignolo has suggested, from categories like race or the law, categories that have pegged bodies to power and prestige within modern political regimes. Instead, *feminismo* accented human dignity and a transnational sense of belonging—being a *"ciudadano de América"* (citizen of America) in a hemispheric sense.[2] The *feminismo* of *Artes y Letras* thus expressed a phase of Pérez's decolonial imaginary for Puerto Rican women, one that could encompass an expansive Pan-American community.[3] Contributors to *Artes y Letras* bridged *"autonoma"* (i.e., nongovernmental) organizing and state-centered organizing, the former being a hallmark of Latina activism usually attributed to indigenous groups but here visible in a more bourgeois, cosmopolitan, and

transnational context.[4] And far from encountering a postsuffrage doldrums—
some called US feminism "dead" by 1935—Silva de Cintrón and her colleagues
embraced a maternalist Pan-American *feminismo* and a gender perspective
otherwise muted in both the national partisan scene and in Harlem's wards
and clubhouses between the wars.[5] The accomplishments and frustrations of
the women activists around *Artes y Letras* challenge a recent scholarly assessment that by World War II, Puerto Ricans were "virtually invisible as historical
actors in New York," and this chapter restores Silva de Cintrón's activities to a
central place in the spectrum of empowerment strategies circulating between
Manhattan and the Caribbean in the tumultuous New Deal era.[6]

Since *Artes y Letras* itself has been mostly overlooked, scholars have missed
the ways in which its editors, amid a plurality of Puerto Rican efforts to subvert the negative effects of racialization in the city, mostly opted out of race
politics altogether.[7] One vehicle for this work, hidden in plain view, was La
Unión de Mujeres Americanas (UMA). A transnational women's organization
established in Mexico in the early 1930s, the New York branch was founded
in 1934 and was recently recognized by the Puerto Rican legislature for its
ongoing and historic achievements.[8] Under the motto *Paz e Igualdad de
Derechos* (Peace and Equality of Rights) UMA carried out a range of activities, notably antiwar and antiwhite supremacist agitation, all reported and
discussed by *Artes y Letras*. By linking local constraints and opportunities in
New York with transnational social formations—some state centered, some
less so—this chapter explores how it was that Silva de Cintrón's genteel culture magazine, filled with New York–based concert promotionals and theater
reviews, was also stuffed with articles about feminism and protest-oriented
social organizing and spoke to readers in at least eight countries in North,
Central, and South America.

The momentum for Silva de Cintrón's work had two main sources. First
was the flowering of Pan-American feminist thought between the wars
and its increased circulation through institutions like UMA and others,
like the International Woman Suffrage Alliance (1904), the Inter American
Commission for Women (1928), and the Asociación Pan Americana de
Mujeres de Puerto Rico (ca. 1920).[9] Key thinkers in these arenas were Margarita
Robles de Mendoza of Mexico, leading light of the UMA, and Mercedes Solá,
pioneer educator and feminist of Puerto Rico.[10] The second element shaping
Silva de Cintrón's work was a popular symbol of identity in the 1930s called
La Bandera de La Raza. This emblem offered leverage against race prejudice
as well as a symbol of solidarity for Spanish-speaking women in New York
City (and beyond). For the women around *Artes y Letras*, *La Bandera* underwrote critiques of mainstream US feminism and US government-sponsored
Pan-Americanism, perspectives that usually entailed colonial-inflected agendas under the sign of "friendship," characteristic of the Good Neighbor Policy
in US foreign relations under Franklin Delano Roosevelt (FDR).[11] *La Bandera*
flew over a range of standpoints on "race" in *Artes y Letras*, including whitening and civilizationist gestures, self-orientalizing flourishes, and antiwhite
supremacist racialist stances against Anglo-Saxonism.[12] Mostly, however, *La
Bandera* waved away "race" in favor of a nondiscriminatory and inclusive
social practice, a decolonizing gesture that refused to play the race game.[13]

Instead, the journal and UMA practiced the kind of solidarity imagined by José Martí in "Our America" back in the 1890s, one that resisted splitting the hemisphere into two, as was so often the case in US official discourses during the heyday of scientific racism and Jim Crow.[14] After years of energetic talk and activity, however, Silva de Cintrón's efforts to define and advance Puerto Rican identity and Pan-American *feminismo* in the public sphere met sore defeat at the New York World's Fair of 1939–40. This event was saturated with eugenic racism, militaristic nationalism, paeans to technology, and hostility to feminism. Local Puerto Ricans—not unlike local African Americans—came up against a rigid and prejudiced establishment concerning their representation at the fair.[15] Black New Yorkers successfully challenged some of the exclusion they faced, but Silva de Cintrón encountered sharp insult and, outside the most narrowly decorative and service-oriented female spaces, UMA was frozen out of influence at the event. This scenario is not quite captured by descriptors like "invisible," nor adequately explained by the "elite-subaltern" dynamic of colonial studies or the racist pitfalls of vote- and ward-based citizenship gambits playing out in Manhattan. Rather, Josefina Silva de Cintrón critically engaged with feminism and related cultural and political endeavors under the aegis of a popular Pan-Americanism in activities neither defined nor contained by categories of "race" or any state-centered rights agenda, yet not fully separable from them either.[16]

Background to Migration

Josefina Silva de Cintrón was born in Caguas, Puerto Rico, a sophisticated small city to the south of San Juan, in 1884. According to her only child, Roberto, her family owned a grocery store in Bayamón, just outside the capital, called La Bayamonesa, and young Josefina (named for her mother, Josefa) spent time in both towns, situated about 20 miles apart. "[S]he grew up there *and* in Caguas," Roberto affirmed, and he recalled stories of her riding on horseback to social events and of her activities in a Catholic church with the altar guild and the women's auxiliary. English was only a small part of her education— "She was never really fluent," her son contends—and she attended an *escuela normal* (normal school) in order to become a schoolteacher, an investment in education likely tied to her status as the eldest of five siblings.[17] In 1920, Josefina's mother, Josefa Silva y Yasty, was a widow living in Rio Piedras (also near San Juan) with her other children: Carmen (28), Cecelia (25), Maria (19), and Guillermo (14). The household included a widowed sister-in-law (*cuñada*) Maria Silva y Acuñoz, age 79, three grandchildren (*nietos*) under the age of six, and the household's *criada* or servant girl, Angelina Leon y Aquiño, age 14.[18] In 1918 or 1919, Josefina married Arcadio Rivera. He worked for the US government as a commission agent but Roberto remembered him as a poet, signaling Josefina's early attraction to the arts and artists. Arcadio Rivera also registered for military service in October of 1918; Josefina gave birth to Roberto a little more than a year later. The 1920 US census lists the married couple as living together in the San Cristobal neighborhood of San Juan, with four-month-old infant Roberto and Joaquina Rivera y Colon (age 25), listed as *criada*. No occupation (*ninguna*) was noted for Josefina.[19]

Josefina and Arcadio's marriage did not last. Possibly, economic need from the couples' families of origin or the demands of the war mobilization strained their marriage. Mother Josefa was also listed as having *ninguna* occupation by the census; she may have lived off an estate from her late husband and/or that of her *cuñada*; it is also possible that the adult daughters of the household engaged in the informal local economy of barter or home production, hidden from view in the US census categories. Around 1923, Josefina secured a position as postmistress at Hato Rey (then a small town, now a suburb of San Juan) and was, according to family lore, the first woman in Puerto Rico to receive such a commission from President Calvin Coolidge, and whose appointment letter was a point of family pride.[20]

Caguas and Bayamón, like most of the island, was strongly Unionist (i.e., pro-statehood) during Josefina's growing up years. The Silvas apparently had welcomed the United States back in 1898, perhaps inclining them toward the Republican Party. Roberto's memory is that "the family wanted to see Spain leave P.R. and wanted the U.S. to occupy P.R." "When the first troops entered her town...[Josefina's] father displayed the U.S. flag from the balcony above the store," he recounts. "It was displayed with the stars down" (in the lower right hand corner). When a passing US military man saw it, he "dismounted from his horse, expressed appreciation for the display and showed her father the correct manner of flag display."[21] It is difficult to interpret this little story. At a minimum, it seems to denote the political attentiveness of the Silva family. It might contain a kernel of humor regarding the new potential for things to be upside down in Puerto Rico, rather than conveying a harmless expression of the family's naiveté about flags.

Roberto also described his mother as "an *activist*" who took "an active 'marching' part in the 'suffragette' movement in Puerto Rico in the 'Twenties,'" predating the securing of the Right to Vote for women."[22] Her activism must have made for a strong family story, told repeatedly, since Roberto was a tiny child in that decade. While it is difficult to place Josefina Silva de Rivera with precision in the island's political milieu, partisanship and woman suffrage figured prominently in Puerto Rican politics in the 1920s, undergirded by the status issue.[23] Two court cases for woman suffrage, those of Genera Pagan (1920) and Mariana Morales Bernard (1924), were conspicuous among organizing efforts and lobbying by island-based women for the vote.[24] Suffrage activism was almost inevitably partisan, and advocates looked to Republicans to extend the Nineteenth Amendment to Puerto Rican women, culminating in a nearly successful end run around the island legislature in 1927–28.[25] Indeed, US-based political parties comprised an important if camouflaged domain of colonial control on the island, one that permitted Theodore Roosevelt (governor 1899–1901) to assert: "We had no colonial service" in Puerto Rico "and we did not develop one."[26]

Josefina's post-office appointment came in the transition between the Harding and Coolidge administrations, a tense moment in which white mainlanders located on the island began to assert partisan-cum-colonial privileges, especially in the capital. In 1923, Robert H. Todd, mayor of San Juan for most of the period 1900–1930, butted heads with newly appointed Governor Horace M. Towner for control of patronage, and he assumed, according to Towner, the right to "dictate post offices."[27] Robert Todd was something of a political boss, one of a group of US-born lawyers and businessmen mostly based in San Juan who declared themselves a branch of the Republican National Committee and assumed the functions of party business: holding conventions, sending delegates to (mainland) national meetings, and, most pointedly, running for office. After the Jones Act of 1917 extended partial citizenship rights to Puerto Ricans, partisan activities on the island became increasingly sharp-elbowed. Over time, amendments to the act shifted patronage and appointment powers away from the governorship and its tight ties to the president and the administration's ruling party and more toward the Puerto Rican legislature and local conditions.[28] Throughout the interwar years, the Puerto Rican delegation (which included the island's nonvoting representative to the US Congress) advanced precisely this agenda, aspiring to have the governor become elected by voters on the island rather than appointed in Washington, DC, a change achieved in 1947.[29] Since the Republican organization rebuffed overtures for fusion from the dominant Unionist Party in Puerto Rico—Towner himself counseled against such a merger as "unwise"—island-based politicians sought to shore up and increase local autonomy by applying pressure on the party system as best as they could. In this scenario, extending patronage positions to educated local women like Josefina Silva de Rivera could advance this agenda toward local control.[30]

The place of women and gender in this partisan-colonial scene has yet to be fully mapped by historians. In the early years of FDR's presidency, a white woman Democrat from Kansas, Mrs. Jean Springstead Whittemore, was a contender for governorship of the unincorporated territory of Puerto Rico. Given the Republicans' snobbery and unwelcome, the Democrats garnered some credibility on the island, with statehood planks in its presidential platforms of 1920 and 1928.[31] The top Democrat in Puerto Rico was Henry W. Dooley, a prosperous Brooklyn-born businessman who came with the New York Naval Militia during the Spanish American War and shortly thereafter returned to stay.[32] Known locally as "Don Enrique," he was a well-placed member of the Democratic National Committee who led the successful nomination fight for John W. Davis of West Virginia, the party's presidential candidate in 1924. Dooley's right hand was Whittemore who, after studying at Columbia Teacher's College, had come to San Germán to teach in a Presbyterian mission school in 1913. Dooley sponsored her political career and Whittemore became one of the highest ranking Democratic women before the New Deal: delegate to three national conventions, the first party committee woman (1928), and the first woman appointed to the Committee on Rules in 1932 at Chicago. Her good looks, unbending partisanship, staunch conservatism, and friends in high places all served her well. In 1924, Whittemore voted with Dooley on the egregious 103 convention ballots for John Davis (a white southerner who openly opposed woman suffrage, child labor laws, and civil rights for African Americans) and later proudly proclaimed that she would "vote as many for [Al] Smith in 1928" (a candidate more in keeping with the spirit of reform). Instead of the governorship, FDR appointed Whittemore to another prestigious and high-profile patronage plum: collector of the Port of San Juan.[33]

Whittemore had a feminized and domesticating view of the US presence on the island, believing that "Puerto Rico's salvation can be worked out in lavender and old lace" (a reference to Myrtle Reed's best-selling novel from 1908).[34] She had a folksy, nostalgic framework for colonial adminis-tration—"Shucks, Puerto Rico is just like Kansas," was how she put it—that is, just like "home" and simply another nearby frontier properly subject to US manifest destiny (looking past the "bleeding Kansas" rent by slavery in the 1850s). Mainland media coverage accented Whittemore's life story as a poor orphan and upwardly mobile working woman was trumpeted in a gushing 1934 article for *Collier's* as a "triumph for feminism."[35] Little of Whittemore's political thinking survives in the scant record of her work, but it seems she was less a gender egalitarian and more an exemplar of suc-cessful (white) womanhood in a colonial setting. She was cultural kin to the female missionaries praised as successful "new women" and harbingers of civilization in the 1890s, worthy of emulation by both "natives" and prop-erly aspiring (white) girls back "home," but not critical of the men of her group in any way.[36] The record is very thin, but at least one woman from mainland was actually discouraged regarding civil service jobs in Puerto Rico before World War I. In 1913, a Miss Adelaide M. Foster of Washington, DC, was told by insular officials that "very few appointments" were made "from the United States," but that "women residing in the island are occa-sionally appointed."[37] These appointments were paltry, however. A decade after Foster's inquiry, a report by the Liga Social Suffragista on "women's work" listed only two female "municipal commissioners of education" in official government service from scores of women active in community-betterment activities on the island.[38]

Only a token among colonizing women moved up the political ranks, and island women struggled to gain recognition. Leading Puerto Rican suffrag-ists used gender critique to advance themselves and their definition of the island's interests under US rule. They well understood the significant power that would accrue to a locally elected governor for Puerto Rico, and some activists opposed such reform until woman suffrage was firmly part of the agenda. Their calls for the acknowledgment of women's educational advance-ment and community activities rested on recognition of gender differentiation and specialization, affirming a comparable sensibility to that of "Continental-American men and women," which obtained "with equal force between the men and women of this territory."[39] Milagros Benet de Mewton of the Liga Social Suffragista argued that women were entitled to the vote as "natural beings and responsible members of the community," and affirmed that in Puerto Rico, "women have progressed to a far greater degree than these same [male] politicians along the lines of stable and sound local government."[40] Benet de Mewton's framework endorsed some of the gender conventions of civilizationist thought: women as naturally disinterested agents of change and the proper uplifters of men. Yet, Puerto Rican men, too, were at pains to por-tray themselves as above politics. "I am very much interested in Porto Rico, but NOT politics," affirmed C. W. Vargas, postmaster in Guayama in 1923. Vargas was careful to count politicians as "all my friends; I treat them so-blacks, whites and socialists," an effort he deemed both necessary to keep his job and as appropriate to his position as a "good faithful and efficient Servant" of "the Administration."[41]

In early 1924, Towner resolved the matter of post offices by continuing all Harding appointees and placing new ones under the civil service exam. Designed to generate "no friction and no publicity" and thereby safeguard the new administration's media image and legitimacy, this resolution also created an opportunity for educated women like Josefina Silva de Rivera who could meet the educational threshold of the exam.[42] Island feminists viewed the Republican party as friendly to woman suffrage; Benet de Mewton admitted as much when she wrote to the chief of the Bureau of Insular Affairs in Washington in 1921, noting that the Liga would "wait[ ] until the present Republican government was duly organized" before resuming their petitions for the vote.[43] Yet, Roberto Cintrón's family story accented gender over partisanship concerning his mother's work as postmistress. "The purpose of politicians at the time was to give the job to a man—in the tradition of a 'man's world,'" recalled Roberto, but "[s]he did not falter, she did not abjectly surrender to the 'machine' and she fought and held on to her position until she left for N.Y.C." Part of her resistance involved making sure that her female assistant could secure the job as next in line, drawing our attention to the constructed nature of "distinterestedness." Roberto also credited his mother with hiring the "FIRST handicapped employee" in the Puerto Rican postal service, an armless man who "requested letter & parcel post recipients to reach into his mailbag and get their mail."[44] In his rendition of the story, Josefina's postal tenure was about competency and charity rather than personal gain or partisan advantage, properly caretaking yet also feminist (as in, female solidarity) and oppositional (against the "machine").[45] These components marked the key features of *feminismo* debate and activity in *Artes y Letras*.

When Josefina Silva moved from island to island in 1927, she brought her son, her education, her credentials in the world of paid work, and a tradition of economic resourcefulness forged in a family of women who managed their own household. She was someone able to broach the partisan doings of Puerto Rico and was a self-identified feminist, comfortable bending Catholic cultural norms. Once in Manhattan, she met up with her fiancé, Felipe Enudio Cintrón, a Catholic priest who left the church in order to wed. Roberto affirmed that their plans "necessitated" leaving Puerto Rico although divorce had been widely available on the island for a generation, and the couple, in their early forties, were hardly impetuous youth flouting parental or church control through elopement.[46] Josefina and Felipe were married in Manhattan in a civil service on May 4, 1927. Felipe later legally adopted Roberto, who never met his "natural father," but his memory was alive in family history.[47]

Despite the Republican flavor of his mother's Puerto Rican years, Roberto contends that over time, she became "a 'card carrying Democrat' [who] worked actively for Dem. Candidates." She was "deep into politics," he affirmed: "P.R., N.Y.C., U.S.A.," a litany of political commitments that highlights border crossing.[48] Silva de Cintrón's shifting party affiliation follows general US voter realignment as social reform moved from the Republican to the Democratic Party in the Roosevelt era. Quite the opposite movement registered on the island of Puerto Rico, however, where labor unrest peaked between 1929 and 1934, and a heavy-handed New Deal fragmented old

3.1   Josefina Silva de Cintrón, ca. 1930.

Photo credit: Roberto Cintrón

political alliances, fanned antiadministration sentiment, and precipitated a sharp uptick in nationalist activity, involving violence on all sides.[49] In this context, Josefina's identification in the pages of *Artes y Letras* as *"no partidarista, sino feminista"* (not partisan, but feminist) gains even more interest.[50] Though her journal held partisan politics to the side, her words signal Silva de Cintrón's complex relationship to intersecting but distinct political affiliations in Manhattan and in Puerto Rico. She also came to New York with experience in journalism, having helped compile a landmark publication back home, *Mujer del Siglo XX*. Issued in 1922 by Mercedes Solá, who was affiliated with the conservative Liga Feminea, Silva de Cintrón's self-description as nonpartisan reflects the feminine, disinterested posture typical of La Liga. Yet Silva de Cintrón's migration might have been a way to distance herself from Solá's conservative tutelage. When Silva de Cintrón cheered UMA members *"¡Adelante, hermanas de la raza!"* in the pages of *Artes y Letras*, she signaled keynotes of her social organizing in New York and the transnational success of her journal: antiracist consciousness and female solidarity including, but not restricted to, suffrage and official politics.[51]

Of Art and Mothers

Consolidating this vision took time. On the first page of *Artes y Letras*'s debut issue in July, 1933, the masthead featured Miguel de Cervantes (1547–1616), author of *Don Quixote* (1605) and an icon for the Golden Age of Spain. In its initial role as the "organ of the Cervantes Artistic Group," *Artes y Letras* claimed the legacy of Spanish contributions to world culture and focused mostly on European arts and musical traditions for a literate, relatively leisured audience.[52] The cover of *Artes y Letras*'s September, 1934, issue carried a photograph of Puerto Rico's El Ateneo, headquarters of high culture in San Juan, and the journal reported on its leading figures like editor and professor Margot Arce and poet Luis Palés Matos.[53] Thus initially, *Artes y Letras* displayed some of the class and cultural orientation more generally attributed to a group of writers and educators known as La Generación del Treinta around El Ateneo in Puerto Rico. This group has been described by Magali Roy-Féquière and other scholars as conservative, elitist, and "vociferously Hispanophilic."[54] A central tenet of La Generación was veneration of the spiritual and cultural legacy of Spain. Members of La Generación also self-identified as *criollo*, a term that throughout Latin America generally meant born in the "new world," but whose race and class inflections tended to efface African-ness and privilege European origins. *Criollo* standpoints also underwrote masculine privilege in the guise of objectivity in ways that limited women's participation. Women found a voice, argues Roy-Féquière, by agreeing to augment rather than challenge the class and racial underpinnings of Puerto Rican cultural nationalism deployed against an invading Anglo-Protestant United States. The group's orientation toward slave-holding *hacendado* paternalism either ignored people of African ancestry in favor of accenting the *jíbaro* (peasant) majority on the island or, by the 1930s, handled "blackness" in distinctly modernist fashion, as the exoticized racial Other. Roy-Féquière underscores the limited vision entailed by La Generación's championing of one colonial model against another through defensive and nostalgic projects that nonetheless was a cultural anchor for Puerto Rico until the 1950s.[55]

The Cervantes image suggests, however, that Silva de Cintrón's coterie in New York did not contend with the politicization of Spanish in precisely the same ways as did teachers and faculty in San Juan or around the Ateneo.[56] The most active writers—Remedios C. de Román, Carmen B. de Córdova, Pedro Caballero, Pura Romo y Silva, Evangelina Antey de Vaughan, and Pedro Juan Labarthe—were Spanish language teachers, mostly in New York City high schools. Rather than bunkering down against an invading English language, the Manhattan group proclaimed itself to students and other interested cosmopolitans as a beacon of world culture via Spanish. "Puerto Ricans work in the two languages most important in America, perhaps the whole world," effused Caballero.[57] The members of the group around *Artes y Letras* were spokes in a wheel linking neighborhood, educational, and social institutions, especially Spanish language and cultural programs at Theodore Roosevelt and Thomas Jefferson high schools, the Eastman School of Music, Columbia University's Spanish Institute (led by Professor Federico de Ónis), and the Roerich Museum, located on the upper west side.[58] Active outreach was key, and El Grupo Cultural Cervantes (later, el Círculo Cultural Cervantes) served the Misión Episcopal Hispana run by (now) Rev. Felipe Cintrón. *Artes y Letras* took pains to describe the mission as "not a religious nor sectarian association, but [one] sincerely cultural, recreational, and benevolent."[59] El Círculo met regularly (its meetings were advertised in the *Sociedades Hispanos* section of *La Prensa*)—and though Felipe was its leader, Roberto remembered that his mother "organize[d] and direct[ed]" much of the group's activities, especially theatricals, including the "casting, [the] choice of Spanish plays, the rehearsing, the total production."[60]

Josefina Silva de Cintrón always had top billing in the *Artes y Letras* masthead as *editora* or *directora*.[61] She was the publisher and also a contributor. Colleague Pedro Caballero wrote most of the front-page editorials and opinion pieces, especially in the early years. Silva de Cintrón's byline occasionally appeared, but she produced most of her copy under the pen name Lidia and sometimes Pepiña (a diminutive of Josefina), feminizing gestures that mediated her authority in the public sphere. Caballero analogized her role to that of a "disinterested captain who sacrifices her time, rest, and even money in the well being of our community." Her writings were "pleasing chronicles and tender compositions" rather than hard-boiled, street-wise reporting. Silva de Cintrón did the bulk of the interviews with visiting artists, as befitting a *salonista*. She also ran a clothing donation center (*un ropero de los pobres*) from the magazine's office at 2085 Lexington Avenue, and publicized it and the work of the Damas Auxilares of Felipe's Misión, in which she was also active.[62] Silva de Cintrón's *Sociales* column reported on clubs and group activities, anniversaries and life-cycle events, and children's accomplishments, and made for important community-building work.

Exactly what the Puerto Rican community, especially its women and young people, looked and sounded like—onstage or off—was of critical importance to fostering identity and social cohesion in the new setting of New York City. Theater, recitation, and public performance were the heartbeat of El Grupo's work, literally an enactment of community. "[M]any anglosaxons do not understand how one sole person simply reciting verses sustains the attention of an audience for three hours," Silva de Cintrón mused, concluding: "In this precisely consists the superiority of the Latin race."[63] She, like other Latina feminists, fused aesthetics and politics, fostering a feminine éntree to public life. Mexican feminist Margarita Robles de Mendoza, in her 1932 pamphlet, "The Citizenship of the Mexican Woman," hoped that her readers might "learn the poetry of rights, and the beauty of action."[64] When Robles de Mendoza spoke in New York in 1934, Silva de Cintrón trumpeted the power of this approach or "mentality" (*mentalidad*) and linked its growth to the "attainment of the rights of woman in all America!"[65]

Focused on the performing arts and literature, this feminist vision informed Silva de Cintrón's role as an impresario of culture:

The plectrum that vibrates the string of the soul of life is in our hands. That is precisely why I am a feminist. Why I am pledged to lending my humble cooperation to the culture of woman; why I study; why I have wanted to teach my sisters to labor for the fair understanding of the progress of woman, because I believe that it is in our hands to provide a tonic: if there is so much disequilibrium in the world, so much disharmony; blame those before who impeded our better preparation; for fortune advances our women and already one will see or, better said, will hear "pleasing sounds," harmonies and sweetness for the happiness of society.[66]

A "fair understanding of the progress of woman" entailed a renarrating of Puerto Rican womanhood, family, and identity in the pages of *Artes y Letras*, rearticulating it as transnational. This work was not just gendered, but political, since in New York, women's full enfranchisement, increased sexual choice, and competence and enterprise in high culture could upend traditional male authority in the public and private realms, authority so carefully guarded back in Puerto Rico by La Generación.

This gendered and transnational reconstruction effort in *Artes y Letras* was especially visible in a clutch of poems about female archetypes: the Spanish gypsy (*la gitana*) and her modern cognate, the flapper.[67] These poems reflect a wondering, reflective state of mind; neither a paean to a "patrimonial Spanish past" á la Pedreira's *Insularismo* (guiding light of La Generación) nor a reflexive condemnation of sexual modernity and its feminine proof texts, the godless rebel or the hapless victim, blamed on Americanization.[68] Grief at the loss of sturdy role models and female connection comes through these writings, understandable for a cohort of women who left their own mothers behind in Puerto Rico to come to New York. Silva de Cintrón, in one of her very few full-length, signed articles, "*Mi Viejo Amigo el Árbol*," longed for the sheltering tree of her childhood where she played and worked with her siblings and parents. She missed her "tender father" and "sainted mother" enough to warrant wearing mourning clothes.[69] In an adoring homage to her daughter Margarita at her first communion, Conchita Francesci Zeno sent up a prayer to her mother "who was a saint in this land and who is protected in my memory."[70] The poetry and testimony published in honor of Josefina's own mother's death in 1935 recalled the pain suffered by all "absent orphans" (*ausentes huérfanos*) in a far-flung Puerto Rican diaspora that included New York and Mexico.[71] As contributors to *Artes y Letras* pondered the legacy of the *gitana* and the impact of flapperism when they looked at their own daughters, they also mourned and deeply missed their Puerto Rican mothers.

In rearticulating womanhood via the arts and modern feminism, *Artes y Letras* vested motherhood and feminine beauty with special import. Especially telling was a cover photograph of a woman named Nemia Vicens in profile, captioned: "*Tipo de belleza puertorriqueña*" (a type of Puerto Rican beauty). In contrast to the *gitana* and flapper, Nemia Vicens is a real woman with a real name. The portrait is of a demure and refined woman, whose moral worth is conveyed through her formal, dignified posture and the symmetry and harmony of facial features (very *not* Picasso). While her name gives her individuality, Vicens is also offered to readers as a representative type in semi-scientific fashion.[72] Her profile accents the facial angle (line from forehead to chin) and allows her face to be read in opposition to racial classifications of the day. In the schema of the facial angle, a steep or flat angle denoted high degree of development or evolution, and a low, sloping angle denoted a more primitive, simian-like status. Thus, Nemia Vicens, with her straight nose and high forehead, might be read as claiming whiteness for the Puerto Rican "type." However, given the overall "racial" politics of *Artes y Letras*, another oppositional reading seems more convincing: no "race" or grouping of humans had an exclusive corner on a high facial angle, as numerous critics of racial science pointed out in the nineteenth and the twentieth centuries.[73] *Artes y Letras* subscribed to a bodily hierarchy that endorsed the "aristocracy of the face," perhaps a necessary counterpoint to the reduction of colonized people to their sick, overreproducing, lazy bodies in the US media. The head shot, with its high forehead, could also accent the intellectual capacity of women, worth emphasizing since Venezuela-born Nomy Bencid was featured in *La Prensa* as the winner of "The Most Perfect Body in New York" contest in 1935, pictured completely nude.[74]

Another key image was the portrait by the expressionist painter James McNeil Whistler (1834–1903), entitled "Arrangement in Grey and Black: The Artist's Mother" (1871) from *Artes y Letras's* May 1935 cover. The painting toured the United States that year and was also honored with a new three-cent postage stamp, "In memory and honor of the mothers of America," recasting this historically controversial painting as "Whistler's Mother," a comforting symbol amid the stress of the Great Depression.[75] *Artes y Letras* offered its own commentary on the painting in a few lines of verse:

> "The mothers with their comfort of poor humanity/through which they teach the goodness that they learned in the sky."

Editors at *Artes y Letras* thus joined a new media association between Whistler's painting with Mother's Day mementoes in the 1930s. *Artes y Letras's* verse suggested that mothers are the heaven-sent gift to all of humanity. The painting and poem provided the keynote for the journal's Mother's Day issue, which annually featured poetry from both internationally famous and local writers in praise of motherhood and of their own mothers, by name. These verses accented mothers' faith, tenderness, and character, inscribing Puerto Rican mothers into not just the U.S. holiday calendar but "American" motherhood, broadly understood.[76] *La Prensa* heartily endorsed observing the holiday. In a land of "violent contrasts," Mother's Day in the U.S. stood out as "noble and humane" because it honored mothers "without distinction of creed or race" and, sounding an inclusive note, *La Prensa's* editors added that "all races of all civilizations" should do likewise.[77] *Artes y Letras* contributor Pedro Juan Labarthe's memoir *The Son of Two Nations: The Private Life of a Columbia Student* (1931) also praised his mother's hard work and sacrifice. "Mother it was all your work," states the protagonist at his college commencement: "You are the heroine of my life."[78]

Labarthe, for one, linked the strength and promise of successful nations to women "gifted with sense," who historically operated "behind [men] and their thrones." "Nowadays women are coming to the top," he cheerily noted, concluding: the "progress of the United States [and other nations] is due to women's activities."[79] *Artes y Letras* energetically debated this kind of popular feminist thinking—more or less an updating of Mill via loose social Darwinism—and cast it in a transnational Latin perspective. Editors held on to the emblem of Cervantes until late in 1938, but rather than look to Spain, they focused more broadly across the Americas. "We offer to our readers a selection of fragments of writings from notable authors of distinct hispanic countries, to sample the racial brotherhood that must unite us."[80] By 1936, *Artes y Letras's* masthead listed an array of *representantes* based in seven countries in Latin America and two US cities, San Bernardino and San Antonio. Of these nine representatives, five can be presumed to be female by their feminine first names. Thus, women appear not merely in supportive, deferential, or symbolic roles, as in the work of La Generación, but in leading ones. The activist and feminist components of *Artes y Letras* stand out especially when compared to *La Prensa's* "For the Ladies" (*Para las Damas*) column that kept exclusively to fashion and home décor topics throughout the 1930s.[81] In addition to its *Sociales* page, *Artes y Letras* had both a *Pagina Feminina,* usually carrying feminist debate and news, as well as a regular *Nuestras Mujeres* feature, specifically dedicated to women in the arts.

Amateur arts might be judged noncontroversial or politically timid for white Protestant women, but Puerto Rican women operated in a very distinct context.[82] First, they claimed authority over classical art forms as well as lighter fare, like comic opera, at a time when women generally did not. Second, by claiming Puerto Rican women and men's competence within European arts traditions, they asserted cultural equity in New York City, a cosmopolitan arts capital. And in contrast to the cultural projects in Puerto Rico surveyed by Roy-Féquière, New York Puerto Rican women exerted pointed leadership in the arts as critics, performers, educators, and boosters, and they used *Artes y Letras* as a platform to explore allied agendas. These agendas included maternalist community-betterment work, like the patronage of local arts institutions, fostering Puerto Rican student successes (both academic and artistic), and political feminism: women's use of the vote, strike, and boycott to advance various policy goals, notably peace, an issue that grew in the aftermath of the devastating loss of life in World War I.[83]

Though inclusive and transnational, *Artes y Letras* especially centered on the interests of Puerto Rican women. Leading contributors were from Puerto Rico; over half its individual subscribers and a solid 30 percent of its international editorial exchanges were located on the island. Caribbean journals claimed a plurality of exchanges (47 percent) with strong showings in the countries of Cuba, Mexico, and Argentina (about 12 percent each). Institutional subscribers within the United States numbered just a few and were all in New York: the 115th Street Library, the 50th Street YWCA, and the Pan American Women's Association (based at the Roerich).[84] The journal was marketed in a handful of bookstalls and newsstands in upper Manhattan for 10 cents each; a year's subscription was $1.00 ($1.50 "*extranjero*") and compares favorably with the

3.2   Cover of *Artes y Letras*, October 1935.

price of the *Bulletin of the Pan American Union* (Washington, DC) and *Puerto Rico Illustrado* (San Juan).[85] With fewer than 100 subscribers in 1934, however, paid advertising and some sort of subvention from Felipe's Misión likely helped get the journal out and pay the rent on the office. Roberto remembered his mother working on articles at the kitchen table at home, and that their apartment was a regular cite of *tertulias* or gatherings of friends for "lively conversation, poem read[ings] [and] instrumental music," which fed the journal's content.[86] As suggested by the almost exclusively local advertisers, sales to the approximately 50,000 Puerto Ricans living in New York City played its part in the journal's viability.[87] Professional services, especially music and dance classes, as well as a range of health-care services were prominent in the ads. Of the latter group, a healthy majority were practitioners with Spanish surnames, and it included pharmacies (like La Farmacia Pan Americana), chiropractors, dentists, physicians, and at least one *comadrona* (midwife), Rosalia M. de Merino. A pair of doctors bragged that they had "25 *años de práctica en Puerto Rico,*" and Jose Monge trumpeted his status as the "*Único undertaker Puertorriqeño*" in Manhattan. Business names like Las Tres Antilles barbershop and the Caribbean Typewriter Shop reflected island-origin readership, and a number of booksellers and printers specializing in Spanish texts and music took out regular ads. Notable, too, are the El Oriente ice cream parlor and the Oriental Wonderland, a shop that sold perfumes, curios, and good luck charms. Bakeries, groceries, and coffee rooms rounded out the *Artes y Letras* directory, and at least one sewing machine retailer put a solidarity spin to its promotional ad: "When you need any service, use people of your own race."[88]

La Bandera de La Raza

These local advertisements in *Artes y Letras* suggest how the term *la raza* figured in a spectrum of oppositional standpoints against white supremacy. At one end of the Caribbean spectrum was the whitening or *blanquearse* of European-focused *criollo* elite and at the other, the Black Imperial (counter) nationalism of a Marcus Garvey. Between these poles, a range of *meztizo*, "new race," or "border" identifications were visible between the wars, the most well known of which is that of *la raza cósmica* propounded in 1925 by José Vasconcelos of Mexico.[89] *Artes y Letras*'s editorial rhetoric on "racial" difference eschewed the category (literally, the word) "white" in favor of "*norteamericanos,*" "*anglosajones,*" or "*sajones*" and, occasionally, "*yanquis,*" that is, accenting geography and culture rather than science or biology. Self-identifying language frequently used the word "*hispanos*" encompassing a far-flung and diverse *latinidad* implying, as sociologist Kelvin Santiago-Valles describes it: "Hispanization regardless of race."[90] A picture of Pedro Caballero costumed in a white turban and a long robe as "*el rey moro*" (the Moorish king) for a production of *La Alhambra* in *Artes y Letras* points up self-orientalizing.[91] Overwhelmingly, however, the ambiguous but capacious phrase *la raza* predominated. And under *La Bandera de La Raza*, *Artes y Letras* moved toward an encompassing vision, embracing not just Puerto Ricans but "*el pueblo hispano*" (the hispanic people).

Devised by an Uruguayan military man, Angel Camblor, in 1932 and embellished by his compatriot, poet Juana de Ibarbourou, *La Bandera* offered a transnational symbol of solidarity under the motto of *Justicia, Paz, Unión y Fraternidad*. In the mix of incentives for its creation was the 440th anniversary of the European "discovery" of America and, in an echo of Martí, a felt need to recast this event in more inclusive terms: "One Sole Flag for Our America" (*Una Sola Bandera Para La América Nuestra*).[92] In his 1935 compendium of media praise for the *La Bandera* movement he sought to encourage, Camblor's framing remarks are striking in two regards: first, in the pains he took to liberate the banner from political ideology in favor of transcendent, spiritual values and second, in his diffidence regarding the word *raza* and, indeed, toward the name of the flag itself. Gesturing toward the decolonial, he stated: "*Llamásele como se quiera*" (Call it what you wish). Camblor reached outward toward the sublime ("*el camino de la perfectibilidad*") rather than toward pathos and loss associated with physically conquered bodies and lands. He celebrated an "America for all Humanity" that was beyond conventional nationalisms and right-left ideologies, "neutral in system, means, partialities, in ideology, in dogmas, etc. etc." *La Bandera*'s symbolic three crosses evoked the flags of the Pinta, Niña, and Santa Maria, but Camblor argued that these symbols had attained universal meaning and eternal sense (*sentido eterno*) of health (*salud*), love (*amor*), and goodness (*bien*). The flag is the image of the sun behind the three crosses and its colors of white and purple and gold represented simplicity, fineness, and hope—generic qualities found in many world cultures, with perhaps an aesthetic nod to the Incas and the Aztecs. Camblor analogized this "*simbolo de las Américas*" to closing a domestic circle; *El Día de La Raza* should be simply "how one says day of the family." "It is the spiritual race, sociologically," he continued, nicely mixing registers of meaning, "more of soul than bone." [93] In this usage, Camblor was consistent with the less rigidly scientific constructions of race in Latin American thought typical of the era.[94]

As of 1935, postage stamps bearing *La Bandera* circulated in Guatemala, Nicaragua, Uruguay, Paraguay, Brazil, and Honduras, all proudly reprinted in Camblor's volume.[95] He was eager to highlight Argentina's possible adoption of the banner, given its status as the southern cone's leading power. As a territory of the United States, Puerto Rico did not qualify for the officialization process, part of which took place at the Conferencia Internacional Americana in Montevideo in 1933. Nor could Puerto Rico issue postage stamps (a fact that Pedro Labarthe's coworkers at the post office had to relearn when they repeatedly asked him for stamps for their "foreign" collections).[96] *Artes y Letras* carried *La Bandera* on its October 1934 cover. When that issue of the journal came to Camblor's attention, he wrote an effusive letter of thanks to Silva de Cintrón, closing his letter with his anticipation of Puerto Rican independence "drop by drop" (*gota a gota*). "Prepare with unbreakable faith that Puerto Rico will soon be master of her destiny," he affirmed. "Hispanic America must in this way have its own vindication."[97] Silva de Cintrón's headline conveyed her pleasure with Camblor's letter; she dubbed it *Una Carta de Gran Significación*. Margarita Robles de Mendoza kissed *La Bandera* in front of 2,000 people when it flew for the first time on "Columbus Day" in October 1934 in New York, a holiday now renamed in *Artes y Letras* as *El Día de La Raza*.[98] Her husband, Dr. Salazar Robles, gave a speech defending *La Bandera* from its critics who defamed it as a meaningless rag (*otro guiñapo más*) and hailed it instead as a hopeful symbol of transformation, "a mantle of simplicity and peace."[99]

La Bandera de la Raza helped *Artes y Letras* articulate a decolonial consciousness, one that was forward thinking rather than nostalgic, dynamic rather than static, and broadly transnational rather than narrowly nationalistic when compared to the work of La Generación. The presence of women at the *bandera*'s creation—the invocation from *poetisa* Juana and its physical creation by Señorita Rosalba Aliaga Sarmiento, "*la bella mujer argentina*," who sewed it with her delicate hands (*sus delicadas manos*), according to Camblor—further enabled women to make it their own.[100] Pura Romo y Silva, Cuban-born Manhattan resident, sewed the first *bandera* in New York, "copied faithfully the Uruguayan original."[101] *La Prensa* noted the singing of a *"Himno de la Bandera de La Raza"* at a UMA gathering in 1934, with music and words written by women.[102] Silva de Cintrón praised the elevating, transcendent ideals (*ideales de elevadisima trascendencia*) embodied in the flag and named Juana de Ibarbouru its *madrina* (godmother).[103] Organized women even made a cake decorated with the *bandera,* which they shared at their gatherings.[104] Spanish language and the *bandera* held UMA women together as they placed racial purity to the side, a stance that mediated the policing, privatization, and subordination of women in the racialist model of nationalism (á la Blyden). And if Silva de Cintrón and her colleagues made no overtures to include neighboring African Americans under the *bandera,* neither did they traffic in terms of imperiled womanhood with its implied racial chauvinism and hostility.[105] "Woman wants, like locomotive Progress, free passage," declared one zesty *Artes y Letras* editorial about *feminismo.* "We do not accept Demarcations."[106]

Más Banderas, Pan-Americanisms, and Orientalist Intersections

Silva de Cintrón and her peers embraced *La Bandera de La Raza* as a more authentic expression of their identity than another flag with some Latin appeal being waved around New York City and Washington, DC, in these same years: Nicolay Roerich's Banner of Peace. An elite, Russian-born painter and theatrical set designer (he also studied law) Roerich founded the Master Institute of United Arts on the upper west side in 1921 to promote his creative projects and house his museum. A world traveler, collector, and self-anointed sage of a hodgepodge spirituality, Roerich, through the Banner of Peace and "Peace Pact" movement, advocated internationally for the protection of artistic and cultural treasures in times of war. According to a recent study, Roerich was a "text book Orientalist," more attuned to Eastern religion than indigenous or *meztizo* America, but his interest in primitivism, mysticism, and rural simplicity led him and his followers to Latin America as well.[107] Backed by wealthy art aficionados in Manhattan, the Peace Pact made its way through the women's clubs and tony lecture circuits in the United States and western Europe, all the way to the League of Nations, where it was approved in 1930.[108] Nominated for the Nobel Peace prize, Roerich also caught the attention of vice president Henry Wallace, a connection that got the Pact in front of the Roosevelt administration and actually signed in a White House Lawn ceremony on April 15, 1935. Conveniently bolstering the "Good Neighbor" image of the administration's foreign policy departure in Latin America, the event was a featured part of "Pan-American Day" in the capital, headlined by the *New York Times* as "2 Americas Join in Cultural Pact."[109] This splashy event, trumpeted loudly by the Pan American Union, based in Washington, DC and whose 21 member nations in Latin America were signatories to the document, likely motivated Angel Camblor to more vigorously wave *La Bandera* that same year and issue his own publication and tribute.

Roerich's Banner of Peace appeared on the cover of *Artes y Letras* in September, 1935. Silva de Cintrón's path to Roerich was a woman whom Roberto described as one of his mother's "great friends": Frances R. Grant (1896–1993).[110] Grant is one of the lesser known of Roerich's New York acolytes, all of whom endure scholarly disdain as "cultists" as does Roerich himself as a "con man."[111] It was Grant, however, as executive director of his Institute and museum, who assiduously worked the women's club circuit in New York and New Jersey to raise money and legitimacy for Roerich's projects.[112] In 1930, Grant established the Pan American Women's Association (PAWA) as a key vehicle for her work. The PAWA served as a ladies' auxiliary for the Roerich Museum and leveraged Grant's éntree to the US-based women's club movement. With a graduate degree in journalism from Columbia, bilingualism (she was born in New Mexico), and flashy travel credentials, Grant parlayed herself into chairmanship of the committee on Latin American Art in the General Federation of Women's Clubs, a perch that gave her access to the networks that fueled her cause and career.[113] Grant was also a regular in the society pages in Manhattan newspapers, and she kept her projects in front of the readers of *La Prensa* and *Artes y Letras* as well.[114]

Press clips preserved in Grant's scrapbooks suggest that she and Silva de Cintrón endorsed one another's work. Notably, however, *Artes y Letras* never editorialized about or explicitly endorsed the Roerich Pact; indeed, the journal's piece on him was written by Grant and appeared some six months after the White House signing event, two years after the pact's endorsement by the Internacional.[115] This silence speaks volumes about what Silva de Cintrón thought of Grant's activities, like her fatuous description of Roerich as a genius (*un genio*) on par with Leonardo de Vinci, as well as Grant's hyperbolic statements regarding women's roles in "the Americas" especially since her own discussions wavered, tellingly, between the "you" plural and "we" form in Spanish: "Women of the Americas, you all must help conserve this sacred torch of liberty and human justice," ran one Peace Pact lecture wrap-up by Grant, "because in our hands is the defense of the heritage of humanity."[116]

Grant's tone and approach were typical of US Pan-Americanism between the wars: high flown and seemingly inclusive, but pocked with bossy condescension and a fickle embrace: You? We? Grant proffered mandates so broad and so vague that they were hard to argue with or, perhaps, even get excited about. Silva de Cintrón publicly remarked that Grant's work was not just talk (*"no es labor de ruidos"*) and conceded that her "altruistic work" was based on empathetic understanding of "our peoples." This endorsement was solid but not effusive, and Silva de Cintrón went on to emphasize that it was Grant's contacts that made the PAWA helpful to UMA: "her effectiveness allows us to see innumerable people of one and the other sex that come here from Latin America bringing greetings of affection through the [PAW] Association which is very well known and esteemed."[117] The stated aims of the PAWA were hardly controversial and practically tautological, namely, "unite the women of the Americas in the idea of mutual interamerican understanding."[118] With Grant as perennial president and her sisters-in-law rotating off and on as officers, it is unlikely that Silva de Cintrón looked to PAWA for a leadership outlet though Remedios de Román did serve as an officer in 1936.[119] Silva de

Cintrón, Carmen de Córdova, and a small handful of women with Spanish surnames residing in upper Manhattan joined the PAWA in early 1932 (paying $2 annual dues), but only Silva de Cintrón retained membership through the end of the decade; Córdova's name was crossed out in the PAWA ledger book with the words *no vuelve* (not returning) written in red.[120]

Grant's orientalism, while perhaps not outright bigoted, bears some discussion because of its intersection with Pan-American discourses of female solidarity, which in turn served as crucial bridges for internationalist feminists between the wars. In "Some Artistic Tendencies in South America" (1929), published in the *Bulletin of Pan American Union*, Grant opined, somewhat contradictorily, about "the *united* cultural destiny of the *two* Americas" (emphasis added) and insisted that through a "mutual devotion to beauty" all "nations may attain a new unity, an impregnable and lasting friendship." Such a friendship hung on a very thin reed of generalization. "As with us [presumably in the United States] the superb experiment of the mixing of peoples is yielding new dynamic racial elements" in other countries as well, affirmed Grant, but her actual observations about Latin American art stuck to a "folk" (indigenous) versus "old Spanish" (European) dichotomy. This essay gives the last word—three paragraphs, actually—to Roerich and his dim-witted prophesy that an "era of happy attainment is predestined for America."[121] Her standard slide-show lecture, "Brazilian Art," heeded the same static "folk" versus "modern" binary, rather than attended to any syncretic or hybrid departures.[122] Overlooking any *meztizaje* in the Americas in favor of a dualistic contest between Europe and Asia, her promotional materials posed questions like "Is the decline of the west at hand?" and "Will the world ascendancy pass again from Occident to Orient?" Grant's other lectures—"The Mystery of Quexlcotl," "Japan's Cult of Beauty," "The Pulse of Asia"—fit the bill for armchair tourism popular in the women's club movement in the interwar years and could also appeal to readers of the still-popular *Lavender and Old Lace*, whose backdrop to romance is the intense domestic consumption of high-end imported furnishings, artwork, and romantic tales from the "east" and which became a play in the 1930s.[123] Grant also worked with ethnicity entrepreneurs like Reconciliation Trips, Incorporated, which specialized in "Group Visits to Chinese, Indians, Japanese, Italians, Russians, Syrians, Jews, Spanish Americans, and Negroes in New York City" and which counted among its solidly respectable "cooperating educators" Gertrude Stein's friend Mabel Foote Weeks at Barnard College and liberal rabbi Stephen S. Wise at the Jewish Institute of Religion (founded in 1922).[124]

Grant's Pan-Americanism belongs to a distinct rhetorical formation with origins in the United States in the 1880s rather than with Martí. US-generated Pan-Americanism between the world wars is usefully understood as an "information industry" with strong ties to US economic agendas and consumer culture.[125] The Pan American Union (PAU) built by Andrew Carnegie in 1910 and located in Washington, DC, published the *Bulletin* and promoted "friendly intercourse, peace, and commerce between the republics of the American Continent." The PAU could take advantage of ideological ground prepared by Latin American thinkers like Martí, who advocated respectful mutuality over default domination of the southern republics by the "collossus" to the north. But US Pan-Americanism typically reflected an engulfing rather than pluralistic frame that defined "the other" as "the same" compared to an Anglo-Saxon or Anglo-American type.[126] For example, this mind-set could define anti-American sentiment as evidence of "Americanism," that is, as "United States-ism" or the desire to self-govern. "Naturally...they wish to direct their own affairs," as a Brookings Institute monograph on Puerto Rico put it in 1930. "Their desire to do so is not anti-American, but American."[127] The PAU's propaganda defined "Pan America as a Whole" to be the United States and the 21 independent nations of Latin America; excluding Canada, "the possessions of Great Britain, France, Holland and Denmark"; and, of course, the possessions of the United States, namely, Puerto Rico.[128]

What, then, to make of PAU's director Leo S. Rowe's appearance on the cover of *Artes y Letras* in 1935 and Roberto's mention of Rowe as another "great friend" of his mother, in the same breath as Frances Grant?[129] What indeed, given that Rowe, while head of the Code Commission for Puerto Rico (1900–1902) made such a gloomy appraisal of the place, especially its women and domestic life? In *The United States and Porto Rico*, Rowe described the "home ideal" as "almost entirely lacking" on the island, where women were practically inert, performing a "relatively small amount of productive and remunerative labor" and "leading lives of comparative idleness," in spite of large families. Rowe could not perceive either women's productive or reproductive labor; he could only see spare dwellings and informal meals taken out of doors, seemingly at random.[130] By contrast, Pedro Labarthe pointed out that though the dominant ideology in Puerto Rico held that women should not work for wages—"women were supposed to stay home even if they were starving"—he took pains to describe how the women in his family worked intensively, mostly in the needle trades, to feed and shelter their children.[131] Unlike contemporary missionary assessments of the Philippines, Rowe did not view Puerto Rican women as particularly "good material" for uplift. The first and last sentences of Rowe's book literally defined Puerto Rico as a "problem," a pattern that became reflexive in the scholarly and periodical literature about the island in English before World War II. "[A] great majority of the peasants simply do not do anything," concluded the predictably named volume, *Porto Rico and Its Problems* in 1930. "The average woman will be found doing her housework on Sundays and holidays, as she does during the week," indicting her as an uncultured drudge rather than acknowledging her as an industrious and active caretaker who juggled multiple, uneven forms of wage earning, barter, and homework to make ends meet.[132]

I would suggest that it was precisely these negative and deficit appraisals of Puerto Rican women that motivated Josefina Silva de Cintrón to call attention to the PAU and its work in *Artes y Letras*. Labarthe advocated for years with the PAU to include Puerto Rican music in its annual concert series; he was finally successful and celebrated by Silva de Cintrón for his advocacy: "*Así se hace patria*" (By this one makes [a] country).[133] Labarthe favored the *plena* and *danzas*, upper class, European-derived dance music, and he explicitly eschewed the Charleston in favor of the waltz and the foxtrot, keeping his distance from working class, African American popular dance forms and the supposedly loose morals and intemperate behaviors that went with them (he was also a strict teetotaler).[134] In a kind but not effusive article accompanying Rowe's portrait in *Artes y Letras*, the writer (probably Silva de Cintrón) emphasized his academic and diplomatic credentials—and Labarthe's successful advocacy—as making the PAU worth appealing to in efforts for Puerto Rican recognition in that body. She called him a "good friend" and cast him as an advocate: "*casi un* 'representative at large'" for Puerto Rico and "a generous patron of ours."[135]

Without such self-assertion, Puerto Rico and its women were either ignored or spoken for by others. Dominant voices in the periodical press in English repeatedly defined Puerto Rico as the "Forgotten Territory" hidden behind a "veil of ignorance and oblivion."[136] "Porto Ricans, therefore, are never heard," complained Leopoldo Cuban in 1930. "They are regarded as inferior intellectually and consequently incapable of understanding even their own problems, which, anomalously as it may seem, are easily understood by the American experts after a few weeks' sojourn in the island."[137] *Artes y Letras* responded to this silencing by waving *La Bandera* and fostering a popular Pan-Americanism that did not take direct cues from Washington, DC. They instead fostered local and transnational institutions. Like *Artes y Letras*, *La Prensa* also cooperated with the Pan American Student League of New York, carrying their weekly newsletter in Spanish and English, and announcing student news, book reviews, and local events associated with Pan American Day.[138]

A final feature of Pan-Americanism and the PAU between the wars would have struck Silva de Cintrón as promising: it housed the Inter American Commission for Women (IACW). At the Conferencia International Americana's 1928 meeting in Havana, the lively demonstrations (including a parade) and advocacy by representatives from international women's organizations convinced the delegates to create a new commission to perform research and advocacy in women's interests. This feminist departure was quite unplanned according to historian K. Lynn Stoner, who suggests that US leadership seized the feminist issue to deflect the palpable hostility of Latin American leaders who were angered by military interventions in Haiti and Nicaragua. Picking up the banner of women's equality raised by female attendees helped the Untied States recoup national prestige and status around a forward-thinking "progressive" issue in the international arena, one with low stakes for diplomacy.[139] Housed at the PAU in Washington and chaired by National Woman's Party leader Doris Stevens, the IACW exhibited much of the condescending and missionizing attitude that historians attribute to Rowe as well as to internationalist US feminists like Carrie Chapman Catt. Among many of her leadership positions dating back to the era of the Nineteenth Amendment, Catt headed the short-lived Pan American Association for the Advancement of Women. On a tour of South America in 1923, she judged the women of the region to be "exceedingly backward" in organizational life.[140] Nonetheless, the IACW was a significant feminist opening in the international arena, and at the 1933 meeting of the Internacional in Montevideo, feminists scored another important benchmark when the conference affirmed married women's nationality. Activists wanted an international treaty to protect the national citizenship of women who married foreign men, a sore point among feminists in the United States since the

Alienage Act of 1907 and an issue that Latin American women could proudly point to in their own countries. Of five nation-states with equal nationality language in their laws or constitutions in 1930, four were in Latin America: Argentina, Chile, Paraguay, and Uruguay (the other was Russia). Margarita Robles de Mendoza was the IACW member from Mexico.[141]

A reenergized and oppositional Pan-Americanism gave migrant Puerto Ricans in New York a platform for reimagining community and social engagement. Pedro Labarthe had something quite "third space" in mind. "Puerto Rico is a Pan American country," he affirmed: a unique, increasingly bilingual, and mixed social and political entity.[142] Those holding to a more strict racial-nationalist model, like Leopoldo Cuban, had a less optimistic view of the Puerto Rican: "He is neither a true American—nor a true Spaniard—nor even a genuine tropical; furthermore, he is not a combination of the three."[143] But Labarthe declared himself a "son of two nations" and "an advocate of peace." In the pages of *Artes y Letras* and his other writings, Labarthe devoted himself to "his ideal, the bringing of the Americas to better understanding," even lobbying Senator William Borah on the matter.[144] Silva de Cintrón emphasized sentiments that transcended nation-state boundaries and imagined a new, pluralistic civilization beyond racial categories:

> ...the women of each nation have the solemn and unavoidable mission to contribute to the instruction of this great friendship and of the new civilization that the Americas *are speaking to provide* the future world.[145] (emphasis added)

Silva de Cintrón's thinking remained less than fully elaborated in the pages of *Artes y Letras*. The phrase "speaking to provide" points to the discursive realm of her actions—the freedom to speak and be heard—and one vitally important in the increasingly media-saturated world she lived in. The most important comment on the relationship between US-based Pan-Americanism and *feminismo* in *Artes y Letras* is the establishment of the New York branch of the UMA in 1934. Taking inspiration from Robles de Mendoza (rather than Rowe or Grant or Catt) Puerto Rican women in Manhattan built upon the UMA's original focus on peace and equality not just as principles but as policy, namely rights. When Carmen de Córdova extended an honorary membership in the organization to Frances Grant in 1938, she added rights to the traditional UMA motto of *Paz e Igualdad* by typing "*DE DERECHOS*" in capital letters onto the printed letterhead.[146]

Things ended badly for Grant and Henry Wallace with Roerich. Wallace's presidential bid in 1948 was rocked by an exposé of the letters he wrote to Roerich in the 1920s with the salutation "Dear Guru" (the so-called Guru Letters). For her part, Grant was evicted from her housing and shut out of the museum when the major Roerich backers made a grab for title to the building and its contents in the later 1930s, embarrassing events discreetly noted in *La Prensa*.[147] By contrast, Silva de Cintrón's fortunes were not harmed by Roerich's falling star and the protracted legal case over his assets in New York. By then, Puerto Rican women in Manhattan women were focused on the New York World's Fair and Puerto Rico's representation in it.[148] And they did so backed by the proudly feminist and transnational organization Silva de Cintrón helped found and foster in the pages of *Artes y Letras*: La Unión de Mujeres Americanas.

Unión de Mujeres Americanas

Reports of UMA in *Artes y Letras* struck several consistent themes: the progress of women toward increasing liberty, female solidarity, mothering values, and legal rights. On this last point, the organization's first president Margarita Robles de Mendoza (who lived part time in New York) insisted, at the founding meeting, that leadership was properly constituted and voted upon.[149] "They receive formally the vote from her sisters of the South," she declared. "This is the only way to make respectable the cause of continental solidarity and the representatives of these causes."[150] UMA was an important turning point since Latin American women's interests at international and Pan American meetings in the preceding decade had often been represented by the wives of diplomats, tapped on the spot to speak on behalf of the women of their nations.[151] In terms of agenda setting, women in New York initially followed the lead set by their Mexican ally: "Peace and Equality is the motto of the institution," ran one early blurb. "We fight for peace first."[152] Like El Círculo's activities, early UMA meetings emphasized building bonds of solidarity through the arts and cultural activities; simply, yet profoundly *"Te Familiar"*: to get to know one another, to become like family.[153] Women from many parts of Latin America gathered and felt welcomed at UMA events—Peru, Ecuador, Puerto Rico, Cuba, and Mexico. In a gesture of "transcendent symbolism" (*simbólica transcendencia*), national flags also hung at these gatherings where flowers and food figured also prominently.[154] In the *Sociales* pages of *Artes y Letras*, readers kept up with the expanding social and mutual benefit societies in Manhattan: Sociedad Madres y Niños, Los Doce Pares, Club-Panamericano, and Pro-Humanidad, just to name a few. Among these, the UMA was notable for its proud claiming of *feminismo*.[155]

UMA also claimed *La Bandera de La Raza* as the "insignia of the association."[156] The women stressed the flag's inclusive potential, describing their platform as "solidarity without distinction of creeds, color, races, or nationalities."[157] The use of the word "Americanas" claimed an encompassing, pluralistic American-ness as the women's rightful domain.[158] Reports from early meetings highlighted feminism as well as conventional patriotism and aspirations to national independence, though the issue of Puerto Rican independence remained muted in the agenda of its international council.[159] *La Prensa's* coverage emphasized the UMA's ceremonial roles in New York, like feting the consul of Peru, entertaining the consul general of Mexico, and honoring dignitaries from Columbia (countries with their own UMA organizations). *La Prensa* recognized the women's efforts as an expression of the "feminine fraternity of the entire Continent" and projected a bit of its own class consciousness onto the group's potential for "the emancipation of woman and the liberation of the proletarian classes."[160]

UMA meetings gave poetry, recitation, theatricals, and musical performance pride of place, reflecting Silva de Cintrón's role as arts impresario as well as the aesthetic and performative aspects of transnational feminist community building. Singing songs and reciting poetry in a group setting enacted solidarity, a solidarity that could have helped Amanda Smith in Liberia. Such activities underscored listening, participation, harmonizing, and, potentially being understood by others. The poem written for UMA by Mercedes Luque and sung as the *"canto civico"* (civic song) of the association conveys this spirit: "Woman of our race, defend your right!" Woman's "redemption" (*redención*) would come not by lawbreaking or overt confrontation with men or the state but by unifying around the larger truth that women had their own voice or power of action in the world. "Unite sisters! Let us break the chains!" she concluded. "But in the name of equals, *compañeras*, not serfs; as in our beautiful saying: Peace and Equality."[161]

Scholarly comparisons of US white women's feminism and Latina feminism usually highlight the former's focus on legal equality between men and women, and the latter's accent on motherhood, an aestheticized elaboration of womanhood, and the caretaking of husbands and sons.[162] Robles de Mendoza's thinking, though strongly maternalist, balanced these elements. Her agenda was highly technocratic and yet suffused with spiritual and aesthetic values. She argued that weak, uneducated, disempowered mothers meant a weak nation–state, and that only informed, socially engaged mothers could rear appropriately patriotic sons. "The modern woman wants to be a mother in the fullness of responsibility and love, not as a victim of biological process."[163] To exclude woman from full citizenship was to create, as Luque also implied, a population of parasites or slaves. Thus, fundamental questions of existence were not matters of feeling or nature, but human-made law. As Robles de Mendoza put it: "The problems of existence can not be resolved with sentimentality, nor left to [chance]...It is preferable, then, to valiantly analyze them and try to give a technical solution."[164] The vote was just and necessary from a general, abstract, disinterested point of view. "We desire to analyze the theme [of the vote] from a point of view much higher [than competition between the sexes], judging it solely as a social thesis." Although women's active citizenship directly shaped the quality of the home, patriotism, and peace, Robles de Mendoza conceded that feminism was not completely contained in the vote ("*El voto no es el todo del feminismo*").[165] Full suffrage for women was not attained in Mexico until 1947. Robles de Mendoza also located herself squarely on the side of the uplifters and assimilators of the Mexican state. Women needed equality so that "they [can] make their own the education of our children and our Indians, [and so] that they [may] use their economic talent in the municipality."[166] Nonetheless, she rooted the justice of women's equality in historical forces and human truths beyond the state's power to confer, especially the shared cultural heritage of the Americas. "The movement for emancipation of women was born almost simultaneously in all America," she affirmed in her speech at Montevideo in 1933. "It is not a local phenomenon of Cuba, Mexico, or Uruguay; it is the whole of America which is rising up."[167]

Robles de Mendoza's maternalism echoed in the *feminismo* of *Artes y Letras*, but Silva de Cintrón and her colleagues focused less on uplift and more on rights, less on "nation" (*nación*) and more on "country" (*patria*) or "peoples" (*pueblos*). Carmen de Córdova was probably the most state centered of *Artes y Letras* feminists. She praised the strides made in New York State toward obligatory jury duty for women, led by the League of Women Voters, National Woman's Party, and a few key white women state legislators. "The reclamation of the rights of woman is an untiring effort and a principle factor in the progress of the nation," she wrote approvingly in the summer of 1937. "Free from prejudice, we recognize her ancient attributes."[168] UMA women tracked and compared legal change concerning the "progress and political status of women," with Ecuador, Nicaragua, and Costa Rica applauded for their constitutional provisions of sex equality.[169] Radio broadcasts spread their message of feminist encouragement. In August, 1938, a short talk by Silva de Cintrón entitled *"Feminismo"* again stressed the New York UMA's themes of "peace and equality of rights." She called upon her listeners to fight for social betterment at the side of men (*"al lado del hombre"*) at a moment when women's *"suavidades femininas"* were sorely needed; Europe was behaving as if problems could be solved with grapeshot (*"con la metralla"*). Silva de Cintrón pointed out that most women made their biggest social impact at church and at home, where "our primary duty" resided; nonetheless "cultivating knowledge" remained vital to "forming from our sons, great men."[170]

In addition to endorsing Robles de Mendoza, Silva de Cintrón's vision also took a page out of Mercedes Solá's important 1921 essay *"Feminismo."* Solá's essay has been incisively analyzed by Roy-Féquière, who points out the elitist and implicitly racist underpinnings—based on *"nuestro tipo criollo"*—of her basically conservative feminism.[171] If Solá's text established important parameters for Puerto Rican feminism within island-based nationalism, New Yorkers extended her thinking transnationally. It is easy to imagine Silva de Cintrón and UMA members in New York warming to Solá's vision of making "the work of motherhood a work of art" (*de la obra maternal una obra de arte*), especially bearing in mind the persistent invisibility and negation of Puerto Rican women's mothering in established Pan-American discourses.[172] "And it is not that woman is tired of motherhood," ran one *Artes y Letras* editorial, "it is that she is tired of only motherhood."[173] Solá's piece also endorsed sex equality a kind of ancient norm, suitable, with updating, for modern times. For Solá, feminism meant "rehabilitating [woman] to her legitimate condition of being human, intelligent, and worthy," neatly disarming the antifeminist bugbear of women desiring to stride past men and become masculine.[174] This was precisely how *Artes y Letras* defined authentic feminism: "the movement that reclaims for woman, the rights that for so many centuries were infringed upon by man."[175] Feminism was, like "world progress" (*progreso mundial*) and "universal democraticization of the people" (*universal democratización de los pueblos*), simply one more enlightened step along the way to global justice.[176]

The most energizing aspect of Solá's feminism playing out in the pages of *Artes y Letras* was her idea of a "feminism of action" (*feminismo de acción*). Solá pointed to the inexorable movement of women into work and school and proclaimed these feminist victories, even if the women involved claimed no feminist principles or consciousness. In *"feminismo,"* she recounted querying young working women about whether they considered themselves feminists, and to their protestations of "Oh, no!" Solá retorts: "But you work, you are a feminist of action." This framing claimed and affirmed the overall propriety and authenticity of Puerto Rican women's presence—and, by extension, their demands—in the public sphere. "We all know that in our country, the feminism of action is triumphant, rather than worrying that our feminism is purely imitative."[177] By closing her long essay with a section on the global sweep of feminism (*"Avance Mundial de la Causa"*) and with an endorsement of organizations like the International Suffrage Alliance, Solá brought to bear another layer of momentum and legitimacy for her cause. And, when she complained that international meetings failed to include sessions in Spanish and told of the unwanted and embarrassing absorption of the Liga Social Suffragista de Puerto Rico into the North American delegation (*"debián unirse a la delegación norteamericana"*) in at least one such meeting, she identified ongoing challenges for Puerto Rican feminists to be visible, heard, and respected in interwar feminist and peace movements.[178]

Newly visible under *La Bandera*, UMA women in New York focused on peace and antiviolence rather than the franchise, the latter remaining, understandably, near the center of Mexican women's activism. Bearing an olive branch like the biblical dove, UMA women could extend peace within and among all people *"interna y externa a todos nuestros pueblos,"* and thereby help "our men" (*nuestros hombres*) with the "progressive work of all America" (*labor progresiva de toda la América*).[179] There was plenty of violence to protest and resist.

UMA's founding year of 1934 witnessed a high point of deaths (eventually totaling some 80,000) in the Chaco War between Bolivia and Paraguay, as well as the conspicuous failure of international mediation of that conflict through the League of Nations.[180] Accusations that the Standard Oil Company was behind aggression in the Chaco region, a charge fanned by Roosevelt opponent Senator Huey Long of Louisiana, were circulated widely in the New York and Latin American news media. US arms companies' active opposition to a congressional embargo on munitions sales to the combatants added fuel to the fire of unrest about this war.[181] In these same years, the Women's International League for Peace and Freedom (WILPF), supported by the Women's Peace Union (advocates of a US constitutional amendment against war), successfully pressed for a senate special investigation of the munitions industry's role in politics around World War I. During the Chaco conflict, the Senate's Nye Committee found that, indeed, "the munitions industry had clearly tried to influence the congressional vote for war in 1917."[182] In at least its outlines, then, the Chaco conflict represented something of a worst-case scenario for violence in South America: neighbors shooting at each other with arms supplied by industrial countries in the interest of those outside nations' most powerful corporations.[183] The Chaco War underscored for Latin American feminists their stark marginality from halls of corporate and military power and at the same time, highlighted the urgency of alternatives to war, evident in the women's *Mandato Pro Paz* active in the southern cone in those years.[184]

The New York UMA fused a peace agenda with antiracism for an additionally good cause: violence on the island of Puerto Rico also reached an all-time high in the 1930s. The New Deal's patchwork of interventions there—hurricane relief, educational mandates, agricultural reorganization—created more turmoil than succor, and protests in the form of labor strikes and nationalist demands for independence sharply increased. The US government's response was, in turn, harsh, punitive, and manipulative. Ernest Greuning, head of the Bureau of Insular Affairs, administered the Puerto Rican Reconstruction Administration (PRRA) with liberal condescension. Then, in the middle of the sputtering reconstruction effort, Senator Millard Tydings attempted to spank the island for a police shooting in San Juan of US-appointed police commissioner and Tydings's friend, Colonel Frances E. Riggs, with an abrupt bill for independence.[185] Tyding's disdain blared across the media: Puerto Ricans were not "grateful" for US citizenship and were indifferent to the teachings of democracy.[186] In the wake of the shooting, the vocal Pedro Albizu Campos and seven other nationalists were jailed for conspiracy against the United States, tried, found guilty, and sentenced.[187] The Tydings bill never came to a vote, but its airing opened the gate for venting prejudice against Puerto Rican people. The *North American Review* opined about the "foulness" and "rotting fungus life" of *jíbaro* existence, and the "fundamental menace" of overpopulation on the island whose "bad elements" would soon be in New York, already the second largest center of Puerto Rican population in the world.[188]

As bloodshed marred island life, Puerto Rican women's frustration with the peace movement erupted in the pages of *Artes y Letras*. In March 1936, nationalist advocate María Más Pozo wrote an article critical of a petition drive spearheaded by Heloise Brainerd (1881–1969), of the PAU (and later of WILPF). Brainerd was organizing Latin American women for a peace petition, aiming for 50,000 supporters.[189] Más Pozo began her article with a stinging critique of the signature campaign. What the peace movement needed was not a "wordy palaver" (*palabrería escrita*) but *"ACCIÓN,"* and Más Pozo was full of ideas. First, women citizens should boycott the vote—*"la abstención del voto"*—and thereby delegitimize violent government actions undertaken in their name. They also should withdraw from employment in war industries and forbid their sons to enlist in the army. The purpose and effect of these actions would be a general women's strike: "Woman declares herself universally on strike against everything implicating war." This strike would contribute to the "great work of humanity" and, in the case of mothers, activate their special skills and duties. Más Pozo questioned the efficacy of merely exercising equal rights with men, and instead stressed the need for female-centered and community-based action in everyday life: "Feminism does not [really] have the name without going to the roots of the ills that afflict humanity and [then] applying the remedy." Equal rights was not necessarily "feminism," in Más Pozo's view, nor had equal rights eliminated the great historic, human afflictions. "Feminism has not eliminated the PAIN OF DEATH," she declared. "Has not eliminated WAR. Has not eliminated prostitution. Has not eliminated crime or robbery. Everything proceeds like before..." Más Pozo combined a more confrontational style of strike and boycott with a more protective stance visà-vis men and family life; for women to protect sons and husbands was to defend love itself, thereby defeating the "pain of death." "Not with signatures, but positively with DOING," she concluded, could other self-identified feminists "support our WORK of redemption."[190]

In the next issues of *Artes y Letras*, the more moderate Carmen B. de Córdova responded in a *carta abierta* (open letter) to Más Pozo, taking a soothing and a tad patronizing tone toward her friend, whom she described as "always amiable and fretful." She argued that it was not the weakness of feminism that slowed the improvement of humanity since the last war, but the backward ways of men, "the resulting fault of masculine feudalism." The gains of feminism, on the other hand, were substantial if not yet fully realized, especially the right to full public expression, including official political power and the vote. Córdova had only admiring words for "*la mujer norteamericana*," who prepared herself carefully and had "won representation and shared responsibility in all areas that were [formerly] the privilege of men" "Let us wait, then," she concluded, "for the law of evolution to complete itself."[191]

Más Pozo responded with an even stronger critique of "*la mujer yanqui*," citing conservative, bureaucratic tendencies that yielded little concrete change. "As soon as you speak of the feminist associations of this country, tell me: what have they DONE? Nothing. Absolutely NOTHING." She challenged their authority to serve as leaders or models for others, citing their complicity with racial violence and "*barbarie*," naming the lynching of African Americans and the invasion of Ethiopia by Italy. "What do you say about lynchings?" Más Pozo demanded, adding a jab at Spanish history. "Has the yankee woman done anything to stop this inquisition in the middle of the twentieth century?" Más Pozo further cited US women's silence in the struggle over federal antilynching legislation during which "not one woman mumbled nor supported the bill."[192] Más Pozo referred to the Wagner-Costigian Act debated in Congress 1934–1938, which the Association of Southern Women for the Prevention of Lynching declined to support and which barely won the endorsement of WILPF's New York branch.[193] Más Pozo did not acknowledge either African American women's antilynching activism or that of more outspoken white southern Methodist women who did press for the bill's passage.[194] Rather, her point was to stake out a more active antiviolence and antiprejudice politics focused on women's everyday actions, which could also respond to matters of the heart and the soul. She reached for a critique that made the link between racial violence and international aggression so lacking in mainstream US peace movement. Harlem congressman Vito Marcantonio did just this when he addressed the Puerto Rican protest march the summer after the Riggs shooting, calling Albizu Campos's jailing a "political lynching" and analogous to a "Tom Mooney or Scottsboro boys frame-up."[195] *Artes y Letras* called the march "overwhelmingly splendid."[196] Más Pozo concluded her letter: "Refuse to cooperate in all acts of barbarism and remove from your soul all expressions that tend to form racial or religious prejudice."[197] Given the silence of *Artes y Letras* on the Harlem Riot of 1935 and Más Pozo's usual distance from race relations concerning African Americans in New York, this later exchange in the journal points to the expanded consideration of the link between racial politics and state violence.[198]

Más Pozo's frustration also stemmed from the changing status of women's international peace petitions by the mid-1930s: stunning successes as acts of social and intellectual mobilization (Jane Addams won the Nobel Prize in 1931 in part for her work with WILPF) and extremely limited as means for lasting policy. It likely, too, reflected the growing rift between feminism and peace, described by historian Harriet Alonso, as the suffragist generation aged and passed on, and attempts to outlaw war by amendment to the US constitution petered out by 1930.[199] For Más Pozo, a strong supporter of independence for Puerto Rico, Brainerd's long-time affiliation with the Pan American Union added a rub, as there was palpable restiveness in New York with its paternalistic style of operation. In the spring of 1934, *La Prensa* reported on the plans of a new group, lead by an Argentinean, called the Confederación Nationalista Hispanoamericanos that intended to call the bluff of good neighborliness: "Our organization opposes panamericanism because with this pretext, the green prairies of our America are converted into camps of...desolation and death," referring to Chaco.[200] In the summer of 1935, a Puerto Rican student disrupted a Simón Bolívar anniversary event at the Central Park statue with sharply worded circulars protesting the "pan-American pageants of the imperialistic United States" and the "lackeys" who staged them, creating "an uproar" that motivated the Roerich Mueseum to request police protection at their evening events that celebrated, among other themes, "Bolivar, The Pacifist" (a stretch even for the expansive cult of The Liberator).[201]

As in the fine and performing arts, prestige and decorum structured authority in the realms of peace and diplomacy. Meetings and rituals touching "this Pan American thing," in Carrie Catt's bumbling phrase, were suffused with theatrics, carefully staged and orchestrated for public consumption (the PAU favored the planting of themed gardens).[202] Leading white women peace advocates in the United States took pride in their exercise of national prestige as part and parcel of advancing their antiwar agenda, especially since Democratic Party women in particular were urged to "drop the sex line in politics," according to New Dealer Emily Newell Blair.[203] The 1935 volume *Why Wars Must Cease*, an eloquent and sophisticated expression of antiwar thought put out by the National Committee on the Cause and Cure of War (NCCCW), contrasts strongly with Más Pozo's antiracist consciousness and emotional urgency. A product of the NCCCW's Book Committee (chaired by Catt), its goal was to foster understanding rather than incite protest. Essays by Jane Addams, Mary E. Wooley, Emily Newell Blair, Eleanor Roosevelt, and Dr. Alice Hamilton, among others, offered incisive and highly readable syntheses of state-of-the-art thinking in psychology, economics, and criminology concerning war—with gender analysis and racial sensitivity conspicuous by their absence. In her concluding essay, writer and educator Dorothy Canfield Fisher noted: "It is an honor to any civilized being to be allowed to testify against war."[204] Fisher's vision of an "imaginary symposium" to make the case against war might well have seemed a comedown to activists looking for fresh approaches. Indeed, Fisher lamented even finding a convener "wise enough, skilled enough" to pull off such a symposium. Her choice for the job, William James, had been dead for 25 years, and she wished aloud: "If anything could bring him out of his grave back to us who need him so, it would be this appeal."[205]

In contrast to this maudlin wistfulness, writers in *Artes y Letras* tested out new ideas, and refurbished a few old ones, too. Articles on pacifism included support of strikes by students and women, suggesting that peace and antiwar themes had a transnational audience. Some of this talk pushed beyond racial/*raza* conventions to more encompassing rhetoric. On the world stage, women could bond in one great "army of Pacifists," who observed not the boundaries of nations but "only Humanity." *Artes y Letras* approvingly quoted editors and commentators from Latin America who answered scientific racism with the idea, "There is but one race...the human race."[206] Editors of *Artes y Letras* also disavowed violence and projected a distinct Puerto Rican heritage of peacefulness compared with the more revolutionary-minded Latin American republics (*"hermanos más revolucionarios"*), a calming, even feminine counterpoint within the region, the *"linda hija boriqueña"* (pretty *boriqueña* daughter) whose natural pacifism was a crucial asset for protecting its cultural heritage.[207] In *La Prensa*, Salvador Mendoza praised Puerto Rico for "sublimat[ing] the patriotism that generated the virulence" of extreme nationalism that could lead to war, commending the special heritage of "the peaceful island."[208] Indeed Puerto Rico, in its metaphorical third-space location betwixt and between nations, "races," and cultures, might have a special role and perspective to offer the international peace movement.

Pedro Juan Labarthe advanced such a plan through *Artes y Letras*: a *"Liga de Naciones Americana"* that could arbiter the interests and conflicts of the hemisphere. Dabbled with on and off for a century, the idea resurfaced in 1936 sparked by a tumult of violent events: the shootings in Puerto Rico, the rickety brokering of the Chaco conflict, civil war in Spain, and the hot tangle of conflicts in the rest of Europe that stretched to Africa. Added impetus came from the US refusal to join the World Court at the Hague (via congressional vote in early 1935) and a general sense among some Latin Americans about feeling "like outsiders" in Geneva.[209] Labarthe reclaimed the *Liga* concept specifically for Puerto Rico and framed it as an expression of authentic Pan-Americanism: "Simón Bólivar was the father of PANAMERICANISM. Not the United States. No. It was an hispanoamerican, light of the Andean heights and ray of the Incas."[210] In the mid-1820s, Bolivar had plans for a Congress of Panama for the new Latin American republics, but it remained mostly a "theoretical structure," according to his most recent biographer.[211] To bolster the contemporary case, Labarthe cited Elihu Root, former US secretary of state, Nobel winner of World Court renown (who died in February 1937), and backer of a "Central American Court" that existed between 1907 and 1917.[212] Labarthe also quoted FDR, who reportedly quipped on his first visit to the island in 1919 that "Puerto Rico was the Switzerland of America."[213] Labarthe retorted: "Let it be so." He embedded the plan in an argument for a "Free Associated State" status for the island viz the United States—*"como Irlanda"*—an interesting twist to the historic inspiration of the Irish freedom movement for Caribbean nationalists of diverse ideological stripes.[214] Like Latin Americans in Europe, he analogized, Puerto Rico "had been ignored by Hispano America." An international court of arbitration in Puerto Rico's "priceless location in the Caribbean sea," promised to raise the island's status and role in the region while restoring a cherished legacy of Bolívar.[215] Ironically, at the New York World's Fair, the island's location would be touted by US officials for precisely the opposite reasons: the ease it allowed for waging war.

The New York World's Fair, 1939–1940

Intended to showcase "The World of Tomorrow," the New York World's Fair was conceived as a hopeful exercise in rationality, planning, and science, but it was shadowed by war. It opened in May, 1939, and in September Hitler invaded Poland, and Britain declared war on Germany. The fair's commemoration of founding father and war hero George Washington included daily military exercises and a Camp George Washington that housed over 700 soldiers on site. Given the martial temper of the moment, it is not surprising that Puerto Rico Day commemorated the landing of US troops on July 25, 1898, a day not marked on the island.[216]

At the dedication of the Puerto Rican pavilion, speeches by male officials stressed the United States' need for national defense. Governor Blanton Winship's remarks declared the island "the keystone of our eastern defense" against "foreign aggression" and described plans to site a submarine and air base there; the same article in the *New York Times* reporting on Winship's speech also burbled on about the "charm of tropic territory" and how "tourists get invitations" to visit. Puerto Rico's Commissioner Eduardo R. Gonzales fell in line, underscoring the "importance that our government is giving to our island as a stronghold for national defense." Such investment proved "that Puerto Rico is a territory faithful to the accepted ideals and traditions of America," adding a pitch for the island as "a land hallowed by a hospitality which, with its enchanting scenery, is a delight to all who visit it."[217] By the end of the year, plans were in motion to build the largest navy base in the world on the island of Puerto Rico: the US station at Roosevelt Roads, completed in 1943.[218]

Artes y Letras's vision of a transnational feminist civic and cultural sphere dedicated to the arts, peace, and Puerto Rican aspirations for equality was difficult to implant in the World's Fair's scientific and militaristic milieu. Instead, Puerto Rico got caught up in the overarching—and eerily complementary—economies of leisure and security. The accent on Puerto Rican tourism at the New York World's Fair belongs in the context of extended "governmental coloniality" on the island during the New Deal, that is, an extension of paternalistic and unequal structures pervading the economy and political life.[219] The repackaging of the island as a "Caribbean Playground" went hand in hand with New Deal spending there during the decade.[220] A media campaign assuaged readers: "Anti-American feeling, so pronounced during former administrations, has entirely disappeared," and: "Life on the island remains easy going and romantic."[221] After the bloody Ponce massacre that took place on Palm Sunday, March, 1937, in which US troops fired into an unarmed group of nationalist protestors, killing 19, the image situation demanded repair, and US elites stepped up. Theodore Roosevelt, Jr. offered a highly romanticized travel guide to Puerto Rico to readers of *House and Garden* in 1938, and the title of his piece, "Island of Enchantment," became a media moniker lasting up to this day, appearing on the 2009 "state" quarter.[222] Fernando Géigel also aided in restoring Ponce's reputation, postmassacre. "What we want very much to do is attract tourists, especially to our annual Mardi Gras carnival in February" in that city, he announced in the

World's Fair's preseason publicity. The Puerto Rican pavilion was to "include a dramatization of that [holiday]."[223]

The pavilion was managed by the Agriculture and Commerce Department of the Government of Puerto Rico, and San Juan officials set up offices in Manhattan to oversee its construction, administer employment, install exhibits, and manage concessions and other activities on the fairgrounds.[224] Politically, Puerto Rican leaders used both the World's Fair and the militarization of the island to raise the stakes for statehood, symbolically abetted by the fair organizers who located the Puerto Rican pavilion in the United States' "Court of States."[225] Not only did this plan backfire, but in the process leadership voices from the New York community became marginalized. Silva de Cintrón and her colleagues raised a strong note of protest over Puerto Rican representation at the fair, only to be mocked at and insulted for their efforts.

The stage was set for conflict a year before the World's Fair opening. In May, 1938, *La Prensa* reported that an investigation was being undertaken concerning the poor appearance of the float representing Puerto Rico in the much ballyhooed preview parade staged that spring. Josefina Silva de Cintrón, Remedios C. de Román, and Carmen B. de Córdova petitioned Fernando Géigel, mayor of San Juan (1939–1941) and on-and-off presence in the Manhattan fair office, with their complaints. The parade was the "first completely mechanized column" in the tradition of American pageantry, and it traveled 16 miles from the Battery to the fairgrounds in Flushing in front of at least a million spectators. Prizes were awarded for various divisions of the parade (including a section on "foreign participation"), and the event featured "many floats containing bathing beauties."[226] It was a long, highly scrutinized international spectacle in which modern technology and the female form mirrored each other as streamlined, pale, sleek, shiny, and alive with electric energy.[227]

According to *La Prensa*, Puerto Rico's float was a ramshackle cart (*"un pobre cajón"*) painted with hasty, careless lettering, implying slovenliness and illiteracy. Silva de Cintrón and her colleagues' letter complained that its presentation "demonstrates the little interest or importance" given to the country by parade organizers and that it reflected inaccurately on Puerto Rican's true "aptitude and knowledge." "What a shame that the lovely young women [traveling aboard] did not have another scenario more appropriate to showcase their attractiveness." The petitioners described their pain for their country (*patria*) as "deep and indelible," and they invoked their "inalienable right" (*derecho inalienable*) as "Puerto Rican women, American citizens" (*mujeres puertorriqueños, ciudadanas americanas*) to "elevate the opinion of our country prevalent in the foreigner." They spoke not just in their own name but in the name of all Puerto Rican women engaged in education, culture, and social-betterment work. Indeed, they claimed the fair as their own (*"nuestra Feria Mundial"*) and declared its purpose to be women's work: "They [feminine] are constructing the world of the future."[228]

In June, *Artes y Letras* recapped the protest and printed the responses of fair officials, which were set pieces in condescension and avoidance. Playing on colonial paranoia, Géigel tried to placate the women by suggesting a hokey twist to the drama: the miserable float was the result of some unnamed "deception" or "trick" on the part of parade organizers.[229] Then Géigel shook his finger at local women for publicizing their protest in the media; *Artes y Letras* replied defensively that "no one had intended to harm anyone, only to salvage the prestige of the country" that had been unacceptably shamed by such a "ridiculous artifact" appearing in the parade.[230] Silva de Cintrón was understandably testy since Millard Tydings had also sounded off again negatively in the press that spring, comparing "ignorant and immoral" Puerto Ricans in New York to the poor whites of Alabama, both of whom overrepresented on New Deal relief rolls according to him. Newly elected NY Assemblyman Oscar Garcia Rivera (R) demanded a retraction, as did Remedios Cruz de Román. Tydings simply denied the statements.[231]

This disrespectful context boded ill for fair attendance by New York Spanish speakers; overall, ticket sales and attendance lagged the first year. In an attempt to drum up local business, fair director Grover A. Whalen himself wrote a letter to *Artes y Letras*, assuring readers that the spectacle was "a 'Fair for Everyman'" with "prices scaled to his purse." "Thus there need be no hesitation on the part of the Latin-American people who are contemplating a trip to the exposition," Whalen wrote in August 1939, acknowledging the transnational reach of the publication. The letter was addressed to Mr. Victor C. de Aragón, the editor of the last, special World's Fair edition of *Artes y Letras*; Josefina Silva de Cintrón had dropped her card at the fair headquarters back in January to no response.[232]

Puerto Rican women fit themselves around the tourism theatricals of the pavilion as best as they could. On the fairgrounds, a woman served as "chief hostess," and 12 "young lady attendants" were charged with hospitality in the "colonial-tropical style" interior, replete with "Spanish patio" with a fountain of youth at the center (Puerto Ricans claimed Ponce de Leon rather than Columbus). So-called native women were on display demonstrating handcraft and lace making.[233] The focus on tourism partly resulted from the boycott of the fair by the major industries of the island: tobacco, distillers, sugar, and, initially, garment and textiles. In his 1939 report, Gonzales recounted business leaders' strong objection to paying for exhibits and their transportation to New York because they understood that funds had been duly raised in the island legislature; the financial burden provoked their "renunciation" of the event. Nonetheless, Gonzalez judged the six months of 1939 "all well worth the investment made" and agreed to sign up for the next year, even extending Puerto Rico's concessions to include a restaurant. He praised the "good-will sown" by the effort though he made no particular mention of the tourism piece; indeed, some of the women employed at the pavilion had come under criticism by inquiring visitors for their lack of fluency in English and reportedly limited knowledge of the island.[234]

Initially, New York's Puerto Rican women had been optimistic about the fair. They understood the event to be, in the words of Carmen Luisa Morales, "*ultra-moderna y ultra-scientífica*" but encompassing various other dimensions, including the "*femenino.*" They understood that women's organizations were an "indispensable key" to the fair's success.[235] Several factors limited the UMA's role, however. First, Pan-Americanism was muted on the fairgrounds; most Pan-American events took place at established and familiar cultural venues midtown rather than out in Queens.[236] Second, the fair organizers eschewed feminism or any kind of female activism. Emily Newell Blair, former chair of the Consumers Advisory Board for the National Recovery Administration, quit the fair's consumer committee (along with her 21 fellow appointees) accusing the corporation of using their names as "window dressing" to advance the overwhelmingly "commercially sponsored" exhibits and promotionals rather than offering space for consumer education and advocacy. The *Times* bumpered its article on the consumer advocates' protest with references to the first "commercially sponsored television broadcast from the Fair grounds"—an Amos and Andy survey of the scene—and the application of Sally Rand, dancer, for a "girl show" venue at the grounds, outlining the fair's commodification of sex and race through minstrelsy and striptease.[237] Finally, women's volunteer roles were tightly scripted and narrowly construed, thematically touching "social and cultural" dimensions of the fair but as a practical matter confined to propaganda efforts. This work historically had accrued as paid labor to local "drummers" and publicity men in past US fairs, and now it was expected to be secured on an unpaid basis by volunteer women, with major media and advertising efforts directed by professionals from Madison Avenue.[238]

Even in these narrow confines, it still took much effort to keep organized women out of the "Hospitality Building" on the fairgrounds, reserved as a perk to all volunteers rather than offered to women's organizations for conferences and meetings, in the tradition of Chicago and other major US expositions.[239] "This is *not* a women's committee," huffed Monica Barry Walsh, chair of the participation division, and "the Hospitality Center is *not* a Women's Building."[240] The center offered cafes, terraces, and meeting rooms for use by committee members and their guests with an English garden décor. Volunteer assignments were distributed through the fair's "Women's Participation" division, chaired by Mrs. Vincent [Brooke] Astor, whose steering committee was populated with well-to-do society ladies. They in turn assigned tasks to local middle-class club women who fanned out in a special "Panel of a Thousand Hostesses." These volunteer women had access to the fair's "Service Center," meeting rooms in the Rockefeller Center in midtown Manhattan.[241]

Josefina Silva de Cintrón was named to this panel of hostesses and became one of the many local women who greeted, transported, entertained, and occasionally housed "distinguished visitors" of the fair, especially "foreign guests" who had language needs beyond English.[242] In the *New York Times* article announcing the hostess panel, the Unión de Mujeres Americanas was listed as both a "local" and a "foreign" organization, in an echo of the island of Puerto Rico's legal status as "foreign in a domestic sense."[243] It was Leo Rowe who put UMA in front of the fair organizers back in 1937, recommending the group over Grant's PAWA, noting that the latter had "not been active lately," and that it "would represent more the native American end than the Latin American."[244] Thus, despite the leadership's penetration of the inner circles of auxiliary female spaces of the World's Fair, UMA made itself felt only faintly and through male patronage. Taking their cues, the then UMA president, Evangelina Antey de Vaughan, invited the fair's head of Foreign Participation to a tea celebrating "Interamerican solidarity and confraternity" in midtown, and UMA women attended similar events with Frances Grant at the rooms in Rockefeller Center.[245] These tracings suggest that Puerto Rican women of New York accessed the fair's workings through a "foreign" rather than an "American" domestic channel; the colonial was unnamed and therefore officially unavailable. The decolonial did not exist. By having Puerto Rico pass as a state and with the Haskell Indian School Honor Guard on duty, presumably performing assimilation and citizenship rather than "colonialism," the fair marked out an exceptionalist, un-imperialist vision of US history.[246]

In the end, *Artes y Letras* put its own spin on tourism, ambassadorship, and promotional work. Through its special editions, editors promoted residents, especially young people, as guides for the fair and experts on New York to Spanish speakers from around the world. *Artes y Letras* reported on the fine showing of Puerto Rican people as skilled consumers of cosmopolitan culture rather than as official representatives of the island of Puerto Rico. Purchasers of the guide were enjoined to take a private guided tour of the fair, led by "*cultos jovenes*" (cultivated youth) who were pleased to give assistance "*a los de nuestra raza*" (to those of our race). Articles proudly described "elegant *neoyorquiñas*" and "*caballeros*" promenading at the fair among the "*gente 'bien.'*"[247] Pride among the youth pushed back against the eugenic undercurrent of the fair, replete with baby contests, beauty pageants, fashion shows, and "typical American" contests that excluded nonwhites and foreigners. *Puerto Rico Illustrado's* coverage saluted the fair as a "living Encyclopedia." Editors remarked with faux horror about the "complete nudity" (*nudismo completo*) of the statuary on the fairgrounds and giggled that the statue of George Washington, at least, was fully clothed. San Juan editors were unwilling to comment more directly about the strip shows and simulated sex acts that met with public outcry in New York, a reminder of which appears in E. L. Doctorow's novel *World's Fair.*[248]

Given the pan-hispanic readership of *Artes y Letras's* fair editions, images and text accented shared roots in Spain and Spanishness. A glowing portrait of "Miss Puerto Rico," Myrtelina Besosa y Silva, crowned queen of the "*Carnaval 'Ponce de Leon' de 1939*," was pictured clasping a fan and wearing a splendid lace *mantón* and high comb, very much the *dama española*.[249] Rather than simply a sop to hispanophilia and *blanquearse*, however, this image must be seen in the context of the public lambasting of Puerto Ricans in general (á la Tydings and the preview parade) and as a counter to the excesses of violence and disorder associated with Puerto Rico, especially in Ponce. Miss Puerto Rico's image of refinement also stood in contrast to the official Puerto Rican souvenir at the fair, the straw hat boutonniere, a likeness of the *jíbaro* "*pava*," with its rustic connotation. Women readers got the message: M. Flores Carrera of Venezuela applauded *Artes y Letras*, echoing Martí, for "creating a publication that vibrates effectively the rhythm of Our America and that reflects clearly hispanic culture in anglo-saxon land."[250]

Conclusion

Though the Puerto Rican flag eventually flew in the "Court of States" at the New York World's Fair, it was under *La Bandera de la Raza* that Puerto Rican women in New York accomplished their most distinctive work.[251] This work interwove several threads within a vibrant Pan-American *feminismo*, drawing on a nonracialist notion of "Our America" and a populist-inflected sense of belonging to the "American people" (*el pueblo americano*) engaged in upbuilding a deterritorialized *americanidad*.[252] The work of UMA shines light on the continuum of Pan-Americanisms circulating in the interwar years, from the missionizing stance of the PAU in Washington (which excluded Puerto Rico) to Latin American traditions that took strength from Bolívar and Martí, then critically reshaped in women's—especially mothers'—interests by Latina feminists active in the transnational realm. To be sure, some of these stratagems, including Angel Camblor's, map onto related hispanic solidarity efforts premised, as Kelvin Santiago-Valles has argued, on "some form of European culture as the ultimate depository of modernity and progress."[253] But contributors to *Artes y Letras* also called out prejudice and racism and organized themselves in opposition to racial exclusivity. "It is exceedingly unjust, this racial preoccupation, as many cases of modest and amiable virtues in persons of color [can be found] and one notes frequently the absence of these [traits] in others of the whitest skin," an exasperated Luz de Selenia wrote in *Artes y Letras* in 1938.[254]

Most of the contributors to *Artes y Letras*—and especially the women associated with UMA and *feminismo*—spent the 1930s balanced on the edge of a contradiction: fostering solidarity via a *raza* that refused to discriminate. In so doing they tried to trace out a third, decolonized space, neither given over to materialism and scientific racism typical of the United States between the wars nor exactly part of the revolutionary or statist political traditions of Latin America. Gender was a significant feature of this work, from Labarthe's construction of a feminized subjectivity for Puerto Rico as a haven of peacefulness and culture in the hemisphere to UMA's assertion of *igualdad de derechos* for the women of the Americas, broadly put. There was nothing essentially gendered about a third space perspective on rights; men as well as women cultivated the stance. "Bear in mind, fellow citizens, that it is not only our representation and patronage which, after all, is not so important, that we are being robbed of," declared Harlem politico Frank Martínez in 1935, "but... something else that has a higher significance in the realm of virtues: Our DIGNITY... "[255] Nonetheless, when the name of Puerto Rico was besmirched in the public sphere, it was Josefina Silva de Cintrón and the leading women of UMA who stepped to the front in defense of the community. This civic sense of right grounded her self-description as "*no partidarista, sino feminista*," though few outside the community gave her a respectful hearing.

The New York World's Fair ran for another year, but it is difficult to track Silva de Cintrón's activities once *Artes y Letras* apparently changed hands as of October, 1939. Though the journal won a Gran Diploma de Honor from the Academia Internacional Americana in Washington, DC, and another citation from a Cuban international press service in 1938, publication was spotty that year, and only two issues, both focused on the fair, were produced in 1939.[256] According to Roberto, the Depression had hit the family very hard, costing them 90 percent of their bank assets. The Cintróns regrouped and ran a small store selling "variety goods." "We lived in the back of the store [and] cooked on a sterno," recalled Roberto, "but it failed." Josefina took in piecework as a garment finisher and even "learned beauty parlor work" and "made money that way." She also took in boarders while Felipe did watch repair, sold "homeopathic medicinal pills," and peddled musical instruments, presumably from the family's collection of theatrical supplies. Felipe also did "cosmetics production at home," likely tied to Josefina's home-based salon. Though sources do not convey all the particulars about the demise of *Artes y Letras*, Roberto hinted that it was successful enough to be worth stealing (though his characterization of the "evil, selfish opportunistic" individuals involved, seeking "to ruin her magazine by fraud and deception," might be overstated).[257] That the Aragón's issue seems to have been the last suggests that the journal gained a small circulation bump with the fair's advent, and tough financial times at home played a part in persuading Josefina Silva de Cintrón to sell.

Puerto Rico's location in the United States' "Court of States" can be read as a gesture of potential "whitening" by inclusion, but ironically the fair's next year accented folk and local color elements in its marketing strategy. The State Department's Division of Cultural Relations urged the promotion of "typical native orchestras" from Latin America, including "Puerotrico" [*sic*]. Anticipating the "Latin craze" in US dance music, this agent continued: "Rapidly growing interest in Latin American popular music and success [of the] Brazilian Pavilion Orchestra indicates such features have great promise."[258] Spanish music became current in the New York and Chicago Philharmonics in 1920s and the 1930s, in part through its "foreign" flavor. Had New York–based dance and music critic Carl Van Vechten discussed what he called the "exotic and non-European" components of Spanish music that "betrayed their oriental origin" and which he analogized to "African negro melodies" at one of Josefina's *tertulias*, I imagine her brow furrowing in confusion, Pedro Caballero offering her a wink and a comforting smile, and Pedro Labarthe puffing himself up for an extended lecture on the purity of the Spanish language throughout Latin America.[259] Little might be resolved, but there was so much worth arguing about.

4
Becoming Mama Maida

Maida Springer in New York City and Africa

If Puerto Rico passed as a state at the World's Fair "Court of States," so too did Liberia perform—or fail to perform—nation-statehood in a range of US venues, like the Columbian Exposition back in 1893.[1] Liberia cancelled its participation in the New York World's Fair of 1939–1940, its pavilion sited, tentatively, in the US "government area" of the fairgrounds. The Liberian legislature's request to the Firestone Corporation to float bonds to fund a stand-alone exhibit was declined by the company. Deeming the expense "out of proportion with the importance and world position of Liberia," Firestone declared that monies so raised "could be much better spent at home than at the New York World's Fair."[2] Entrenched in Liberia since the 1920s, the company made profitability in its rubber plantations a priority.[3] In New York, Firestone represented Liberia not as a nation but as a "jungle hinterland" where the company's "extensive plantations" were located and through which visitors walked on their way to the "modern tire factory" installed at their exhibit.[4] Firestone's neocolonial posture found support in Liberian president William V. S. Tubman's economic "Open Door Policy," a policy echoed in Governor Luis Muñoz Marin's "Operation Bootstrap" for Puerto Rico in the postwar period. Free-trade enthusiasm and heightened commerce—economic, intellectual, and political—between New York, Puerto Rico, and west Africa provide the context for Maida Springer's peak years of postwar international labor activism, work that met a sobering conclusion in Liberia in 1965.

Maida Springer has been appraised by scholars as "indispensable" and a "vital liaison" between African labor movements and the American Federation of Labor and Congress of Industrial Organizations (AFL-CIO) in the 1950s.[5] This chapter situates such appraisals within the gender and racial politics of her membership union, the International Ladies Garment Workers Union (ILG). My treatment places Springer's ILG work in the liberal internationalist milieu that accented human rights, prosperity, and free trade during the Cold War, a milieu very much absorbed and reflected by her union. I follow scholars of

129

anti-imperialism who suggest that as the Victorian era's gendered and overtly racialist frameworks receded sharply in the wake of World War II, a language of nondiscrimination opened up some space for black women's participation in international freedom struggles.[6] Though Maida Springer was highly visible in the media and often highly effective behind the scenes in the labor movement, I argue that ILG officers sharply constrained and disciplined her public voice and political choice-making in both the domestic and the international arenas. These constraints point up the sexist and white chauvinist assumptions beneath the expansive language of human rights and the spirit of pluralism especially alive in New York City, home to the United Nations and lively experiments in multicultural education.[7] I also suggest that gender did not so much recede from transnational realms in this era as become rearticulated, at least in the context of Pan-Africanism. Springer's moniker "Mama Maida," conferred by her African friends and allies, points to a gendered domain of historical meaning and action in this period, one strongly endorsed by feminist scholars of Africa, namely, that family, kinship, and lineage are crucial to understanding African realities of culture, politics, and society.[8]

When Maida Springer's Africa-minded contemporaries sought space outside Cold War suppositions, women and family matters sometimes went missing. "The Negro's fundamental loyalty is...to *himself*," Richard Wright intoned in his laudatory preface to George Padmore's *Pan-Africanism or Communism? The Coming Struggle for Africa* (1956). "The Negro, even when embracing Communism or Western Democracy, is not supporting ideologies, he is seeking to use *instruments* (instruments owned and controlled by men of other races!) for his own ends." He "stands outside of those instruments and ideologies," asserted Wright. "He has to do so, for he is not allowed to blend with them in a natural, organic and healthy manner."[9] If there was an "outside" to those "instruments and ideologies"—and there may not have been very much—it was, in Maida Springer's handling, the domain of family. Gendered language and familial attachment allowed Springer to operate in the tense and polarized atmosphere of labor internationalism and Cold War politics. Carried out under the aegis of the International Confederation of Free Trade Unions (ICFTU) and strongly supported by the ILG, this work involved events and programs that Springer participated in on both sides of the Atlantic. Some of these activities were fraught by the threat of violence, especially in Tanganyika and, as we shall see, in Liberia.[10] In addition to writing articles for the *Free Trade Union News* (an AFL, and later AFL-CIO publication) and *Opportunity Magazine* (organ of the Urban League), Springer attended educational conferences, developed student scholarship and training programs, participated in various goodwill ventures, and supported union and job training efforts, involving almost a dozen trips to Africa between 1955 and 1965.

Unlike the prolific authors Wright and Padmore, Springer spent considerable time visiting and traveling in Africa and had experiences that were rich with gendered meanings and dynamics. In some African settings, Springer was considered "nonfemale," that is, outside society's norms of femininity.[11] Nevertheless, family was the enabling metaphor for Springer's trade union advocacy in Africa, as shaped by Cold War anticommunism. "Communism's lack of impressive adherents in Africa will be because this ideology does not countenance those mores which are the warp and woof of African culture—respect for family life, traditions, and the aged," she told a New York audience in 1959. "Africans see their children as the jewels of the nation. Communism sees children as grist for the future collective mill."[12] Further, Springer claimed a kind of political kinship with African figures like Tom Mboya, whom she regarded as "my second son," and the Padmores, who enfolded her in the "warm familial relationship of the revolutionaries."[13] These connections worked both ways. Across the continent, African friends and colleagues referred to her as "Sister" or "Mama." "She is 'Sister Maida' in more than a conventional sense," wrote Tanganyikan labor leader Julius Nyerere to A. Philip Randolph in 1957. "She is one of them."[14] Fictive kin points to another generative space within the decolonial imaginary that this study has traced, a gendered domain through which Springer could recuperate an African identification in an era in which skin color politics were increasingly scouted. In this context, gender gave Springer some traction to create a viable labor internationalism to the side, if not completely outside, of Cold War imperatives, notably in her 1959 proposal to the ILG for a women's needle trades training school in west Africa. Springer's final efforts in Liberia in 1965 underscore her commitment to acting forthrightly in the interest of supporting African labor as well as to the enduring and significant obstacles—some gendered, some not—to her success.

As the older-style racialism of Blyden (d. 1912) and Garvey (d.1940) lost currency, the metaphors of kinship and extended family allowed Springer to reclaim an African connection. She did so in a gendered idiom, a feminized counterpoint to both Wright's masculinist rhetoric and to the "continental" sensibility to be found in Padmore's political Pan-Africanism.[15] Enabled by the immigrant culture of her union—which Springer also claimed as her "second family"—the language of kinship helped her mediate between the spirited Garveyism of her Manhattan upbringing and the color-blind egalitarianism espoused (if not fully enacted) by her union and her adopted country, the United States.[16] "I have an unending love affair with the American labor movement," she contended in an extensive oral history interview conducted by her biographer, Yevette Richards, in 1990.[17] "My union, the International Ladies garment Workers Union, is a family of some thirty-two national origins," she proclaimed, and as a Panamanian immigrant, she was a proud constituent member.[18] Further, as "Mama Maida," Springer could connect to African people and politics without, at least to her own thinking, becoming compromised by the Cold War polarities that Wright held in disdain. Rather like Amanda Berry Smith, Springer's pan-Africanism was part of the spiritual, poetic, and kinship-based streams of transnational identification within the diaspora.

Thus several threads wove through Maida Springer's approach to work in Africa. First, her roots in Panama—especially women's foodways—enabled her to connect with a broad spectrum of people in the diaspora. Second, the ILG's "social unionism"—an embrace of the whole life of the worker—helped to put feet under her emerging transnational vision. As we shall see, however, ILG worker training and official politics were steeped in super patriotism, colonial ignorance, and mostly symbolic treatments of antiblack racism within the United States, limiting Springer's scope of analysis and field of action. Finally, Garveyite pride in Africa nourished cultural sensibilities like deference to elders, gender flexibility, and the entwinement of political relations with family relations, all of which enabled Springer's development as a practicing pan-Africanist.[19]

Together, these streams of identification made familial attachment into a form of transnational politics. This stance allowed Springer some latitude in an era in which African Americans' US citizenship was newly bounded and regulated, as in the denial of passports to leftists W. E. B. Du Bois and Paul Robeson in the early 1950s.[20] It should be noted, however, that the family sensibility prized and utilized by Springer sheltered her from some aspects of the Cold War politics in which she participated. Whether she knew it or not, Springer's cooperation with the Free Trade Union Committee, headed by Jay Lovestone, put her in the orbit of his connections to the Central Intelligence Agency. Springer affiliated with Lovestone—a key advisor to ILG president David Dubinsky—because she felt confident in her authentic relationships to Africans, maintained an earnest connection to the ILG and its patriotic unionism, and had an independent and long-standing anticommunist views forged in the 1930s, predating the Cold War.[21] Springer made a primary commitment to, as she put it, "share with the workers of Africa the feeling of solidarity beyond their beleaguered borders" (195). "I empathized with the people of Africa," she asserted in her oral history. "I couldn't be objective!" (220).

Maida Springer thus practiced politics in the idiom of family feeling, an idiom sometimes muted in the brilliant flowering of recent scholarship on black diasporic politics in the mid-twentieth century.[22] The pages that follow root Springer in face-to-face relationships with workaday people rather than in the state-centered political registers of the manifesto, editorial, or diplomatic protocol usually favored by scholars of foreign relations and elite internationalism. Hers is a quieter, feminized speech heard only up close, for example, in the whispered and pantomime greetings of taxicab drivers who, surrounded by armed guards, insisted on showing traditional hospitality to their "Mama Maida" at Dar-Es-Salaam airport in 1953, or in the passionate study sessions at the Padmore kitchen table in London, or in the heartfelt letters from Liberia to Brooklyn inquiring after "Mama's" health (179). A transnational sensibility helped Maida Springer steer through a tumultuous international politics that she did not control but that nonetheless, as the *New York Times* announced in 1945, made her "the first American Negro woman to represent American labor abroad."[23]

Daughter, African, Citizen, Unionist

The *Times'* designation of Springer as a "first" and as an "American Negro woman" stands out from a range of identifications and media monikers operating in Springer's life in the public eye. She claimed to have "very little respect for the semantics of race" as practiced in the United States and referred repeatedly in her oral history to her personal "paint job," that is, to the constructed, even distracting nature of the labels associated with skin color (76,

138, 220). Growing up in New York City, Springer identified with a group she called "foreign-born blacks," a category only recently coming into focus in the scholarship on African ethnicity and migration to the United States.[24] This "foreign" identification connected her to the vibrant immigrant culture pervading the ILG. Springer's belief that "your union book was your passport" underscores the attractive and rewarding features of the ILG's internationalist outlook and the mobility it promised (111). Garvey would have been chagrined by her union fervor, but ironically the momentum had been set by his Universal Negro Improvement Association (UNIA), where family feeling, expansive female roles, and race pride worked its way into powerful new solidarities in polyglot black Manhattan. "I didn't know anything about the word 'integration,'" Springer remarked of her growing up years in the city, "that came later" (36).

Foodways and home-based sociability gave New York Garveyism a family feeling. "Many meetings…were held at my house," Springer recalled. "My mother was an extraordinary cook. She would cook fricasseed chicken and friend plantain and rice and peas and coconut bread or coconut cake in the summer when you could get all these special things" at outdoor markets (41). Springer's friend Pauli Murray fondly remembered the "bubbling exuberance and international flavor" of their household, brought together by Adina Stewart's "exotic Caribbean dishes."[25] Springer's mother was enterprising and vivacious. "There were always hot political issues and my mother was always there, and I was with her." Adina invested in the UNIA's Terry Association and was a Black Cross Nurse, parading proudly in the smart uniform, cap, and cape with her daughter in hand.[26] From UNIA meetings and soapbox speakers, Springer heard "compelling" oratory and she came to believe in its potential for "reshaping the world." Outstanding women like Henrietta Vinton Davis and Amy Jacques Garvey—women who, like her own mother, "held a room"—made a very strong impression. Springer first heard about "Back to Africa" and "Don't buy where you can't work" in a UNIA hall. Garvey's emphasis on black autonomy led him to his own version of anticommunism in the 1920s, when the Stewarts were most active. In one sweep against the "whiteman," Garvey warned that "between Communism, white trade unionism, and workers' parties he [The Negro] is doomed…" His separatism earned belated praise from George Padmore as "the first black leader to force them [the communists] to keep their hands off Negro organizations."[27] Such was the migrant Caribbean context of the New York UNIA that Springer did not realize until many years later that Davis was "an American woman" and "not part of the West Indian entourage" (39). When she met Chicago labor activist George McCray, she had similar realization: "This was unusual. I thought only New Yorkers (laughs) were Garveyites and Caribbean people" (179).

Unlike in the Canal Zone, where anglophones were played off Spanish speakers, New York migrants found commonality as newcomers and as "blacks from the Caribbean and Central America."[28] Next door, on west 142nd street, the Murray family of New Orleans mentored Springer and her mother. Springer got her first library card with Clara Murray's guidance, and she helped to "fold and stuff leaflets" with daughter Dora for her father, Atwood "Pops" Murray during his organizing drives with the Brotherhood of Sleeping Car Porters.

The Murrays were part of the "enclave" of people whom Springer described as "culturally like us." In 1927, she enjoyed a "typical Caribbean wedding" in Madame C.J. Walker's Hall in her marriage to Owen Springer, whose family was from Barbados and whom she met in her neighborhood. The couple lived in the building that the Murrays owned on Edgecombe Avenue. Dora and Clara outfitted the nursery and layette for Eric Springer, born in 1929. "Until Mrs. Murray's death," Springer acknowledged, "she was my second mother."[29]

Unlike Jamaican-born Una Marson, who later befriended Springer in London in the 1940s, Springer stayed close to home and family in the 1920s. Compared to her garrulous mother—whom Pauli Murray remembered as a woman of "mischievous sparkle and infectious gaiety"—Springer described herself as quiet, readerly child.[30] Marson, born in 1905 and from a middle-class family, reached into the public sphere through the arts, like Josefina Silva de Cintrón, and she edited her own journal, *The Cosmopolitan*, in Kingston 1928–1931.[31] But Springer's oral history does not convey a strong vision of her youthful self apart from the world of family and neighborhood. Frustrated by the vocational track foisted on her child in New York public schools, Adina sent her daughter to Bordentown School in New Jersey, a historic black institution organized along Tuskegee lines. Maida graduated in 1926 with only a vocational diploma, but she gained two important assets: inspiration from campus visitors like Du Bois and Robeson and a life-long mentor, school headmaster Lester Granger (later head of the Urban League in New York).[32] When Springer marched, Eric in hand, in the parade celebrating the first union contract for the Brotherhood of Sleeping Car Porters in the summer of 1937 as "a *delegate* from the dressmaker's union," it was a watershed moment, one Springer felt was "*inconceivable*" in her younger days (66–67). That same year, Springer decided to become a US citizen. Typed into the blank line on the naturalization form after the phrase "my race is" appeared the answer: "African Black."[33]

Springer joined the paid labor force in 1932, when the Depression hit especially hard. The Springers did not suffer serious deprivation or hunger, but when her husband endured a "massive pay cut," Maida turned to wage labor. Initially, she did piecework going "shop to shop" in the garment district and joined Local 22 of the ILG in May of 1933. The general strike of that year was soon upon her in August, and she signed up as a member of the strike committee. This brief but politicizing experience was a turning point, and colleagues quickly recognized her ability. In addition to the approval of unionism from the Murray family, crucial to Springer's attraction to the ILG was the promise of education, the beating heart of storied Local 22. After the Wagner Act, unions ramped up internal training to take advantage of their new legitimacy and power in the bargaining and contract process. "I was excited and wanted to know more because I felt so limited," Springer recalled. "I *drank in* everything and people began to point me out and a lot of other [new union] people, black and white" (69). In spirit, Springer was not unlike Alabama's Hosea Hudson, whose loyalty to the Communist Party derived in part from the party's educational program that helped him claim himself as a political actor.[34] Business agent Smoliah Margolin, who serviced the first shop where Springer worked, made an immediate difference. "And Margolin was the person who kept challenging me to learn more and to do more," including classes in contract and parliamentary procedure, Springer recalled. Margolin also embodied the immigrant mythology of the union, and he told stories about the "East side ghettos" of Jewish workers and of himself walking to work with his sewing machine "on his back." "He was one of those who represented that history," a history that Springer was expected to understand and, to some extent, identify with as a union member.

Springer was especially drawn to the "intellectual ferment" within the ILG, people who "called themselves the *active*." "Most of them were college graduates," Springer observed, "a great intellectual cadre of young people" whose "families were foreigners," like her own. The *active* included members of the Progressive Club within Local 22, many of whom went on to become officers, educators, and leaders in the union. In the churning days of the mid-1930s, the union was "force feeding" promising new members who were then sent to "different classes in order to develop some sense of history." Not just a job but a "whole new world" and a "whole education" was before her (70). Mentoring and family feeling also fostered a sense of possibility and belonging. Springer would count Leon Stein, editor of the union newspaper *Justice*, and his wife Miriam as "firm family friends." "They were part of that young group of intellectuals that we knew," she stated in her oral history, noting carefully: "I wasn't a part of the intellectual group." Nonetheless, Springer claimed a sense of belonging as a student: "This involvement in the union was my university and has taken me to all kinds of universities and provided me with many experiences" (71).

Maida Springer's long attachment to the ILG derived from a particular set of opportunities for wage earning and training—she called it "the hope and self-respect that it held"[35]—which meshed with values deeply held in her family and community. Her new unionist identity was also tied up with citizenship politics and, however she resisted it, "race." Springer held at bay some of Garvey's racialism in order to enter into a multiethnic, multilingual, and strongly patriotic organization that was the ILG as led by David Dubinsky, president from 1932 to 1966. Over time, Springer became a mediator and translator between groups within the union, rather than someone who "held the room" on her own as an advocate of a "racial" or any other standpoint.

In an emblematic scenario at a plant in lower Manhattan, the ILG bumped up against Father Devine and his followers during a strike in 1937. Springer was called in to translate. The union wanted Devine to recall his followers, called "angels" and "children," who were serving as strikebreakers for the company. Marty Feldman of the ILG "couldn't talk to them, because he didn't understand the language," Springer recalled, he being as stumped by "angels" and "children" as the cultist's people were by a word like "strikebreaking." They only saw jobs. Springer, who knew neighbors and associates in the movement, "gave Feldman a crash course in Father Devine language" (114). She also translated "race" for ILG members. Regarding union outings and activities, women would come to her, "cry and say" that their families "would kill [them] if [they] went anywhere with niggers." Springer personally went to members' homes to talk to families. "Fortunately, I knew enough political history that I could cite simple examples of how prejudice played a part in their lives from the country from which they came," she explained. "And since I was also a foreigner, I think it was acceptable, grudgingly. Because no matter what I did, no matter what I said, I still wore this brown skin" (106–107).

The ILG put Springer's skills at mediation and translation to work in the complaint department of the Joint Board of Dress and Waistmakers. In her oral history, Springer spoke poignantly of her own "failures" and limitations in counseling, especially with the black women workers who were segregated in the low-wage end with hope of little mobility. "I used to say to some of them, 'Look, you've been in the industry X number of years. You're only going to get raises when we renew a contract. Go to school. You don't have to leave your job. Your union book is your passport. Go to the Needle Trades School'" (later, SUNY's Fashion Institute of Technology). Springer took these women's resistance to further training personally; "my failure" she called it, a memory that made her "sad." She felt "lacking in something... [that could] have persuaded more young women to take advantage of what was offered to them as part of their union membership" (111).

In her oral history, Springer neither deeply analyzed the race prejudice in the ILG nor grappled with larger pressures facing the union, namely, manu-facturing's outsourcing in the later 1950s (initially called the "out of town" or, more ominously, the "run away" shops). Instead, her oral history personalized an issue that was structurally out of her hands. The scenario further points to the other deficits in the ILG: its circumscribed engagement with racism in its ranks and the leadership's limited grasp of the global political economy that came to dominate it after World War II. These weaknesses derived from the union's very strength: its proud vision of patriotic "Americanism," an assimi-lationist ethos, and an accent on labor peace rather than contestation, all of which served Springer so well and all the way to Africa. I now turn to a detailed examination of ILG Americanism as a context for Springer's own "passport" to labor internationalism during and after World War II.

Locating Black Women in ILG "Americanism"

Throughout the decades of Maida Springer's activism, *Justice* articulated the ILG's sense of being a union "family" on a multicultural landscape, as a gateway of "Americanism" for immigrants. Americanism meant citizenship rights—especially suffrage—fair wages, and a patriotic love of the United States. "Family" gave authenticity and coherence to unionism through a common-place metaphor. ILG leaders trumpeted the success of an "Americanism" that successfully "assimilated [its members] into the Union body" and, by exten-sion, the US body politic. The union blended work and citizenship obliga-tions with blaring headlines in *Justice*: "POLITICS Is Your Job!"[36] Americanism also had a social side of education and fun that made the ILG "More than a Union—a Way of Life."[37] Union rhetoric was welcoming and encompassing. "We never concern ourselves with the race, religion, nationality or color of our sisters and brothers," insisted David Dubinsky. "We know them only as garment workers."[38] Dubinsky (born David Isaac Dobnievski in Brest-Litovsk, Poland, 1892) thus voiced an inclusive vision of family, one that waved away the kind of racial boundary keeping around family-making and voting rights that, for example, Marcus Garvey, southern white supremacists, and other racial purists would never countenance.[39]

Americanism and its assimilationist cognate the "Melting Pot Spirit" in the ILG were roomy, imprecise formulations, signifiers in the most generous and capacious sense.[40] The union gave new life to the idea of the "melting pot," first voiced by playwright Israel Zangwill at the turn of the century and then declared a failure by intellectual Randolph Bourne in 1916.[41] It drew energy from the excitement of the new United Nations (UN) in nearby midtown. Popularly referred to as the "family of nations," commentators repeatedly analogized the work of the UN and ILG in a kind of mirror of mutual recognition and legitimacy.[42] Photographs of "ILG Day at the U.N." and multinational holiday celebrations of locals reflecting "The U.N.—Union Style" were standard fare in *Justice*.[43] The choir of Local 60-A, the heavily African American dress-shipping clerks' local, sung a "Labor Hymn to [the] U.N." on WEVD New York, on the organization's tenth anniversary in 1955.[44] This linkage was picked up and reinforced by local political leadership. New York State Governor Herbert Lehman called the "ILG—A 'United Nations'" in an anniversary address in 1960. He described the union as a parallel "workshop of tolerance," an "example of how people of different national origins, colors and creeds can work together in vibrant and constructive harmony, in total and fraternal solidarity." It did so by turning "an insurgent force" into "one of the basic balance wheels of our national economy and our system of democracy," much as similar hopes were pinned to the UN's peacekeeping and arbitration authority in the international realm.[45]

The successful mixing of "family," "melting pot," and "U.N." in the ILG social imaginary hinged on several factors. One factor, as Lehman suggested, was the accent on incorporating rather than contestatory political modes, in which "dangerously disruptive" class consciousness morphed into something like a harmony of interests. "Family" like the "UN"—and labor relations—managed conflict through differentiation and segmentation, leaving unequal power relations and hierarchies largely intact. Within the ILG, language and gender structured much of this segmentation. The union organized language-based locals from its earliest inception at the turn of the twentieth century, mainly for Yiddish, Italian, and English speakers. By 1930, Italian-speaking Local 89 was the union's largest and under the leadership of Luigi Antonini, boasted of its own radio show, extensive cultural activities, and active outreach to postwar Italy.[46] The Cutters Local 10, for decades the incubator for the highest levels union leadership, conducted business in Yiddish and maintained Yiddish publications until well after World War II. These accommodations came from and served the men at the top of the organization. When Puerto Rican women requested their own local in 1934, they were turned down, given only a language "section" within Local 22, without their own leadership structure.[47] By 1950, Local 22's Education Department focused extensively on English education, "necessary" according to director Mark Starr, "because of the number of new members who are Puerto Rican."[48] Despite these fractured practices, the multilingual tradition of the ILG was repeatedly cited by the leadership as proof that diversity and solidarity worked together. As Zimmerman bragged during the seven-state dressmakers' strike of 1958: "neither race nor color nor creed nor nationality of origin mattered" on the streets during protests. "Many languages were spoken on the picket line, for ours is a union of many origins," alluding to the segments contained within the whole.[49] The ILG spoke the language of pluralism but politically practiced assimilation. Building on Jennifer Guglielmo's work for the World War I era, I further suggest that within the ILG, assimilation as "whitening" entailed a rejection of radical politics and disciplining of women's bodies and voices around bourgeois standards of femininity.[50]

At the pinnacle of its power in the 1950s, the ILG was 450,000 workers strong, and its highly visible president Dubinsky publicly self-identified as a "foreign-born U.S. patriot."[51] African Americans and Africans might be hard-pressed to identify with the European focus of the union's cultural milieu. The lively internationalism in the pages of *Justice* ran along charity and advocacy lines through family and heritage linkages focused almost exclusively on Europe. Key themes in the 1940s were "adopting" (actually, financial sponsorships) of war orphans, sending clothing and food drives to hungry children in the former Allied countries, and liberalizing the movement of displaced persons into the United States.[52] *Justice* headlines emphasized the spread of democracy, both in formerly fascist Italy and newly created Palestine.[53] Editors enthusiastically endorsed the Marshall Plan with no debate about whether rebuilding England might implicitly or explicitly bolster its empire in Africa, about which George Padmore railed in the postwar 1940s. Rather, *Justice* focused on local and national partisan fortunes, eager to keep up with the political gains of the British Labor Party.[54] The union made a strong bid to shape such an outcome through the American Liberal (formerly Labor) Party, and it played the spoiler in New York City and New York State election politics in the mid-twentieth century. Thus, on the global as well as the local political map the analogy drawn by the union between the ILG and the UN was all too apt, as both organizations gave short shrift to Africans; the latter organization initially excluded "small nations" and "colonials"—that is, much of the African continent—as *Justice* itself acknowledged, though only in a cartoon sketch.[55] The ILG was internationalist rather than transnational; it channeled its agency and political commitment through the nation-state.

As numerous Cold War scholars have noted, US-based white supremacists rejected ILG style Americanism in the postwar 1940s. But in *Justice's* crazy quilt of ethnicities, "Dixie" was simply another patch to be stitched into the union "family." The column "Dixie News and Views" connoted a folksy, local color attitude on the part of the editors, and its relentlessly upbeat and overblown headlines portrayed "Dixie" as part of the ILG family.[56] A captured local was counted a victory, even if it was a Jim Crow shop, and white women needle workers were praised and celebrated as exemplars of the best of the "Old Dominion."[57] Southern swings reported by organizer John Martin stepped around racial exclusion in textile mills and garment shops, eager to portray the region as a place where "union hostility [was] overcome" and that "southern labor [was] no longer cheap and docile."[58] ILG internationalism proved a liability among southern whites and the union's championing of civil rights provoked defenders of Jim Crow in the region.[59] Violence, injunctions, right-to-work laws, and Taft-Hartley open-shop provisions beat back ILG organizing efforts, especially in Mississippi and Tennessee.[60] In terms of electoral politics, white southerners operated far outside the reach of Dubinsky's American Liberal Party and thus could be safely ignored. The conservative commentator Westbrook Pegler scorned Dubinksy's "Americanism," labeling his union tactics a "paternal and patronizing program [that] comes from Europe" and ridiculing his questionable "version of English" (he spoke with a heavy Yiddish accent), linking anticommunism with long-standing nativist and xenophobic sentiment.[61] Southern white conservatives staunchly rejected a range of liberal and universalist "human rights" projects in this period, targeting the UN with determined opposition at the grass roots and the congressional levels.[62]

In its effort to project an ILG "family" that could reach into the deep south, it is of little surprise that black women were all but invisible in the pages of *Justice*. Part of assimilationist politics entailed the "Americanizing" of the working woman, and glamorized, sexualized, and "whitened" images of womanhood plastered its pages with ample space allotted to "the traditional charm of the southern belle."[63] Women needle workers appeared in photographs captioned as "beauties," "belles," "gorgeous girls," "maids," "queens," even "mermaids," pictured in leisure, artsy, recreational, romantic, and athletic—especially bathing suit—settings.[64] These portrayals cut against the sexist stereotype of the wage-earning woman as masculinized. But *Justice's* "Our Women" column featured a profile sketch of a narrow-featured, long-haired female face, and events featuring a "Professional [Hair] Stylist" for female bonding among members likely distanced African American women from the prevailing terms of femininity.[65]

Maida Springer was the only black woman leader visible in *Justice* after World War II; she was also the only woman leader *period*.[66] As numerous scholars have pointed out, the officer ranks of the ILG between 1925 and 1960 were virtually static, a tight cohort of Jewish men, many of whom had roots in the organization predating World War I. In the case of Local 10, family ideology and union power fused, and the intergenerational tie of fathers and sons was trumpeted as the "Cutter's Chips," sons of elite cloak cutters.[67] The few Jewish women in leadership roles included Pauline Newman and Fannia Cohn, whose unionism also predated World War I, and who were, by 1930, cordoned in feminized sectors, health care and education, respectively. Cohn had her budget cut to zero and funded her projects out of family money, and Newman was only marginally visible after World War II. Rose Pessotta actually quit the executive board in 1944 in protest of her token female status, after years of complaint.[68] Indeed, Local 22 Dressmakers was created precisely to divide and manage its burgeoning female ranks after 1919, now empowered with the vote, and to isolate its radicals during the first Red Scare. (Pessotta was an anarchist.) Charles Zimmerman, though beloved, held firm as the Local's manager and union vice president from 1932 to his retirement three decades later.[69]

When the ILG turned from "Dixie" to the southwest, *Justice* carried folksy pictures of Spanish-surnamed women dancing, wearing ponchos, or with guitars, and captioned a headshot of union organizer Carlotta Rodriguez as

"San Antonio Rose."[70] The label "Spanish" rhetorically "whitened" a range of Spanish-speaking women in the orbit of the ILG. As voluntary (if colonial) migrants to New York, who spoke a European language and had active family ties "back home," Puerto Ricans analogized more easily to the ILG's model of ethnic membership and US national citizenship than did those who claimed a more remote African heritage.[71] *Justice* melded Manhattan-based Puerto Rican women workers into a polyglot Euro-American-ness by labeling them "Spanish" whereas Caribbean-based workers remained "Puerto Ricans." Such reframings slid into Eurocentrism that passed all too quickly over the state of "white-Negro relations," and shrank to almost nothing the space for African Americans who identified as black or African. As Governor Lehman put it: "The ILGWU has shown in a practical way how integration can work.... not just the integration of whites and Negroes, but integration of Poles, Italians, Puerto Ricans, Hungarians, Cubans Mexicans, Finns and Slovaks, Turks and lots more." This flattening could normalize the case for black-white integration but also decenter or even ignore it, as in the headline: "Dressmakers Have No Minorities."[72] Thus, Governor Lehman celebrated an ILG-style Americanism tied to European immigrant mythologies and to "American" standards of wages, consumption, and electoral participation, standards that were actively rejected by the deep south and that fared only slightly better in the colony of Puerto Rico.[73]

For their part, Puerto Rican elites—sons and daughters of *La Generación*—hardly smiled on ILG unionization efforts on the island expressly packaged as Americanization.[74] Only dimly conversant in categories of empire, Dubinsky was inclined to view the island as a state, or potential state, and he tried—and failed—to get the 1955 rise in minimum wage for US workers extended to Puerto Rico. Addressing a mass meeting in New York, Dubinsky argued: "You here and your brothers and sisters in Puerto Rico are all Americans. You are entitled to live as Americans," and opponents of the minimum wage were "pleading an inhuman, un-American cause."[75] Accenting patriotism, *Justice* built on FDR's legacy in Latin America with Labor's own "Good Neighbor Policy: Join the Union."[76] After fits and starts at organizing—and dueling in the *New York Times* with Puerto Rico's Labor Commissioner Bernando Berdicia—Dubinsky and Governor Luis Muñoz Marin cut a deal giving the union a freer hand in organizing in exchange for leaving wage differentials between the island and the mainland intact. The result widened the wage differential and sent manufacturers scurrying to the island from the mainland.[77] By 1959, 7,000 Puerto Rican workers, almost 22 percent of all garment workers on the island, were in the ILG fold, portrayed in *Justice* as highly assimilable to the union "family."[78] *Justice* carried the stunning Ruth Hererra pictured as the "*Reina* [Queen] *de Aguja*," crowned in a Labor Day celebration, a holiday from the US calendar now observed on the island.[79]

Given the transnational context of Puerto Rican workers' lives, the spoiler partisan tactics Dubinsky advanced in Manhattan actually exported better to the Caribbean than to the US south. Yet, the overall weakness of free-market unionism ultimately failed to hold jobs for "American" workers. As the AFL-CIO tried to assert itself in the US government's overall anticommunist agenda abroad, they simply got manipulated by stronger actors at the State

Department.[80] Between 1945 and 1965, Maida Springer would play a role in this international scenario as it touched Africa.

Springer's status in the overall gender division of power in the ILG was also tied to managing racism. So-called interracial work was segmented into the education program rather than centered in the contract process. The education program carried "Intercultural" workshops for members aimed at overcoming prejudice, mainly defined as a question of attitudes. "With great ingenuity and speed [the facilitator] got people to talking about their childhood scenes and common customs," went one workshop report. "Soon they were singing and dancing together."[81] Educational talks headlined "Western 'Cultures' Described...as Basically Same" left little room for consideration of so-called nonwestern ones.[82] Indeed, race relations experts split the "daily affairs" of workers off from their "wage and work conditions," in the belief that the "elimination of prejudice" on an individual personal level was a "prerequisite" for challenging "industrial gains...through traditional [i.e., collective bargaining] channels."[83] Often enough, black women were lectured on how to not stereotype all whites as racists.[84] *Justice* carried proud declamations that the ILG had "Jim Crow Powdered," and the leadership backed the postwar efforts to maintain the Fair Employment Practices Commission (FEPC) as a "crucial fight."[85] But just as often, there was simply silence where discussions of anti-black racism might have been. The little ditty sung by members, "What Makes a Good American?" was typical of this posture. "Oh, I may not know a lot of things, But one thing I can state:/ Both native born and foreign born / Have made our country great."[86] Presumably African Americans could identify as "native born," but such formulations talked around institutional racism and virtually precluded identification with Africa via an enslaved versus migrant past. Historian Daniel Katz has recently described the ILG education program's gendered dimensions, with women flocking to dancing, theatrics, and sports, while men crowded into the public speaking and political economy classes.[87] Another layer of segmentation touched "intercultural" and antiprejudice work on the "personal" and "feminine" side of the equation, leaving women to do work that male leadership could then take public credit for, leaving segregation and low wages firmly in place on the shop floor.

This scenario raised expectations for Maida Springer without exactly powering her. During the war, for example, Springer found sympathy rather than active support for her antiracist positions. For example, she declined to donate blood in the segregated Red Cross drives, and instead directed her local to raising money for a blood machine for a "Chinese blood bank" downtown. *Justice* steered clear of commenting on any of this tension within the ILG, which was a very sore point among New York City African American leaders during the war.[88] In her oral history, Springer called the courageous labor activist Charlotte Adelmon, from Trinidad, publicly "outspoken, outrageous," and "Fierce!" in her opposition to the Red Cross's racist policy. "She could cook!" Springer added, noting the women's cultural camaraderie, even as she kept her own protests much quieter than Adelmon's (121–122).

The war witnessed stepped-up activism in New York City. In addition to the March on Washington Movement and the Double V strategy endorsed by civil rights organizations, protests around the death sentence facing Odell

Waller of Florida centered in Manhattan. During the mobilization to save Waller, Springer met Pauli Murray, whom she described as "on fire" for racial justice. Given the important role of labor in the war effort, the ILG pressed its power in the electoral realm, and the Liberal Party tapped Springer to run for office. The Liberal Party appealed to Springer's basic disenchantment with the major parties—"I didn't like the Republicans, I didn't like the Democrats," as she put it, and in 1942, party strategists "twisted [her] arms" to run for a seat in the New York State Assembly (131). She called the run "a real misadventure," because though the party handlers assured her that she would lose the primary, she actually won it (though she lost the general)—plus her husband Owen was a "die-hard" Democrat and her friend Lester Granger, a Republican.[89] Pauli Murray later praised Springer's run as giving much needed "visibility to minority women in politics," an example she herself drew strength from when she ran for office on the Liberal ticket (with Springer's devoted help) in 1949.[90] But Springer recalled the episode "to my shame" in her oral history, a comment that points to her discomfort with wheeling and dealing of politics and perhaps to some retrospective regret for playing along (129).

While she was sometimes labeled and "read" by ILGers as "black," her status as a naturalized citizen and some-time native speaker of Spanish portended broader zones of identification within the union's cultural landscape, zones that did not materialize. "Coming as I did from somewhere else, a foreigner," she explained, Springer's oral history repeatedly identified a need for more education in order to construct and connect with a history that was so important to her organization but that she did not precisely share (154). She also admitted to being "so emotionally involved in the history of this country [the U.S.A.] and that this was the be-all, the mecca for people who were oppressed all over the world" (231). This situation gave Springer a "divided feeling" about ethnic bulwarks within the union that could be reinforced in a prejudicial manner by employers as well as union officials. She explained, "we, the garment workers, were challenged about racial policy" within the union, and noted, "there were officers who really could never see the black worker or the Spanish worker moving straight across the board" into power and leadership roles.[91]

Springer's Internationalism

Given the European focus of ILG internationalism, it is no surprise that Springer's path to Africa was through Europe. Her February, 1945, appointment to the US women's labor delegation to England under the auspices of the US Government's Office of War Information (OWI) fits squarely within the patriotic and media-minded war work of the ILG. Her selection as one of the AFL's two delegates was intended to cast a shadow on its rival, the CIO, allowing the former to appear more progressive and inclusive, and benefit from the media bounce that surrounded the delegation's activities. The papers "always...said that there were two women representatives from the AF of L, [and that] one of them was an American Negro," recalled Springer, looking back. "Not just two women representatives of the AF of L" (147).

4.1   US Labor Delegation to England, 1945. Left to right: Grace Woods Blackett, Maida Springer, Julia O'Connor Parker, and Anne Murkovich.

Photo credit: Schlesinger Library, Radcliffe Institute, Harvard University

If Springer regretted some of her wartime sacrifices for the ILG, none appeared in the press coverage of her OWI labor delegation service. In the pages of *Justice*, Springer highlighted her status as a symbol of progress and integration and underscored her loyalty to her union. "I have been a member of Local 22 for 12 years. During all of that time I have enjoyed all the opportunities offered to every member," she remarked. "To try to do my best on this mission to England is a grand way for me to pay back in some small measure the debt I owe to my union."[92] NAACP commentators endorsed her participation as fanning hope for the Double V strategy, issues Springer endorsed but could not always directly act upon.[93]

For its part, the OWI propaganda mission of "helping hands across the ocean" between England and the United States meshed easily with the ILG's homefront war work and charity support to the Allies in Europe. During the seven-week trip, *Justice* carried regular photographs and articles about the delegates largely based on OWI press releases; Springer's own voice is completely absent. The coverage touched rationing, union organizing, and diplomatic receptions and press conferences.[94] *Justice* readers were to be humbled by British women's sacrifice amid hardship, and goaded by British workers' "pressenteeism" compared with US workers' "absenteeism," so deplored by the OWI.[95] The articles made breezy analogies between US working women and their "British sisters" abroad, tracking the "girl labor delegates" as they confronted the difficult straits of England's war orphans and child workers.[96] The two articles written by Springer herself lost much of their bite as they appeared after V-E (Victory in Europe) day. Her essays "What I Saw in Britain" kept to uncontroversial, feminine fare, mostly travelogue copy about the London blackout, the weather, and seasickness. Some of the diction, in fact, sounds very state department describing of "effective mobilization of manpower and the tight control over the civilian phases of wartime life," especially rationing.[97]

By contrast, Springer's later oral history gave voice to the racism she experienced as a member of the delegation and to the consciousness-raising experiences around anticolonialism that occurred outside of the delegation's official duties. Upon arrival in Washington, DC, Springer was whisked to Bethune House, a property of the National Council of Negro Women, rather than checking in at the Statler Hotel with the other delegates. Now, Mary McLeod Bethune stepped in to translate. Despite the "bitter truth" of the Jim Crow arrangements, Springer was "lectured gently" over tea and pound cake to accommodate the situation. "In effect, she said that I did not have the right or the luxury of popping off and wanting to go back to New York," Springer recalled. Holding herself out as a mother figure, Bethune addressed Springer as "my daughter," and emphasized the "extraordinary opportunity" to travel, investigate, learn, and "come back and report to the Council." "She said *that* was my right; *that* was my duty," rather than to oppose Jim Crow on the spot. "When that dear lady got through talking to me, I felt like a worm," Springer recalled.[98] When Springer received an award from the National Council of Negro Women in 1946, *Justice* took ample and public pride in her recognition.[99]

While *Justice* articles about Springer in England read as if she were a Red Cross nurse or innocuous lady volunteer at the USO, her oral history documents a broader set of contacts with military personnel and activists in London. "I met a large number of Caribbean soldiers in England," she recalled, and "spent a lot of interesting time listening to the soldiers from the islands" (148–149). She was introduced to these men by Una Marson, now a journalist for the BBC.[100] Marson tapped Springer for BBC radio addresses aimed at Caribbean listeners, and she shared her activist world with her guest. Springer made decisive contacts through Marson—who also "cooked West Indian food" at her home, after hours. There, Springer listened to people who "had a vision of the future, and they were looking to the day when they were going to have a country, not a colonial dependency. So it was very good talk at night" (148). During one of the press conferences of the tour, journalist George Padmore sent Springer a note to speak to her later. Padmore, the "empire basher" (and former communist), made a huge impression. The war would soon be over, "[b]ut by this time [1945] between George Padmore and Una Marson," Springer declared in her oral history, she "had a whole different agenda also" (148).

The precise contours of this "different agenda" are hard to document from the extant record of Springer's return to the United States. Her 1946 article "Toward a New Job Outlook" in *Opportunity* magazine, the publication of the National Urban League, suggests some continuing pressures and constraints on Springer's speech. *Opportunity* carried a fair share of Africa-minded and Caribbean-themed pieces in the 1940s, reflective of the expanding transnational consciousness in the anglophone black diaspora in that decade.[101] However, little in Springer's piece reflects any "different agenda" learned in England or of transnational connections. Instead, it was a human-resources-type essay, which contrasted the "spirit sucking" quality of "money-focused culture" with a deeper, yet illusive "job satisfaction," which dogged workers in both the "white collar" and "assembly line" sectors.[102] She plugged the ILG's Needle Trades High School and Institute for Fashion Design, praising its combination of "cultural education with a broad and comprehensive training for employment in the garment industry."[103] Springer pointed to international issues only twice, and fleetingly, first in a negative allusion and then in a strikingly flattened analogy. She opened the essay with an anecdote she attributed to Eugene V. Debs, former Socialist Party leader and now dead some 20 years, who used to tell a story about a "foreign potentate" visiting the United States "from his semi-feudal country in Asia." This king gawked at the "strange" American factory "slaves" who returned to work at the lunch bell, since in his own country, he averred, "They'd never come back." Readers would presumably chuckle at this Orientalist parable, with its stock characters of "despots" and "slaves." Springer also referred to the boredom and empty competitiveness of white collar or "front office" employment typical of government workers in "Washington, let's say, or the British Colonial Office." Springer lumped these two institutions together as part of a "cumbersome bureaucratic structure that threatens to enslave us all"—establishing neither exactly a political equivalency, as a strident anti-imperialist might, nor any particular contrast, as to superiority or faults. Here, generic bureaucracy is the enemy, in need of leavening by "quality" jobs. The essay thus flattens out and devalues paid work in general—perhaps, especially for women—refocusing the discussion from conditions of labor to matters of "personality," "creativity," and the necessity for "leisure time and opportunity to live a complete human life."[104]

Certainly, the Urban League and the ILG shared a powerful consensus around values: an upbeat and assimilative Americanism, a cheerful ethnocultural pluralism, and an antiprejudice ethic.[105] Yet, Springer's essay, with its ultrafeminine accent on "personality" points to a narrow bandwidth of acceptable commentary concerning the political economy of wage labor at the dawn of the Cold War. Her article also gives a fair index to the deficits in training offered to ILG women, which in 1946 featured things like "science lectures," "Esperanto," and "current events," classes outnumbered 2:1 by "charm talks," bowling tournaments, and other amusements.[106] It was a long stretch from an ILG workshop on Robert's rules to the workings of international capitalism and colonialism. In *Justice*, colonialism was only referred to as a subset of racist bias rather than as a crucial feature of expansive capitalism and largely as a European defect to be swept away with other prejudices after the US-led allied victory. Tipping its anticommunist hand, ILG editors tagged the Soviet Union as the "war-mongering imperialist" or "red imperialist" and painted charges of racism within the ILG as "commie smears."[107]

In both its teaching and propaganda (perhaps the two were not so far apart), the ILG foreclosed analytical connections between capitalist economic exploitation and racism; neither were any such reflections evident in Springer's published article. Such links were important to southern black workers like Hosea

Hudson, who responded warmly to the Communist Party's inspiring if vague call to "self determination in the black belt." *Justice* claimed that the union already had Jim Crow "powdered" in its own ranks, and the leadership held itself as exemplars of democracy by promoting unionism for the rest of the world. The union's Education Department led the way as "ILGWU Educational Missionaries" traveled to foreign countries, and its head, Mark Starr, jetted around (often at State Department's behest and on their tab) to Asia ("Starr Teaching Japs Union Democracy") and to Latin America ("Program for a Free Latin America.")[108] These efforts evolved into a cozy, and later secretive, set of operations on the international labor scene involving the AFL's Free Trade Union Committee (founded in 1942) and subsequently, into a series of labor institutes that functioned as an arm of state department policy during the Cold War.[109]

If Springer's internationalism remained muted in the immediate postwar 1940s, so too did her civil rights work proceed mainly in coordination with her employer's political agenda. Her role in the Madison Square Garden rally for a permanent Fair Employment Practices Commission of 1946 is emblematic. Springer's competent assistance with the wartime protests against the Waller execution brought her to the attention of A. Philip Randolph, who was also leading the FEPC fight. Randolph called on Dubinsky and Zimmerman to tap her as an organizer. "Randolph believes in you," explained Zimmerman, "and we are going to release you," conveying a fait accompli. Springer recalled feeling shock and anxiety at this assignment, though she pulled it off very well indeed. Some 20,000 people attended the event at which she coordinated renting space, ticketing, flyers, and some elements of the program (a choir was one contribution). But Springer's own voice was not especially strong in this event; as she put it, she "worked in the community" behind the scenes to get things done (126, 131).

Where matters of national policy were concerned, Springer cooperated with her superiors and towed the line. In 1948, she gave a radio broadcast to London on "Women in Industry." She stressed the importance of union contracts in advancing equal pay for equal work in the United States, and touted her union's "outstanding record in raising the status of women" by virtue of the principle of "no discrimination on the grounds of sex, religion, or race."[110] The idea that that contract—rather than legislation—was the place to work out equity issues was logically consistent with the ILG's opposition to the Equal Rights Amendment, against which Springer and Pauline Newman both testified in Washington as a "threat to women."[111] Thus, Springer's promotion that year to business agent for the New York Dress Joint Board was a reward for her competency, her loyalty, and her ongoing usefulness as symbol of ILG nondiscrimination.[112] Looking back, she did not quite have the language to deeply analyze the forces around her and downplayed her own agency in feminine, self-deprecating terms: "I do not know why it was my good fortune to have been selected to share in these experiences," she marveled in her oral history. "If I had been very smart I would not have dared to do some of the things I did. So I've been lucky on that score. And I have had people with great faith in me" (128–129). One of those people was George Padmore.

Studying Empire

Springer reconnected with Padmore in 1951 when she again traveled to England, this time for study. She attended an eight-month training program at Ruskin Labor College in Oxford University. She went abroad on an Urban League Fellowship, a program they had offered since 1912 in the area of social work, but Lester Granger raised private funds for her attendance.[113] Springer turned to Padmore because while at Ruskin, she was rocked personally and intellectually. Hungry for knowledge but more comfortable listening than performing in academic settings, Springer was taken aback by the oral, debate-centered pedagogy. "I never mastered it," she later admitted (155). In her report to the Urban League, she hinted that the "weekly personal tutorials" seemed to "point up one's woeful lack of comprehension of the subject."[114] In her oral history, she admitted being close to tears at school. "I wasn't able to answer and I was embarrassed and I maybe was nearly crying" (156); she never sat for her exams.[115] To cope, Springer escaped to London to spend weekends with the Padmores, where George's library and his willingness to talk to her steadied and, in effect, trained her.

> George Padmore, I considered, was my PhD education without going to a university for it. In a half hour we would sit down and over a cup of tea and cognac he would—not discuss with me, because I wouldn't have known what I was discussing—but he would lay out to me part of the history of what he called "empire." What his presentation of the histori-cal facts gave to me, one would have had to spend a semester in school getting the lectures. So he was a great educator, and he didn't have a problem proselytizing me. I was a very *willing* subject. (150)

The passage above is notable for the one-way flow of information and her assent to his authority. "I'm very indebted to George Padmore," she main-tained. "He was a liberal education," which colloquially means generous but also suggests, given the Cold War tenor of the times, rather not leftist. Springer also described coping adroitly with her ingénue status in the interna-tional swirl around the Padmore apartment. When Padmore would relay his lists, plans, and social obligations to her and expressed concern that she might be overwhelmed, Springer graciously offered up the following: "George, I can just listen" (151).

There was so much to learn. In the activist black diaspora, Padmore func-tioned as "the elder of the anti-colonial family," in his biographer's words.[116] Born Malcolm Nurse in Trinidad in 1903, he became a journalist and left for the United States in 1924 for education that included study at Howard University and New York University. He joined the Communist Party and did his organizing mostly in the eastern states before the Depression. Padmore also traveled abroad under party auspices, including to Russia, and allowed himself to be elected an officeholder in that country where he could not speak the language. Padmore was good-humored and clear-eyed about the symbol-ics involved; nonetheless, the Soviet state's constitutional ban on racism left a lasting impression on him, and its legacy became a kind of transnational black folk wisdom on antiracist possibility.[117] Immediately after World War II, he trumpeted the Soviet Union as "a unique multi-national State" and a "Multi-National Federated Socialist Commonwealth"—which offered a promising template for a postcolonial order in Africa.[118] He also spent time in Paris and London in the 1930s, settling in the latter in 1935. Padmore earned a living in journalism and founded the International African Service Bureau in 1937, a news gathering agency, while keeping a hand in local as well as international politics (even running unsuccessfully for London city council). He is best remembered as the trusted mentor and advisor to Kwame Nkrumah, first leader of independent Ghana, whom he met through his childhood friend and long-time London collaborator, C. L. R. James.[119]

Padmore left the Communist Party in the early 1930s because, his biographer contends, the leadership refused to weigh in on a major crisis in Liberia, Africa. An international scandal broke in 1929–30 involving exploitative labor practices in Liberia, and the findings of the League of Nations' investigating commission nearly resulted in putting the country under mandate. Padmore would have learned of the trouble through the on-site investigations of Richard L. Buell of Harvard and the widely read *Pittsburgh Courier* journalist George Schulyer. They documented forced labor trafficking from Liberia to cocoa plantations on Fernando Po, a Spanish possession off the African coast, and the traffic's entanglement with labor demands of the Firestone rubber plantation, involving tens of thousands of Liberian native workers.[120] The imbroglio did not resolve until 1936, when Liberian President Edward Barclay essentially stared down the League of Nations through inaction, allowing the mandate paperwork to expire to the indifference of the international news media (by then preoccupied with events in Ethiopia and Spain). The Spanish, for their part, paid a small fine and eventually relinquished Fernando Po in 1956; the Liberian legislature passed laws technically outlawing labor exportation and "pawning" of youthful workers. Firestone extracted a refocused Liberian labor policy more congenial to its plantation requirements. The closest scholar of these events declares them a "trauma" in Liberian national history, with indigenous leadership and the suffering of workers violently subordinated to US corporate and Americo-Liberian interests.[121]

Padmore's 1931 pamphlet "How American Imperialism Enslaves Liberia" skewered US pretension as a "land of the free and home of the brave." He called out its "most vicious and brutal systems of peonage and Jim Crowism, segregation and Mob Law" in North America and the nation's hypocritical stance as "Yankee slave masters" who played "the role of 'champions' of human rights" in Africa.[122] Padmore quoted US officials who plainly identified Liberia as a "protectorate" and described highly exploitative Firestone practices enabled by sycophantic Americo-Liberian leaders. "This is how Dollar Diplomacy operating through Firestone has been able to enslave millions of colonial toilers by saddling loans upon this little West African Republic, through the machinations of a corrupt clique of native bourgeois politicians who prostitute themselves as the lackeys of Yankee imperialism."[123] Padmore had little to say about Spain but raked Garvey and Du Bois for their pretension and duplicity toward Liberia in the 1920s. Garvey had vainly sought to use the country to launch a continental liberation program (declaring himself "Provisional President of Africa"), and Du Bois had permitted himself to be flattered as the American Plenipotenary back in 1924 during the much-publicized swearing in of President C. B. King.[124] Padmore's pamphlet borrowed as much from Martí as from Marx, invoking the Cuban's phrase, "colossus to the north" and repeatedly referring to "Yankee Imperialism." Padmore's emphasis on "national freedom" in this pamphlet is also salient, and he spent much of his energy after World War II mapping nationalist rather than communist paths to African liberation from European colonialism.

Padmore's book *Africa: Britain's Third Empire* (1949) constitutes a major statement of his thinking; it was a text that Maida Springer studied with him carefully. "There is where I want you to intervene," she recalled him directing her from the tutorial in his kitchen.[125] *Africa* was produced as follow-up to the watershed 1945 Pan African Congress in London. This event set in motion the ideas and activist energy leading to Ghanaian independence in 1957, and it inspired many of the figures active in the "magical year" of 1960 that ushered in over a dozen new African nations. Padmore's book offered a trenchant and sweeping overview of British Empire across the continent, "an indictment of a social system—Imperialism—from the point of view of an African."[126] The signifier "African" was something of a rhetorical flourish, not to be mistaken for a celebration of indigenism. Padmore thought grandly, in continents, and by identifying himself as "An African" he opposed himself to Europeans. He viewed indigenism or tribalism as "backward," "tawdry," and even "retarding" to the cause of African nation building and advised that only by modernization and trade unionism would the "spur be brought to national unity" needed to defeat colonialism. Such dynamics would "open the door to Africa's future process, unity and amity and the realization of the United States of Africa," that is, a continent-wide political structure.[127] The "American" echoes of this formulation are worth noting, even as Padmore remained suspicious of the United States as an actor in the world and a resolute eclectic in his political vision.

Unlike Edward Blyden—for whom Padmore named his only child by his first wife—Padmore's Pan-Africanism took an ecumenical view of diversity of African religion, culture, and language and trucked not at all in "racial" thinking. Padmore believed that homogeneity was unnecessary to foster a coherent and stable nationalism needed for successful decolonization. Echoing Booker T. Washington more than the former elder statesman of Liberia, Padmore insisted:

> History has provided us with examples of heterogeneous communities united nationally without sacrificing local loyalties, and there is no reason why the Africans of Nigeria—or, for that matter, of any other territory on the continent—cannot be as separate as the five fingers in things purely tribal, and yet be as united as the hand in all things essential to common progress.[128]

While scholars note that after World War II, Padmore "followed a Pan-Africanist, rather than a Communist, logic," few have commented on his US-inflected sensibilities, or on the very keen hope he placed in the Atlantic

Charter's language of self-determination for all peoples—to the point of urging colonized people to aid in the British war effort and "fight to the death against the Nazi and the Japanese peril."[129]

The Padmore who mentored Springer in 1951 thus spoke in a recognizable if skeptical "American" idiom. His passion for decolonization echoed in the talk of the "many African students" Springer met at Ruskin. In her report back to the Urban League, she called it a "bit ironic" that "lectures on Colonial Development" were given at Rhodes house on the Oxford campus, and she marveled that the Asian and African men studying there would "return home to serve their countrymen with ability, compassion, dignity and insight, thus giving the lie to the Rhodes-Kipling concept of the 'White Man's Burden.'"[130] The "urgency" and "vastness" of "finding solutions to [colonial] problems" took firmer root in her mind in Springer's second experience abroad. At the same time, she gravitated toward her mediating role and reported correcting "African...misconceptions about the position of the Negro in the United States," and that discussions of racial injustice were "supercharged with deep and abiding emotional implications."[131] Springer was defensive when Britons looked down on the United States as a land of "*lynchings*," which she then countered with "some British history about where my father came from" (Barbados, 158). As in her ILG role, Springer translated racial issues across boundaries of country, culture, and political orientation. "The job of interpreting to other countries the dynamics of American race relations by those actively engaged in the process of furthering integration is one which needs to be performed as much as the work of speeding up the process," she stated to the Urban League.[132] It was to this work of mediation that Springer retained her strongest commitment and comfort level. Indeed, even after her work at Ruskin she declared it "presumptuous of me to attempt to make detailed and specific conclusions" about international labor struggles, demurring "that is a job for the expert."[133]

George Padmore was both an agitator and an expert. His *Pan Africanism or Communism? The Coming Struggle for Africa* (which Springer had on her personal bookshelf) is consummately a work of interpretation of African anticolonialism savvy to Cold War geopolitics.[134] In it, he positioned Pan-Africanism in a decolonial third space between "Imperialism" and "Communism," a kind of anti-ideology ideology, never settling on someone else's definition of freedom. Padmore traced out a "neutral camp, opposed to all forms of oppression and racial chauvinism—white or black—[that] associates itself with all forces of progress and goodwill, regardless of nationality, race, colour or creed, working for universal brotherhood, social justice and peace *for all peoples everywhere*." This decolonial stance meant, according to Padmore, that Africans "prefer to attain freedom under the standard of Pan-Africanism, a banner of their own choosing."[135] Further, Padmore's text proffered a history of Pan-Africanism that was older, tested, vibrantly transnational, and a more authentic fit to African needs than the Johnny-come-lately of Cold War binaries. In this history, Liberia is the star. Padmore likely took cues from Du Bois, whose 1940 essay "What Is Africa to Me?" answered : *Liberia*.[136] In Padmore's work, Liberia is not a product of US bad faith or mixed motives, nor is the local elite corrupt and dominated by outsiders. Instead, Liberia is celebrated for outwitting and outlasting the manipulations of European aggressors and the "dollar dictatorship" of the United States. The labor crisis of the 1930s is rewritten as a laudable episode of Liberian resistance to both a high-handed League of Nations and the offer of a US Congress-backed loan as well.[137] Padmore was silent on historic and ongoing native unrest, and it is possible to discern gritted teeth in his carefully parsed support for President William V. S. Tubman (elected in 1946, he had been indicted in the Fernando Po scandal). Stepping around Tubman, Padmore reached back to Blyden, whom he quoted generously on the theme of Liberia as being "triumphant over all obstacles" in laying "the foundation of a State."[138] Du Bois is accorded a prominent role in Pan-African organizing and Garvey, despite his "obvious limitations" as a statesman, figured as a "visionary" and "undoubtedly one of the greatest Negroes since emancipation."[139] Padmore nodded to his marxist roots with a clarion call: "Colonial and subject peoples of the world, Unite!"[140]

Given Padmore's encompassing vision, what might be said of his influence on Springer as a thinker and activist? Several issues stand out. First, Padmore made an important critique of "objectivity" as a disciplining and silencing mechanism used against native or other oppositional analyses of colonialism. Only colonizers "make a fetish of 'objectivity,'" Padmore declared. "No nationalist can be objective where the fate of his country's freedom is concerned."[141] Springer took strength from this insight as she sought to get her own footing in talk of empire. "I don't know any objective people," she asserted to Yevette Richards. "I hear people say they are objective, but they're objective about their point of view that they're putting forward" (213). This perspective helped Springer see through the interested standpoints that sought to limit and discredit criticism of colonialism in general and black voices in particular in the academic, trade union, and activist settings through which she moved. Indeed, Jay Lovestone was particularly severe on this count. A report to him by Springer on Africa initially "read like a manifesto of a member of the I.R.A.," so she "tore it up" to start over. "I think you now have a fair job of observation," she finally told him.[142] In such an environment, Springer's own views had little chance to develop fully. The second area of consensus between Springer and Padmore was around education. "Illiteracy is the backbone of reaction," he asserted. "It is not accidental that the education of the native races of Asia and Africa is neglected, for history shows that as soon as an intelligentsia emerges among subject peoples it becomes the vanguard of the political struggle against alien rule."[143] Like Amanda Smith, Maida Springer shared the modernizationist assumptions of Padmore's position. In this view, the labor movement was a crucial ingredient in bringing colonized people the skills and solidarity needed to leverage a fight against imperialism. "What they [unions] lack in strength under colonial domination," insisted Springer regarding the African labor movement, "they more than make up for in their service as an educational forum generally, and specifically, in their attempts to learn and apply the methods of our twentieth century social order." Despite its handicaps, she argued, "The African labor movement is one of the most important links in our attempts at world accord economically and politically."[144]

Beyond this common ground, however, Padmore and Springer diverged in both style and substance. The differences in each approach—oppositional versus mediating—took cues from gender, of course, but there is an important ideological dimension as well. Padmore consistently named—if not fully theorized—the United States as an imperialist power in the 1930s and the 1940s. But as an "American" trade unionist abroad, Springer felt "home free" and liberated from the charge of oppression: "We [the United States] didn't have any colonies" (174). Padmore's view of Liberia has already been described; in the postwar context, he could only tersely acknowledge: "In an imperialistic age, America, the greatest Imperialist Power, must play lead, and all other interests will finally be subordinated to hers." Padmore approved of increases in the right to self-government in Puerto Rico and applauded Philippine independence, changes he would have welcomed in west Africa. "When you are rich you can afford to be generous," he sardonically remarked. Padmore was unhappily resigned about US status but determined to end the sacrifice of African freedom on the altar of England's desire for postwar prosperity, endorsed by a "bankrupt" British labor movement.[145] The political economy of the United States never came in for sustained critique by Padmore, though throughout his career he consistently called out colonial domination on the left as well as the right. "To fascist and democratic imperialists we declare: 'A plague on both camps!' Africa for the Africans!"[146] In acceding to a US-defined postwar international scene, however, Padmore could claim Maida Springer as an ally. "George gave me the blessing, I guess," was how she put it in her oral history (150).

Like Padmore, Springer also rarely spoke in a "racial" idiom. Sometimes he indulged in references to "typical white man's thinking" or pointed to the "Coloured World," but in the main, he steered clear of the racialism of Garvey—or even the more mediated view of Du Bois ("two-ness"). He was intolerant of positions that smacked of "racial chauvinism."[147] As the International African Service Bureau announced: "Our organization is AFRICAN. But we repudiate hostility to any other race as a race," a formulation that left room, like *la raza* did, for solidarity without prejudice or discrimination by skin color.[148] Padmore had only praise for the "educated or 'Europeanized' Africans" who functioned as in the "vanguard of the national and progressive movements." "This is," he affirmed, "a natural development."[149] He approvingly noted that in reformed Russia, Jews "evince no separatist tendencies. Rather the process is the reverse, one of assimilation," and he predicted exactly the same for "the American Negro."[150] He also defended interracial marriage, "one of the inevitable concomitants of any policy of equality," and Dorothy Pizer Padmore, a white Briton, was his long-standing common-law wife.[151] For Padmore, there was nothing particularly "racial" about imperialism or nationalism or capitalism. In theorizing power, he observed that political domination could even "turn them [the British] into 'natives'—as all conquered people are called."[152] He was well aware that capitalist economic formations exceeded the nation-state but accommodated conventional nationalism for emotional and strategic reasons. Padmore theorized that nationalism's power to underwrite racism, war, and the owning class's right to trap and control capital would eventually recede as socialist reform eroded its economic basis.

Thus defanged, nationalism would become harmless sentiment or an ornament of "culture," uncontroversial and nontoxic.[153] That economic decision making, in fact, became more rigidly fused with the state apparatus in an array of postcolonial state formations in Africa and elsewhere puts in even sharper relief Padmore's hopefulness and idealism.

The idealism she imbibed, but Springer never engaged in Padmore's level of theorizing or generalization. "Therefore you never find any documents in which I made speeches against this, that and the other," she pointed out in her oral history (186). Given the hedged political and social environment she moved in, there was hardly any room. For Padmore, the "acid test of national freedom" was the "right of peoples to decide their own foreign policy."[154] He embraced universal rather than gendered or racial basis for such authority, and human rights-style assumptions carried the message. The African Woman figured as an icon in Padmore's *International African Opinion*. She was a Lady Liberty–like figure with torch held aloft, head held high and confident, with striped robe worn over one shoulder, and a rather more lively visage than her stolid counterpart in New York Harbor. With the African Woman as a distant emblem and she herself demurring the authority of "the expert" within anti-colonialist circles led by Padmore, Maida Springer turned to—as much as she was left to—family.

Maida Springer in Africa

Maida Springer's bridge to Africa came from organized labor in 1955. The year was a difficult one, as she faced personal health challenges that required some leave time from work as well as the dissolution of her marriage. Springer was in demand as a speaker with the Young Women's Christian Association (YWCA) and the ladies auxiliary of the Brotherhood of Sleeping Car Porters (BSCP), and she also played host for the ILG to African visitors when the labor world came to New York, like Francis Edward Tachie-Menson of the Ghana Trade Union Congress. This role enhanced the internationalist status of the ILG in Manhattan, though the mold for Springer had already been set by her mother, Adina, who took in exchange students from Africa during their summer breaks from college.[155] Casting about for surer direction in her career, Springer approached Zimmerman about a new administrative job with the ILG, possibly looking for job security as her district lost 25 percent of its shops and anticipated further closures. She also complained to Pauli Murray of being so "busy with silly discharge cases" that she didn't have time for anything else.[156] As it happened, Tachie-Menson approached the ICFTU leadership in Brussels suggesting Springer as a participant in the first ever Trade Union International Seminar in Accra. At this news, a despondent Springer came to life. She wrote to Zimmerman that the meeting date "happily" fell within the timeframe of her current sick leave, and that she very much wanted to attend.[157] According to his letter, Tachie-Menson thought Springer could appeal to African women, a group he termed "stubborn" and "shallow minded" and who believed that "only men join trade unions." Not only was Springer a "wonderful coloured American lady trade unionist of international fame," according to him, but she had "the magic colour (black, laughter)." Tachie-Menson flattered

Oldenbrook by paying tribute to his "great Organization the ICFTU" and its defense of "the free labour world and for freedom loving people," hitting anti-communist high notes for good measure.[158] He also played to civilizationist stereotypes about so-called backward native women in this appeal and even made light of racial politics ("black, laughter"). Springer was derisive about such matters, rolling her eyes about "my 'passport of dark skin.'"[159]

Springer attended the Accra seminar as an observer. Despite her sponsor's pitch about connecting with local women, she recalled being "the only woman" at events. Overall, Springer found the attendees "very impressive" and serious; she noted the participants' thirst for knowledge and strong work ethic; they "studied very hard" (172). In her "Thumbnail Sketch" of this first trip, likely presented to her ILG colleagues who apparently footed the bill, Springer mostly described her experiences on a safari, commenting only obliquely on labor issues: "I wish I could convey to you the interest of the African workers in the American Trade Unionist."[160] In two articles for the *Free Trade Union News*, Springer averred strong views. "It is not my intention to offer expert analysis or final conclusions about the situation on the Gold Coast," she explained, keeping her remarks to tracing out opportunities for the ICFTU to provide a constructive role, with no mention of women workers.[161] In her oral history, she noted that Padmore had written letters ahead of her trip enabling Springer to meet Gold Coast labor leaders Kojo Botsio and Kwame Nkrumah, future prime minister. Botsio met Springer at her hotel in a car with "flags flying," a scenario that "had everybody's eye's popping and mine, *too*," she recalled (173). Timing and theater counted for much. Just six months earlier, the Bandung Afro-Asian Conference and its declaration of principles—articulated in contradistinction to the Charter of the U.N.—caught the West by surprise; Springer's connections in Accra to well-placed African leaders hinted at yet more surprises in politics for the United States and gave her unanticipated political currency back in Washington.[162]

If Springer was not completely sure what to make of these African connections yet, the State Department had some ideas. In late 1956, the United States Information Service (USIS) approached Zimmerman with the idea that Springer would make a good subject for a film on the benefits of US-style free trade unionism to be shown in Africa. The USIS had long-standing connections to the AFL from the war years; Springer also publicized her Accra visit to Leon Stein at *Justice* and to Jay Lovestone of *Free Trade Union News,* and it was the latter who probably put her name in the hopper in Washington.[163] The planned film was to highlight the union's "[r]acially mixed membership...including Arab and Asian" and feature mild, uncontroversial forms of dispute resolution and contestation—"preferably about a safety issue" read one prompt.[164] It is unclear if this film ever came to fruition, but the propagandistic designs on Springer, begun a decade earlier with the OWI, remained a signal feature for her Africa work. Then world-shaking events in west Africa put her in transatlantic circulation to Africa in the years 1957–1959.

Outstanding among these events was Ghana's independence from Britain, official on March 6, 1957 and marked in an international celebration that inspired a global constituency for black freedom. Attended by leading US civil rights activists like Dr. Martin Luther King Jr., A. Philip Randolph, Lester

Granger, and Ralph Bunche, the event had special power in the United States where African Americans had launched a "second reconstruction" against racism via the Brown decision and the Montgomery Bus Boycott. The leftist orientation of Du Bois and Robeson put them under suspicion, and they were denied passports, though their wives attended the event.[165] The independence celebration was widely hailed in the US black press, but Springer's own article in the *Courier* was self-effacing and modest. She warned readers that what she had to share might sound like "an odd bit" given the intense emotion released by the excitement in Ghana and the media sensation around the sparkling Nkrumah. "I have a nagging feeling that perhaps I have not fully grasped the significance of the colorful, dramatic and dignified climax of this phase of the African revolution," she tentatively began. Her essay built into an oblique homage to some unnamed heroes of independence—she likely had Padmore in mind—when she described how "my mind kept going back to 1945 when I met some of the men who were then, and in many cases still are, the leaders in political thought for African independence." She placed these leaders' success in "western" tradition: they "all had one crime in common, they believed in the tradition of British democracy, the ideals of the French Revolution, and in the Declaration of Independence." Springer also admitted to a bit of immigrant nostalgia; she was "a little envious of my African brother" because he "always knew he had a country and belonged."[166] Elegiac rather than emboldened, Ghana brought Springer to the edges of her own citizenship journey, and she did not have a ready container for the emotions that swirled in her. Standing next to A. Philip Randolph as the Ghanaian flag was raised, she recalled: "I wept like a baby on that evening" (213). If Springer was wistful, she was also resolved. Later that year, she wrote a pointed and angry letter to the editor of the *New York Times* for running an article from a "settler orientation" describing a kind of white flight from Ghana, and she recommended Tom Mboya of Kenya, Harry Nkumbula of Rhodesia, and Julius Nyerere of Tanganyika as resources for a more balanced view of African independence. The letter was not printed.[167] In early 1958, she was still unclear about a viable connection to Africa. To AFL-CIO leadership, she noted that it was "difficult to evaluate the usefulness of discussions of the struggles of the American Negro in the U.S." in African settings. "One can only judge by the amount of time these eager men and women want to spend" together that "in their mind [we are] a symbol of hope."[168]

Soon enough, however, Springer was back in contact with Padmore in anticipation of the All Africa People's Conference (AAPC) to be held in Accra in December, 1958. As a leading light behind the event, Padmore pulled out all the stops in this historic forum designed to chart the course of Africa's freedom from colonialism. Springer recounted his directive to her in her oral history: "We do not have a lot of money, and we are trying to make sure that they [trade unionists] are all here," she recalled. "We expect you to come and find money to help *your* (laughs) trade union colleagues" attend (emphasis in original). Springer agreed, "on one condition": anonymity.[169] At the conference, Springer was again swept by this "extraordinary" and "history making" event. She experienced the Conference as part of a plurality. "I say we, because I felt so deeply involved in and a part of the conference," she recalled.

"For once in my life, I was somewhere I had the right paint job" ([*sic*], 220). Because she was not African, Springer could not be an official delegate, but she threw herself into volunteering by greeting people at the airport, working at the registration table, and "doing whatever I was asked to do." In addition to Randolph, unionist George McCray, now based at the Kampala Labor College in Uganda, represented African Americans in the US labor movement. In these men's communications during the buildup to the AAPC, McCray counted Springer as an "African nationalist," and Randolph observed back to him that Springer and he had "been talking about this question [of supporting African independence] for a long, long time."[170]

Gender figured in a very complex way for Springer at the AAPC, a setting in which she felt Africans viewed her as "nonfemale" (221). Such assessments were based on status dimensions that westerners call "gender" that in an African context pegged age, lineage, and family status to social belonging and identity. "Number one, my age always…made a difference," Springer noted. By African custom, she was accorded deference and respect as an elder in a union movement where youth predominated. "Many of these people were young people in their twenties"(221). "I didn't look my age but I was the old lady in Africa," she later joshed (156). Being "a woman alone, moving around the world" also set her apart from African gender norms (221). Thus, in the heavily male African union movement, Springer became gender neutral or an honorary male. "There were young men who respected me and wanted my support, but they called me Brother Maida" (267). As a representative of the United States, she had "a certain standing" in terms of both prestige and foreignness that aligned more with masculinity than femininity. "I was in a peculiar position in any case," Springer admitted. "A woman, in the labor movement, and black" (173). At the AAPC, these dynamics were especially evident, since African women were in very active attendance. "Women didn't pay much attention to me," she recalled. "I was an observer. I did not sit in their closed meetings." Springer was emphatic on this point in her oral history concerning African women and the AAPC: "I had no voice." "Now the *men* thought I was an important factor," mainly because she had access to "some concessions, some support, some understanding." "I could help move an agenda" (221, emphasis in original). In these male settings, family-like solidarities could also emerge, as Nyerere and others made clear.

From the record, it is hard to assess precisely what Springer made of the issue of gender, belonging, and status in Africa. What is more clear is that like the Ghanaian independence ceremony, she found the All Africa Peoples' conference elating, but also sobering and even daunting. Springer's report to Jay Lovestone at the *Free Trade Union News* was terse; a few paragraphs barely covering a half page. In perhaps a protective veiling of a precious, personally momentous experience, she noted simply that the conference resolutions were "very satisfying" and enclosed only "random news article and pictures" to give him "a window on the proceedings."[171] Her report back to the ILG was more emphatic, yet, still circumspect. "It is difficult to communicate to one of the Western world the impact of a conference held in the capital of an independent African state upon the African delegates, most of whom are still colonial subjects." She implied that there really was no language to convey this reality, and instead quoted a black South African delegate who exclaimed at the generous and respectful treatment he received in Accra compared to his home country: "It is hard to believe this is real."[172]

Springer's rising expectations about the United States' role in Africa derived in part from the federal's government's significant increase in propaganda efforts to a budget of over 30 million dollars in 1959; in excess of a third of the USIS total budget for cultural programming abroad.[173] For its part, the AFL-CIO (joined together in 1955) could wax inspirational about anticolonialism: "American labor, today as always, supports the aspirations of all colonial and oppressed peoples to national independence and human freedom."[174] But in practice, Springer used her voice at home, quietly. Her proposal to the ILG for a vocational school for women and girls in west Africa attempted to get to what McCray called "the ground roots" in his own educational work in Uganda.[175] The school Springer envisioned would be "organized and financed by the ILGWU with the technical assistance of Histadrut [the Israeli trade union organization] and in cooperation with an African government." The purpose: "To train girls and women in the skills and industrial techniques of garment making." Here, Springer appealed to tried and true ILG approaches. "[O]ur union, with its long history and tradition as a pioneer in so many areas of human development, would again demonstrate its social vision and foresight." Her framework to "treat[ ] the Africans as friends and colleagues rather than adversaries" reflected something of the conciliating tone of the American Committee on Africa with which Springer also had contact with during the preceding year at Zimmerman's behest, and she took pains to map her plan on to an "American" style pure-and-simple unionism severed from any overt anticolonial agenda.[176] Thus constrained, Springer postulated that African society was "not unlike our own [U.S.] early development" with indus-trialization in which "opportunities for training of women are extremely lim-ited," a situation remediable through education. In Springer's view, the ILG's female membership would also have "profound significance in Africa" as an example and an inspiration. She believed that such a school would "raise the standard of living" and promote the "internal economy" of the host country, citing "Israel [as] a good model." "The dividends in good will for the American labor movement and the social satisfactions for the African community will justify the investment," she optimistically concluded.

Rather than adopt Padmore-inspired vanguardism or elaborate upon Nkrumah's vision of the "African Personality," which he rang out at the AAPC, Springer stuck with the familiar.[177] She had a long tradition of ILG worker edu-cation to draw on, and Springer now recommended an institution for Africa modeled on the Needle Trades School that she had broadcast to US readers back in 1946 in *Opportunity*. Springer could also point to the ways that the union exported many of the signal features of its "social unionism" to Puerto Rico in the 1950s, including medical services, hurricane relief, and housing initiatives.[178] The proposal perhaps reflected the rising fortunes of Springer's friend Bibi Titi Mohamed of Dar-es-Salaam, where urban women participated in the wage labor economy and had considerable enthusiasm for the union movement in the 1950s, though these conditions were less salient in the rural economy of west African nations.[179] The previous summer, Springer and Lester

Granger, who was also highly enthused by his introduction to Africa in Ghana, percolated about a "workers cooperative" in Nigeria. This idea, focused on cotton and not especially on women, may have taken cues from work by Tuskegee in Togo at the turn of the century, and they even approached Premier Nnamdi Azikiwe by letter about a plan.[180]

Springer's proposal to the ILG also responded to a loyalty question that had been raised on the job, indicating the Cold War tone of internal ILG relations, even among old friends. Just after her return from the AAPC, Jay Lovestone referred to Springer as a "double fanatic" in a curt letter.[181] Such was Springer's enthusiasm for Africa that Zimmerman himself remarked in an off-hand comment that he did not want her to go back to Africa because she might "forget about the union." She was hurt: "On the contrary, it is precisely because of my trade union roots...that I feel impelled to speak on this matter," Springer affirmed, even as she admitted that it was "no secret that I want to work in Africa for a time as an American trade unionist."[182] In a kind of counteroffer to the vocational school proposal, Local 22 recommended Springer for a promotion to education director, a position of no little influence. In her letter to the Local's leadership, Springer described the "good deal of anxious thought" the offer generated in her mind but stated, "reluctantly" that she was unable to accept the "challenge" offered her. Like her vocational school proposal, Springer's letter pointed out her own need for further education, indicating an interest in "training in Israel," where she had toured after the AAPC from December 1958 to January 1959.[183] The vocational school would have granted a high school diploma that Springer herself did not hold.

Springer's school proposal did not grapple with the international political economy of the garment industry, nor did it undertake an analysis of west African sociology of gender, work, and relationships of production. Later in life, Springer evinced a clearer understanding of indigenous African women's history of home-based production, agriculture, and market traditions (212). If she had an inkling of the changing relationship between wage labor, gender, and trade unionism in west Africa—such as has been recently elaborated for mid-twentieth century Nigeria by Lisa A. Lindsay—Springer did not indicate it at the time.[184] Her proposal's appendix was a list of African countries that tallied up to a grand total of population—231,281,189 people—alluding, perhaps, to some future consumer or voter potential. "Any event in Africa, no matter how seemingly minute," she asserted, "will have important reverberations in nearly every corner of Africa." This butterfly wing theory of social change probably was less than a clinching argument for the $200,000 budget she requested from Local 22.[185] Had she asked him, sociologist E. Franklin Frazier would have asserted that indigenous Africans had far more experience in industry than did African Americans, particularly with cooperatives, though Springer knew quite a bit about Scandinavian and Israeli models. "I am convinced that Israel climactically, agriculturally and in the approach of the Israeli to community development can be of great value to the eager African communities," she asserted to Lester Granger in the summer of 1959, but she never got the chance to try.[186]

The Vocational School for African Women stands as a marker of Springer's struggle for a forthright and fulfilling connection to the work of social unionism in Africa. It also indexes the pressure on African Americans to prove their loyalty and advance programs in line with local political and US foreign policy interests. Lacking her own financial resources (like Fannia Cohn's family money), she triangulated US-Israeli-west Africa cooperation to potentially make the school go, appealing to the repatriation and homeland beliefs cherished by some of the Jewish ILG leadership. Springer also appealed directly and personally to Zimmerman's role as her mentor, reminding him of his "confidence and trust" in her and the "unqualified support" he had shown her "down the years."[187] It also highlights the ideological distance between ILG style internationalism that proceeded in close coordination with the AFL-CIO and State Department compared to the expansive transnational and pan-African beliefs that Springer held personally dear and that met with welcome and encouragement within the black diaspora.

Broaching Liberia

In the 1950s, Maida Springer tried on the role of "American trade unionist" in Africa. A culminating expression of this effort was her position as "Africa representative" to the AFL-CIO's International Affairs Department (IAD) in 1960, involving a move to Washington, DC. Springer's participation in the first-ever industrial relations conference held in Liberia in 1965 highlights all the weaknesses and contradictions of both these roles. First, the weak charity component and overburdened symbolics of US labor's presence at that meeting made no lasting difference on the direction of unionism in the country and indeed, the heightened media scrutiny her presence entailed may have actually increased the vulnerability of labor activists who put themselves forward in the highly repressive and violent Tubman regime. Second, the agenda that Springer endorsed at the meeting—essentially, New-Deal-style protective labor legislation—was a woeful mismatch for the Liberian political economy, completely dominated since the mid-1920s by international corporate interests in mining and rubber. Finally, the placating and condescending response of her superiors at the IAD put an exclamation point on her subordinated status in US labor circles. To be sure, Springer understood Liberia to be one of the "ultra-conservative non-Socialist countries in Africa," and there is merit to her assessment of the conference as a *"truly historic* occasion."[188] But that her recommendations went ignored back home and that her main contact, "Brother" James E. Bass, secretary general of the Liberian CIO, wound up in jail for sedition for his activities at a Firestone plantation strike the next year encapsulates the dire situation of the Liberian labor movement and the highly inadequate response of US labor to it.

President Tubman's willingness to convene an industrial relations conference in 1965 pointed up Monrovia's lack of control over both corporate and labor sectors, as strikes in the early 1960s by Liberian workers made international news.[189] In 1958, an independent-minded group lead by Joseph McGill of the Monrovia-based mechanics union broke with the government-sponsored Labor Congress of Liberia (LCL), taking the name Congress of Industrial Organizations(CIO), a clear nod to the more risk-taking sector of U.S. labor movement. The LCL was mainly an arm of the administration (dues went

4.2   "Woman of the Year" award given to Maida Springer from the Delta Alpha Zeta Chapter of Zeta Phi Beta sorority, 1960, in honor of her new position as Africa representative with the International Affairs Department of the AFL-CIO. Left to right are Janice Suderis, Florence Coffin, E'thlyn Lamos, Maida Springer, and Almida Coursey-Barileus. Note kente cloth on Coffin, who was the guest speaker.

Photo credit: Schlesinger Library, Radcliffe Institute, Harvard University

directly to Tubman's True Whig Party) and was headed by the president's son, William Shad Jr.[190] In this environment, most worker protests were nonunion (or "wildcat"), and notable in the highly exploited rubber plantation sector dominated by Firestone. Led by skilled tree tappers, a strike exploded there in July, 1963. An estimated 20,000 workers shut down operations at multiple divisions of Firestone in Liberia for two weeks and wrung demands out of the company largely outside government (or union) agencies, who nervously reported on the "strategic advantage" workers gained from successfully bringing production to a halt.[191]

Firestone had enjoyed a free hand for decades. In the wake of the forced labor scandal of 1930, company representatives negotiated face to face with local headmen to secure their employment needs. Possibly taking cues from the New Deal across the Atlantic, Monrovia attempted to assert wage scales and other reforms in the 1930s and was pointedly rebuffed.[192] World War II did little to enhance Liberia's bargaining power with US corporate and government entities. Firestone negotiated on behalf of the United States to build an airfield (dubbed Robertsfield) to enable its military actions in deliberations so secret they were held orally only, later trumpeted by the company as serving interests "vital to our nation's—and the United Nation's—survival."[193] Referred to condescendingly in *Time* and *Newsweek* as "Uncle Shad," *Fortune* hailed Tubman as "a staunch friend of free enterprise" and one whose open door policy "offered foreign investors complete freedom in repatriating capital and earnings," behaviors that elsewhere in Africa, it was admitted, were "usually equated with neo-colonialism."[194]

Padmore looked ahead to a modern future for Africa, but Tubman's deferral to US economic interests had a quaint, laissez-faire ring to them. His "Open Door" policy echoed John Hay's approach to Asia from the previous century.[195] Indeed, Tubman opposed a continental political organization for Africa and rejected Padmore-inspired nonalignment in foreign policy.[196] Instead, Tubman plotted a new entity through a "Second Conference of African States," which became, by 1963, the "Organization for African Unity," and whose "Monrovia group" remained explicitly friendly to the west.[197] Though a founding member of the International Labor Organization (an agency of the League of Nations later adopted by the United Nations), Liberian officials viewed international affiliation outside of great power diplomacy with caution, notwithstanding their steadfast opposition to European colonialism.[198] Even in this, Tubman invoked Victorian-era affinities: "Abraham Lincoln would understand the temper of Africa's millions whose aspirations have been too long dammed up."[199] Liberia was present at the founding meeting of the UN, praised by Tubman as a means for "the eventual fashioning of a world based on the brotherhood of man and Fatherhood of God." Yet, he also parsed his Victorian clichés, not pressing too hard on universalist assumptions: "If scientific inventions have taught any lesson, it is that we are neighbors, if not brothers, and that each one's welfare is inextricably bound up with the other's."[200]

Within Liberia, the president accented family and comported himself as a patriarch. Tubman, "like the responsible father" as he put it in a radio address, laid out various austerity measures involving taxes and cutbacks in what he called "Operation Production," putting government imprimatur on stepped-up corporate demands on employee output in 1963.[201] Workers had seen little of the profits from the postwar auto boom from either Firestone or Liberia (whose gross national product grew 7 percent in some years). Highly skilled rubber tappers earned a pitiful 50 cents a day (roughly per "task," a set number of trees) but were subject to additional unpaid tasking that extended their workday to 10–14 hours. A minimum wage law passed by the Liberian legislature in May, 1963, raised agricultural workers hourly rate to 8 cents; in complying, Firestone cut food subsidies and the workers struck. The *New York Times* identified the point of contention as "fringe benefits," but food, housing, and medical subsidies were not fringe but essential components of employees' compensation used, in turn, to justify low wages.[202] The strike also took place in the context of falling world prices for rubber, which threatened Liberian government revenues as well as Firestone profits. In short, Monrovia saw the 1963 strike of Firestone workers as a major affront. "Heretofore, proposed changes [in wages] such as this were communicated to, and discussed with the Government," averred a government study of the strike. "This procedure was not followed in the present instance."[203] The 1965 conference was staged in part to reinsert the administration's authority across a number of domains and Tubman knew the world—specifically, the International Labor Organziation—was watching.[204]

From the record, it is difficult to assess Maida Springer's understanding of the Liberian labor situation or political economy in 1965. She had to have Padmore in mind when she noted: "In Africa, as well as in other circles, Liberia has been pointed to derisively as the example of what (Democratic America) wants to foist on the hapless toiling masses."[205] On a personal note, her health remained a challenge; she viewed her travel to the country as a "test" of her own physical strength, though she suffered "exhaustion, hypertension, and [was] a candidate for a stroke."[206] She studied up on the Department of Labor's "Summary of the Labor Situation in Liberia" from 1959, which mouthed vacuous probusiness clichés and contained nothing about the recent organizing or strike activity there.[207] Nonetheless, the Liberian CIO proposed an agenda that would be familiar and uncontroversial to Springer. Their preconference working paper accented reform of "labour legislation" in order to "establish a proper atmosphere for sound industrial relations." At the top of their list were pensions and workmen's compensation. Liberian labor law recognized only two categories of worker: "industrial" and "agricultural." Firestone spokespeople admitted that Liberia had "no legal minimum wage for skilled labor" and job categories were arbitered through the Labour Commission, also headed by Shad Jr. McGill and Bass wanted to reclassify segments of the rubber industry workforce into the "industrial" or "professional category." To some extent, the men spoke for a nascent labor aristocracy who wanted access to "Company Stores" and other perks that were off limits to "labourers." They also desired general rules for all workers, like an eight-hour day and made a poignant demand for "respect [for] the human beings." These issues were among many "inequities which should have been abolished many decades ago."[208] The Liberian CIO's postconference interest in a training center to issue certificates that could help qualify workers for the higher "industrial" wage likely reflects Springer's hand; this was a standard recipe for empowering workers both in the US and in her work in Africa. "This is of utmost importance because management here in Liberia have always regarded the entire working class in this country as being UNSKILLED," declared Bass and McGill. They were "certain that Government would undertake to lend full support and cooperation because it would be an upward trend to offer the quality of artisans for this industrial revolution."[209]

Such "upward trends" were, however, precisely opposed by Firestone. The government-commissioned study of the 1963 strike expressly identified several sectors, "notably rubber," as being "least attractive to the floating unskilled labor force" and pinpointed "increased education" as the culprit. Firestone looked attractive to Liberian workers who faced forced labor in Fernando Po two generations earlier, but times had changed, and the company admitted that the "acquisition of even a base minimum of education is causing workers to seek other employment."[210] For their part, plantation workers exhibited sensibilities cross cut by corporatist and citizenship thinking. "[W]e told Firestone that we know our rights," stated a striker named Boimah Bage, even as he pledged deference and loyalty to Monrovia: "We can not refuse what our Government will say to us." "Government is the only source of remedy that heal this sore therefore what representatives of Government will tell us if we are satisfied with it, we shall be compelled to submit [*sic*]," added a colleague. "We are your children working for Firestone," declared Peter Paye, acknowledging Tubman as "father" and adding, pointedly: "I have been here for about 24 years and no improvement is seen whatever."[211]

The Liberian CIO's agenda as presented to Springer reflected little of this political and cultural complexity. It was, however, one that she could endorse, as it merely proposed to bring Liberian labor law roughly in line with the norms of "most industrialized countries of the world." Glaringly absent from both the CIO's proposed agenda and Springer's initial appraisal of the conference's potential was the fact that strikes were essentially illegal in Liberia. Since the first modern job actions in 1945, government troops consistently suppressed strikes; since then, Liberian law required strikes to be approved in advance by the labor commission.[212] The lack of violence in the 1963 stoppage appears to have been something of an anomaly and a fair index to Monrovia's remove from Firestone's day to day operations. It is worth noting that Firestone's unionized workers in Iowa wildcatted to press their contract and grievance issues during the 1950s with notable success, despite the strictures of Taft-Hartley and a Cold War media environment that beat the drum for labor peace.[213]

At the Liberia conference itself, Tubman backed away from even touching what labor legislation existed. Instead, he pushed "experiment and cooperation, rather than...legislation" to achieve "better industrial relations."[214] Bottom line for Tubman? "Operation Production is Priority No. 1."[215] According to Springer, labor's performance at the meeting was mixed. She alluded to the presence of some "few poor souls who could contribute nothing" to the proceedings, a possible allusion to language and translation issues. These participants were, in her mind, outshone by a "few delegates" who performed "magnificently," one of whom was offered a "job as a Personnel Officers by one of the large construction companies." Rather than sniffing out the cooptive potential lurking at the meeting, Springer singled out "Chief of Cabinet, William V. Tubman, Junior" for praise, as one of the "younger men" who seemed open to "labor's right to be represented."[216] The conference chairman, A. Romeo Horton, addressed his conference remarks exclusively to Tubman—"Mr. President"—and asserted: "I do believe that both Labour and Management would elect to maintain our way of life come hell or high waters."[217] Attesting more to the feeling than the substance of the situation, Springer reported to Saul Miller at the AFL-CIO in Washington that "Management" would not "get over the shock of this confrontation for some time." She anticipated that a "change in Liberia's Labor Policy" was in the offing "with the President's blessing," a conclusion hard to square with Tubman's actual remarks (which she also forwarded to Miller and Lovestone).[218]

Part of the confrontation Springer referred to was quite personal. Though not listed in the official program, she participated on the conference's "Committee on Productivity" as a "Labour Expert." The corporate side challenged her at the meetings. In subsequent notes, Springer indicated that she was "officially an observer" but that "Management...challenged my right to speak with the authorities and official action was taken...which gave me full delegate rights and later [I] was elected to the drafting committee." Without further elaborating, she noted: "No dull moments on this panel." Tubman apparently let Springer speak up against management—so he didn't have to—and then let Firestone play the cat's paw against her. In a later addendum to conference documents, Springer noted being listed in the "final documentation as one of those creatures I abhor (A specialist)."[219] Here Springer deprecated her status as an expert in favor of her more authentic connection to the CIO leadership itself.

Indeed, Bass and McGill needed her expertise and legitimacy for their agenda and made her an ally. At the end of the conference they, as part of the Supreme Council of the Congress of Industrial Organization of Liberia, inducted Springer as a "Knight Commander of the Venerable Order of Human Rights." The gesture highlights the strong ties of Liberian unionism to the historic fraternal movement in the country as well as an instance of African gender flexibility and adoptive strategies. A woman could be a "knight," and Springer's diploma empowered her with "all the rights, power and emoluments appertaining thereto."[220] The warmth of this gesture echoed in the welcome given to a male African American Peace Corps volunteer as a "returning son" in these same years. Carl Meacham worked in a government school in Maryland County during 1965–66, noting that Liberians viewed African Americans as "brothers in several ways," a reception that made him feel "at the same time uncomfortable and proud." Meacham even met with President Tubman in an "uneventful" gathering during which the president "talked incessantly about the same innocuous subject while the rest of us listened."[221] Whether and how Tubman answered Springer's letter of February, 1965, that noted "I am trying many approaches to

4.3   First National Industrial Relations Conference, Monrovia, 1965. Springer is in print dress with beaded necklace, near the center of the group.

Photo credit: Schlesinger Library, Radcliffe Institute, Harvard University

hasten support both technical and financial for the CIO," is not known; most of his presidential papers were destroyed in the civil war that began in 1979. In a postscript to her letter, she thanked him personally "for an evening of good company and talk."[222] One might fairly presume, given Tubman's proclivities and Springer's comfort zone, that much of it was one way.

Much the same dynamic obtained back in Washington, DC. Springer suggested to Jay Lovestone that $5,000 would "demonstrate the AFL-CIO's understanding and solidarity" to the Liberian CIO, and she further recommended sending two US consultants for short-term mentoring. None of this came to pass. She did write to James Bass in April that "Brother McCray" and another consultant would be available for follow-up. In the end, she secured the Liberian CIO $750 for car repairs and some back salary for officers; McGill and Bass's nine-month budget for following up on what they termed the "Apparent Gains" of the conference ran to $40,000.[223]

McGill and Bass aimed high, but Liberian labor's status actually deteriorated in the coming year. In February, 1966, 10,000 Firestone workers struck for five days for a wage increase pegged to the "industrial" rate of 15 cents an hour. The government dispatched troops and shot at workers, killing at least one and wounding others.[224] In a radio broadcast to the nation, Tubman declared that the primary "obligation and responsibility of the Government" is the "preservation of the state," and that workers' defiance of the law requiring government approval for strikes—skipped over in 1963 and now again ignored, according to him, by these new insurgents—amounted to an attack on the government. "The law does not contemplate violence unless violently assailed; the law is a mighty organ and must prevail and be upheld," he intoned, "because it involves *individual liberties* and the security and *safety of the State*," though clearly the latter trumped all others.[225] By jailing Bass on the charge of sedition, Tubman retained full police authority over the laboring population while being able to deny active opposition to trade unionism or even strikes, per se.[226] He announced a new law requiring strict separation of "Industrial Unions" and "Agricultural Unions" and, for good measure, warned listeners against the "mysticism of unrealistic ideologies that are illusionary and fantastic."[227]

In such an environment, Maida Springer's translation skills would have been helpful, to say the least. When Liberian representatives appeared before the International Labor Organization concerning state violence against workers the following year, the delegation defined such outside pressures and regulation as a form of "blackmail" that would never be countenanced by the government.[228] The Liberians probably meant extortion rather than blackmail per se, but both words point to excruciatingly unequal power relations on the world stage. On the issue of translation and its bearing on transnational politics in the diaspora, President Tubman noted that few in Liberia shared even a definition of "strike," since workers apparently made a distinction between work stoppage and "strike." "Isn't this what 'strike' means in English: to hit, to strike, to fight?"[229] A Lovestone informant later reported that Firestone clamped down on unionization and that "many attempts [to organize] have...met with failure." "It is now evident that Firestone Company operating in Liberia does not want to recognize [any] union and uses devices to blackmail...to prevent organization in the plant."[230] Here, blackmail probably named the power dynamic more aptly, since the company could tattle on unsanctioned (law-breaking, "seditious") union activities by workers to Monrovia and fairly expect disciplinary action.

Back in Washington, the AFL-CIO's paltry response to Springer's initiative in Liberia underscored her tightly managed and subordinated status in the IAD. In March, 1966, Lovestone reached out to Springer with supreme condescension about a possible return to east Africa for "what is left of what was the Tanganyika Federation of Labor" convention in Dar-es-Salaam. Lovestone's Europe-based associate, Irving Brown, had raised the idea of sending Springer as "fraternal representative"; Lovestone countered with a recommendation that she attend as a "fraternal observer." "Now, note the distinction between representative and observer," he lectured Springer. "A fraternal representative implies some form of participation, having a voice but no vote," he continued. "A fraternal observer has neither voice nor vote but a couple of good strong and yes, good clean ears and very little use of the lips—none at all, if possible." Springer was advised to take it or leave it, with Lovestone's patronizing closing comment: "we give you the confidence and power to act."[231] How Springer was supposed to "publicize and advocate openly and energetically" any AFL-CIO policy or position in such circumstances amounts to pure insult. She chose not to attend.[232] Within the year, she quit the IAD.

Conclusion

Maida Springer's efforts in Africa reveal much about the promise and pitfalls of transnational black labor activism in the Cold War era. The ILG's limited grasp of African political economy and blinkered understanding of imperialism make for a sobering portrait of colonial ignorance, even as Springer's "passionate feelings about Africa" spurred her on to persist in finding a forthright and workable connection to the continent. That connection had two key components. First was the training and education she received in the ILG in which critical analysis of postwar economic and political agendas of both the United States and Africa—to say nothing of their interconnections—were conspicuous by their absence. Second, of course, was the Cold War, which severely circumscribed activists' ability to cultivate a transnational sense of citizenship that could vigorously challenge the foreign policy agenda of the US nation-state. Much as E. Franklin Frazier posited, Springer identified herself as an "American trade unionist" in the 1950s and the 1960s. Frazier penned a stern challenge to individuals looking Africa-ward in these years. "An increasing number of American Negroes may to go Africa as advisors and specialists," he wrote in 1958, "but they go as Americans representing American interests, not African interests."[233]

What, then, of the other standpoints and strategies available to Maida Springer? Clearly, she struggled—and mostly deigned—to adopt the stance of trained expert or professional consultant. And though she briefly identified herself as "African Black" during at least one moment in her life, she never adopted either a Blyden-like "racialist" standpoint or a "continental" standpoint, as did George Padmore, in order to place herself in the world and analyze power relations. Yet, neither did Springer subscribe to what she called Pauli Murray's "301% American" patriotism. Murray's deep and complex family roots in the United States and her outstanding accomplishments as a lawyer gave her a deep attachment to citizenship and the US constitution quite distinct from that of a worldly cosmopolitan like Padmore or that of Springer, who attached to a New York–based immigrant sensibility.[234] Friends like Pauli Murray and Lester Granger knew very well the toll that Springer's work took on her. Murray even nominated her friend for the NAACP's Spingarn Medal in 1959 to offer comfort and affirmation for her efforts, especially on behalf of younger African unionists.[235] The highlights of Springer's transnational career were accomplished during her IAD years under the auspices of the USAID, and these would never have happened without her: a motor drivers school in Nigeria, a Kenyan institute of tailoring and cutting, and the successful training program for a contingent of African unionists in New York City, pictured happy and smiling in the pages of *Justice*.[236]

What remained strongest for Maida Springer was a gendered language of family that connected her to the African diaspora, a connection she refused to surrender and that she risked much to sustain, even working with the dubious and difficult Lovestone. Her more trustworthy allies, like Lester Granger, wanted Springer out of Washington, DC, and back in New York City, where she would be protected from unspecified "attacks" that plagued her work in the AFL-CIO's operation.[237] "I have been *bloodied, battered, misunderstood*," Springer later declared (197). The situation could have cost her her life, particularly during her abortive trip to Tanganyika in 1957 so well described by Yevette Richards, in which Springer was followed and harassed by the police.[238] Given the intense and taxing pressures on Maida Springer, it is might be easy for historians to miss her deep connection to the African people, fostered over years of visiting villages, schools, and homes in addition to workplaces and union halls, because she never got the chance to really write about it. "To have been welcomed into family and other intimate activities of the African community was a real privilege," she wrote after Ghanaian independence. "In this atmosphere, one was able to sense much that was never said."[239] Her Caribbean heritage, feisty Garveyite upbringing, and proud membership in the multiethnic ILG convinced Maida Springer that she and the union movement could "play a significant role" in Africa, and the encouragement of inspiring colleagues like A. Philip Randolph, George F. McCray, and George Padmore only strengthened this conviction. Of but not in the civil rights upsurge in the United States, Springer nonetheless believed in its "impact on the African mind...such that we get a response from Africans not accorded to our European and British labor counterparts," and she struggled mightily to find a way to realize this potential.[240] The very real constraints on her voice add poignancy to her admission that "a book was one of the things I would never write" about Africa.[241] A skilled and practiced mediator, she sighed over all these contradictions with a characteristic graciousness. "And if [my presence in Africa] would make for some cohesion," she told Yevette Richards, "the least I could do was listen" (192).

Conclusion

Failed Escapes and Impossible Homecomings

This study followed four women's paths of engagement with the world through their writing, institution building, and activism. By attending to pressures of racialization in a transnational framework, my analysis contextualized their geographic and ideological (re)positionings vis-a-vis the United States between 1880 and 1965, its cultural formations (missions, higher education, publishing), as well as its political ones (feminist organizations, political parties, and labor unions). Following Emma Pérez, I argue that their repositionings are usefully understood as decolonial in intent and effect, that is, as critical of and resistant to the normalizing categories of national belonging and racial identification associated with the modern nation-state, including citizenship and coloniality. Their decolonial imaginings frequently took gendered cues, as in the feminized subject position of Puerto Rico as a "pretty daughter" in the Caribbean or the identification of Gertrude Stein with the conquering hero U. S. Grant or a saintly Susan B. Anthony. At its most provocative, the decolonial imaginary opened spaces beyond the binaries of male/female, black/white, nation/colony, making Puerto Rico a political "Switzerland" among nation-states or making a person "transparent" rather than "colored."

As a contribution to transnational approaches in scholarship, these chapters join works that show how even the most nationalistic of historical undertakings, like Reconstruction and the New Deal in the United States, took cues from imperialism and had implications well beyond the "lower 48," notably in places like Liberia and Puerto Rico. Each chapter thus points up the connections between the politics of national belonging and the politics of empire, topics often studied separately, with race and racialization as a unifying theme. Amanda Smith's identification as a "saint" within a putatively race-neutral empire of Christ and her emotional attachment to an African "fatherland" hedged her tenuous claim on US citizenship. This citizenship was hard-won in her family's struggle against enslavement but became severely circumscribed by racism over the course of the nineteenth century, despite Reconstruction. Holiness offered Smith a sphere of action that was both more emotionally intimate and more morally ambitious than did national citizenship and she recoiled from the violence of state-building and colonialism during her mission to Liberia. Also intrigued by divinity and human transcendence, Gertrude Stein's rejection of women's medicine and married motherhood made a critique of racial reproduction and nation building as entailed in each domain. Though Stein held fast to her legal citizenship throughout her decades of writing in France, it could not completely protect her during World War II. Her opera about Susan B. Anthony highlighted the nefarious entanglements of racism and sexism with state-sponsored institutions like marriage and citizenship and made for a sobering portrait of "American" political ideology on the cusp of the United States' rise to global power. Josefina Silva de Cintrón had US citizenship thrust upon her in Puerto Rico during the World War I era. She used the mobility it offered her to build a transnational sense of belonging to "the americas" via *Artes y Letras*, one that was resistant to the colonizing and prejudicial dynamics shot through her citizenship. In the mid-twentieth century, Maida Springer stretched the boundaries of naturalized US citizenship via transnational, family-inflected connections to Africa. Like the other figures in this study, Springer was frustrated by racial hierarchy at home and racial chauvinism abroad. Of the four, Springer probably faced the most debilitating constraints on the use of her voice and political choice-making. Cold War pressures and policies threatened her health and well-being on the job and her physical safety overseas even as she worked for years to build constructive links between the US and African labor movements.

I have focused on women who were US citizens either by choice, by the imposition of law, or by accident of birth. The nature of their ideological and practical attachment to their citizenship provides the context of their sense of transnational possibility in the world. The detailed fabric, the very fine threads, of that citizenship-attachment gives their transnationalism texture and meaning. I offer no predictions or theories as to "strong" or "weak" commitments to citizenship as tending toward (or away from) the transnational. Rather, a transnational framework that encompasses empire brings into view the full implications of modern nation-state citizenship as either mobile or brittle, enabling or restrictive. The issue of race is important for historians of gender because women's bodies and labors are deployed within and across linked domains of rule, communication, and trade that are constituent of nation-states and empires. Marriage, missions, education, medicine, the arts, and labor organizing are just few of the activities that intersect with these domains.

Reading for the decolonial illuminates the ways in which women sought to leverage their needs, interests, and desires transnationally in order to reconfigure pressures and opportunities in their lives. The word has a number of uses. First, it can enable the comparisons encouraged by globally-minded scholars by putting into relief the historicity of dominant political entities like nation-states.[1] Second, it can name standpoints that do not fit neatly into the normative labels of state-sponsored identities and thereby open up obscured fields of power, identification, and solidarity. Finally, the word decolonial can specify a politic within a spectrum of transnational realms and social formations, one that touches back on conventional disciplinary concerns in historiography, like citizenship and racism and feminism. The category decolonial conveys my interest in a group of women who have mostly slipped through the canons of nation, race, and citizenship in US historiography. Their failed escapes and impossible homecomings offer us stories that we can reconsider and learn from in our own time of neo-empire and globalizing capital.

The work I did on this book grew out of the transnational and imperial turns in historiography. It also grew from and bears on my teaching. The main question I brought from the classroom to this work came from a student in my US history survey class on women and gender: "Will this class be taught from an American perspective?" When I read this question aloud to the class—it was part of a "free write" assignment in which I asked students to respond anonymously to a series of prompts, including one to voice questions or concerns about the course—I stumbled to answer it. I was better able to praise the question for its acuity and generative potential than to offer much of an answer, which was at first rambling and awkward. (I can hear my family saying: "academic.") "Depends on how one defines 'American,'" I said. "Do you, students, interpret the syllabus from an 'American' perspective? If so, how would you define that perspective and why?" Is it a matter of technical citizenship, emotional patriotism, or physical residence in a particular part of the globe? The nationalistic temper (or not) of the reading material? I ended with something like: "The course is United Statesian in focus but not restrictively so, and treats the nation state as a political outcome of on-going struggle, a story of uneven exclusions and inclusions over time."[2] In developing courses on transnational themes, I sometimes ask students (and myself) to locate on any world map the "Eastern Hemisphere." Students usually point to a small handful of somewheres for the "Western Hemisphere" (they are less sure if I just say: "The West"). The full title of my US history course on the "colonial" period is "Women and Gender in Parts of North America, Some of Which Become the United States," a title that does not fit in the allotted spaces in the online computerized listing of the course. This fit issue gives us pertinent matters to discuss on the first day of class, like whose perspectives and interests are reflected in and served by the commodification, marketing, and circulation of certain types and units of knowledge in higher education and beyond.

The issue of mapping, labels, and boundaries is as salient in the archives as in the classroom and it echoed strongly during the research I did for this book.[3] In the archives, I encountered the forgetting of colonialism and the erasure and displacement of things "foreign." For example, does the lack of documentation in the New York World's Fair archives concerning the Puerto Rican "cart" in the 1938 preview parade indicate that the episode was, in fact, a sneaky trick on the part of somebody official within the Fair Corporation that was successfully covered up, or that I simply can't adequately verify that the cart ever existed? The Claude A. Barnett and Associated Negro Press papers at the Chicago Historical Society contain substantial international coverage. Unfortunately, the University Publications of America microfilm edition produced in 1985 notes that "[p]ortions of the original collection" were "not included in the microform" version, "particularly the African and Other Foreign Interests series, [as well as] the World News Service correspondence and news releases."[4] Post Thomas Bender's writing of a decade ago, the professional legitimacy of transnational work pins its hopes on "international, multi-archival research," and "[m]ulti-sited, multi-lingual, multi-archival work"; yet, clearly there is much to be learned in English, within the United States, as long as we dig beneath publishers' and archivists' editing (and can afford to travel to do so).[5] In a related strain, what does it mean for transnational scholarly practice—calls to "go to the archives of places we write about"—when the main body of material open to researchers about the country of Liberia is housed in Bloomington, Indiana, Washington, DC, and New York City rather than in Monrovia?[6] Or that about the same number of Puerto Rican heritage people live in the US mainland as in the Caribbean? The conventional boundaries of geography, language, and demography—indeed, biography also—that make academic knowledge visible can break down outside the domesticating container of the nation-state. Such boundaries and labels need to remain part of scholarly inquiry and teaching and could put in motion a new, initially disorienting vocabulary, for students and practitioners. In using a few new words, this study has tried to suggest that colonial ignorance is a structuring if unnamed feature of US Protestant missions, anglophone new woman literature, establishment Pan-Americanism, and Cold War free trade unionism, a feature that also shapes the extant archival record of each and all of these historic endeavors. Might not it figure in others?

Notes

Introduction

1. José Martí, "Our America," in *José Martí: Selected Writings*, ed. Esther Allen and Roberto González Echevarría (New York: Penguin Books, 2002), 295.
2. Regarding empire, Sinha emphasizes the importance of framing female agency as the "outcome of specific struggles in history" rather than measuring women's ideas and actions according to past or contemporary theories or foundationalisms. Mrinalini Sinha, "Mapping the Imperial Social Formation: A Modest Proposal for Feminist History" *Signs* 25 (Summer 2000) 4: 1077–1082. Julian Go refers to a "global inter-imperial field" in "Crossing Empires: Anti-Imperialism in the US Territories" (paper presented at American Anti-imperialism since 1776 Conference, Oxford University, England, April 29–30, 2011, cited with author's permission). Paul A. Kramer, "Race, Empire and Transnational History," in *Colonial Crucible: Empire in the Making of the Modern American State*, ed. Alfred W. McCory and Francisco A. Scarano (Madison: University of Wisconsin Press, 2009), 199–209, emphasizes a dynamic distinct from the one I focus on: "Not simply that difference made empire possible; empire remade difference in the process" (200). On white supremacy, see Marilyn Lake and Henry Reynolds, *Drawing the Global Colour Line: White Men's Countries and the International Challenge of Racial Equality* (Cambridge: Cambridge University Press, 2008).
3. In this extensive literature, most influential on my thinking have been Antoinette M. Burton, *Burdens of History: British Feminists, Indian Women, and Imperial Culture, 1865–1915* (Chapel Hill: University of North Carolina Press, 1994); Kevin K. Gaines, *Uplifting the Race: Black Leadership and Politics in the Twentieth Century* (Chapel Hill: University of North Carolina Press, 1996); Glenda E. Gilmore, *Gender and Jim Crow: Women and the Politics of White Supremacy in North Carolina, 1896–1920* (Chapel Hill: University of North Carolina Press, 1996); Gail Bederman, *Manliness and Civilization: A Cultural History of Gender and Race in the United States* (Chicago, IL: University of Chicago Press, 1996); Louise Newman, *White Women's Rights: The Racial Origins of Feminism in the United States* (New York: Oxford, 1999); Peggy Pascoe, *What Comes Naturally: Miscegenation Law and the Making of Race in America* (Oxford: Oxford University Press, 2009).
4. In this tremendous literature, see Peggy Pascoe, "Miscegenation Law, Court Cases, and Ideologies of 'Race' in Twentieth-Century America," *Journal of American History* 83 (June 1996) 1: 44–69; Joanne Meyerowitz, "'How Common Culture Shapes the Separate Lives': Sexuality, Race, and Mid-Twentieth Century Social Constructionist Thought," *Journal of American History* 96 (March 2010) 4: 1057–1086; Nell Irvin Painter, *The History of White People* (New York: W. W. Norton, 2010), chapters 16 and 24; George M. Fredrickson, *The Black Image in the White Mind: The Debate over Afro-American Character and Destiny, 1817–1914* (New York: Harper & Row, 1971); and Reginald Horsman, *Race and Manifest Destiny: The Origins of American Racial Anglo-Saxonism* (Cambridge: Harvard University Press, 1981).
5. Thomas Bender, ed., *Rethinking American History in a Global Age* (Berkeley: University of California Press, 2002); "AHR Conversation: On Transnational History,"

American Historical Review 11 (December 2006) 5: 1140–1464; Ann Curthoys, ed., *Connected Worlds : History in Transnational Perspective* (Canberra: ANU Australian National University, 2005.); Ian R. Tyrrell, *Transnational Nation: United States History in Global Perspective since 1789* (Basingstoke: Palgrave Macmillan, 2007); Caroline F. Levander and Robert S. Levine, eds., *Hemispheric American Studies* (New Brunswick, NJ: Rutgers University Press, 2008); Manning Marable and Vanessa Agard-Jones, eds., *Transnational Blackness: Navigating the Global Color Line* (New York: Palgrave Macmillan, 2008); Kimberly Jensen and Erika A. Kuhlman, eds., *Women and Transnational Activism in Historical Perspective* (Dordrecht: Republic of Letters Publishing, 2010).

6. Irene Lara, "Goddess of the Americas in the Decolonial Imaginary: Beyond the Virtuous Virgin/Pagan Puta Dichotomy," *Feminist Studies* 34 (2008) 1: 99–127, and Walter D. Mignolo, "Citizenship, Knowledge, and the Limits of Humanity," *American Literary History* 18 (2006) 2: 312–331. Exile and exodus have had long purchase in African American history written in the United States. For a fresh departure, see the innovative work of Elizabeth Anne Pryor, "'Jim Crow' Cars, Passport Denials and Atlantic Crossings: African-American Travel, Protest and Citizenship at Home and Abroad, 1827–1865," PhD diss., University of California Santa Barbara, 2008.

7. Laura Briggs, Gladys McCormick, and J. T. Way, "Transnationalism: A Category of Analysis," *American Quarterly* 60 (September 2008) 3: 625–648. Very stimulating treatments can be found in Rita de Grandis and Zilà Bernd, eds., "Unforeseeable Americas: Questioning Cultural Hybridity in the Americas," *Critical Studies* vol. 13 (Atlanta: Rodopi, 2000), and Nancy L. Green, "Expatriation, Expatriates, and Expats: The American Transformation of a Concept," *American Historical Review* 114 (April 2009) 2: 307–328.

8. Frederick Cooper and Ann Laura Stoler, eds., *Tensions of Empire: Colonial Cultures in a Bourgeois World* (Berkeley: University of California Press, 1997); Ruth Roach Pierson, Nupur Chaudhuri, and Beth McAuley, eds., *Nation, Empire, Colony: Historicizing Gender and Race* (Bloomington: Indiana University Press, 1998); Caren Kaplan, Norma Alarcón, and Minoo Moallem, eds., *Between Woman and Nation: Nationalisms, Transnational Feminisms, and the State* (Durham, NC: Duke University Press, 1999); Inderpal Grewal, *Transnational America: Feminisms, Diasporas, Neoliberalisms,* (Durham, NC: Duke University Press, 2005); Tony Ballantyne and Antoinette Burton, eds., *Bodies in Contact: Rethinking Colonial Encounters in World History* (Durham, NC: Duke University Press, 2005); Tony Ballantyne and Antoinette Burton, eds., *Moving Subjects: Gender, Mobility and Intimacy in an Age of Global Empire* (Urbana: University of Illinois Press, 2009).

9. Anne McClintock, *Imperial Leather: Race, Gender, and Sexuality in the Colonial Contest* (New York: Routledge, 1995), chapter 1, especially page 24; Ann Laura Stoler, *Carnal Knowledge and Imperial Power: Race and the Intimate in Colonial Rule* (Berkeley: University of California Press, 2002), 57.

10. Linda Gordon, "Internal Colonialism and Gender" in *Haunted by Empire: Geographies of Intimacy in North American History*, ed. Ann Laura Stoler (Durham, NC: Duke University Press, 2006), 444, 450.

11. Laura Briggs, "Gender and US Imperialism in Women's History," in *The Practice of US Women's History: Narratives, Intersections, and Dialogues*, ed. S. J. Kleinberg, Eileen Boris, and Vicki Ruiz (New Brunswick, NJ: Rutgers University Press, 2007), 156.

12. Chris Bayly, quoted in "AHR Conversation: On Transnational History," 1452.

13. Stephanie M. Camp, *Closer to Freedom: Enslaved Women and Everyday Resistance in the Plantation South* (Chapel Hill: University of North Carolina Press, 2004) and James C. Scott, *Weapons of the Weak: Everyday Forms of Peasant Resistance* (New Haven, CT: Yale University Press, 1985).

14. For the idea of the native helper and related themes, see Peggy Pascoe, *Relations of Rescue: The Search for Female Moral Authority in the American West, 1874–1939* (New York: Oxford University Press, 1990), and Catherine Ceniza Choy, *Empire of Care: Nursing and Migration in Filipino American history* (Durham, NC: Duke University Press, 2003).

15. Kristin L. Hoganson, "'As Badly off as the Filipinos': US Women's Suffragists and the Imperial Issue at the Turn of the Twentieth Century," *Journal of Women's History* 13 (2001) 2: 9–33; Leila Rupp, "Challenging Imperialism in Women's Organizations, 1888–1945," *NWSA Journal* 8 (Spring 1996) 1: 8–27; Allison L Sneider, *Suffragists in an Imperial Age: US Expansion and the Woman Question, 1870–1929* (Oxford: Oxford University Press, 2008); Rosalyn Terborg-Penn, "Enfranchising Women of Color: Woman Suffragists as Agents of Empire," in *Nation, Empire Colony*, 41–56. See also Ian R. Tyrrell, *Reforming the World: The Creation of America's Moral Empire* (Princeton, NJ: Princeton University Press, 2010), especially chapter 6.

16. Laura Briggs, "In Contested Territory," *The Women's Review of Books* XVII (March 2000) 6: 21.

17. Alessandra Lorini, "Cuba Libre and American Imperial Nationalism: Conflicting Views of Racial Democracy in the Post-Reconstruction United States," in *Contested Democracy: Freedom, Race and Power in American History*, ed. Manisha Sinha and Penny Von Eschen (New York: Columbia University Press, 2007), 191–214; Laura Lomas, *Translating Empire: José Martí, Migrant Latino Subjects, and American Modernities* (Durham, NC: Duke University Press, 2008); Maria DeGuzmán, *Spain's Long Shadow: The Black Legend, Off-Whiteness, and Anglo-American Empire* (Minneapolis: University of Minnesota Press, 2005).

18. Emma Pérez, *The Decolonial Imaginary: Writing Chicanas into History* (Bloomington: Indiana University Press, 1999), xiii–xix.

19. "No Dictionary Entries Found for 'decolonial.'" *Oxford English Dictionary*, http://www.oed.com/(viewed on January 1, 2011). For early works citing Spivak, see Laura E. Donaldson, *Decolonizing Feminisms; Race, Gender & Empire Building* (Chapel Hill: University of North Carolina Press, 1992), and Linda Tuhiai Smith, *Decolonizing Methodologies: Research and Indigenous Peoples* (Dunedin, New Zealand: University of Otago press, 1999). See also Briggs, *Reproducing Empire: Race, Sex, Science and US Imperialism in Puerto Rico* (Berkeley: University of California Press, 2006), 193–209.

20. Gayatri Chakravorty Spivak, "Can the Subaltern Speak?" in *Can the Subaltern Speak?: Reflections on the History of an Idea*, ed. Gayatri Chakravorty Spivak and Rosalind C. Morris (New York: Columbia University Press, 2010), appendix.

21. Marilyn Lake, "Nationalist Historiography, Feminist Scholarship, and the Promise and Problems of New Transnational Histories: The Australian Case," *Journal of Women's History* 19 (Spring 2007) 1: 180–186.

22. Margot Canady, *The Straight State: Sexuality and Citizenship in Twentieth-Century America* (Princeton, NJ: Princeton University Press, 2009), 54.

23. Stoler, *Carnal Knowledge*, 12; Antoinette Burton, "Introduction: On the Inadequacy and Indispensability of the Nation," in *After the Imperial Turn: Thinking with and through the Nation*, ed. Antoinette Burton (Durham, NC: Duke University Press, 2003), 7; Bender, "Introduction: Historians, the Nation, and the Plentitude of Narratives," in *Rethinking American History*, 10.

24. Amy Kaplan, *The Anarchy of Empire in the Making of US Culture* (Cambridge, MA: Harvard University Press, 2002), especially chapter 1.

25. See remarks in the AHR conversation cited above as well as Frederick Cooper, "Postcolonial Studies and the Study of History," in *Postcolonial Studies and Beyond*, ed. Ania Loomba et al. (Durham, NC: Duke University Press, 2005), 401–422, and Geoff Eley, "Imperial Imaginary, Colonial Effect: Writing the Colony and Metropole Together," in *Race, Nation and Empire: Making Histories, 1750 to the Present*,

ed. Catherine Hall and Keith McClelland (Manchester: University of Manchester Press, 2010), 217–236.

26. Delsey Deacon, Penny Russell, and Angela Wollocott, "Introduction," *Transnational Lives: Biographies of Global Modernity, 1700 to the Present* (New York: Palgrave Macmillan, 2010), 2–3. See also David Lambert and Alan Lester, eds., *Colonial Lives across the British Empire: Imperial Careering in the Long Nineteenth Century* (Cambridge, UK: Cambridge University Press, 2006).

27. Following usages found in Gaines and Meriwether, I distinguish capital "P" Pan-Africanists who focus on political, legal, and military confrontation with formal colonialism from lower case "p" pan-Africanists who work primarily in social and cultural domains and have uneven connections to organized political movements. See Kevin K. Gaines, *American Africans in Ghana: Black Expatriates and the Civil Rights Era* (Chapel Hill: University of North Carolina Press, 2006), and James H. Meriwether, *Proudly We Can Be Africans: Black Americans and Africa, 1935–1961* (Chapel Hill: University of North Carolina Press, 2002).

28. Emmet J. Scott, "Is Liberia Worth Saving?" *Journal of Race Development* 1 (January 1911) 3: 277–301, and Luis Muñoz Morales, "Autonomous Government for Puerto Rico," in same issue, 363–366. Christina Duffy Burnett and Burke Marshall, "Between the Foreign and the Domestic: The Doctrine of Territorial Incorporation, Invented and Reinvented," in *Foreign in a Domestic Sense: Puerto Rico, American Expansion, and the Constitution,* ed. Christina Duffy Burnett and Burke Marshall (Durham, NC: Duke University Press, 2001), 1–36.

29. Edward W. Said, *Orientalism* (New York: Vintage Books, 1979), 1–28.

30. Adrienne M. Israel, *Amanda Berry Smith: From Washerwoman to Evangelist* (Lanham, MD: Scarecrow Press, 1998); Yevette Richards, *Maida Springer: Pan-Africanist and International Labor Leader* (Pittsburgh, PA: University of Pittsburgh Press, 2000). On Stein, I rely on Brenda Wineapple, *Sister, Brother: Gertrude and Leo Stein* (New York: G. P. Putnam's Sons, 1996). Edna Acosta-Belén, "Silva de Cintrón, Josefina Pepiña (1885–1986)" in *Latinas in the United States: A Historical Encyclopedia*, vol. 3, ed. Vicki L. Ruiz and Virginia Sánchez Korrol (Bloomington: Indiana University Press, 2006), 682–683; anonymous reader reports in author's possession.

31. Patricia A. Schechter, *Ida B. Wells-Barnett and American Reform 1880–1930* (Chapel Hill: University of North Carolina Press, 2001), 187, 213; Alfred M. Duster, ed., *Crusade for Justice: The Autobiography of Ida B. Wells-Barnett* (Chicago, IL: University of Chicago Press, 1971), 373.

32. Gertrude Stein, "Picasso [1938]," in *Picasso: The Complete Writings,* ed. Edward Burns (New York: Liveright, 1970), 34.

33. Gaines, *American Africans in Ghana*; Brenda Gayle Plummer, *Rising Wind: Black Americans and US Foreign Affairs, 1935–1960* (Chapel Hill: University of North Carolina Press, 1996); Brenda Gayle Plummer, ed., *Window on Freedom: Race, Civil Rights, and Foreign Affairs, 1945–1988* (Chapel Hill: University of North Carolina Press, 2003); Mary L. Dudziak, *Cold War Civil Rights: Race and the Image of American Democracy* (Princeton, NJ: Princeton University Press, 2000); Penny M. Von Eschen, *Race against Empire: Black Americans and Anticolonialism, 1937–1957* (Ithaca, NY: Cornell University Press, 1997).

34. Bender, "Historians, the Nation, and the Plentitude of Narratives," 1.

1   A Kind of Privileged Character

1. Mrs. Amanda Smith, *An Autobiography: The Story of the Lord's Dealings with Mrs. Amanda Smith, the Colored Evangelist: Containing an Account of Her Life Work of Faith, and Her Travels in America, England, Ireland, Scotland, India, and Africa as*

an Independent Missionary [Chicago: Meyer & Brother Publishers, 1893] introduction by Jualynne E. Dodson (New York: Oxford University Press, 1988), 414–415 (emphasis in original). Hereafter, all references to this text will be to this edition, cited parenthetically.

2. Claude A. Clegg, III, *The Price of Liberty: African Americans and the Making of Liberia* (Chapel Hill: University of North Carolina Press, 2004), 6. See also Marie Tyler-McGraw, *An African Republic: Black & White Virginians in the Making of Liberia* (Chapel Hill: University of North Carolina Press, 2007), and Bruce Dorsey, "The Transnational Lives of African American Colonists in Liberia," in *Transnational Lives: Biographies of Global Modernity, 1700 to the Present*, ed. Desley Deacon, Penny Rusell, and Angela Woollacott (New York: Palgrave Macmillan, 2010), 171–182.

3. Elsa Barkley Brown, "To Catch the Vision of Freedom: African American Women's Political History, 1865–1880," in *African American Women and the Vote, 1837–1965*, ed. Ann D. Gordon, et al. (Amherst: University of Massachusetts Press, 1997), 66–99; Tera W. Hunter, *To 'Joy My Freedom: Southern Black Women's Lives and Labors after the Civil War* (Cambridge: Harvard University Press, 1997); Glenda Gilmore, *Gender and Jim Crow: Women and the Politics of White Supremacy in North Carolina, 1896–1920* (Chapel Hill: University of North Carolina Press, 1996); Patricia A. Schechter, *Ida B. Wells-Barnett and American Reform, 1880–1930* (Chapel Hill: University of North Carolina Press, 2001).

4. A. N. Cadbury, *The Life of Amanda Smith: The African Sybil, the Christian Saint* (Birmingham, England: Cornish Brothers, 1916); Edith Deen, *Great Women of the Christian Faith* (New York: Harper, 1959); E. F. Harvey, ed. *Amanda Smith: The King's Daughter* (Hampton, TN: Harvey & Tait, 1977); Nancy Hardesty and Adrienne Israel, "Amanda Berry Smith: A 'Downright Outright Christian,'" in *Spirituality and Social Responsibility: Vocational Vision of Women in the United Methodist Tradition*, ed. Rosemary Skinner Keller (Nashville, TN: Abingdon Press, 1993), 61–79.

5. Darlene Clark Hine and Kathleen Thompson, *A Shining Thread of Hope: The History of Black Women in America* (New York: Broadway Books, 1998); Beverly Guy Sheftall, ed., *Words of Fire: An Anthology of African-American Feminist Thought* (New York: The New Press,, 1995); Paula Giddings, *When and Where I Enter: The Impact of Black Women on Race and Sex in America* (New York: W. Morrow, 1984); Nell Irvin Painter, *Creating Black Americans: African-American History and Its Meanings, 1619 to the Present* (New York: Oxford University Press, 2006).

6. Smith is not mentioned in C. S. Smith, *A History of the African Methodist Episcopal Church...from 1856 to 1922* (Philadelphia Book Concern of the AME Church 1922), electronic edition http://docsouth.unc.edu/church/cssmith/smith.html.

7. Hallie Q. Brown, "Amanda Smith, 1837–1915," in *Homespun Heroines and Other Women of Distinction*, intro. Randall K. Burkett ([1926] New York: Oxford University Press, 1998), 128–132.

8. Adrienne Israel, *Amanda Berry Smith: From Washerwoman to Evangelist* (Lanham, MD: Scarecrow Press, 1998), and Michelle Mitchell, *Righteous Propagation: African Americans and the Politics of Racial Destiny after Reconstruction* (Chapel Hill, NC: University of North Carolina Press, 2004), chapter 1.

9. Mia Bay, "The Improbable Ida B. Wells," *Reviews in American History* 30 (2002): 439–444.

10. "Holiness," *Evangelical Dictionary of Theology*, ed. Walter A. Elwell (Grand Rapids, MI: Baker Book House, 1984), 375–376.

11. Israel, *Amanda Berry Smith*, 154.

12. Nell Irvin Painter, *Sojourner Truth: A Life, a Symbol* (New York: W. W. Norton, 1996); Painter, "Sojourner Truth's Knowing and Becoming Known," *Journal of American History* 81 (September 1994) 2: 461–492.

13. Smith's narrative put the date in 1870 or 71, but the General Conference met in Nashville in May, 1872. Her appearance is not noted in Smith, *History of the African Methodist Episcopal Church*, 99–103. The Fisk singers numbered ten in 1875, the third group of "Jubilees" according to Andrew Ward. See Andrew Ward, *Dark Midnight When I Rise: The Story of the Jubilee Singers Who Introduced the World to the Music of Black America* (New York: Farrar Strauss, 2000). Smith's favorite hymn, "A Little More Faith in Jesus," was also a Jubilee staple. See J. B. T Marsh, *The Story of the Jubilee Singers, with Their Songs* (Boston, MA: Houghton, Mifflin and Co., 1880), 178.

14. Stephen Ward Angell, "The Controversy over Women's Ministry in the African Methodist Episcopal Church during the 1880s: The Case of Sarah Ann Hughes," in *This Far by Faith: Readings in African American Women's Religious Biography*, ed. Judith Weisenfeld and Richard Newman (New York: Routledge, 1996), 94–95.

15. James Campbell, *Songs of Zion: The African Methodist Episcopal Church in the United States and South Africa* (New York: Oxford University Press, 1995), 46.

16. Cheryl Townsend Gilkes, *"If It Wasn't for the Women": Black Women's Experience and Womanist Culture in Church and Community* (Maryknoll, NY: Orbis Books, 2001), 4, 68. See also Susie C. Stanley, *Holy Boldness: Women Preachers' Autobiographies and the Sanctified Self* (Knoxville: University of Tennessee, 2002), chapter 5, especially 112–128.

17. Smith, *An Autobiography*, "at great liberty," 267, 76, 301, 322, 340, 372, 383, 401, 157, 210; "perfect freedom," 226, 239. Such language was certainly a convention among evangelicals of the day.

18. "Letter from Amanda Smith," *Christian Standard,* June 3, 1882.

19. "Amanda Smith," *Christian Standard*, July 19, 1888; Smith, *An Autobiography*, 185, 223.

20. Israel, *Amanda Berry Smith*, 11–13.

21. The area to the south of Washington Square teemed with religious meeting houses and churches, including three "African" congregations—Methodist, Episcopal, and Baptist. Roger H. Pidgeon, *Atlas of the City of New York* (New York: E. Robinson, 1881), plate 18; Dripps New York City Maps, (New York: M. Dripps, 1864), plates 6 and 7. Israel, *Amanda Berry Smith*, 38–40.

22. Smith, *An Autobiography*, 299; Israel, *Amanda Berry Smith*, 63–64. Williams, *Black Americans and the Evangelization of Africa*, 93.

23. "Letter from Amanda Smith," *Christian Standard*, August 2, 1884.

24. "Amanda Smith," *Guide to Holiness* (November 1879): 150. See also "Amanda Smith," *Christian Standard* July 19, 1888; an 1882 text reprinted in the *Christian Standard* seems closer to the version in her later autobiography. See "Experience of Amanda Smith," *Christian Standard*, February 4, 1882; and Brown, "Amanda Smith," in *Homespun Heroines*, 128.

25. Israel, *Amanda Berry Smith*, 61.

26. See "A Modern Pentacost: Embracing a Record of the Sixteenth National Camp-Meeting for the Promotion of Holiness, held at Landisville, Pa., July 23 to August 1, 1873," ed. Rev. Adam Wallace (Salem, OH: Convention Book Store, n.d.), 203–204. "Sister Smith" conducted a meeting "for the benefit of the colored people, quite a number of whom were in attendance as waiters, and some as visitors at the encampment."

27. See, for example, train car discrimination notes in *The Helper* (August 1903): 4; and Jim Crow conditions in the south, "Jottings by the Way," *The Helper* (September 1902): 5.

28. Williams, *Black Americans and the Evangelization of Africa*, 93, suggests that Smith "identified with whites" and was "accommodating in her social attitudes."

29. From *African Repository* (October 1875), quoted in Debra Newman, "The Emergence of Liberian Women," PhD diss., Howard University, 1984, 352.
30. "Sunday Sermon Delivered by Amanda Berry Smith," (1877) in Israel, *Amanda Berry Smith* (appendix), 161.
31. Israel, *Amanda Berry Smith*, 60.
32. Nell Irvin Painter, *Exodusters: Black Migration to Kansas after Reconstruction* (New York: Knopf 1977), chapter 11; Walter L. Williams, *Black Americans and the Evangelization of Africa, 1877–1900* (University of Wisconsin Press, 1982), 40; and Mitchell, *Righteous Propagation*, 19–49.
33. Tyler-McGraw, *An African Republic*, 173.
34. Jane Hunter, *The Gospel of Gentility: American Women Missionaries in Turn-of-the-Century China* (New Haven, CT: Yale University Press, 1984); Ian Tyrell, *Woman's World/Woman's Empire: The Woman's Christian Temperance Union in International Perspective* (Chapel Hill: University of North Carolina Press, 1991), 101–102.
35. Smith, *History of the African Methodist Episcopal Church*, 221–223.
36. Eunjin Park, *"White" Americans in "Black" Africa: Black and White American Methodist Missionaries in Liberia, 1820–1875* (New York: Routledge, 2001); Sylvia M. Jacobs, ed., *Black Americans and the Missionary Movement in Africa* (Westport, CT: Greenwood Press, 1982).
37. Williams, *Black Americans and the Evangelization of Africa*, appendix D.
38. C. T. O. King to William Coppinger, October 4, 1887. Records of the American Colonization Society, Incoming Correspondence, 1819–1917; Letters from Liberia, 1833–1917, microfilm edition, hereafter, RACS. For the northern context, see Edward J. Blum, *Reforging the White Republic: Race, Religion and American Nationalism* (Baton Rouge: Louisiana State University Press, 2005), especially chapter 6.
39. This is Park's conclusion as well as that of Donald F. Roth, "The 'Black Man's Burden': The Racial Background of Afro-American Missionaries and Africa," in *Black Americans and the Missionary Movement in Africa*, 34.
40. J. R. Oldfield, "The Protestant Episcopal Church, Black Nationalists, and the Expansion of the West African Missionary Field, 1851–1871," *Church History* 57 (1988) 1: 31–35. Wilson Jeremiah Moses, *Alexander Crummell: A Study of Civilization and Discontent* (New York: Oxford, 1989), chapters 8–10.
41. Smith, *History of the AME Church*, 312.
42. Sylvia M. Jacobs, "Their 'Special Mission': Afro-American Women as Missionaries to the Congo, 1894–1937," in *Black Americans and the Missionary Movement in Africa*; Ann Streaty Wimberly, "Called to Witness, Called to Serve: African American Methodist Women in Liberian Missions, 1834–1934," *Methodist History* 34 (1996) 2: 67–77.
43. Walter L. Williams, "William Henry Sheppard: Afro-American Missionary in the Congo, 1890–1910," in *Black Americans and the Missionary Movement in Africa*, 135–154.
44. Jacobs, "The Historical Role of Afro-Americans in American Missionary Efforts to Africa," in *Black Americans and the Missionary Movement in Africa*, 20. See also Williams, *Black Americans and the Evangelization of Africa*, 175.
45. Ibrahim Sundiatia, *Black Scandal: America and the Liberian Labor Crisis, 1929–1936* (Philadelphia, PA: Institute for the Study of Human Issues, 1980), 86.
46. Park, *"White" Americans in "Black" Africa*, 189–194.
47. William Taylor, *Story of My Life* (New York: Hunt and Eaton, 1896), 692–699. Taylor puts the story of his ordination in the mouth of a witness, Rev. M. D. Collins of the Des Moines Conference, since he himself had strongly taken the position against sending whites to Africa. The General Conference accepted Taylor's name as "the will of God" and deemed it "utterly irresistible" (744–750).

48. J. A. Newby, "African Emigration," *Christian Recorder*, January 31, 1878. See also Rev. R. F. Hurley, "Why We Should Not Go to Africa," February 21, 1878; Rev. Andrew Chambers, "America versus Africa," March 7, 1878; Rev. J. H. Scott, "Shall We Colonize Africa with American Negroes?" January 25, 1883; Rev. Jas. H. Turner, "The African Question," February 22, 1883; Hon. William Nesbitt, "The Liberia Question," March 23, 1883, all in *Christian Recorder*.

49. Rev. Samuel Williams, "Four Years in Liberia: A Sketch of the Life of the Rev. Samuel Williams with Remarks on the Missions, Manners and Customs of the Natives of Western Africa Together with an Answer to Nesbitt's Book [1857]," in *Liberian Dreams: Back to Africa Narratives from the 1850s*, ed. Wilson Jeremiah Moses (University Park: Penn State University Press, 1997), 165.

50. Smith, *History of the AME Church*, 27, 127–128; 180–181. See also "The African ME Church in Liberia," *The Observer* [Monrovia] September 9 and November 11, 1880; James Campbell, *Middle Passages: African American Journeys to Africa, 1787–2005* (New York: Penguin, 2006), 109–111, and Williams, *Black Americans and the Evangelization of Africa*, 45–47.

51. Rev. C. C. Felts, "Missionary Prospect in the African ME Church," *Christian Recorder*, March 31, 1887. On black women's support for African missions, see Mrs. Hattie Nicholas, "What Can the Ladies Do?" *Christian Recorder*, June 23, 1887; Smith, *History of the AME Church*, 149. Interestingly, Smith mentions the work of Jennie Sharp, an African American woman working under the auspices of the ME church in Liberia on page 179, but entirely neglects Amanda Smith. For a photograph of Sharp with her students, see Catherine Reef, *This Our Dark Country: The American Settlers of Liberia* (New York: Clarion Books, 2002), 118.

52. Smith, *History of the AME Church*, 21–22. Williams, *Black American and the Evangelization of Africa*, 53. Charles S. Smith, *Glimpses of Africa, West and Southwest Coast* (Nashville, TN: Sunday School Union, 1895), especially the chapter "Missionary Enterprises."

53. Campbell, *Middle Passages*, chapter 2. A revisionist appraisal can be found in Eric Burin, *Slavery and the Peculiar Solution: A History of the American Colonization Society* (Gainesville: University Press of Florida, 2005), who finds that overall "colonization tended to undermine slavery," 2.

54. Burin, *Peculiar Solution*, 151. Emigrants received ten acres of land but only acquired full title after they could show "improvements." See appendix D "Title Deed Grant for Completion of Improvement Requirement" in Tom W. Shick, *Behold the Promised Land: A History of Afro-American Settler Society in Nineteenth-Century Liberia* (Baltimore, MD: Johns Hopkins University Press, 1980), 149–150.

55. Wilson Jeremiah Moses, *The Golden Age of Black Nationalism, 1850–1925* (New York: Oxford University Press, 1988), and Gail Bederman, *Manliness and Civilization: A Cultural History of Gender and Race in the United States, 1880–1917* (Chicago, IL: University of Chicago Press, 1997).

56. Rev. William Rankin Dorvee, "The Present Success of Liberia: Its Extent and Meaning," *The African Repository* (July 1882): 66.

57. Augustus Washington, "Thoughts on the American Colonization Society, 1851," in *Liberian Dreams*, 194.

58. "The Two Voices," *The African Repository* (July 1888): 96–104.

59. W. E. B. Du Bois, "The Conservation of Races," in *Classical Black Nationalism: From the American Revolution to Marcus Garvey*, ed. Wilson Jeremiah Moses (New York: New York University Press, 1996), 228–240. See also Mia Bay, *The White Image in the Black Mind: African-American Ideas about White People, 1830–1925* (New York: Oxford University Press, 2000), chapter 3.

60. T. McCants Stewart, *Liberia: The Americo-African Republic* (New York: Edward O. Jenkins' Sons, 1886), 54.

61. Du Bois, "The Conservation of Races," 232.
62. Edward Wilmot Blyden, "Liberia at the American Centennial," *Methodist Quarterly Review* (July 1877): 461.
63. Dr. E. W. Blyden, "America and Africa's Evangelization," *African Repository* (October 1888): 108.
64. Hollis R. Lynch, ed. *Black Spokesman: Selected Published Writings of Edward Wilmot Blyden* (New York: Humanities Press, 1971), xi–xxxv.
65. Wilson Jeremiah Moses, *Classical Black Nationalism from the American Revolution to Marcus Garvey* (New York: New York University, 1997), 1–42, and Williams, *Black Americans and the Evangelization of Africa*, part II.
66. "Letter from Amanda Smith," *Christian Standard*, December 17, 1881.
67. Stewart also referred to a "Christian Negro Nationality," *Liberia*, 103. See also Blyden, "The Men for Liberia," *African Repository* (October 1888): 105–107.
68. Blyden, "Origin and Purpose of African Colonization," in *Black Spokesman*, ed. Lynch, 43.
69. Edward Blyden to Hon. J. J. Gibson, April 18, 1882, RACS.
70. Edward Blyden to William Coppinger, November 19, 1887, RACS.
71. On Blyden's heritage, see Stewart, *Liberia*, 32; Blyden to Coppinger, November 19, 1887, RACS.
72. King to Coppinger, October 22, 1883, RACS.
73. William Nesbitt, "Four Months in Liberia, or, African Colonization Exposed" in *Liberian Dreams*, 107.
74. Blyden to Coppinger, February 1883 [*sic*], RACS. These cases involving H. D. Brown and A. B. King were marked "private and confidential."
75. King to Coppinger, June 27, 1887; Blyden to Coppinger, March 27, 1884; King to Coppinger, May 17, 1884, RACS. US consul John Smyth also raised eyebrows by his "free talk" with married and unmarried women in Monrovia and reportedly fathered a child out of wedlock in Sierra Leone.
76. Wrote a Mrs. Brierly (Episcopal) in 1884 to the American Board of Missions: "…of course I still plead for your educational establishments to continue under the control of white Americans & surely it matters not to a true Htian [Christian] who is our earthly captain…" Brierly also fretted over leaving native girls under the control of a Mr. Merriam, a native convert, whom she suspected of selling off marriageable girls in the bush. Mrs. Brierly to Rev. Thimber, August 20, 1884, both in Mission Archives, Liberia Collection, Indiana University, Bloomington, Indiana.
77. Freetown petition to Bishop Ferguson dated March 22, 1888, signed by R. H. Marshall, R. H. Gordon, Jacob Wolff, and E. A. Barr to Rt. Rev. L. D. Ferguson, March 20, 1888 (dateline Robertsport); petition to Ferguson March 9, 1888; Ferguson's response to Robertsport petitioners, letter dated March 19, 1888, Mission Archives.
78. Mary A. Sharp to William Coppinger, May 16, 1887, RACS.
79. Deuteronomy 23: 2–7 specifies that Ammonite and Moabite unions with Hebrews required a ten-generation waiting period; Hebrew unions with Edomites and Egyptians only required three generations, in the latter's case, "because you lived as an alien in his country." Blyden expounds on these matters in a letter to William Coppinger, October 19, 1887, RACS. When contents of his letters were reprinted in the *African Repository* as articles, biblical sections on race were eliminated and only the quantitative matters (i.e., figures on mortality, longevity, fertility, etc.) remained. Blyden, "The Term Negro," *African Repository* (October 1888): 107–109.
80. "Dr. Blyden's Influence," *Christian Recorder*, November 8, 1882. See also "Dr. Blyden's Opinion," *Christian Recorder*, June 24, 1880.
81. [Ben?] Anderson to C. T. O. King, undated, RACS, emphasis in original. For related ideas, see Reginald Horsman, *Race and Manifest Destiny: The Origins of American Racial Anglo-Saxonism* (Cambridge: Harvard University Press, 1981).

82. George Fredrickson, *The Black Image in the White Mind: The Debate on Afro-American Character and Destiny, 1817–1914* (Middletown, CT: Wesleyan University Press, 1971), chapters 3, 7, and 8; Eric T. L. Love, *Race Over Empire: Racism and US Imperialism, 1865–1900* chapters 1 and 2. For a treatment that emphasizes the staying power of monogenesis in Christian theology and its power to mitigate racial science, see Colin Kidd, *The Forging of Races: Race and Scripture in the Protestant Atlantic World, 1600–2000* (New York: Cambridge University Press, 2006), chapters 5 and 8.

83. Former Liberia critic Martin Delany actually changed his mind about emigration as his ideas about race shifted. In 1879 he argued that the "three original races" were "indestructible," and, therefore, "*miscegenation* as popularly understood—the running out of two races, or several, into a new race—cannot take place." In such circumstances, emigration to Liberia should be neither feared nor thwarted. Martin R. Delany, *Principia of Ethnology: The Origin of Races and Color, with an Archeological Compendium of Ethiopian and Egyptian Civilization, from Years of Careful Examination and Enquiry* (Philadelphia, PN: Harper & Brother, Publishers, 1879), 91–92, 30–40. See also Campbell, *Middle Passages*, 97–98.

84. Blyden to Coppinger, March 16, 1887, RACS.

85. Blyden to Coppinger, March 13, 1884, RACS.

86. Blyden to Coppinger, April 19, 1887, RACS.

87. William Coppinger, *Winning an Empire* (Hampton, VA: Normal School Steam Press, 1884).

88. "Letter from Bishop Taylor," *Christian Standard*, July 9, 1887.

89. Smith, *An Autobiography*, 379.

90. Blyden to Coppinger, December 1, 1887 refers to the "sacredness of individual rights and of the rights of races." Blyden to Coppinger, August 20, 1887 refers to "mongrel Christianity," RACS.

91. For the elaboration of the idea that "the negro is, at this moment, the opposite of the Anglo-Saxon," see Blyden, "Ethiopia Stretching Out Her Hands unto God; or, Africa's Service to the World," in *Black Spokesman*, ed. Lynch, 35–37; on African civilization, and how "its great peculiarity will be its moral element," see Blyden, "The Call of Providence," in *Black Spokesman*, ed. Lynch, 32. See also Blyden, "A Chapter in the History of Liberia [1892]," in *Black Spokesman*, ed. Lynch, 117. For related sentiments, see also Du Bois, "Conservation of the Races" (1897).

92. Blyden, "The Three Needs of Liberia," [1908] in *Black Spokesman*, ed. Lynch, 125.

93. Blyden claimed Abbeokuta, Nigeria as "my fatherland" in Blyden to Coppinger, November 28, 1881, RACS. King refers to Africa as the "*Fatherland*" in a letter to Coppinger, March 9, 1882, RACS. So did Martin Delany, as described in Campbell, *Middle Passages*, chapter 2. Blyden referred to Africa as "the continent of my fathers and my race" in *Liberia's Offering: Being Addresses, Sermons, etc.* (New York: J. A. Gray, 1862), ii. At some moments, though he switched genders, "*Africa is to be redeemed by her own children—but mulattoes and quadroons are not Africa's children and every effort to make them the instruments of her redemption must end in disastrous failure*" in Blyden to Coppinger, October 6, 1884, RACS. On Du Bois wavering between motherland and fatherland, see Brent Hayes Edwards, *The Practice of Diaspora: Literature, Translation and the Rise of Black Internationalism* (Cambridge, MA: Harvard University Press, 2003), 145. See also Henry McNeal Turner, "The American Negro and His Fatherland," in *Classical Black Nationalism*, 221–227.

94. Blyden to Coppinger, August 20, 1887, RACS; A Female Observer, "Our Native Sisters Are Still in Gross Darkness," *The Observer* [Monrovia], November 25, 1880. It's important to note that Blyden was extremely critical of white missionary education that would produce "effeminate training" among the men and deskilling among

the women. He was particularly critical of Mary Sharp's work among the Kru, since disrupting the maritime traditions among the men and teaching the women town-style domesticity would lead to "social disintegration." He noted scathingly that American churches send money to the tune of $30 a head, effectively "buying" the children in exchange for naming them. "But she is making money on her system," he scowled. Blyden to Coppinger, June 6, 1887, RACS.

95. Blyden to Coppinger, October 13, 1887, RACS.
96. Blyden to Coppinger, May 24, 1884, RACS.
97. "I did not send her away and I shall not send for her," asserted Blyden to Coppinger, January 25, 1887, RACS.
98. Jennie Davis to William Coppinger, August 25, 1884, RACS.
99. Blyden to Coppinger, October 13, 1887, RACS. Blyden to Coppinger, June 6, 1887, RACS. See "Visitors in Liberia by Bishop Ferguson," *African Repository* (July 1888): 92.
100. Blyden to Coppinger, October 22, 1887, RACS.
101. Shick, *Behold the Promised Land*, 100; Newman, "The Emergence of Liberian Women," 344. Blyden believed that if it were "put to a vote and left up to the women to decide," polygamy "would be abolished by an overwhelming majority." Quoted in Newman, "The Emergence of Liberian Women," 360.
102. "Mrs. Amanda Smith," *The Observer*, February 23, 1882.
103. Blyden to Coppinger, April 11, 1885, RACS.
104. "An Oration, by H. R. W. Johnson, Delivered in Monrovia at the Thirty-Five Celebration of Liberian Independence," [1882] (Monrovia: Government Printing Office, 1883), 28, in United States, *Despatches from the United States Ministers to Liberia, 1863–1906* (Washington, DC: National Archives and Records Service, 1962). Hereafter, *Liberia Dispatches*.
105. "Mrs. Amanda Smith," *The Observer*, February 23, 1882.
106. Taylor quoted in "Improvement in West Africa," *Christian Standard*, August 30, 1888.
107. "Bishop Taylor's Quadrennial Report of Our Church Work in Africa," supplement to the Baltimore *Methodist*, May 26, 1888, 2; "Letter from Bishop Taylor," *Christian Standard*, May 7, 1887.
108. Letter dated June 20, 1884, reprinted in *Christian Standard*, October 25, 1884. See also "Temperance and Education," *African Repository* (October 1882): 110–111.
109. King to Coppinger, November 14, 1882, RACS.
110. King to Blyden, July 18, 1885, RACS.
111. Smith, *An Autobiography*, 362. To the Honorable Senate and House of Representatives from H. R. W. Johnson, January 18, 1884: "I beg leave to inform you that I have this day approved Senate Bills as follows: No. 8 "Amendatory Act to the Act entitled an Act regulating the liquor traffic." Government documents—Executive Correspondence, Liberia Collection. *The Observer*, "Notes," December 31, 1880, and "The Liquor Bill," January 27, 1881. The bill imposed an annual licensing fee of a hefty $2,000 on importers. "Acts Passed by the Legislature of the Republic of Liberia, During the Session 1882–83" "An Act Regulating the Liquor Traffic" (Monrovia: Government Printing Office, 1883), 9. The law may have reflected the advocacy of the US Consul, John Smyth, who wrote to the US State Department : "I must not fail to mention...the importance of so amending the Revenue Laws as to impose higher duties on the importation and sale of Alcoholic Liquors, gun powder fire arms and tobacco," he noted, continuing: "Many of the tribal difficulties...may be attributed to the use of Alcohol." Smyth to Anthony W. Gardner, December 6, 1882; both in *Liberia Dispatches*.
112. "Message of the President of the Republic of Liberia to the First Session of the Nineteenth Legislature, December 1883" (Monrovia: Government Printing Office, 1883), 6, in *Liberia Dispatches*.

113. Blyden to Coppinger, May 14, 1887; Blyden to Coppinger, November 24, 1881. The "Baptists of Clay-Ashland" resolved to forbid their members from "dealing in ardent spirits" according to local press in Monrovia. "Religious," *The Observer*, October 20, 1881.
114. King to Coppinger, February 2, 1882, RACS.
115. "Letter from Amanda Smith," *Christian Standard*, June 3, 1882.
116. Johnson, "An Oration," 28.
117. Samuel D. Ferguson was born in 1842 in South Carolina. His parents migrated to Liberia around 1850, and after the death of his father he was raised in the Episcopal mission. He became bishop in 1885. George F. Bragg, *History of the Afro-American Group of the Episcopal Church* (Baltimore, MD: Church Advocate Press, 1922), 201–207, electronic edition, http://docsouth.unc.edu/church/bragg/bragg.html.
118. "Letter from Mrs. Amanda Smith to Mrs. Liddie H. Kenney," *Christian Standard*, June 11, 1887.
119. King to Coppinger, July 8, 1884, RACS.
120. "Letter from Amanda Smith," *Christian Standard*, March 1, 1884.
121. "Amanda Smith Letter," dateline Mt. Olive, *Christian Standard*, June 27, 1885. Taylor elaborated on building up vocabulary and written language in Africa in *Story of My Life*, 704, and his *The Flaming Torch in Darkest Africa* (New York: Eaton and Mains, 1898), 533–534.
122. On the AME Zion church in Liberia in the 1880s, see Williams, *Black Americans and the Evangelization of Africa*, 58.
123. Tyrell, *Woman's World/Woman's Empire*, 83.
124. Campbell, *Middle Passages*, chapters on Delany and Turner. For twentieth-century case studies, see Manning Marable and Vanessa Agard-Jones, ed. *Transnational Blackness: Navigating the Global Color Line* (New York: Palgrave Macmillan, 2008).
125. Albert S. Broussard, *African-American Odyssey: The Stewarts, 1853–1963* (Lawrence: University Press of Kansas, 1998). On Sheppard, see Williams, *Black American and the Evangelization of Africa*.
126. Blyden to Coppinger, September 12, 1887, RACS.
127. Blyden to Coppinger, May 31, 1884, RACS.
128. "Letter from Bishop Taylor," *Christian Standard*, July 9, 1887. See also Williams, *Four Years in Liberia*, 138.
129. Taylor, *The Flaming Torch*, 545–546. Taylor claimed to personally restrain himself when confronted with native custom: "For example, I have never attacked their custom of wearing ornaments and charms, but have often seen them tear these emblems of heathenism from their persons and cast them under their feet as they rushed to the altar of prayer" (543).
130. Mrs. B. F. Kephart "drew my umbrella through" the offerings left to the Devil by natives in Harper, near Cape Palmas, Liberia, as she reported in the *Christian Standard*, September 26, 1889. On similar details in Nigeria, see Chinua Achebe, *Things Fall Apart* (1958).
131. See also "Facts about Africa" and "A Great Need," *The Helper* (April 1900): 1, and "The Right Text," *The Helper* (May 1900): 1.
132. Quoted in Newman, "The Emergence of Liberian Women," 297.
133. Ibid., 356.
134. "A Letter from Cape Palmas," *African Repository* (October 1888): 123. Educated girls were then re-sold *by missionaries* for an even higher price. Mrs. Brierly to Mr. Thimber, August 24, 1883, dateline Monrovia, inquired of her American board: "What are we to do about our Vey girls [for] as soon as they are of an age to become useful, they are taken away to the 'Grebo' bush where they are betrothed or rather sold to the highest purchaser?" Mission Archives.

135. Informant phrasing quoted in Mary H. Moran, *Civilized Women: Gender and Prestige in Southeastern Liberia*, (Ithaca, NY: Cornell University Press, 1990), 3–7. See also Moran, "Civilized Servants: Child Fosterage and Training for Status among the Grebo of Liberia," in *African Encounters with Domesticity*, ed. Karen Hansen (New Brunswick NJ.: Rutgers University Press, 1992), 98–115.

136. "Amanda Smith's Letter," *Christian Standard*, October 11, 1885.

137. "Amanda and Bob's First Meeting," *The Helper* (January 1900): 4; "Answers to Inquiries about Bob," *The Helper* (March 1900): 2; "Bob, The African Boy," *The Helper* (May 1900): 2. On adoption and purchase of Chinese girls abroad, see Hunter, *The Gospel of Gentility*, chapter 6 and 179, 192.

138. Blyden to Coppinger, November 19, 1887, RACS.

139. Stewart, *Liberia*, 66.

140. Hon. John H. Latrobe, "Cape Palmas, Liberia," *African Repository* (January 1885): 4. Latrobe recounts a dialogue with a representative of a local King Freeman, one Simleh Ballah, who pronounced Liberian laws of monogamy to be "good law for pickaninny, bad law for Simleh Ballah," apparently referring to Americo-Liberians as "pickaninny."

141. When B. Y. Payne visited the United States at the turn of the century, he visited with Smith and referred to her as "Auntie." See "Jottings by the Way," *The Helper* (October 1900): 4.

142. "Letter from Amanda Smith," *Christian Standard*, June 3, 1882. Burrin suggests that patterns of marriage resistance fostered autonomy for women in Liberia, which in turn protected migrant women from "sexism," 157–159.

143. "Letter from Amanda Smith," *Christian Standard*, April 2, 1887.

144. Ibid., and Smith, *An Autobiography*, 429: "I never was homesick but about five minutes the whole eight years I was in Africa." "From Amanda Smith," *Christian Standard*, July 23, 1887: "I am not homesick one bit, thank God, and would rather stay than not."

145. "Letter from Amanda Smith," *Christian Standard*, May 1, 1886.

146. "From Amanda Smith," *Christian Standard*, January 29, 1887.

147. Bishop Taylor, "Founding the Kroo Coast Stations," *Christian Standard*, June 27, 1889.

148. "From Amanda Smith," *Christian Standard*, July 23, 1887.

149. Bishop William Taylor, "Liberia Methodism," *Christian Standard*, April 29, 1887. He was inclined to blame "Arab traders" for much of the trouble in the Liberian hinterland. See *Story of My Life*, 708–710.

150. *An Autobiography*, 457; Taylor, *Flaming Torch*, 718, recounts this same reaction.

151. Blyden to Coppinger, May 31, 1885, RACS. "The people of Liberia are now too much of one kind. They are 'stewing in their own juice.' This is why it would be such a blessing to us if a white man could be sent from America as Minister Resident.... We need the influence of a neutral official."

152. Blyden to Coppinger, September 12, 1887, RACS.

153. "Bishop Taylor's Quadrennial Report," [1888], 14.

154. Some Africans regarded "Afro-Americans as...black-skinned white men," again underscoring the social rather than biological construction of "race." See Williams, "William Henry Sheppard," 146, and Clegg, *Price of Liberty*, 97.

155. Rev. Marshall W. Taylor, D. D., *The Life, Travels, Labors, and Helpers of Mrs. Amanda Smith*, (Cincinnati, OH: Cranston & Stowe, 1886), 62; See also "Liberian Methodism," *African Repository*, (July 1886): 99–100. It seems that Marshall was the bishop's son, who helped with a range of publication projects back in the United States during his father's international career.

156. Taylor, *Life, Travels, Labors*, 58–59.

157. Smith, *AME Church History*, 177–178.

158. "From Amanda Smith," *Christian Standard*, June 28, 1888.
159. George Lansing Taylor, "The New Africa," *Christian Standard*, December 20, 1888.
160. Blyden to Coppinger, January 25, 1887; March 14, 1887, King to Coppinger; May 14, 1887, Proclamation by C. T. O. King to citizens of Monrovia (re: aid to exiles) RACS. See also C. Clifton Penick to Bishop Ferguson, dateline Louisville, KY, May 19, 1887, and August 10, 1887, Bishop L. D. Ferguson to Hon. E. J. Barclay, August 10, 1887, Domestic Correspondence, Liberia Collection. Taylor, *Story of My Life*, 716.
161. Coppinger, *Winning an Empire*, 11.
162. Blyden to Coppinger, May 14, 1887, RACS.
163. "Letter from Amanda Smith," *Christian Standard*, August 20, 1887.
164. "Letter from Amanda Smith," *Christian Standard*, April 2, 1887.
165. "From Amanda Smith," *Christian Standard*, September 10, 1887.
166. Quoted in "The Two Voices," *African Repository* (July 1888): 103. Greener received an honorary degree from Liberia College in 1873.
167. Blyden to Coppinger, August 20, 1887, RACS.
168. "Bishop Taylor's Quadrennial Report of Our Church Work in Africa," [1888], 12.
169. Taylor, *Story of My Life*, 717.
170. "Letter from Bishop Taylor," *Christian Standard*, July 9, 1887.
171. Bishop William Taylor, "Liberia Methodism," *Christian Standard*, April 29, 1887.
172. "From Amanda Smith," *Christian Standard*, January 29, 1887.
173. "From Amanda Smith," *Christian Standard*, December 17, 1887.
174. "Mrs. Amanda Smith," *Christian Standard*, September 3, 1887.
175. "Letter from Amanda Smith," *Christian Standard*, August 20, 1887. Taylor actually noted that a Julia Fletcher was also along as Smith's "companion and sister" in *Story of My Life*, 717.
176. "Letter from Bishop Taylor," *Christian Standard*, July 9, 1887.
177. "Letter from Amanda Smith," *Christian Standard*, August 20, 1887.
178. Taylor, *Story of My Life*, 727.
179. "From Amanda Smith," *Christian Standard*, November 14, 1885.
180. "Amanda Smith," *Christian Standard*, February 20, 1886.
181. "Letter from Amanda Smith," *Christian Standard*, March 1, 1884.
182. Blyden to Coppinger, January 25, 1887, RACS.
183. Blyden to Coppinger, August 20, 1887, RACS.
184. "From Amanda Smith," *Christian Standard*, July 23, 1887.
185. Blyden left the Presbyterian Church in 1886 but remained nominally Christian. On Islam, see his *Christianity, Islam and the Negro Race* (London: W. B. Whittingham, 1887). See also Blyden, "Mohammedanism in Africa," *African Repository* (October 1887): 108–112.
186. "Letter from Amanda Smith," *Christian Standard*, August 20, 1887.
187. King to Coppinger, October 4, 1887, RACS.
188. W. A. Warner to Mr. Richard Grant in *Christian Standard* (dated September 24, 1887) January 19, 1888; see also J. S. Pratt to Brother Grant, (dated October 1, 1887), *Christian Standard*, January 19, 1888, on details of negotiating in goods and cash for native labor to build schools promised by treaty.
189. Letter to R. C. S. Miller, March 13, 1895, reprinted in C. S. Smith, "Liberia in the Light of Living Testimony: A Pamphlet" (Nashville, AME Church Sunday School Union, 1895), 34–35.
190. Campbell, *Middle Passages*, chapter 3.
191. Ida B. Wells, "Afro-Americans and Africa," *AME Church Review* (July 1892): 40–44. "Jesse Sharp, Esqr." *The Observer* [Monrovia] September 23, 1880. This short biography held out Sharp as "an aristocratic, well-to-do Southern Planter" to inspire newcomers to turn their "trammeled and unacknowledged manhood into material success and prosperity by immigrating to Liberia."

192. Hunter, *Gospel of Gentility*, 174, 223, 228. Nancy Boyd, *Emissaries: The Overseas Work of the American YWCA, 1895–1970* (New York: The Woman's Press, 1986), especially part I.
193. Smith, *An Autobiography*, 199, 201; 495–496. Pamela E. Klassen, "The Robes of Womanhood: Dress and Authenticity among African American Methodist Women in the Nineteenth Century," *Religion & American Culture* 14 (2004) 1: 39–82.
194. Letter from K. V. Eckman, April 19, 1989 writing from Sas Town, Liberia, in *The African News*, (August 1889): 344.
195. Smith, *Glimpses of Africa*, 256; 90–92. He ignored Smith's book and quoted Crummel and Stewart instead.
196. The journal *Illustrated Africa* was coedited with Henry M. Stanley, the English adventurer and MP, (who searched out Livingstone in east Africa) and was managed by Taylor's son in New York, for profit. Taylor, *Story of My Life*, 750. See his *Africa Illustrated, Scenes from Daily Life on the Dark Continent from Photographs Secured in Africa by Bishop William Taylor, Dr. Emil Holub and the Missionary Superintendents.* (New York: Illustrated Africa [ca. 1895]). "While waiting for heathen potentates I took photographs of men, women, and children and other objects of interest" notes Taylor in *Flaming Torch*, 528. On the *Christian Standard's* Africa appeals, see "The Dark Continent," July 16, 1891, 5, and "Bishop Taylor's African Mission," August 6, 1891, 5, and June 30, 1892, 15.
197. "Mountain Lake Park," (July, 16–23–30, 1891); "National Camp Meeting" (June 23, 1892); letter (December 1, 1892); (January 20, 1893); (February 2, 1893), all in *Christian Standard*. She remained popular for more than another decade. See "12,000 at Love Feast" August 28, 1905, and "30,000 attend 15 services," August 20, 1906, *New York Times*.
198. Christopher Reed, *All the World Is Here!: The Black Presence at White City* (Bloomington: Indiana University Press, 2000). Description of Liberia exhibit is from Carol Bowen Johnson, "World's Fair Letter," *The Independent* (July 20, 1893): 977. May Sewall and World's Congress of Representative Women, *The World's Congress of Representative Women* (Chicago, IL: Rand McNally, 1894).
199. Quoted in Israel, *Amanda Berry Smith*, 105. The 1910 census identifies The Amanda Smith Industrial Orphan Home with Smith, a handful of staff, and 32 children in residence. Ancestry.com, *1910 United States Federal Census* (database online). Provo, UT, USA: Ancestry.com Operations Inc, 2006 (viewed September 30, 2008).
200. James M. Thoburn, "Introduction," in Smith, *An Autobiography*, vi.
201. Moses, *The Golden Age of Black Nationalism*, chapter 5, and, in general, see Deborah G White, *Too Heavy a Load: Black Women in Defense of Themselves, 1894–1994*, (New York: W. W. Norton, 1999), chapters 1 and 2.
202. Blyden quoted in Newman, "Emergence of the Liberian Woman," 310.
203. Lawrence S. Little, "AME Responses to Events and Issues in Asia in the Age of Imperialism, 1880–1916," *Journal of Asian & African Studies* 33 (1998) 4: 317–330. In general, see George P Marks, *The Black Press Views American Imperialism (1898–1900)* (New York: Arno Press, 1971), Mitchell, *Righteous Propagation*, 60–62.
204. Editorial, *The Helper* (September 1900): 7.

2   Unmaking Race

1. Gertrude Stein, *Everybody's Autobiography* (New York: Vintage, 1973), 22–23.
2. Stein, "Poetry and Grammar," in *Lectures in America* (Boston: Beacon Press, 1985), 220–221. She described commas in eugenic language as "enfeebling" and "degrading."
3. For reviews of the opera's performance, see "The Mother of Us All," *Theatre Journal* 51 (1999) 2: 212–214, and from the *New York Times*: James R. Oestreich, "A Suffragist

in Her Den, Bracing for the Circus"(March 21, 2000); Donal Henahan, "Opera: Virgil Thompson, 'The Mother of Us All'" (March 23, 1983); Allen Hughes, "Lexox 'Mother of Us All' Lacks Nothing but Seats for the Crowd," (July 3, 1972); Rosalyn Regelson, "Was She Mother of Us All?" (November 5, 1967); Bernard Holland, "Thomson and Stein Serve Up Shards of a Life," (September 13, 2003).

4. Stein guarded her citizenship quite closely, filling out an "Affidavit to Explain Foreign Residence and to Overcome Presumption of Expatriation" in January 1918 at the American consular service in Marseilles in anticipation of her service as a "delegate of the American Fund for French Wounded" during World War I. See application number 9059 from NARA RG 59 in Ancestry.com. *U.S. Passport Applications, 1795–1925* (database online). Provo, UT, USA: Ancestry.com Operations, Inc., 2007, (viewed September, 2010). For a normative treatment of Stein as an "expatriate writer," see Alissa Karl, "Modernism's Risky Business: Gertrude Stein, Sylvia Beach, and American Capitalism," *American Literature* 80 (March 2008) 1: 83–109. For a more critical perspective, see Benjamin Townley Spencer, "Gertrude Stein, Non-Expatriate," in *Literature and Ideas in America: Essays in Memory of Harry Haden Clark*, ed. Robert P. Falk (Athens: Ohio University Press, 1975), 204–227.

5. Gertrude Stein, *The Autobiography of Alice B. Toklas* (New York: Vintage Books, 1960), 83.

6. Stein and Van Vechten met in 1913 and grew closer with each passing decade. After Stein's US lecture tour in 1934-5, during which Van Vechten squired her and Toklas around a great deal, the "Woojums" family connection seems to have been sealed. "Woojums" strikes me as a possible variant on "we chums." Gertrude Stein, *The Letters of Gertrude Stein and Carl Van Vechten, 1913–1946* (New York: Columbia University Press, 1986), vols. 1 and 2.

7. "She [GS] says a landscape is such a natural arrangement for a battle-field or a play that one must write plays," notes "Alice" in *The Autobiography* (132).

8. For an incisive analysis of generations of Stein detractors, see Karin Cope, *Passionate Collaborations: Learning to Live with Gertrude Stein* (Victoria, BC: ELS Editions, 2005), especially chapter 3.

9. Stein devised her own clichés about herself: "They always say, she says, that my writing is appalling but they always quote it and what is more, they quote it correctly, and those they say they admire they do not quote. This at some of her most bitter moments has been a consolation." Stein, *The Autobiography*, 70.

10. Gertrude Stein, "Cultivated Motor Automatism: A Study in Character and Its Relation to Attention," *Psychological Review* 5 (May 1898): 295–306. And with Leon Solomons, "Normal Motor Automatism," *Psychological Review* 3 (September 1896): 495–512.

11. See reviews in Kurt Curnutt, ed., *The Critical Response to Gertrude Stein* (Westport, CT: Greenwood Press, 2000), 9–13.

12. Barbara Will, *Gertrude Stein, Modernism, and the Problem of "Genius"* (Edinburgh: Edinburgh University Press, 2000). Stein's most cited line about genius is in *The Autobiography*, where "Alice" states: "The three geniuses of whom I wish to speak are Gertrude Stein, Pablo Picasso and Alfred Whitehead," (p. 5).

13. Shari Benstock, *Women of the Left Bank: Paris, 1900–1940* (Austin: University of Texas Press, 1986), chapter 5. Robert Morse Crunden, *American Salons: Encounters with European Modernism, 1885–1917* (New York: Oxford University Press, 1993), book IV, and Crunden, *Body & Soul: The Making of American Modernism* (New York: Basic Books, 2000), chapter 10. Stein is outside the geographical frame of Christine Stansell, *American Moderns: Bohemian New York and the Creation of a New Century* (New York: Metropolitan Books, 2001).

14. Cushing Strout, "The Unfinished Arch: William James and the Idea of History," *American Quarterly* 13 (1961) 4: 505–515, especially 508. See also John

Whittier- Ferguson, "Stein in Time: History, Manuscripts, and Memory," *Modernism /modernity* 6 (1999) 1: 115–151.

15. Stein, *The Geographical History of America, or the Relation of Human Nature to the Human Mind* (Baltimore, MD: Johns Hopkins University Press, 1985), 109.

16. "Introduction by William H. Gass," in Stein, Ibid., 23.

17. Gertrude Stein, "Portraits and Repetition," in *Lectures in America*, 198. William James, *The Principles of Psychology*, authorized ed., unabridged (New York: Dover Publications, 1950), especially chapter 5 ("The Perception of Time") and chapter 11 ("Attention"). James theorizes, for example: "If then we prove ideal construction of the object to be present in *sensorial* attention, it will be present everywhere," 439. See also Stephanie L. Hawkins, "The Science of Superstition: Gertrude Stein, William James, and the Formation of Belief," *Modern Fiction Studies* 51 (2005) 1: 60–87, and Liesl M. Olson, "Gertrude Stein, William James and Habit in the Shadow of War," *Twentieth Century Literature* 49 (2003) 3: 328–359.

   Scholars are about split on James's influence overall, but most take Stein at her word in her notebooks around 1910 when she declared she was "not a pragmatist"—though the statement is more a rejection of her brother Leo's incessant systematizing and an emotional declaration of independence from him than a carefully considered break with James, as Wineapple suggests. In a notebook written during *The Making of Americans*, Stein wrote: "...then realizing that I was not a pragmatist just recently do not believe all classification is teleological, then realize, that aesthetic has become the whole of me..." DB-66, Box 285, folder 17, MS 77, Yale Collections in American Literature (hereafter, YCAL).

18. William Wasserstrom, "The Sursymamericubealism of Gertrude Stein," *Twentieth Century Literature* 21 (1975) 1: 90–106.

19. Stein, *Matisse Picasso and Gertrude Stein with Two Shorter Stories* (Minneola, NY: Dover Publications, 2000), 252. This delightful passage reads: "The music of the present tense has the presentation of more accent than the best intention multiplies. The method in it is not more to be deplored than the unification is represented. The best passage is not more likely."

20. Jennifer Ashton, *From Modernism to Postmodernism: American Poetry and Theory in the Twentieth Century* (Cambridge, UK: Cambridge University Press, 2008), chapters 1 and 2 focus on Stein in relation to Whitehead, Russell, and F. L. G. Frege.

21. Stein, "The Gradual Making of *The Making of Americans*," in *Lectures in America*, 147–148.

22. Ashton, *From Modernism to Postmodernism*, 52. Elsewhere, Ashton suggests that the shift takes place in "A Long Gay Book." See her introduction to *Matisse Picasso and Gertrude Stein with Two Shorter Stories*, 3 and 6. See also, Ashton's "Gertrude Stein for Anyone," *ELH* 64 (1997) 1: 289–331 and "'Rose is a Rose': Gertrude Stein and the Critique of Indeterminacy," *Modernism/modernity* 9 (2002) 4: 581–604.

23. Leon Katz, "The First Making of *The Making of Americans*: A Study Based on Gertrude Stein's Notebooks and Early Versions of Her Novel (1902–1908)" PhD diss., Columbia University, 1963. In an 1986 essay, Katz restates his basic thesis that Weininger enabled Stein to pursue systematizing for her own none-too-generous purposes. "Weininger and *The Making of Americans*," in *Critical Essays on Gertrude Stein*, ed. Michael J. Hoffman (Boston, MA: G. H. Hall, 1986), 141. On Weininger, see Nancy A. Harrowitz and Barbara Hyams, eds., *Jews & Gender: Responses to Otto Weininger* (Philadelphia, PA: Temple University Press, 1995) and Chandak Sengoopta, *Otto Weininger: Sex, Science, and Self in Imperial Vienna* (Chicago, IL: University of Chicago Press, 2000).

24. Feminist literary scholars mostly appraise *The Making* as an apprenticeship piece and hang their big judgments about modernist form on "Three Lives" (1909) and

"Tender Buttons" (1914). Most helpful on *The Making* are: Marianne DeKoven, *A Different Language: Gertrude Stein's Experimental Writing* (Madison: University of Wisconsin Press, 1983); Lisa Cole Ruddick, *Reading Gertrude Stein: Body, Text, Gnosis* (Ithaca, NY: Cornell University Press, 1990); Jayne L Walker, *The Making of a Modernist: Gertrude Stein from Three Lives to Tender Buttons* (Amherst: University of Massachusetts Press, 1984); Janice L Doane, *Silence and Narrative: The Early Novels of Gertrude Stein* (Westport, CT: Greenwood Press, 1986); Melanie Taylor, "A Poetics of Difference: *The Making of Americans* and Unreadable Subjects," *NWSA Journal* 15 (2003) 3: 26–42; Kelley Wagers, "Gertrude Stein's 'Historical' Living," *Journal of Modern Literature* 31 (2008) 3: 22–43.

25. For literary treatments of mostly white British women and "new woman fiction," see Ann Heilmann, *New Woman Strategies: Sarah Grand, Olive Schreiner, Mona Caird* (Manchester, UK: Manchester University Press, 2004); Sally Ledger, *The New Woman: Fiction and Feminism at the Fin De Siècle* (Manchester, UK: Manchester University Press, 1997); and Ann Heilmann, *New Woman Fiction: Women Writing First-Wave Feminism* (Houndmills, Basingstoke, Hampshire: Macmillan Press, 2000). The Bodley Head's best sellers in these genres date from the mid-1890s, the Grant Allen, *The Woman Who Did* (1894) and the response, Victoria Crosse, *The Woman Who Didn't* (1895). On Emma Goldman as a "New York Jew," see Stansell, *American Moderns*, chapter 4.

26. Priscilla Wald, *Constituting Americans: Cultural Anxiety and Narrative Form* (Durham, NC: Duke University Press, 1995), 242. Maria Damon, "Gertrude Stein's Jewishness, Jewish Social Scientists, and the 'Jewish Question,'" *Modern Fiction Studies* 42 (1996) 3: 489–506.

27. Gertrude Stein, *Tender Buttons: Food, Objects, Rooms* (Los Angeles, CA: Sun and Moon Press, 1991), 1. My reading of *Tender Buttons* is indebted to Allegra Stewart, *Gertrude Stein and the Present* (Cambridge: Harvard University Press, 1967), especially chapter 3.

28. William James, "The One and the Many," in *The Writings of William James*, ed. John H. McDermott (Chicago, IL: University of Chicago Press, 1977), 405–417.

29. The construct "new woman" is usually treated as part of discreet British or US national domains; they have yet to be rigorously connected in the scholarly literature. On the US side, see Martha H. Patterson, ed., *The American New Woman Revisited: A Reader, 1894–1930,* and Fannie Barrier Williams, *The New Woman of Color: The Collected Writings of Fannie Barrier Williams, 1893–1918* (DeKalb: Northern Illinois University Press, 2002). See also Martha H. Patterson, *Beyond the Gibson Girl: Reimagining the American New Woman, 1895–1915* (Urbana: University of Illinois Press, 2005). For a mostly English perspective, see Carolyn C. Nelson, ed. *A New Woman Reader: Fiction, Articles, and Drama of the 1890s* (Peterborough, UK: Broadview Press, 2001).

30. Sarah Grand, "The New Aspect of the Woman Question," *North American Review* 158 (March 1894): 270–276. Grand literally described men as preferring to "sleep late."

31. Ouida, "The New Woman," *North American Review* 158 (May 1894): 610–619.

32. Ella W. Winston, "Foibles of the New Woman," *Forum* 21 (April 1896): 186–192, more or less repeats the "Ouida" side of the question, as does Winifred Kirkland in "The Woman Who Writes," *Atlantic Monthly* 118 (July 1916): 46–54; Margaretta M. Tuttle, "Maternity and the Woman Intellectual," *Colliers* 44 (January 29, 1910): 18–19 revived the "cow woman" metaphor.

Critical, mocking, or merely appeasing views of the new woman can be found in: "The New Woman Under Fire: Is the Vote Necessary for Woman's Influence?" *The Review of Reviews* 10 (December 1894): 656–657; "The Psychology of Woman," "The Education of Woman," "Advice to the New Woman" all in *The Review of Reviews* 12 (July 1895): 82–85; Sigmund Spaeth, "The Real New Woman," *Colliers*

47 (July 15, 1911): 16–17; M. L. H. Harris, "The New Woman Who Would Do Things," *Ladies Home Journal* 24 (September 1907): 17; Boyd Winchester, "The Eternal Feminine," *The Arena* 27 (April 1902): 367–373; "A Word to the New Woman," *Atlantic Monthly* 118 (October 1916): 574–576; Harriet Abbott, "What the Newest New Woman Is," *Ladies Home Journal* 37 (August 1920): 160; James Henle, "The New Woman," *Harper's Weekly* 61 (November 20, 1915): 502–503.

Generous, sympathetic discussions can be found in the following: Louise Connoly, "The New Woman," *Harper's Weekly* 57 (June 7, 1913): 6; Edwin Bjorkman, "The Meaning of the New Woman," *Colliers* (January 29, 1910): 12; Clare deGraffenried, "The 'New Woman' and Her Debts," *Popular Science Monthly* 49 (September 1896): 664–672; Lilliam W. Betts, "The New Woman," The *Outlook* 52 (October 12, 1895): 587; Anne Warner, "A New Woman and the Old," *The Century* 79 (November 1909): 85–92; Guglielmo Ferrero, "The New Woman and the Old," *Hearst's Magazine* 22 (July 1912): 70–77; Josephine K. Henry, "The New Woman of the New South," *The Arena* 11 (February 1895): 353–362; "The New Woman" (discussion) *Harper's Weekly* 61 (December 18, 1915): 597–600 (responses to Henle, cited above); Julia Magruder, "The Typical Woman of the New South," *Harper's Bazaar* 33 (November 3, 1900): 1685–1687. See, additionally, entries in Patterson, ed., *The New American Woman Revisited.*

33. Florence Kelley, "The Home and the New Woman," *The Outlook* 93 (October 16, 1909): 363.

34. "The New Woman under Fire" [1894] and Henle, "The New Woman" [1915].

35. On hysteria as a ploy or indulgence by "soul sick" women who want to trump up power and attention in their households and churches, see: "Hysteria," *The Independent* 58 (March 30, 1905): 736–738; For a review of Charcot's translated work, see "Mind and Body," *The Independent* 54 (March 20, 1902): 697–698. For a nicely demystifying view, see William Hirsch, "Epidemics of Hysteria," *Popular Science* 49 (August 1896): 544–549.

36. Laura Briggs, "The Race of Hysteria: 'Overcivilization' and the 'Savage' Woman in Late Nineteenth-Century Obstetrics and Gynecology," *American Quarterly* 52 (2000) 2: 246–273.

37. H. B. Montgomery, "New Woman of India," *World Outlook* 2 (November 1916): 22–23; S. N. Singh, "The New Woman in the Mohammedan World," *The Review of Reviews* 46 (December 1912) 716–720; A. Kinnosuké, "The New Woman in China and Japan," *The Review of Reviews* 46 (July 1912): 71–73; H. Davies, "New Woman in China," *Missionary Review of the World* 31 (May 1908): 374–375; A. B. Dodd, "New Woman in Turkey," *The Century* 66 (October 1903): 925–933. A number of Anglo-American commentators reviewed women in France, Italy, and Germany as rather primitive and resistant to change. On France, see "New Phases of the Woman Movement throughout the World," *The American Review of Reviews* 47 (March 1913): 364–385; Margaret P. Boyle, "The 'New Woman' in Germany," *Outlook* (October 23, 1897): 468; F. B. Clark, "The New Woman in Italy," *World Outlook* 3 (October 1917): 23.

38. G. A. Miller, "New Woman in the Orient," *The Overland Monthly* 52 (December 1908): 501–509. Here, I align rather than distinguish the US and British views in colonial contexts. Some work on British white women suggests that the new woman actually threatened to stir up trouble among the natives. See Iveta Jusová, *The New Woman and the Empire* (Columbus: Ohio State University Press, 2005). On the US side, the only negative appraisal of modernized, Christianized "native" women I encountered was in the China case at the turn of the twentieth century. One US missionary noted that "The 'emancipated woman' of China who has broken all the old conventions is both masculine and immoral," quoted in Jane Hunter, *The Gospel of Gentility: American Women Missionaries in Turn-of-the-Century China* (New Haven, CT: Yale University Press, 1984), 176.

39. "The Women's Movement and Foreign Missions," *The American Review of Reviews*, 47 (1913): 366–367.

40. A. C. Wallace, "Higher Hysterics," *Critic* 41 (September 1902): 213–217.

41. Etsu Inagaki Sugimoto, "The House of the New Woman," *World Outlook* 4 (September 1918), cover and 14–16.

42. Charles F. Thwing, "The Best Thing College Does for a Man," *Forum* 21 (March 1896): 44–52. Despite the manly title, this essay was inclusive and upbeat concerning women undergraduates, whose answers to his survey were remarkably similar to those by the male undergraduates. See also, William James, "The Social Value of the College-Bred," *McClure's Magazine* 30 (February 1908): 419–422; "College-Bred Wives," *Current Literature* 38 (January 1905): 41–43; W. E. B. Du Bois, *The College-Bred Negro American* (Atlanta, GA: Atlanta University Press, 1910).

43. Rosalind S Miller, *Gertrude Stein: Form and Intelligibility: Containing the Radcliffe Themes* (New York: Exposition Press, 1949), 120. Emphases in the original.

44. Brenda Wineapple, *Sister Brother: Gertrude and Leo Stein* (New York: G. P. Putnam's Sons, 1996), 56–58; 124. On sexism in medical school, see Maria Farland, "Gertrude Stein's Brain Work," *American Literature* 76 (2004) 1: 117–148.

45. Miller, *Gertrude Stein*, 140–141.

46. Gertrude Stein, *Fernhurst, Q. E. D., and Other Early Writings* (New York: Liveright, 1971), 118.

47. Gertrude Stein, "The Value of a College Education for Women," typescript copy in Dr. Claribel and Miss Etta Cone Papers, Archives and Manuscript Collection, the Baltimore Museum of Art. Envelope postmarked 1899.

48. Charlotte Perkins Gilman, *Women and Economics: A Study of the Economic Relation between Men and Women as a Factor in Social Evolution* (New York: Harper & Row, 1966), 33.

49. Gilman, *Women and Economics*, 159–160.

50. Ibid., 180.

51. Minutes of the Maryland State Federation of Women's Clubs, 1899–1900–1901, Box 8, MSA-SC #4307, Maryland State Archives. Adelaide Nutting discussed army nursing on March 20, 1900. The Teachers & Educators Union, Baltimore Women's College Alumnae, and the Baltimore section of the National Council of Jewish Women were among the "original clubs to vote for Federation," March 21, 1900. Of note is that the clubs regularly gathered as a group on the Johns Hopkins campus.

52. On Stein and Keyser family Baltimore origins, see Linda Wagner-Martin, *Favored Strangers: Gertrude Stein and Her Family* (New Brunswick, NJ: Rutgers University Press, 1995). On the city in general, see William T. Brigham, "New England in Baltimore," *New England Magazine* 22 (April 1900): 218–31, and Stephen Bonsal, "The New Baltimore," *Harper's New Monthly Magazine* 92 (February 1896): 331–350. See also Crunden's chapter on Baltimore in *American Salons*, 165–193.

53. Stein might have been right, up to a point. Baltimore schools were in serious disrepair in the 1890s, with over half needing physical replacement. However, 1898 brought charter reform and a new school board structure to the city, and a newly elected Republican administration committed to change. Andrea R. Andrews, "The Baltimore School Building Program, 1870 to 1900: A Study of Urban Reform," *Maryland Historical Magazine* 70 (1975) 3: 260–274.

54. Stein, "The Value of a College Education for Women."

55. Cynthia Horsburgh Requardt, "Alternative Professions for Goucher College Graduates, 1892–1910," *Maryland Historical Magazine*, 74 (1979) 3: 274–281. On college and the marriage market for female graduates, see Dorothy Dix, "College-Bred Wives," *Current Literature* 38 (January 1905): 41–43. M. W. Shinn, "Marriage Rate of College Women," *Century* 50 (October 1895): 946–948. Marion Talbert, "The

College, the Girl, and the Parent," *North American Review* 192 (July/December 1910): 349–358.

56. Stein, *Everybody's Autobiography*, 254.

57. Gilman, *Women and Economics*, 136; 317.

58. Vernon Lee, "The Economic Dependence of Women," *North American Review* 175 (July 1902) 1: 71–90. Lee wrote several volumes of literary criticism and art history, was a regular contributor to the NAR and other elite journals, and published many stories. Her late work *The Handling of Words, and Other Studies in Literary Psychology* (1926) reveals her to be tentative about modernism, praising Henry James but overall much more comfortable in the eighteenth century. Mencken relied on her reading of Nietzsche in his own work *The Philosophy of Friedrich Nietzsche* (Boston, MA: Luce, 1908). On imperial feminism, see Antoinette Burton, *The Burdens of History: British Feminism, Indian Women and Imperial Culture, 1865–1915* (Chapel Hill: University of North Carolina Press, 1994).

For other positive reviews of *Women and Economics*, see: Anne E. Muzzey, "The Hour and the Woman," *The Arena* 22 (August 1899): 263–271; Jeanette Barbour Perry, "Women and Economics," *The Critic* 35 (October 1899): 890–893; Arthur B. Woodford, "Present Trends in Economic Thought," *The Dial* 26 (February 1, 1899): 83–86. On Gilman's socialism and economic views, see Mark W. Van Wienen, "A Rose by Any Other Name: Charlotte Perkins Stetson (Gilman) and the Case for American Reform Socialism," *American Quarterly* 55 (2003) 4: 603–634. Louise Newman, *White Women's Rights: The Racial Origins of Feminism in the United States* (New York: Oxford, 1999), especially the introduction and chapters 1 and 6. See also Gail Bederman, *Manliness & Civilization: A Cultural History of Gender and Race in the United States, 1880–1917* (Chicago, IL: University of Chicago Press, 1995), chapter 4.

59. Quoted in Louise M. Phail, "An Historical Sketch of the Maryland Federation of Women's Clubs, 1899–1930 (n.p., 1930), 30–31, and 3. Copy in MSA-SC #4307, Maryland State Archives.

60. Wineapple, *Sister Brother*, 117–118, suggests the speech was of a piece with Gertrude and Leo's self-distancing gestures from the conventional respectability of Jewish Baltimore, in anticipation of their departure from the United States. On Jews and the most-favored immigrant status, see Eric L. Goldstein, "The Unstable Other: Locating the Jew in Progressive-Era American Racial Discourse," *American Jewish History* 89.(2001) 4: 383–409; on Theodore Roosevelt's fondness for Jews' assimiliability, see Gary Gerstle, "Theodore Roosevelt and the Divided Character of American Nationalism," in *Racially Writing the Republic: Racists, Race Rebels, and Transformations of American Identity* (Durham, NC: Duke University Press, 2009), 163–195.

61. Beth Wenger, "War Stories: Jewish Patriotism on Parade," in *Imagining the American Jewish Community*, ed. Jack Wertheimer (Lebanon, New Hampshire: Brandeis University Press, 2007), 93–119, especially 95.

62. Stein, "The Value of a College Education for Women."

63. Jane Addams, "The Subtle Problems of Charity," *Atlantic Monthly* 83 (February 1899): 163–178, emphasis added.

64. Gertrude Stein, *The Making of Americans: Being a History of a Family's Progress* (Champaign-Urbana, IL: Dalkey Archive Press, 1995), 43. All future references to this volume will be to this edition and cited parenthetically by page number within the text.

65. Amy Kaplan, *The Anarchy of Empire in the Making of US Culture* (Cambridge, MA: Harvard University Press, 2002); Kristin L. Hoganson, *Fighting for American Manhood: How Gender Politics Provoked the Spanish-American and Philippine-American Wars* (New Haven, CT: Yale University Press, 1998). Jennifer Rae Greeson, "Expropriating

The Great South and Exporting 'Local Color': Global and Hemispheric Imaginaries of the First Reconstruction," in *Hemispheric American Studies*, ed. Caroline F. Levander and Robert S. Levine (New Brunswick, NJ: Rutgers University Press, 2008). Alice Fahs, "The Feminized Civil War: Gender, Northern Popular Literature, and Memory of War, 1861–1900," *Journal of American History* 85 (March 1999) 4:1461–1494.

66. Merle T. Cole, "Defending Baltimore during the 'Splendid Little War,'" *Maryland Historical Magazine* 93 (1998) 2: 158–181.

67. Gertrude Stein, *Wars I have Seen* (New York: Random House, 1945), 41.

68. Discovered by biographer Brenda Wineapple in 1995, the essay has gone unremarked by Stein scholars since. Brenda Wineapple, "Gertrude Stein and the Lost Ark," in *The Critical Response to Gertrude Stein*, 344–352. All quotations from Stein's "Degeneration in American Women" are drawn from the appendix in Wineapple, *Sister Brother*, 411–414.

69. George J. Engelmann, "The Increasing Sterility of American Women," *Journal of the American Medical Association* 37 (October 5, 1901): 890–897.

70. Stein, *The Autobiography*, 82. See Wineapple, *Sister Brother*, 151–154. On Englemann, see Regina Markell Morantz-Sanchez, *Conduct Unbecoming a Woman: Medicine on Trial in Turn-of-the-Century Brooklyn* (New York: Oxford University Press, 1999), and for context Deborah Kuhn McGregor, *From Midwives to Medicine: The Birth of American Gynecology* (New Brunswick, NJ: Rutgers University Press, 1998).

71. For example, the Maryland State Federation of Club Women's main campaign in 1900 was "purity of the press": the removal of "medical advertisements which offended the modesty of women," that is, birth control, from the newspapers. See Phail, *An Historical Sketch*, 30–31.

72. Wineapple, *Sister Brother*, 410. Diane Dillon, "Indians and 'Indianicity' at the 1893 World's Fair," in Nancy K. Anderson, *George deForest Brush: The Indian Paintings* (Washington, DC: National Gallery of Art, 2008).

73. Max Simon Nordau, *Degeneration* (London: W. Heinemann, 1895). For a helpful overview mostly focused on Europe, see William Greenslade, *Degeneration, Culture, and the Novel, 1880–1940* (Cambridge: Cambridge University Press, 1994).

74. Nordau, *Degeneration*, 16, 19.

75. Quotation from unsigned review in *Psychological Review* 2 (May 1895)3: 289. Additional negative reviews can be found in *The Critic*, 26 (March 30, 1895): 233–234; *The Arena* 15 (December 1895): 147–152; *The Outlook*, 52 (July 6, 1895): 24–25; and W. D. Howells, "Degeneration," *Harper's Weekly* 39 (April 13, 1895): 342. William James, "*Genie und Entartugn, eine psychologische Studie*," reviewed in *Psychological Review* 2 (May 1895) 3: 293.

76. J. J. Stevenson, "Is This a Degenerate Age?" *Popular Science Monthly* 60 (April 1902): 484.

77. Lewellyn F. Barker to Miss Stein, January 30, 1902 in *The Flowers of Friendship: Letters Written to Gertrude Stein*, ed. Donald Clifford Gallup (New York: Octagon Books, 1979), 24.

78. Gilman, *Women and Economics*, 149. Farland carefully points out, however, that "the turn away from biology [and the rise of 'gender'] did not do away with [sex] determinism" in science or social science. In fact it may have made it more urgent and more ethereal, locating it in the realms of psychology, history, and culture. Farland, "Gertrude Stein's Brain Work," 142.

79. Wineapple, *Sister Brother*, 146–149; 202–205.

80. Steven Meyer, *Irresistible Dictation: Gertrude Stein and the Correlations of Writing and Science* (Stanford, CA: Stanford University Press, 2001), especially chapter 3.

81. Ralph Waldo Emerson, "History," *The Complete Essays and Other Writings of Ralph Waldo Emerson* (New York: Random House, 1950), 139, 143.

82. Emerson, "Self-Reliance," *The Complete Essays*, 164.

83. On Emerson's racialism, see Nell Irvin Painter, *The History of White People* (New York: W. W. Norton, 2010), chapters 10, 11, and 12. For the "transparent eyeball," see Emerson, "Nature," *The Complete Essays*, 6. The distinction between these two Emersons may be very slim. He wrote: "But if the man is true to his better instincts or sentiments, and refuses the dominion of facts, as one that comes of a higher race; remains fast by the soul and sees the principle, then the facts fall aptly and supply into their places; they know their master, and the meanest of them glorifies him" in "History" in *The Complete Essays*, 139.

84. Stein, "Poetry and Grammar," 236.

85. Adam Begley, "The Decline of the Campus Novel," *Lingua Franca: The Review of Academic Life* 7 (1997) 7: 39–46. Begley associates the campus novel as a genre almost entirely with the post–World War II period.

86. Stein, *Fernhurst, Q.E.D., and Other Early Writings*, 3. All future references to this volume will be to this edition, cited parenthetically by page number in the text.

87. Joyce Antler, "'After College, What?' New Graduates and the Family Claim," *American Quarterly* 32 (Autumn 1980) 4: 409–434. Addams, *Twenty Years at Hull House*, 64–65, 93–94. See also Addams, *Democracy and Social Ethics*, especially the chapter "Filial Relations," (New York: Macmillan, 1902).

88. Emma Goldman "The Tragedy of Woman's Emancipation," in *The Feminist Papers: From Adams to de Beauvoir*, ed. Alice S. Rossi (Boston, MA: Northeastern, 1988), 508–516.

89. Henry Adams, *The Degradation of the Democratic Dogma* (New York: Macmillan, 1919) and Adams, *The Education of Henry Adams* (New York: Modern Library, 1931), especially chapter 25.

90. Elyse Blankely argues that Stein identified with sharply elitist and individualistic strains of feminism as necessary to the cause of her art and to the demands of her emotional life. "The New Woman was, in short, derivative; and since Stein wanted to be an original, she had to rid herself of the eager New Woman in order to become her own woman." Elyse Blankley, "Beyond the 'Talent of Knowing': Gertrude Stein and the New Woman" in *Critical Essays on Gertrude Stein*, 196–209.

91. Henle, "The New Woman," 503.

92. Quoted in Farland, "Gertrude Stein's Brain Work," 124.

93. Stein, *The Autobiography*, 79.

94. Stein to Van Vechten, [postmarked] August 22, 1925, *Letters of Gertrude Stein and Carl Van Vechten*, vol. 1, 121. See also the admission by Stein in *Everybody's Autobiography*, 71.

95. Of printing a "popular edition" of *The making*, Stein wrote: "That would please me more than anything" (Stein, *Everybody's Autobiography*, 99).

96. Katz, "The First Making of *The Making of Americans*," note 1, p. 214. "In the Nineteen Thirties, GS in effect retracked the arguments she had already accepted as conclusive during the writing of *MA* [The Making of Americans]."

97. Gertrude Stein, *Everybody's Autobiography*, 99–100.

98. Stein's notebooks indicate that little inspiration is to be had from the "spinster type." Of the "spinster quality," she noted a "lack of generosity and sentimentality." Conceive themselves heroes but do nothing heroic (DB-50). See also "The Spinster Group" (DB-66), folder 284, box 17, MS 77, YCAL.

99. A-3 #6, folder 287, box 17, MS 77, YCAL.

100. Farland, "Gertrude Stein's Brain Work," stresses the sexist (rather than feminist) thrust of *The Making*, given that David is the hero. Stein, *The Autobiography*, 113, notes: "But in spite of all this there was a hero and he was to die."

101. Emerson, "Nature," 156. Here, I draw on Stewart, *Gertrude Stein and the Present*. Tirza True Latimer makes a similar point about Stein's art and archive: "The completion of the collection denotes, in effect, stasis, or death." Tirza True Latimer,

"'In the Jealous Way of Pictures': Gertrude Stein's Collections," *Women's Studies* 39 (2010): 583.

102. James, "The One and the Many," 405–417.
103. Miller, *Gertrude Stein*, 108.
104. Stein,"The Gradual Making," in *Essays in America*, 148–149.
105. Deuteronomy 6:4. See Judith Plaskow's commentary in *The Sh'ma and Its Blessings*, edited by Rabbi Lawrence A. Hoffman (Jewish Lights Publishing, Woodstock Vermont, 1997), 99. It is very difficult to get at the extent of Stein's Jewish education. She seems to have been at least familiar with the some traditional prayers, as she acknowledges one of the morning *brachot* that thanks God for "not having made me a woman." See "Q. E. D.," in *Fernhurst, Q. E. D. and Other Early Writings*, 58. Linda *Wagner-Martin, Favored Strangers: Gertrude Stein and Her Family* (New Brunswick, NJ: Rutgers University Press, 1995), chapters 1 and 2, notes that she did attend Sabbath school, at least briefly, in her childhood years in California. In "Grant," Stein wrote: "Each one is all." Stein, *Four in America* (New Haven, CT: Yale University Press, 1947), 30.
106. Stein, *Everybody's Autobiography*, 153. Ashton suggests that math's grammatical correlatives are "I" and "it," which she identifies as infinitely substitutable words. See her "Gertrude Stein for Anyone," 289–331. I'm suggesting "one."
107. In the text, see 388, 393–394, and 407.
108. See especially, Beckson, *London in the 1890s*, chapter 6, and on the Bodley Head, Wendell V. Harris, "John Lane's Keynotes Series and the Fiction of the 1890's," *PMLA* 83 (October 1968) 5: 1407–1413.
109. Hugh H. M. Stutfield, "The Psychology of Feminism," *Blackwood's* 161 (January 1897): 104–107 in *A New Woman Reader*. See in same volume, Stutfield's 1895 much-cited essay "Tommyrotics." On Grande's sales, see "Literary Encyclopedia: Sarah Grand," http://www.litencyc.com/php/speople.php?rec=true&UID=1836 (viewed December 18, 2008). For reviews of *The Heavenly Twins* in the United States, see *The Outlook* 48 (November 18, 1893): 905; *The Nation* 57 (November 16, 1893): 374; *The Critic* 23 (August 5, 1893): 92. The latter review described characters in the novel as "hysterical," but the book overall as full of "cleverness," "charm," "freshness," and "poetic feeling."
110. Wineapple characterizes this document as part of a draft letter intended for May Bookstaver, Stein's first love. Wineapple, *Sister Brother*, 202–203. For original, see (unnumbered) page 10 of notes and fragments in Box 139, folder 3274, MS 76, YCAL.
111. Roger Fry to Gertrude Stein, April 6, 1913, Box 107, folder 2133, MS 76, YCAL.
112. Dana Cooper, "Country by Birth, Country by Marriage: American Women's Transnational War Efforts in Great Britain, 1895–1918," in *Women and Transnational Activism in Historical Perspective*, ed. Kimberly Jensen and Erika Kuhlman (St. Louis, MO, Republic of Letters Publishing, 2010), 44–47.
113. Stein, *Everybody's Autobiography*, 48.
114. John Lane to Gertrude Stein, January 28, 1913, Box 113, folder 2349, MS 76, YCAL. Stein, *The Autobiography*, 128. Lewis J. May, *John Lane and the Nineties* (London: John Lane, 1936), states: "Mrs. Lane was, unofficially, one of the chief literary advisors to the Bodley Head, and Lane always placed great reliance on her judgment" (168).
115. John Lane to Gertrude Stein, January 31, 1913 for rejection of *The Making*, and April 4, 1913 for acceptance and terms for *Three Lives*, both in Box 113, folder 2349, MS 76, YCAL.
116. See Edward Burns's notes in *Letters of Gertrude Stein and Carl Van Vechten*, vol. 1, 38, note 6. The only change was a new title page. Robert B. Harmon notes "Of these 1,000 [Grafton Press] editions, 300 were subsequently used for the first British

edition published in 1915." Robert Harmon, *The First Editions of Gertrude Stein* (Los Altos CA: Hermes Publications, 1978), 20.

117. Lane to Stein, January 28, 1913, Box 112, folder 2349, MS 76, YCAL.

118. Lane to Stein, January 31, 1913: "If you are in town Sunday we shall be very pleased to see you and your friend." Annie Lane to Stein, September 30, 1914: "It would give me much pleasure to see you and your friend again," both in Box 113, folder 2349, MS 76, YCAL. In the John Lane Papers at the British Library, only 11 items between the two remain, all mostly undated letters. See Gertrude Stein to John Lane [possibly 1921]: "Kindest remembrances from Miss Toklas and myself to Mrs. Lane" (Reel #3).

119. Stein, *The Autobiography*, 142. Stein named her Joseph Stalin character "Joseph Lane," in her later novel, *Mrs. Reynolds*.

120. May, *John Lane and the Nineties*, 87. Not too much detail is offered in J. W. Lambert and Michael Ratleff, *The Bodley Head* (London: Bodley Head, 1987), 105–107. Of Wilde's arrest, Lane remarked: "It killed [the journal] the *Yellow Book*, and it nearly killed me" (107). See also Beckson, *London in the 1890s*, 216–217. The media mistakenly reported that Wilde carried a copy of the *Yellow Book* under his arm as he was taken to prison.

121. Stein, *The Autobiography* , 128.

122. Stein, *Tender Buttons*, 29.

123. DeKoven sees "a parallel mutuality between progressive politics and avant garde art," symbolized by *Tender Buttons* and Hull House, but I see dissonance and rejection. Marianne DeKoven, "'Excellent, Not a Hull House': Gertrude Stein, Jane Addams and Feminist-Modernist Political Culture," in *Rereading Modernism: New Directions in Feminist Criticism*, ed. Lisa Rado (New York: Garland Publishing, 1994), 32–350.

124. Stein, *Tender Buttons*, 75.

125. On the *Atlantic Monthly*, see Stein, *The Autobiography*, 195. Sedgwick petted and praised Mary Antin, who practiced "assimilation with a vengeance," according to Jacobson in *Barbarian Virtues: The United States Encounters Foreign Peoples at Home and Abroad, 1876–1917* (New York: Hill and Wang, 2000), 205–219. On Sedgwick's stern rejection of Stein's work, see his letter in Gallup, ed., *The Flowers of Friendship*, 130.

126. Stein, *The Autobiography*, 154.

127. Ibid., 69.

128. RG 59 Records of the US Department of State, Passports, Great Britain, vol. 143, passports # 3609-3642 (3621 and 3021 for Toklas and Stein). For a representative busy day in August, see vol. 138, August 11, when 174 passports were issued all to "natives" and verified mostly by "personal examination." Passports were not required for foreign travel until 1918. John Torpey, *The Invention of the Passport: Surveillance, Citizenship, and the State* (New York: Cambridge University Press, 2000), and Mae Ngai, *Impossible Subjects: Illegal Aliens and the Making of Modern America* (Princeton, NJ: Princeton University Press, 2001), especially chapter 1.

129. Stein describes another go-round with the American embassy in Paris in *The Autobiography*, 161, in which she demands a passport over the objections of the clerk, who meekly submits. In addition to the 1914 emergency passport in London, Stein and Toklas had two additional passports issued, one in March 1915 another in August 1916. See passport applications numbered 53623 and 53624 and 32226 and 32227 in Ancestry.com. *U.S. Passport Applications, 1795–1925* [database online]. Provo, UT, USA: Ancestry.com Operations, Inc., 2007 (viewed December 2, 2009).

130. M. A. Heiss, "Evolution of the Imperial Idea and U.S. National Identity," *Diplomatic History* 26 (Fall 2002) 4: 515–521. Rowe points out that Henry Adams reveled in

the weakening of the British empire as it made room for new and improved US power in the world. John Carlos Rowe, *Literary Culture and U.S. Imperialism: From the Revolution to World War II* (Oxford: Oxford University Press, 2000), chapter 8.

131. Stein, "What Is English Literature?" in *Lectures in America*, 40.
132. Ibid., 49, 50–51. On Stein and imperial geographies, see Sonita Sarker, "Race, Nation and Modernity: The Anti-Colonial Consciousness of Modernism," in *Gender in Modernism: New Geographies, Complex Intersections*, ed. Bonnie Scott (Urbana: University of Illinois Press, 2007), 472–482. See also Stein's *Geographical History of America*.
133. Stein, *Everybody's Autobiography*, 233.
134. Transcripts of notebooks marked C-46, Box 285, folder 17, MS 77, YCAL.
135. Addams, *Twenty Years at Hull House* (New York: Signet, 1981), chapter 2, "Influence of Lincoln." Gertrude Stein, *Four in America* (New Haven, CT: Yale University Press, 1947), 54. Her "four" are Washington, Wilbur Wright, Henry James, and Grant. She wrote in *Wars I Have Seen*, "I was a passionate admirer of General Grant and the Northern army," 6.
136. Stein, *The Autobiography*, 78; see also, Stein, *Everybody's Autobiography*, 235, 247.
137. Stein, *The Autobiography*, 16.
138. Neil Schmitz, "Doing the Fathers: Gertrude Stein on U. S. Grant in *Four in America*," *American Literature* 65 (1993) 4: 751–760. Gerald Horne, "Race from Power: U.S. Foreign Policy and the General Crisis of White Supremacy," in *Window on Freedom: Race, Civil Rights, and Foreign Affairs, 1945–1988*, ed. Brenda Gayle Plummer (Chapel Hill: University of North Carolina Press, 2003), 54. See also Barbara Will, "Lost in Translation: Stein's Vichy Collaboration," *Modernism/modernity* 11 (2004) 4: 651–668 and Phoebe Stein Davis, "Even Cake Gets to Have Another Meaning": History, Narrative, and Daily Living in Gertrude Stein's World War II Writings," *Modern Fiction Studies* 44 (1998) 4: 568–607. On World War II as a global crisis of racial ideology, see Marilyn Lake and Henry Reynolds, *Drawing the Global Colour Line: White Men's Countries and the International Challenge of Racial Equality* (Cambridge: Cambridge University Press, 2008), chapter 14.
139. Stein, *Wars I Have Seen*, 36–37. All future references to this text will be to this edition, cited parenthetically.
140. Malcolm Cowley praised the book as an "utterly convincing picture of a people and a time," in his review of *Wars* in the *New York Times Book Review* (March 11, 1945), 22.
141. *Passeport de protection* dated February 12, 1944 in Box 140, folder 3295, MS 76, YCAL. Stein's 1915 passport application listed four "identifying documents" including her emergency passport issued in London in 1914 and a "police declaration" dated 1911.
142. See earlier, notes 4, 128, and 129.
143. Stein's distinction between saint and hysteric bears mentioning here. See Stein, *The Autobiography*, 228. So too is the pop remedy for hysteria in her day. "What she [the hysterical woman] needs is not spiritual advice, but outdoor exercise and a course in mathematics," asserted a writer in the *Independent* in 1905. "Arithmetic is often a very good antidote for some foolish ideas." This view casts the long walks and conversations with Alfred Whitehead in the summer of 1914 in an interesting light. Stein, *The Autobiography*, 152–153. "It was beautiful weather and beautiful country and Doctor Whitehead and Gertrude Stein never ceased wandering around in it and talking about all things." On the cure for women's nervousness, see "Hysteria," *The Independent*, 737.
144. Gertrude Stein, "The Mother of Us All," in *Plays by American Women, 1930-1960*, ed. Judith E. Barlow (New York: Applause, 1994), 280. All future references to this opera will be to this edition cited parenthetically in the text. See also Gabor Boritt, ed.,

War Comes Again: Comparative Vistas on the Civil War and World War II (New York: Oxford University Press, 1995); Chris Myers Asch, "Revisiting Reconstruction: James O. Eastland, The FEPC and the Struggle to Rebuild Germany, 1945–1946," *Journal of Mississippi History* 67 (2005) 1: 1–28.

145. Daniel was "yet not a very real name to me and I never have found out whether it is a name that I like or not" Stein wrote in *Everybody's Autobiography*, 138.

146. See Louis Francis Hartman and Alexander A. Di Lella, *The Book of Daniel* (Garden City, NY: Doubleday, 1978) for useful commentary and context.

147. Alma Lutz, *Susan B. Anthony: Rebel, Crusader, Humanitarian* (Boston, MA: Beacon Press, 1959), chapter 1, "Quaker Heritage" and Ida Husted Harper, *Life and Work of Susan B. Anthony* ([1898] Salem, NH: Ayer Co, 1983), vol. 1, chapter 1.

148. Blackbeard's legend was fanned by one of Stein's favorite authors, Defoe—whose first name was also Daniel. Daniel Defoe, *The History and Lives of All the Most Notorious Pirates and Their Crews...from Captain John Avery, Who First Settled at Madagascar, to Captain John Gow* (Glasgow: printed by Robert Duncan, 1788). Blackbeard the pirate also appears in Stephen Vincent Benét's short story "The Devil and Daniel Webster" (1938) as "Teach," one of the dastardly jury members. Stein met Benét and seems to have known this very popular story well.

149. On the Stein brothers' rivalry, see Wagner-Martin, *Favored Strangers*, 6. On Baltimore family and the Civil War, see Stein, *Wars I Have Seen*, 6. Stein's mother's brother served on the Confederate side.

150. Stein, *Everybody's Autobiography*, 133, 139, 142.

151. See, for example, her description of independent, self-supporting unmarried women's domestic instincts and pleasing housekeeping skills in "Homes of Single Women," from 1877. In *Elizabeth Cady Stanton, Susan B. Anthony, Correspondence, Writings, Speeches,* ed. Ellen Carol DuBois (New York: Schocken Books, 1981), 146–151.

152. Abraham Lincoln, "House Divided Speech," delivered at Springfield, Illinois, 1858. See http://www.historyplace.com/lincoln/divided.htm (viewed September 2010).

153. Stein to van Vechten, November 20, 1945, in *Letters of Gertrude Stein and Carl Van Vechten,* vol 2, 197–198. Rheta Childe Dorr, *Susan B. Anthony, the Woman Who Changed the Mind of a Nation* (New York: Frederick A. Stokes, 1928); Julie Des Jardins, *Women and the Historical Enterprise in America: Gender, Race, and the Politics of Memory, 1880–1945* (Chapel Hill: University of North Carolina Press, 2003), chapter 6. It's likely that Stein also looked at Harper's biography, as it contains language from the letters quoted in her opera's libretto. Harper, *Life and Work of Susan B. Anthony,* vol. 1, 343. Stein quoted from a letter by Anthony to her mother: "My constantly recurring thought and prayer now are that no word or act of mine may lessen the might of this country in the scale of truth and right." Stein did the same for Webster, drawing directly on his speeches "Reply to Maine" and "America," drawn, possibly, from Williams Jennings Bryan, *The World's Famous Orations* (New York: Funk and Wagnalls, 1906).

154. The cryptogram can be found in Stein, *Everybody's Autobiography*, 122 and 290.

155. "Suffrage Memorial Halted at Capital," *New York Times,* February 9, 1921; "Women Plan Fight for Legal Equality," *New York Times,* February 5, 1921; "3 Suffragists (in Marble) To Move Up in the Capitol," *New York Times,* September 27, 1996.

156. Kathryn Kish Sklar and Jill Dias, *How Did the National Woman's Party Address the Issue of the Enfranchisement of Black Women, 1919–1924?* (Binghamton, NY: State University of New York at Binghamton, 1997) in *Women and Social Movements in the United States, 1600–2000,* ed. Kathryn Kish Sklar and Thomas Dublin http://asp6new.alexanderstreet.com/was2/was2.index.map.aspx (viewed August 2, 2010).

157. "A Black Group Assails Statue of Suffragists," *New York Times*, March 9, 1997. "Remarks by the First Lady at the Sojourner Truth Unveiling," April 28, 2000, see http://www.whitehouse.gov/the-press-office/remarks-first-lady-sojourner-truth-bust-unveiling (viewed August 6, 2010).

158. *Gertrude Stein: In Words and Pictures: A Photobiography* (Chapel Hill, NC: Algonquin Books of Chapel Hill, 1994), 166. The fetishes were given to them in 1934 by Van Vechten during the US lecture tour to protect them during air travel, which Stein feared (initially).

159. Bennett Cerf, *At Random: The Reminiscences of Bennett Cerf* (New York: Random House, 1977), 107.

160. Stein, *Everybody's Autobiography*, 133.

161. Cerf, *At Random*, 103–105.

162. Ibid., 108.

163. Gertrude Stein to Bennett Cerf, March 20, 1945, Cerf Papers, Columbia University.

164. Stein, *Fernhurst, Q. E. D.*, 118.

165. Stein, *Everybody's Autobiography*, 200. On use of stereotypes from minstrelsy by Stein, see Barbara Webb, "The Centrality of Race to the Modernist Aesthetics of Gertrude Stein's Four Saints in Three Acts." *Modernism/modernity* 7 (2000) 3: 447–469.

3   ¡Adelante Hermanas de La Raza!

1. "Misa Para Josefina Silva de Cintrón," *El Diario-La Prensa* (November 18, 1988), 9, identifies her death date as October 29, 1988. The Social Security Death Index confirms this date and further indicates 1884 as her year of birth. Ancestry.com, *Social Security Death Index* [database online]. Provo, UT: Ancestry.com Operations Inc, 2010 (viewed June 7, 2011). Edna Acosta-Belén, "Silva de Cintrón, Josefina Pepiña (1885–1986[sic])" in *Latinas in the United States: A Historical Encyclopedia*, ed. Vicki L. Ruiz and Virginia Sánchez-Korrol (Bloomington: Indiana University Press, 2006), vol. 3, 682–683; Virginia Sánchez-Korrol, "The Forgotten Migrant: Educated Puerto Rican Women in New York City, 1920–1940," in *The Puerto Rican Woman: Perspectives on Culture, History, and Society*, ed. Edna Acosta-Belén (New York: Praeger, 1986), 170–179; and Sánchez-Korrol, *From Colonia to Community: The History of Puerto Ricans in New York City* (Berkeley: University of California, 1994), 113–114.

2. Walter D. Mignolo, "Citizenship, Knowledge, and the Limits of Humanity," *American Literary History* 18 (2006) 2: 312–331. Though Mignolo refers to a "decolonial idea of humanity," his article does not cite Pérez's work or touch on gender. Sonia Dmitrowna, "*Nuestro América Ante el Futuro*," *Artes y Letras* [hereafter *AL*] (June 1939): 4.

3. Emma Pérez, *The Decolonial Imaginary: Writing Chicanas into History*, (Bloomington: Indiana University Press, 1999), 33. See also Irene Lara, "Goddess of the Americas in the Decolonial Imaginary: Beyond the Virtuous Virgin/Pagan Puta Dichotomy," *Feminist Studies* 34 (2008) 1: 99–127, and Angie Chabram-Dernersesian, "Chicana! Rican? No, Chicana Riqueña! Refashioning the Transnational Connection," in *Between Woman and Nation: Nationalisms, Transnational Feminisms, and the State,* ed. Caren Kaplan, et al. (Durham, NC: Duke University Press, 1999), 264–295. See also Jorge Duany, "The Rough Edges of Puerto Rican Identities: Race, Gender, and Transnationalism," *Latin American Research Review* 40 (2005) 3: 177–190 and Gervasio Luis Garcia, "I Am the Other: Puerto Rico in the Eyes of North Americans, 1898," *Journal of American History* 87 (June 2000) 1: 39–64.

4. Breny Mendoza, "Unthinking State-Centric Feminisms," in *Rethinking Feminisms in the Americas,* ed. Mendoza (Ithaca, NY: Cornell University Press, 2000), 6–18.

5. G. Parkhurst, "Is Feminism Dead?" *Harper's Magazine* 170 (May 1935): 725–745. Scholars apply the word "doldrums" to the period of strategic flux for the organized suffrage movement around the turn of the twentieth century or to the period following World War II, a period of feminist backlash. Lisa Tetrault, "The Incorporation of American Feminism: Suffragists and the Postbellum Lyceum," *Journal of American History* 96 (March 2010), and Leila J Rupp, *Survival in the Doldrums: The American Women's Rights Movement, 1945 to the 1960s* (New York: Oxford University Press, 1987).

6. Lorrin Thomas, *Puerto Rican Citizen: History and Political Identity in Twentieth-Century New York City* (Chicago, IL: University of Chicago Press, 2010), 132. Thomas's study neglects *Artes y Letras,* though her introduction describes "cultural citizenship" and "diasporic citizenship," concepts which resonate with the idea of a third space or decolonial approach to rights. See also Lorrin Thomas, "Resisting the Racial Binary? Puerto Rican's Encounter with Race in Depression-Era New York City," *Centro: Journal of the Center for Puerto Rican Studies* 21(Spring 2009) 1: 5–35.

7. Juan Manuel Carrión has wearily stated that the "deconstruction of the Hispanic myth of racial democracy has almost become an industry" within the academy. Juan Manuel Carrión, *"Two Variants of Caribbean Nationalism: Marcus Garvey and Pedro Albizu Campos,"* Centro: Journal of the Center for Puerto Rican Studies 17 (2005): 31. For the vagaries of claiming legal whiteness by Mexicanos/as, see Mae M. Ngai, *Impossible Subjects: Illegal Aliens and the Making of Modern America* (Princeton, NJ: Princeton University Press, 2005), chapter 1 and Natalia Molina, "'In a Race All Their Own': The Quest to Make Mexicans Ineligible for U.S. Citizenship," *Pacific Historical Review* 79 (May 2010) 2: 167–201.

8. *Senado de Puerto Rico, Resolucion* 2198 http://www.senadopr.us/Archivo_Digital /2005-2008/Radicaciones/Resoluciones_del_Senado/2006/rs2198-6.pdf (viewed on April 3, 2009).

9. Megan Threlkeld, "How to 'Make This Pan American Thing Go?' Interwar Debates on U.S. Women's Activism in the Western Hemisphere," in *Women and Transnational Activism in Historical Perspective,* ed. Kimberly Jensen and Erika Kuhlman (St. Louis, MO: Republic of Letters Publishing, 2010), 173–192 and K. Lynn Stoner, "In Four Languages but with One Voice: Division and Solidarity within Pan American Feminism, 1923–1933," in *Beyond the Ideal: Pan Americanism in Inter-American Affairs,* ed. David Sheinin (Westport, CT: Greenwood Press, 2000), 79–94. See also Ellen DuBois and Lauren Derby, "The Strange Case of Minerva Bernardino: Pan American and United Nations Women's Rights Activist," *Women's Studies International Forum* 32 (2009) 1: 43–50 and Donna J. Guy, "The Politics of Pan-American Cooperation: Maternalist Feminism and the Child Rights Movement, 1913–1960," *Gender & History* 10 (1998) 3: 449–469. A foundational essay is Leila J. Rupp, "Constructing Internationalism: The Case of Transnational Women's Organizations, 1888–1945," *American Historical Review* 99 (1994) 5: 1571–1600.

10. Sarah A. Buck, "The Meaning of the Women's Vote in Mexico, 1917–1953" in *The Women's Revolution in Mexico 1910–1953,* ed. S. E. Mitchell and Patience A. Schell (Lanham, MD: Rowman and Littlefield, 2007), 84. Anna Macías, *Against All Odds: The Feminist Movement in Mexico to 1940* (Westport CT: Greenwood Press, 1982), chapter 6, and Shirlene Soto, *Emergence of the Modern Mexican Woman: Her Participation in Revolution and Struggle for Equality, 1910–1940* (Denver CO: Arden Press, 1990), 103–105.

11. The policy somewhat revised the Monroe Doctrine of 1823 that claimed for the United States a right to intervene in Latin American affairs (against Europe) with an ideal of nonintervention. Fredrick Pike, *FDR's Good Neighbor Policy: Sixty Years of*

Generally Gentle Chaos (Austin: University of Texas Press, 1995) and James William Park, *Latin American Underdevelopment: A History of Perspectives in the United States, 1870–1965* (Baton Rouge: Louisiana State University Press, 1995), chapter 5. Mark T. Berger, "A Greater America? Pan Americanism and the Professional Study of Latin America" (45–56), and Richard V. Salisbury, "Hispanismo versus Pan Americanism; Spanish Efforts to Counter U.S. Influence in Latin American before 1930" (67–77), both in *Beyond the Ideal*. For exceptionalist apologetics, see Joseph Burne Lockey, *Essays in Pan-Americanism* (Port Washington, NY: Kennikat Press, 1967), especially "The Meaning of Pan Americanism" (1925) and "Pan Americanism and Imperialism"(1938).

12. Reginald Horsman, *Race and Manifest Destiny: The Origins of American Racial Anglo-Saxonism* (Cambridge, MA: Harvard University Press, 1981).

13. Juan Flores, "The Latino Imaginary: Dimensions of Community and Identity" (183–193), and Frances R. Aparicio, "On Sub-Versive Signifiers: Tropicalizing Language in the United States" (194–212) in *Tropicalizations: Transcultural Representations of Latinidad*, ed. Frances R. Aparicio (Hanover, NH: University Press of New England, 1997).

14. José Martí, "Our America," in *José Martí: Selected Writings*, ed. Esther Allen and Roberto González Echevarría (New York: Penguin Books, 2002): 288–296.

15. Robert Rydell, *World of Fairs: The Century-of-Progress Expositions* (Chicago IL: University of Chicago Press, 1993), chapters 3 and 6; Rydell, *All the World's a Fair: Visions of Empire at American International Expositions, 1876–1916* (Chicago, IL: University of Chicago Press, 1984), chapters 5–8.

16. Magali Roy-Féquière, *Women, Creole Identity, and Intellectual Life in Early Twentieth-Century Puerto Rico*, (Philadelphia, PA: Temple University Press, 2004); Laura Briggs, *Reproducing Empire: Race, Sex, Science, and U.S. Imperialism in Puerto Rico*, (Berkeley: University of California Press, 2002), and Eileen Findlay, *Imposing Decency: The Politics of Sexuality and Race in Puerto Rico, 1870–1920*, (Durham, NC: Duke University Press, 1999).

17. Roberto Cintrón, personal communication to author, April 16, 2009. Rosa E. Carrasquillo, *Our Landless Patria: Marginal Citizenship and Race in Caguas, Puerto Rico, 1880–1910* (Lincoln: University of Nebraska Press, 2006), 111. J. C. S. [Josefina Silva de Cintrón], "*Mi Adhesión*," *AL* (June 1936): 15. Solisirée del Moral, "Negotiating Colonialism: 'Race,' Class, and Education in Early-Twentieth-Century Puerto Rico" (131–134), and Pablo Navarro-Rivera, "The Imperial Enterprise and Educational Policies in Colonial Puerto Rico" (163–174), both in *Colonial Crucible: Empire in the Making of the Modern American State*, ed. Alfred W. McCoy and Francisco A. Scarano (Madison: University of Wisconsin Press, 2009).

18. Ancestry.com, *1920 United States Federal Census* [database online]. Provo, UT, USA: The Generations Network, Inc., 2005 (viewed May 4, 2009).

19. Roberto Cintrón, April 16, 2009. Ancestry.com, *1920 United States Federal Census* and Ancestry.com., *World War I Draft Registration Cards, 1917–1918* [database online]. Provo, UT, USA: The Generations Network, Inc., 2005 (viewed May 4, 2009).

20. Roberto Cintrón, April 16, 2009. President Calvin Coolidge destroyed most of his personal papers before leaving office. My search of extant records concerning the post office revealed no letter of appointment for Josefina Silva de Rivera. See *Index to the Calvin Coolidge Papers* (Washington, DC: Library of Congress, 1965), 5–6, and in the microfilm collection, reels #24–25–26 concerning "post offices" and reel #128 concerning "Porto Rico." Hereafter, CC Papers.

21. Roberto Cintrón, April 16, 2009. On political opinion regarding the United States ca. 1909, see "Questionnaires," Box 1–3, entry 80, RG 350, Records of the Bureau of Insular Affairs relating to Puerto Rico, 1898–1934, NARA II.

22. Roberto Cintron, April 16, 2009, emphasis in the original.

23. Allison L Sneider, *Suffragists in an Imperial Age: U.S. Expansion and the Woman Question, 1870–1929* (Oxford: Oxford University Press, 2008), especially chapter 5; Norma Valle Ferrer, "Feminism and Its Influence on Women's Organizations in Puerto Rico," in *The Puerto Rican Woman: Perspectives on Culture, History, and Society*, ed. Edna Acosta-Belén (New York: Praeger, 1986), 75-87; Yamila Azize-Vargas, "The Emergence of Feminism in Puerto Rico, 1870–1930," in *Unequal Sisters: A Multicultural Reader in U.S. Women's History*, ed. Vicki L. Ruiz and Ellen Carol DuBois (New York: Routledge, 2000): 268–277; María de Fátima Barceló-Miller, "Half-Hearted Solidarity: Women Workers and the Women's Suffrage Movement in Puerto Rico During the 1920s" (126–142), and Gladys M. Jiménez-Muñoz, "Literacy, Class, and Sexuality in the Debate on Women's Suffrage in Puerto Rico During the 1920s" (143–170), in *Puerto Rican Women's History: New Perspectives*, ed. Félix A. Matos Rodríguez and Linda C. Delgado (Armonk, NY: ME Sharpe, 1998). Gladys Jiménez-Muñoz, "Deconstructing Colonialist Discourse: Links between the Women's Suffrage Movement in the United States and Puerto Rico," *Phoebe: An International Journal of Feminist Scholarship, Theory, and Aesthetics* 5 (1993): 9–34, and Jiménez-Muñoz, "Carmen Maria Colon Pellot: On 'Womanhood' and 'Race' in Puerto Rico during the Interwar Period," *CR: The New Centennial Review* 3 (2003): 71–91. See also Rosalyn Terborg-Penn, "Enfranchising Women of Color: Woman Suffragists as Agents of Empire," in *Nation, Empire, Colony: Historicizing Gender and Race*, ed. Ruth Roach Pierson and Nupur Chaudhuri (Bloomington: Indiana University Press, 1998), 41–56.

24. Azize-Vargas, "The Emergence of Feminism in Puerto Rico," 271–272, and Sneider, *Suffragists in an Imperial Age,* 129–131. "H.B. 1 An Act To grant woman suffrage, to declare her right to be elected to public office in Porto Rico, and for other purposes," February 15, 1921, file 27260, Box 1217, RG 350, NARA II. See also related clippings and legal opinions in this file.

25. Sneider, *Suffragists in an Imperial Age,* 129–134. On Puerto Rican women's support for amending the Jones Act, the Asociación Puertorriqueña de Mujeres Sufragistas wrote to Coolidge encouraging him to sign the bill if it should pass the Senate. See Ana L. Velez [president] to Hon. Calvin Coolidge January 16, 1929, in file 27260, Box 1217, RG 350, NARA II.

26. Theodore Roosevelt, *The Colonial Policies of the United States* (New York: Arno Press, 1999), 99.

27. H.M. Towner to General New [Postmaster General of the United States] November 28, 1923, CC Papers. See also Towner to C. Bascom Slemp, Setpember 6, 1923 and November 15, 1923, and Robert H. Todd to Slemp, September 19, 1923 in CC Papers. Todd was a Harding appointee, initially, to the Immigration Commission in San Juan.

28. Henry Wells, *The Modernization of Puerto Rico: A Political Study of Changing Values and Institutions* (Cambridge, MA: Harvard University Press, 1969), 108–111. Truman R. Clark, "'Educating the Natives in Self-Government': Puerto Rico and the United States, 1900–1933," *The Pacific Historical Review* 42 (1973) 2: 220–233.

29. *Memorial to the President and to the Congress of the United states Presented by the Porto Rican Delegation to the United States* [ca. 1924], CC Papers.

30. Towner to New, November 28, 1923, CC Papers.

31. On partisan matters in Puerto Rico, see Wells, *The Modernization of Puerto Rico*, chapters 3 and 4. "Will Ask Statehood Plank," May 30, 1928; "Porto Ricans Ask Statehood Planks," May 27, 1928; "Porto Rico May Go for Gov. Roosevelt," April 17, 1932, all in *New York Times*. "Political Phenomena of Porto Rico" from Pedro Boricua, May 12, 1916, and "Democrats in Puerto Rico" from Henry W. Dooley, June 12, 1916 in *New York Times*. Governor Horace M. Towner opined in 1924: "It is utterly impossible for

the Democrats to organize any effective opposition against the President." Towner to Slemp, May 14, 1925, CC Papers.

32. "Henry W. Dooley of Porto Rico Dies," *New York Times*, March 13, 1932.
33. "On Way to Inauguration" (February 27, 1933); "Resigns in Puerto Rico" (October 17, 1933); "Few Committeewomen" (June 27, 1928); "Democratic Women on Duty in Chicago" (June 21, 1932); "William Whittemore [obit], September 30, 1942), all in *New York Times*.
34. Myrtle Reed, *Lavender and Old Lace* (New York: G.P. Putnam's Sons, 1908).
35. W. B. Courtney, "Kansas on the Carib," *Colliers* 94 (December 29, 1934): 10–12.
36. Kelvin A. Santiago-Valles, "'Higher Womanhood' Among the 'Lower Races': Julia McNair Henry in Puerto Rico and the 'Burdens' of 1898," *Radical History Review* 73 (1999): 47–74.
37. [Chairman] to Miss M. Adelaide Foster, October 25, 1913, file 21061, Box 957, RG 350, NARA II.
38. "Acting Commissioner" to Hon. E. J. Saldaña, December 20, 1922, and attached report by Miss Beatrix Lassalle in file 21061, Box 957, RG 350, NARA II.
39. Ricarda Ramos Casellas [Liga Social Suffragista de Puerto Rico] and Milagros Benet Mewton [Asociación Pan-Americana de Mujeres de Puerto Rico] to Calvin Coolidge, October 14, 1927, in CC Papers.
40. Benet de Mewton to General Frank McIntyre, June 10, 1921, file 27260, Box 1217, RG 350, NARA II.
41. C. W. Vargas to Hon. Frank B. Willlis, September 10, 1923, CC Papers. Vargas seems to have been removed from Puerto Rico by the 4th Ohio regiment as their "mascot" and received some education and employment in the postal service in Columbus. He was apparently the first Puerto Rican postmaster named by President Harding. See Frank B. Willis to Bascom G. Slemp, September 24, 1923, CC Papers.
42. H. M. Towner to C. Bascom Slemp, February 17, 1924, CC Papers. On the Crowder memo, see Sneider, *Suffragists in an Imperial Age*, 129–130. See also Towner to Frank McIntyre [Chief, Bureau of Insular Affairs], May 21, 1925, file 27260, Box 1217, RG 350, NARA II.
43. Milagros Benet de Mewton to General [Frank] McIntyre, May 5, 1921, file 2760, Box 1217, RG 350, NARA II. Benet de Mewton did not "insist upon universal suffrage" but remained interested in language that would include "ALL" potential voters after certain literacy thresholds had been met. Mewton to McIntyre, May 19, 1921. See also Rosario Bellber [also of the Liga Social Suffragista de Puerto Rico] to McIntyre, January 23, 1924 in Box 1217, RG 350, NARA II.
44. Roberto Cintrón, April 16, 2009, and Pedro Caballero, "*Doña Josefina* S. de Cintrón Ante Los Hispanos," *AL* (June 1935): 14.
45. Not until 1919 were all civil service examinations open to women according to Patricia Ingraham, *The Foundation of Merit: Public Service in American Democracy* (Baltimore, MD: Johns Hopkins University Press, 1995), 33.
46. The new Civil and Penal Codes of 1902 "greatly expanded divorce provisions" and enjoyed wide popular support. Eileen J. Findlay, "Love in the Tropics: Marriage, Divorce, and the Construction of Benevolent Colonialism in Puerto Rico, 1898–1910," in *Close Encounters of Empire: Writing the Cultural History of U.S.-Latin American Relations*, ed. Gilbert M. Joseph et. al. (Durham, NC: Duke University Press, 1999), 139–172.
47. Roberto Cintrón, April 16, 2009. The San Lorenzo probably arrived in May; see *New York Times*, May 17 and 27, 1927. State of New York Certificate and Record of Marriage, no. 13636. Municipal Archives, City of New York.
48. Roberto Cintrón, April 16, 2009.
49. Manuel R. Rodríguez, "Representing Development: New Perspectives about the New Deal in Puerto Rico, 1933–36," *Centro: Journal of the Center for Puerto Rican Studies*

14 (2002) 2: 148–179. See also Thomas G Mathews, *Puerto Rican Politics and the New Deal* (Gainesville: University of Florida Press, 1960), and César J. Ayala and Rafael Bernabe, *Puerto Rico in the American Century: A History Since 1898* (Chapel Hill: University of North Carolina Press, 2007), chapter 5, and Blanca G. Silvestrini, *Historia De Puerto Rico: Trayectoria De Un Pueblo* (San Juan, PR.: Ediciones Cultural Panamericana, Rotedic, S. A. Grupo Novograph, 1992), capítulo 13. For a more critical overview, see Ronald Fernandez, *The Disenchanted Island: Puerto Rico and the United States in the Twentieth Century* (New York: Praeger, 1992), chapter 5.

50. Josefina S. de Cintrón, "*Mi Adhesión,*" *AL* (June 1936): 15.
51. Lidia, "'UMA' *Unión de Mujeres Americanas,*" *AL* (September 1934): 7.
52. "*Ufanemonos del Español,*" *AL* (June 1934): 1, 8. Editors maintained opposition to bilingual education in Puerto Rico: "*Enseñanza Bilingue,*" *AL* (September 1934): 1, 8. See also Ricardo Leon, "*La Lengua Castellana,*" *AL* (June 1934): 7, Tomas R. Gares, "*El Idioma Castellaño y P.R.*" *AL* (September 1934): 3, and José Pérez Lozada, "*Un Español 'Nuestro,*" *AL* (July 1936): 6, 13.
53. "*Ateneo Puertorriqueño,*" *AL* (September 1934). See also "*Interesante Conferencia,*" *AL* (September 1933): 4.
54. Roy-Féquière, *Women, Creole Identity,* chapter 1 and Kelvin Santiago-Valles, "The Imagined Republic of Puerto Rican Populism in World-Historical Context: The Poetics of Plantation Fantasies and the Petit-Coloniality of Criollo Blanchitude, 1914–48," in *Race, Colonialism, and Social Transformation in Latin America and the Caribbean,* ed. Jerome Branche (Gainesville: University Press of Florida, 2008), 59–90.
55. Roy-Féquière, *Women, Creole Identity,* especially chapter 1.
56. Roosevelt mandated English instruction in the public schools of Puerto Rico for the first time in 1937. Maria Josefa Canino, "An Historical Review of the English Language Policy in Puerto Rico's Educational System, 1898–1949," PhD diss., Graduate School of Education of Harvard University, 1981, 183. *Artes y Letras* opposed this policy. See "*La Intranquilidad de Puerto Rico,*" *AL* (May 1937): 1.
57. Pedro Caballero, "Bertha Singerman," *AL* (December 1934): 6
58. "*El Centenario en honor de Lope de Vega Aquí,*" April 25, 1935. The *Círculo* celebrated Mothers' Day at the Eastman School: "*Celebración del Círculo Cultural Cervantes,*" April 29, 1935, and regularly met there. See "*Baile de Primavera del C. Cultural Cervantes,*" May 24, 1935. For praise of the work of Professor Ónis and the Insitutos de las Españas see "*Resultó Brillante La Velada Literaria,*" October 15, 1934. The *Círculo* also met in the Roerich for various events; see "*Festival del Círculo Cultural Cervantes,*" February 12, 1934, which included skits and a dance. All in *La Prensa.*
59. "*Círculo Culturtal Cervantes,*" *AL* (October 1933): 1.
60. Cintrón, *Ibid.* "*Una Velada Del Grupo Artistico 'Cervantes,'*" January 6, 1934; "*Un Almuerzo Del Círculo Cultural Cervantes,*" January 27, 1934; "*Una Veleda Del Círculo Cultural Cervantes,*" October 8, 1934; "*Circulo Cultural Cervantes,*" April 1, 1935; all in *La Prensa.* The paper also carried a list of the *oficiales* for "*La Misión Episcopal Hispana*" that listed women who did friendly visiting and directed the choir. "*Damas Auxiliares,*" and "*Oficiales de la Mision Episcopal Hispana,*" April 1, 1935. The *Círculo* hosted Luis Muñoz Rivera in a summer visit in 1934: "*El Homanje de C.C.C.*" and "*Velada del C.C. en Honor de Muñoz Rivera,*" (16 and 19 July 1934) all in *La Prensa.*
61. Sometimes Rev. Cintrón was titled in the masthead as *jefe de redacción* basically, editor; The September 1935 masthead described the journal as a "*Revista Mensual Fundada por Josefina Silva de Cintrón, Directora-Propietaria.*" (p. 5).
62. Caballero, "*Doña Josefina S. de Cintrón,*" *AL* (June 1935): 1, 14. "*Ropero de los Pobres,*" *AL* (August 1936): 18, and "*Damas Auxiliares,*" *AL* (November 1936): 29.
63. "*El Verso Castellano con Barral,*" *AL* (May 1936): 7. This reflected popular belief, according to opinion shapers in New York. See editorials in *La Prensa*: "*Espectaculos*

Hispanos en Nueva York,"(April 20, 1936) and *"Teatro Hispano 'Amateur,'"* May 24, 1935.

64. Margarita Robles de Mendoza, *Ciudadanía De La Mujer Mexicana* (Morelia, MI: A. Obregon, 1932), frontispiece.

65. Lidia, *"Margarita Robles de Mendoza,"* AL (June 1934): 4. "Amelia Earhart *honrada en Mejico con Medalla de oro por la 'UMA.'"* La Prensa April 25, 1935.

66. J. S. de Cintrón, *"Vida Nueva,"* AL (July 1936): 12.

67. On Spanish cultural heritage, see Remedios C. Román, *"Las Descendientes de la Reina Isabel de España,"* AL (October 1933): 1, 4 and (December 1933): 1, 4, which pointed out woman suffrage under the Second Republic (1931). Pura Romo Silva, *"A La Mujer Español,"* AL (March 1937): 10.

68. Trina Padilla de Zanz, *"España,"* AL (April, 1934): 4; *"La Flapper,"* AL (July 1934): 5; Dylis Vaugham, *"Gitana,"* AL (May 1934): 5. An unidentified New York writer penned a poem called *"La Gitanilla"* and dedicated it to Fatima de Mendez of Cuba, portraying a kind of resigned attraction to the *"Linda Gitanilla"* despite her ambiguous moral value as neither *"bueno"* or *"malo."* See AL (August 1934): 5. Jiménez-Muñoz, "Literacy, Class, and Sexuality," and Juan Flores, "The Insular Vision: Pedreira and the Puerto Rican *Misère,"* in his *Divided Borders: Essays on Puerto Rican Identity* (Houston, TX: Arte Publico Press, 1993), 23.

69. Pepiña, *"Mi Viejo Amigo el Árbol,"* AL (December 1934): 7.

70. Conchita Zeno, *"La Comunión de me Hija Margarita,"* AL (May 1936): 4.

71. M. Flores Cabrera, *"Necrología: Hacia Su Patria,"* and Pura Romo Silva, *"Un Recuerdo,"* AL (March 1935): 7. The journal also carried a photograph of the deceased.

72. AL (August 1934), cover. There was no accompanying article about her, as was the case with famous artists and performers whose pictures appeared on the AL cover.

73. Nicole Rafter, "Apes, Men and Teeth: Earnest A. Hoonton and Eugenic Decay" in *Popular Eugenics: National Efficiency and American Mass Culture in the 1930s,* ed. Susan Currell and Christina Cogdell (Ohio University Press, 2006), 248–268. See also Vicki L. Ruiz, "Star Struck: Acculturation, Adolescence, and Mexican American Women, 1920–1950," (343–361), and Kathy Peiss "Making Faces: Cosmetic Industry and the Cultural Construction of Gender," (324–345) in *Unequal Sisters,* 4th ed. (New York: Routledge, 2008), 343–361. For an earlier intervention, see Martin R. Delany, *Principia of Ethnology* (Philadelphia, PA: Harper & Brother, Publishers, 1879).

74. *"Una hispanoamericana tiene aquí el cuerpo más perfecto,"* La Prensa, April 1, 1935. The phrase "aristocracy of the face" is from Susan Sontag, *Illness as Metaphor; and, AIDS and Its Metaphors* (New York: Macmillan, 2001), 128. On the Puerto Rican body under colonialism, see Benigno Trigo, "Anemia and Vampires: Figures to Govern the Colony, Puerto Rico, 1880–1904," *Comparative Studies in Society and History* 41 (January 1999)1: 104–128.

75. "For many years it has become the custom for Mother's Day greetings to carry a reproduction of the famous "Whistler's Mother." So read an advertisement for Hern's Store on 14th street in *New York Times,* May 11, 1935. On Whistler, see Robert M. Crunden, *American Salons: Encounters with European Modernity, 1885–1917* (New York: Oxford University Press, 1993), chapter 1. On the Whistler stamp, see http://www.nwhm.org/exhibits/stamps/mothers.html. (viewed December 13, 2009).

76. One writer made an elaborate case for Christmas as more spiritually appropriate and historically accurate for Mother's Day: Jaime Vilar Lago, *"Navidad: El Día de las Madres,"* AL (December 1934): 1, 14. *"La Madre: Divagaciones Sentimentales,"* AL (May 1937): 13–14, 18. See also *"Celebración del 'Dia de las Madres' en Iglesias,"* La Prensa, April 25, 1935.

77. *"El Dia de la Madre,"* La Prensa, May 7, 1938.

78. Pedro Juan Labarthe, *The Son of Two Nations: The Private Life of a Columbia Student* (New York: Carranza & Co., 1931), 173.

79. Labarthe, *Son of Two Nations*, 145–146.
80. Editorial squib, *AL* (October 1935): 4.
81. Beatriz Sandoval edited the *"Para Las Damas"* page that included the series *"Modas de Paris"* and *"La Mujer y La Casa"* written by Mll. Daré and Lydia le Baron Walker, respectively. *La Prensa* did cover mainstream and pan-American feminist activity, following the work of labor secretary Frances Perkins and Sophonisba Breckenridge (December 12, 1933) and the 1933 Montevideo conference, with NWP leader Doris Stevens making the headline "Doris Stevens *Alaba el Triunfo de la Mujer en la Conferencia de Montevideo"* (January 25, 1934).
82. Karen J. Blair, *The Torchbearers: Women and Their Amateur Arts Associations in America, 1890–1930* (Bloomington: Indiana University Press, 1994). *La Prensa* did carry notices of a small number of art groups in New York, including *"Los Hijos Del Arte,"* which, interestingly was made up of all women, and *"Club Pro Arte"* seemed to have more of an accent on folk and sacred arts rather than high European forms. *"Actividades de 'Los Hijos Del Arte" La Prensa* (May 24, 1935).
83. Diana Selig, "World Friendship: Children, Parents and Peace Education in America between the Wars," in *Children and War: A Historical Anthology*, ed. James Marten (New York: New York University Press, 2002), 135–146. On celebrating local student success, see: La Directora, "Triunfo de Puerto Rico," *AL* (April 1935): 1. Silva de Cintrón enthused over the success of Puerto Rican student from "our university" (in Puerto Rico) who won debate tournaments held in Washington, NY, and in San Juan. This tournament was likely related to student exchanges sponsored by Carnegie Endowment for Peace. Its "Division of Intercourse and Education" sponsored various student exchanges mostly with Europe but also with "the Orient" and "Interamerica." Between 1928 and 1938, Puerto Rico appeared only once in the annual yearbook, when the Yale debate team received $560 grant to visit University of Puerto Rico in April 1929 (to debate in English). UPR students had visited Yale to debate in Spanish in 1928 (1930, 76–77). Carnegie Endowment for International Peace, *Year Book* (Washington, DC: The Endowment, 1912+)]
84. *"Nuestros Canjes," AL* (October 1937): 15; *"Suscriptores de 'Artes y Letras' en este año," AL* (December 1934): 12.
85. *AL* (January 1935) (inside cover); *Bulletin of the Pan American Union* (February 1937), ii, cost 10 cents per issue, 12 cents for *Puerto Rico Illustrado* 28 (July 1939), cover.
86. Roberto Cintrón, April 16, 2009.
87. Sánchez-Korrol, "Survival of Puerto Rican Women in New York Before World War II," in *Historical Perspectives on Puerto Rican Survival in the United States*, ed. Clara E. Rodriguez and Virginia E. Sánchez-Korrol (Princeton, NJ: Marcus Weiner Publishers, 1996), 55–67, and Frederick Douglass Opie, "Eating, Dancing, and Courting in New York Black and Latino Relations, 1930–1970," *Journal of Social History* 42 (2008) 1: 79–109.
88. *AL* (July 1933; December 1934; May, and October 1937); quotation from February 1935 issue, 11.
89. Marilyn Grace Miller, *Rise and Fall of the Cosmic Race: The Cult of Mestizaje in Latin America* (Austin: University of Texas Press, 2004). José Vasconcelos, *The Cosmic Race: A Bilingual Edition* (Baltimore, MD: Johns Hopkins, 1997). See also Vicki L. Ruiz, *"Morena/o, Blanca/o, y Café con Leche*: Racial Constructions in Chicana/o Historiography," in *The Practice of U.S. Women's History: Narratives, Intersections, and Dialogues*, ed. S. J. Kleinberg, Eileen Boris, and Vicki L. Ruiz (New Brunswick, NJ: Rutgers University Press, 2007), 221–237.
90. Santiago-Valles, "The Imagined Republic of Puerto Rican Populism," 78. *La Prensa* referred to *"las españas"* as a social formation unique to the world's peoples (*"como ningún otro pueblo de la historia"*). Editorial, *"El Españolismo Integral," La Prensa* (April 1, 1935).

91. Photograph on p. 13 with caption, *AL* (March 1935). Caballero had a mostly playful approach to these categories; he praised *"tres aspectos étnicos de nuestra poesia: I. Lo Negro. II Lo Mulatto. III Lo Jíbaro."* Sometimes he accented "whiteness," holding up *"el puro español blanco."* See *"Neustro Primer Declamador," AL* (September 1936): 5.

92. Capitán Angel Camblor, *"Una Sola Bandera Para La América Nuestra," AL* (October 1934): 1, 8.

93. Angel Camblor, *La Bandera de La Raza,* (Montevideo: Editorial Unión Hispanamericana, 1935): 16.

94. Nancy Stepan, *The Hour of Eugenics: Race, Gender, and Nation in Latin America* (Ithaca, NY: Cornell University Press, 1991), and Richard Graham, *The Idea of Race in Latin America, 1870–1940* (Austin: University of Texas Press, 1990).

95. For Mexican enthusiasm for La Bandera, see *"La 'Bandera de la Raza' flamerar el 12 en todas las escuelas de Méjico," La Prensa,* September 27, 1934.

96. Carnegie Endowment for International Peace, *Conferencias Internacionales Americanas, 1889–1936,* (Wáshington, Dotación Carnegie Para la Paz Internacional, 1938), 487, 529. Labarthe, *Son of Two Nations,* 95.

97. Capitán Angel Camblor, *"Carta de Gran Significación que Agredecemos al Creador de La Bandera de la Raza," AL* (October 1936): 7.

98. *"Día de la Raza. Día de Colon," AL* (October 1934): 6. *La Prensa* only mentioned that Robles de Mendoza lead celebrants in a pledge or prayer—*"la plegaria de la Bandera de la Raza."* See *"Vibrante Afirmación de Hispanidad Fue la manifestación columbina de ayer"* (October 13, 1934): 6, which glossed the event as follows: *"Fue un memorable y típico 'Día de la Raza.'"* See Editorial, *La Prensa,* *"El Día de Colon,"* October 12, 1934, which actually accented the "Spanishness" of Colon. At other moments, *la raza* was in focus: *"La Glorias del Descubrimiento fueron remomoradas en el banquete de la raza,"* (October 6, 1934), *La Prensa.*

    On Puerto Rico's need for its own flag in the pages of *Artes y Letras,* see Marta Lomar, *"Nuestras Banderas"* (November 1935): 4; *"Bandera de Puerto Rico"* (May 1938): 8; Alice Esteva Menéndez de Williams, *"El Niño Que no Tiene Bandera,"* (October–November 1938): 11. The men and women gathered in somber protest of the Ponce massacre carried small flags as pictured in *La Prensa,* 26 March 1937. For a bracing and brilliant discussion of the Puerto Rican flag, see Juan Flores, "The Lite Colonial: Diversions of Puerto Rican Discourse," in his *From Bomba to Hip Hop: Puerto Rican Culture and Latino Identity* (New York: Columbia University Press, 2000), 31–47.

99. *"El Dr. Mendoza Pronuncio un Magnifico discurso de la bandera de la raza," La Prensa,* October 25, 1934.

100. Camblor, *La Bandera de la Raza,* 11.

101. Lidia, "UMA," *AL* (September 1934): 7.

102. *"Sociedades," La Prensa,* November 20, 1934. The words were by Maria Piedad Castillo de Levy and music by dona Estrella de Diaz.

103. "UMA" *AL* (September 1934): 7. *"Unión de Mujeres Americanas," AL* (June 1936): 17, *"La Unión de Mujeres Americanas Celebra el Segundo Aniversario de su fundación," AL* (July 1936): 9.

104. *"Tercer Aniversario de la Únion de Mujers Americanas," AL* (July 1937): 12.

105. Thomas, "Resisting the Racial Binary?" 35, and fuller treatment in Thomas, *Puerto Rican Citizen,* 76–83. Thomas attributes the silence around the Puerto Rican identity of the young man at the center of events leading to the Harlem Riot of 1935 to distancing by Puerto Rican leaders from the African American community and the stigma associated with violence and "blackness." For his part, Pedro Caballero likened sharing the neighborhood with *"la raza negra"* to enjoying good cognac (*"como copita de cogñac"*) and the warming of the tropical sun (*"calcinate sol tropical"*) a primitivizing, commodifying, and objectifying gaze, to be sure. Pedro Caballero, *"El Harlem Arrabalero," AL* (January 1936): 1. Some racial-sexual anxieties were documented

in other segments of the Puerto Rican community at this time. "Conditions are so bad in this section that no decent girl of the upper class would walk on these streets at night," stated one informant. "I have three girls," noted another business owner, "I must protect them." Chenault, *The Puerto Rican Immigrant*, 139; anonymous quotations from his fieldwork. *La Prensa* tracked the debate over the marriage between Woodrow Wilson's grand daughterEllen Wilson McAdoo and a Philippine-born actor, Rafael López de Oñate. *"¿Tiene o No Sangre Filipina?" La Prensa*, October 25, 1934. *"Y como allí no se permiten matrimonios entre personas de la raza blanca con orientales, los cosa parece en un* 'impasse.'" "And because there [in California] they do not permit marriage between people of the white race with orientals, the thing appears at an 'impasse.'"

106. *"No Aceptamos Demarcaciones," AL* (August 1938): 1.

107. Karl Meyer, *Tournament of Shadows: The Great Game and Race for Empire in Central Asia* (Washington, DC: Counterpoint, 1999), 451. See also Jacqueline Decter and Nikolai Rerikh Museum, *Nicholas Roerich: The Life and Art of a Russian Master* (Rochester, VT: Park Street Press, 1989).

108. "To Protect Art by Neutral Flag," *New York Times*, August 8, 1930. The Pact and *La Bandera* were each adopted in December 1933 by the Seventh International American conference. Carnegie Endowment for International Peace, *Conferencias Internacionales Americanas, 1889–1936*, 487–488; 529–530. *La Prensa* noted the slow and steady progress of *"El Pacto Roerich"* on October 3, 1934.

109. "The Roerich Pact and the Banner of Peace," ceremonial pamphlet (New York: Roerich Museum, 1935), copy in France R. Grant Papers, Rutgers University Archives (hereafter Grant Papers). "2 Americas Join in Cultural Pact," *New York Times*, April 16, 1935.

110. Roberto Cintrón, April 16, 2009. Grant was the daughter of prosperous and secularized Jewish parents. She was born in Abiquiu, New Mexico, in 1897.

111. See "Arthur Schlesinger Jr./Who Was Henry A. Wallace?," http://www.cooperativein-dividualism.org/schlesinger_wallace_bio.html (viewed December 30, 2009). Equally dismissive is Frederick Pike's assessment of the apostles of mystical arts in the 1930s in *FDR's Good Neighbor Policy*, 72–74. Negative evaluations can also be found in Wallace's recent biography, John C. Culver, *American Dreamer: The Life and Times of Henry A. Wallace* (New York: Norton, 2000), 143, 483.

112. See letters in Frances Grant papers in Box 9, folders 56, 57, 59, and 63, date ranges 1930–1938 to women in the following organizations: Newark Section of the National Council of Jewish Women, Board of Education, New York City; Young Men's and Young women's Hebrew Association of Hartford; Federation of Jewish Women's Organizations, Inc.; Sisterhood of the Hebrew Institute of University Heights; Women's Division, American Jewish Committee; New Jersey State's Nurses's Association; Women's National Republican Club, Inc.; New York State Federation of Women's Clubs.

113. On some of the PAWA's activities, see: "Chilean Envoy Honored," *New York Times*, April 9, 1933. Sadie Orr-Dunbar [GFWC President] to Frances Grant, May 26, 1939; Grant responds May 31, 1939, Box 9, Folder 48, Grant Papers.

114. "Pan American Women's Association," *La Prensa*, January 20, 1934. For clippings, see Box 22, folder 43, in Grant Papers. See also Por Lidia, *"Sociales,"* Pan American Women's Association of the R.M. in *AL* (January 1934): 2.

115. Roerich banner on cover and see article *"Nicholas Roerich y Su Obra," AL* (September 1935): 10.

116. Undated and untitled typescript commentary in Spanish, *"Hermanas de la America Latina [sic]"*, Box 9, folder 68, Grant Papers.

117. "Pan American Women's Association/Asociación Panamericana de Mujeres," clipping in Box 22, folder 43, Grant papers. See also clipping from *Columbia* magazine,

edited by Abraham Martinez, from 1939, where Josefina Silva de Cintrón is noted as a participant in a PAWA dinner in 1939.

118. PAWA Pamphlet, Box 17, folder 6, Grant Papers.
119. *"Nuestra Portada," AL* (June 1936): 12.
120. PAWA notebooks, "Dues Collected," Box 16, folders 50 and 51, Grant Papers.
121. "Some Artistic Tendencies in South American Art," *Bulletin of the Pan American Union,* vol. 63 (October 1929): 972–983. See also her articles "The Brotherhood of Art," *Musician* 20 (February 1924), and "Tibet's Sacred Art," *Art and Archeaology* 22 (September 1926).
122. "Brazilian Art," *Bulletin of the Pan American Union,* vol. 65 (January 1931).
123. See promotional materials in Box 9, folders 63 and 64 in Grant Papers. Kristin L Hoganson, *Consumers' Imperium: The Global Production of American Domesticity, 1865–1920* (Chapel Hill: University of North Carolina Press, 2007), chapter 4. Rose Warner and Myrtle Reed, *Lavender and Old Lace: A Modern Dramatization of Myrtle Reed's Most Popular Novel in Three Acts* (New York: S. French, 1938).
124. Clarence V. Howell to Frances Grant, September 30, 1936 and October 15, 1948, Box 9, folder 57, and Box 17, folder 7, Grant Papers. More information on reconciliation trips can be found in New York World's Fair Papers (hereafter NYWFP), Box 175, folder 4. Howell hoped to market his services for those interested in touring New York City, "our choice, for it has the greatest variety of races, isms, and religions." He continued: "The purpose: is to reconcile group to group, as well as person to person—not to convert those we visit, not to be converted. Friendship, fellowship, love between groups have their intrinsic worth, regardless of ideas either group holds." See Howell to "Miss Why and Mr. Wherefore," ca. December 4, 1936.
125. Ricardo D. Salvatore, "The Enterprise of Knowledge: Representational Machines of Informal Empire," in *Close Encounters of Empire,* 69–105 Pike, *FDR's Good Neighbor Policy,* especially chapters 7 and 8 takes a much more benign view of intercultural activities, and assigns them less historical weight and value as well.
126. José Martí, "Our America," in *Jose Martí,* 289. See also Lomas, *Translating Empire,* 219. Elizabeth A. Cobbs, "Why They Think Like Gringoes: The Discourse of US-Latin American Relations," *Diplomatic History* 21 (Spring 1997) 2: 307–316. For the PAU's self-definition, see inside cover of representative issues of the *Bulletin,* like February 1937, ii.
127. Victor S. Clark, "A Word to Porto Rican Readers," in *Porto Rico and its Problems.* (Washington DC: Brookings Institution, 1930), ix.
128. John Barrett, *The Pan American Union: Peace Friendship Commerce* (Washington, DC: Pan American Union, 1911), 14. Akira Iriye, *Cultural Internationalism and World Order* (Baltimore, MD: Johns Hopkins University Press, 1997), chapter 2.
129. Roberto Cintrón, April 16, 2009; *AL* (June 1935), cover. Leo S. Rowe, *The United States and Porto Rico: With Special Reference to the Problems Arising out of Our Contact with the Spanish-American Civilization* (1904), 9–13 warned of a "lapse into barbarism" for the entire Caribbean without US guidance.
130. Rowe, *The United States and Porto Rico,* 106–108.
131. Labarthe, *Son of Two Nations,* 19–22.
132. Appendix A, José C. Rosario, "The Puerto Rican Peasant," in *Porto Rico and Its Problems,* 568. For some details on Puerto Rican home life, see the home economics movement on the island. Editorial, "Home Economics in Porto Rico," *Journal of Home Economics* 19 (July 1927): 388–390. Grace J. Ferguson, *Home Making and Home Keeping: a Text Book for the First Two Years' Work in Home Economics in the Public Schools of Porto Rico,* ([San Juan, P.R.: Bureau of Supplies, Printing, and Transportation, 1915); Maria Teresa Orcasitas, "The Development of Home Demonstration Work in Puerto Rico," 31 (April 1939): 229–231; Katherine Rogers, "Homemaking Education for Puerto Rico," 30 (January 1938): 28–29; Marie Vestal, "Home Economics at the

University of Puerto Rico," 30 (January 1939): 29–31; Rosa Marina Torres, "Twenty-Five years of Home Economics in Puerto Rico," 31 (April 1939): 239–40; A. S. Baylor, "Homemaking Education on the Island of Puerto Rico," 24 (August 1932): 679–682. All in *Journal of Home Economics*. Of these Rogers is the most condescending and negative.

133. "Pedro J. Labarthe," *AL* (November 1933): 2.
134. Labarthe, *Son of Two Nations*, 62.
135. "Dr. Leo S. Rowe," *AL* (June 1935): 1, 14.
136. Murray M. Paddack, "Puerto Rico's Plight," *Current History* 44 (June 1936): 91–92.
137. Leopoldo Cuban, "Porto Rican View of American Control," *Current History* 31 (March 1930): 1158.
138. "The Pan American Student," May 13, 1938, and *"Notas Escolares,"* April 2, 1935 in *La Prensa*. See *"Actividades Escolares," AL* (May 1937): 19, and *"Notas Escolares," AL* (March 1935): 13 and (May 1935): 13.
139. Stoner, "In Four Languages but with One Voice," and Jiménez-Muñoz, "Deconstructing Colonialist Discourse." Bernardino was taken seriously enough by *La Prensa*, *"La Mujer Dominicana tiene consciencia...del ejercicio del sufragio,"* (February 3, 1934) and editorial *"El Feminismo Hispano-Americana,"* same issue.For detailed treatments of Stevens, see Esther Sue Wamsley, "'A Hemisphere of Women': Latin American and U.S. Feminists in the IACW, 1915–1939," PhD diss., Ohio State University, 1998, and a very generous appraisal in Mary Trigg, "'To Work Together for Ends Larger Than Self': The Feminist Struggles of Mary Beard and Doris Stevens in the 1930s," *Journal of Women's History* 7 (1995) 2: 52–85.
140. David Barton Castle, "Leo Stanton Rowe and the Meaning of Pan Americanism," in *Beyond the Ideal* assesses Rowe as fundamentally missionizing and paternalistic (33–44). For a favorable evaluation, see Sumner Welles, "In Memoriam: Dr. Leo S. Rowe," *The Americas* 3 (January 1947). Catt quoted in Threkeld, "How to 'Make this Pan American Thing Go,'" 185.
141. Bertha Lutz, "Nationality of Married women in the American Republics," *Bulletin of the Pan American Union* (April 1926): 1–8. Flora de Oliveira Lima, "The First Conference of the Inter-American Commission of Women," *Bulletin of the Pan American Union* (April 1920): 1–8. See also Candice Lewis Bredbenner, *A Nationality of Her Own Women, Marriage, and the Law of Citizenship* (Berkeley: University of California Press, 1998), chapter 6, *Conferencias Internacionales Americanas, 1889–1936*, 492–493.
142. Labarthe, *Son of Two Nations*, 112.
143. Cuban, "Porto Rican View of American Control," 158.
144. Labarthe, *Son of Two Nations*, 159, 116. LaBarthe sent the senator an inscribed copy of his book.
145. *"Orientaciones,"* May 1941, 22, 43; FG Papers. See also hearty endorsement of *"El feminismo Hispano-Americano," La Prensa*, February 3, 1934.
146. Cordova to Grant, June 28, 1938, Box 17, folder 25, FG Papers.
147. "'Riverside Museum' *será ahora el antiguo Roerich," La Prensa*, May 17, 1938.
148. Byline March 27, 1939, *Voz de Atlantida*, clipping inGrant Papers, Box 22, folder 43.
149. "De Nuestro Lectores," *La Prensa*, July 16, 1934. "Feminist Reviews Mexican Victory; Mrs. M. R. de Mendoza Played a Leading Role in the 18th-Year Fight for the Ballot," *New York Times*, September 8, 1935. "Montevideo Hotel Upset by a Feminist's Husband," *New York Times,* December 1, 1933. Alicia I. Rodriguez-Estrada, "Dolores Del Rio and Lupe de Velez: Images on and off the Screen, 1925–1944," in *Writing the Range: Race, Class and Culture in the Women's West*, ed. Elizabeth Jameson and Susan Armitage (Norman: University of Oklahoma Press,

1997), 475–492. Margarita Robles de Mendoza to Plutarco Elias Calles, March 6, 1932, document reprinted in Buck, "The Meaning of the Women's Vote in Mexico, 1917–1953," 84–85.

150. Soto, *Emergence of the Modern Mexican Woman*, 103–105. "*La Unión de Mujeres Americanas Recibirá las Primeras Delegadas Iberoamericanas,*" *La Prensa* (October 17, 1934). See also "*Unión de Mujeres Americanas,*" *AL* (June 1936): 9, 17. At other moments, press coverage pointed out the informal nature of the UMA, that is, as one not consecrated or designated by state government: "*sin carácter official.*" "*Aprobo las bases la Unión de Mujeres Americanas en la sesión celebrada,*" *La Prensa,* June 18, 1934.

151. Isabel Keith Macdermott, "A Significant Pan American Conference," *Bulletin of the Pan American Union* 55 (July 1922): 10–35, Guy, "The Politics of Pan-American Cooperation," and Threlkeld, "How to 'Make This Pan American Thing Go.'"

152. "*Unión de Mujeres Americanas,* 'UMA,'" *AL* (October 1934): 8; "UMA," *AL* (June 1935): 6.

153. "*Actividades Hispanas,*" *AL* (March 1936): 13.

154. "*La Unión de Mujeres Americanas celebra el Segundo Aniversario de su fundación,*" *AL* (July 1936), 9. See also "*Doña Josefina S. de Cintrón,*" *AL* (June 1935): 14. At another event, Caballero waxed enthusiastic about the attendance of "*mejicanos, peruanos, cubanos, venezolanos, colombianos, chilenos, puertorriquenos, y representatnes de otros pueblos hermanos!*"

155. Pérez, *The Decolonial Imaginary*, chapter 7, especially 87–88.

156. "*Unión de Mujeres Americanas,* 'UMA,'" *AL* (June 1936): 17.

157. "*Unión de Mujeres Americanas,* 'UMA,'" *AL* (October 1934): 4.

158. The International Council for Women of the Darker Races, active in the early 1920s, declined admission to "women of the Anglo-Saxon race." See Lisa Materson, "African American Women's Global Journeys and the Construction of Cross-Ethnic Racial Identity," *Women's Studies International Forum* 32 (2009): 38.

159. "*La Unión de Mujeres Americanas celebra el Segundo Aniversario,*" *AL* (July 1936): 9. Betances Jaeger was the Puerto Rican representative to the larger UMA branch, and in the 1934 New York meeting "promised to fight for the independence of her country and defend the cause of all women" (*prometiendo luchar por la independencia de su patria y defender la causa de todas las mujeres*). Maria Luisa de Casto, "*Unión de Mujeres Americanas,*" *AL* (November 1934): 4, 8.

160. "*Homenaje al Peru de la U. de Mujeres Americanas,*" April 25, 1935; "*'La Ola' Puesta en Escena por la Unión de Mujeres Americanas,*" April 29, 1935; "*Una Velada de la Unión de Mujeres Americanas,*" May 17 and 24, 1935; "*Celebración del Primer Aniversario de la Unión Mujeres Americanas,*" June 11, 1935 (with photo) all in *La Prensa.*

161. Mercedes Luque, "*Unión de Mujeres Americanas,*" *AL* (September 1936): 13.

162. Asuncion Lavrín, "Suffrage in South America: Arguing a Difficult Case," in *Suffrage and Beyond: International Feminist Perspectives,* ed. Caroline Daley and Melanie Nolan (New York: New York University Press, 1994), 184–209; Francesca Miller, "Latin American Feminism and the Transnational Arena," in *Women, Culture, and Politics in Latin America,* ed. Emilie Bergmann et al (Berkeley: University of California Press, 1990), 10–27, and Corinne A. Pernet, "Chilean Feminists, the International Women's Movement, and Suffrage, 1915–1950," *Pacific Historical Review* 69 (November 2000) 4:663–688.

163. Robles de Mendoza, *Ciudadanía De La Mujer Mexicana,* 19.

164. Margarita Robles de Mendoza, *La Evolución De La Mujer En México* ([México, Imp. Galas], 1931), 10.

165. Ibid., 67. See also "*Espiración Feminista Mexicana,*" *AL* (June 1938):1

166. Robles de Mendoza to Elias Calles, in *The Women's Revolution in Mexico,* 85.

167. Robles de Mendoza quoted in "How History Was Made at Montevideo," *Equal Rights* (January 6, 1934): 382.
168. Carmen B. de Córdova, "*Victoria Feminista en el Estado de Nueva York,*" *AL* (August 1937): 5.
169. "*Unión de Mujeres Americanas, 'UMA,'*" *AL* (April 1937): 12. "*La unión de Mujeres Americanas celebra la Independencia de Costa Rica,*" *AL* (October 1936): 18.
170. J. S. C. [Josefina Silva de Cintrón] "*Feminismo,*" *AL* (August 1938): 10
171. Mercedes Solá, *Feminismo: Estudio Sobre Su Aspecto Social, Económico Y Político* (San Juan, P.R: Cantero, Fernández & Co, Inc., 1922), 29.
172. Ibid., 24.
173. "*No Acemptemos Demarcaciones,*" *AL* (August 1938): 1.
174. Solá, *Feminismo,* 9.
175. "*Feminismo Autentico,*" *AL* (June 1937): 1
176. Solá, *Feminismo,* 9.
177. Ibid., 13–14.
178. Ibid., 37–40. Solá also attended the 1922 meeting in Baltimore. See also Maude Wood Park [President, National League of Women Voters] to Frank McIntyre, February 9, 1922, file 27260a, Box 1217, RG 350, NARA II (includes conference flyer).
179. "*Unión de Mujeres Americanas,*" *AL* (October 1934): 4, 8.
180. "League Body Fails to End Chaco War," *New York Times*, March 13, 1934; "*La Inutil Hecatombe Del Chaco*" (November 20, 1934) and "*La Guerra del Chaco sigue*" (February 5, 1934), both in *La Prensa*.
181. Michael L. Gillette, "Huey Long and the Chaco War," *Louisiana History* 11 (1970) 4: 293–311. See also William R Garner, *The Chaco Dispute: A Study of Prestige Diplomacy* (Washington, DC: Public Affairs Press, 1966), 92–94, and Leslie B. Rout, *Politics of the Chaco Peace Conference, 1935–39* (Austin: Published for the Institute of Latin American Studies by University of Texas Press, 1970), 89–91. Rout is highly dismissive of an oil-driven interpretation of the Chaco conflict (48). Bryce Wood concludes that Bolivia's charges against Standard Oil were nothing if not self-interested, since in 1937, the government confiscated the properties of the company. Bryce Wood, *The United States and Latin American Wars, 1932–1942* (New York: Columbia University Press, 1966), 65–67.
182. Harriet Hyman Alonso, *Peace as a Women's Issue: A History of the U.S. Movement for World Peace and Women's Rights,* (Syracuse: Syracuse University Press, 1993), 124.
183. "*La Mediacion en el Chaco,*" April 2, 1935; "*El Momento de la Paz,*" April 25, 1935; "*La Diplomacia en el Chaco,*" June 10, 1935; all in *La Prensa*. See Leo S. Rowe, "Latin America," January 1, 1936, *New York Times,* and Pan American Union, *Bolivia and Paraguay Make Peace…* (Washington DC: Pan American Union, 1938). For a fairly cynical view of all participants in the peace process, and the war as a matter between stubborn, squabbling neighbors in the southern cone, see Pike, *FDR's Good Neighbor Policy,* 241.
184. Miller, "Latin American Feminism," in *Women, Feminism and Social Change,* 282. "La Lucha por la Paz," *AL* (January 1938): 12; Esther J. Crooks, "*Gira de Buena Voluntad por Damas Latinoamericanas Auspiciada por el Mandato Pro-Paz,*" *AL* (October 1939): 30. See also the poem: "*La Paz de Chaco,*" *AL* (October 1934): 3.
185. Frank Otto Gatell, "Independence Rejected: Puerto Rico and the Tydings Bill of 1936," *Hispanic American Historical Review* 38 (1958): 43–44. Gattell describes the Tydings Bill as "the act of an angry man; there was no statesmanship about it." Robert David Johnson, "Anti-Imperialism and the Good Neighbor Policy: Ernest Gruening and Puerto Rican Affairs, 1934–1939," *Journal of Latin American Studies* 29 (February 1997) 1: 89–110.

186. Tydings quoted in "Puerto Rico Bill May Call 'Bluff,'" *New York Times,* April 26, 1936. For ingratitude comments, see "Gruening Favors Tydings Plan for Free Puerto Rico," *Evening Star* [Washington, DC] (April 24, 1936): 1.
187. Ayala and Bernabe, *Puerto Rico in the American Century,* 110–111; "2 kill police and shot dead," February 24, 1936, *New York Times; "Los Asesinatos de Puerto Rico," La Prensa,* February 27, 1936.
188. Eric M. Matsner and William Laidlaw, "Puerto Rico: Old Woman in a Shoe," *North American Review* 242 (Winter 1936–37): 277–278; 280–281. More generous appraisals in Paddack, "Puerto Rico's Plight," William H. Haas, "The Jibaro, An American Citizen," *The Scientific Monthly* 43 (July 1936)1: 33–46; Harwood Hull, "Better Times for Puerto Rico," *Current History* 43 (January 1936) 4: 367–372.
189. Brainerd, a Smith graduate, was a staff person at the PAU sometime communicant with *Artes y Letras,* writing a short verse for mother's day issue in May, 1935. Heloise Brainerd, *Intellectual Cooperation Between the Americas...,* [Pan American Union] Education series, no. 15 (Washington, DC: Pan American Union, 1931); Heloise Brainerd, "Introducing Children to the Other Americas," *Parents Magazine* 9 (May 1934): 15–16. See also "Petitción Contra La Guerra" *La Prensa* (December 5, 1936): 1, 8, and Concha Romero James, *"La Cooperación Intelectual en América, 1933–1936," AL* (September-October 1937): 9.
190. Maria Más Pozo, *"Recogiendo Firmas contra la Guerra," Dedicado a mi culta amiga Petronilla Angélica Gomez, directora de "FEMINA" en Santo Domingo,* R.D., *AL* (March 1936): 12, 14, emphasis in original.
191. Carmen B. de Córdova, *"Carta Abierta de Feminismo: para Maria Más Pozo," AL* (April 1936): 5.
192. Maria Más Pozo, *"La Mujer y el Feminismo: A mi excellent amiga Carmen B. de Córdova," AL* (June 1936): 5, 18.
193. Alonso, *Peace as a Women's Issue,* 103; Jacquelyn Dowd Hall, *Revolt Aagainst Chivalry: Jessie Daniel Ames and the Women's Campaign against Lynching* (New York: Columbia, 1979), 237–249. See also Robert L. Zangrando, "The NAACP and a Federal Antilynching Bills, 1934–1940," *Journal of Negro History* 50 (April 1965) 2: 111.
194. It bears further investigating whether Más Pozo viewed "An Art Commentary on Lynching," the NAACP antilynching art exhibition at the Arthur U. Newton Galleries on 57th Street in the winter of 1935."Protests Bar Show of Art on Lynching," *New York Times,* February 12, 1935. *La Prensa* carried a report on the lynching of Claude Neal in Marianna, Florida, on p. 1 on October 29, 1934, and also described the NAACP efforts on his behalf.
195. Marcantonio quoted in "10,000 Parade Here for Puerto Ricans," *New York Times,* August 30, 1936.
196. "La Manifestacion Nationalista," *AL* (September 1936): 8.
197. Maria Más Pozo, *"La Mujer y el Feminismo."* Más Pozo claimed Silva de Cintrón as her "spiritual friend" (*spiritual amiga*). Más Pozo, *"Sensibilidad Femenina," AL* (August 1935): 11.
198. On Más Pozo's earlier position viz African Americans and the Harlem Riot see, Thomas, *Puerto Rican Citizen,* 61–77. Though Más Pozo publically criticized lynching earlier in the decade, Thomas stresses her investment in the myth of racial democracy in Latin culture and suggests that her suburban, elite status kept her from mixing in Harlem politics, especially across the color line. *AL* also made space for conservative views, *"Sobre Feminismo," AL* (May 1936): 10, 14.
199. Alonso, *Peace as a Women's Issue,* 117–122. Alonso, *The Women's Peace Union and the Outlawry of War, 1921-1942* (Knoxville: University of Tennessee Press, 1989), chapter 6. Mary Ann Glendon, "The Forgotten Crucible: The Latin American

influence on the Universal Human Rights Ideal," *Harvard Human Rights Journal* 16 (2003): 26–39.

200. *"Una Confederación que Combatirá a la únion panamericana,"* La Prensa, March 9, 1934.

201. "Discord Arises at Bolivar Fetes," *New York Times,* July 25, 1935. *AL's* report on the Roerich event did not note any unrest or disturbances. *"Liga Internacional de Accion Bolivar"* (August 1935): 11. On the cult of Bolivar, see John Chasten, "Simon Bolivar: Man and Myth," in *Heroes & Hero Cults in Latin America,* ed. Samuel Brunk and Ben Fallow (Austin: University of Texas Press, 2006), and Christopher B Conway, *The Cult of Bolívar in Latin American Literature* (Gainesville: University Press of Florida, 2003). *AL* rounded up a wide range of scholarly and popular Bolivar opinion from throughout Latin America and proclaimed Bolivar as all these—prophet, hero, emblem, peacemaker, and, of course, liberator. *"El Héroe Epónimo de América"* (June 1935): 5.

202. See, for example, "The Garden of Peace," *Bulletin of the Pan American Union,* 71 (October 1937): 777–779. Located in La Plata, Argentina, "This garden, which was dedicated in November, 1936, unites forty-six nations and all races of the world in a living monument." Catt quoted in Threkeld, "How to 'Make This Pan American Thing Go.'"

203. Emily Newell Blair, "Why I Am Discouraged about Women in Politics," in *Major Problems in American Women's History,* ed. Mary Beth Norton and Ruth M. Alexander (Lexington, MA: DC Heath, 1996), 332.

204. Rose Young and National Committee on the Cause and Cure of War (U.S.), *Why Wars Must cease* (New York: The Macmillan Co., 1935), 141.

205. Ibid., 149.

206. Pedro Caballero, *"Huelgas Pro-Paz,"* AL (May 1936): 5; Angela Graupere, *"Pacifismo,"* AL (July 1936): 13; *"raza humana"* quoted from *"La Nueva Democracia,"* in *"De Nuestros Canjes,"* AL (March 1936): 13.

207. *"¡Aguarda!"* AL (June 1936): 1.

208. *"El Dr. Mendoza Pronunció,"* La Prensa, October 25, 1934.

209. See also Chenault, *The Puerto Rican Immigrant,* 153. On the international context, see Garner, *The Chaco Dispute,* 85. See also "League of Nations in Americas," April 15, 1936; "League of Nations on This Side Urged," July 12, 1936; "Chilean Backs American Court," all in *New York Times.*

210. Pedro Juan Labarthe, *"Puerto Rico y la Liga de Naciones Americana: El Tirunfo del Panamericanismo,"* AL (February 1937): 12, 18; and continued (March 1937): 14, 18.

211. John Lynch, *Simón Bolívar: A Life* (New Haven, CT: Yale University Press, 2006), 212–217.

212. James Brown Scott, "Elihu Root-His Latin American Policy," *Bulletin of the Pan American Union,* 71 (April 1937): 298 notes the court "passed out of existence because of the unfavorable attitude of the Government of the United States."

213. Labarthe, *"Puerto Rico y la Liga de Naciones Americana-El Triufo del Panamericanismo"* AL (March 1937): 12, 14, 18. For his part, Bolivar analogized the Isthmus of Panama for Latin Americans to the Isthmus of Corinth for the Greeks; see Lynch, *Simon Bolivar,* 213. In a more cynical analogy, Bernardo Vega complained: "But Puerto Rico, it seems, had to rest content as the 'Gibraltar of America.'" Bernardo Vega, *Memoirs of Bernardo Vega: A Contribution to the History of the Puerto Rican Community in New York* (New York: Monthly Review Press, 1984), 206.

214. George Bornstein, "The Colors of Zion: Black, Jewish, and Irish Nationalisms at the turn of the Century," *Modernism/modernity* 12 (2005) 3: 369–384.

215. Labarthe, *"Puerto Rico y La Liga de Naciones Americana,"* AL (March 1937): 14. For earlier versions of his plan, see *Son of Two Nations,* 143. Labarthe sent a copy of his

book to former Senator William Borah, former opponent of the League of Nations and would-be presidential challenger to Roosevelt in 1936.

216. "Puerto Rico to Mark Its day at the Fair," July 24, 1939; "Puerto Rico Astir over Leahy Plan," July 26, 1939, both in *New York Times*. Blanton Winship to Maude Emery Lennox, November 2, 1938, NYWFP, Box 721, folder 9.

217. "Winship Phones Greetings to Fair," *New York Times*, May 14, 1939. For *La Prensa's* coverage, also duly noting the military agenda for the island, see *"Fue Muy Concurrida y Lucida La Fiesta Conmemorativa de Puerto Rico en La Exposición,"* July 26, 1939. For more on the military buildup on the island during the World's Fair, see "Puerto Rico Marks End of War," November 12, 1939, *New York Times*, which took the occasion of veterans' day to update readers on "current military activities" on the island and commend the "loyalty of our citizens here."

218. Marco Durati, "Utopia, Nostalgia and the World War at the 1939–40 New York World's Fair," *Journal of Contemporary History* 41 (2006) 4: 663–683.

219. New Deal programs, notably land reform and relief through the PRRA, entailed an expanded government employment center, adding about 11,000 jobs to the island. Rodriguez, "Representing Development" and Fernandez, *The Disenchanted Island*, chapter 5.

220. Dennis Merrill, "Negotiating Cold War Paradise: U.S. Tourism, Economic Planning, and Cultural Modernity in Twentieth-Century Puerto Rico," *Diplomatic History* 25 (2001) 2: 175–214, Faye C. Caronan, "Colonial Consumption and Colonial Hierarchies in Representations of Philippine and Puerto Rican Tourism," *Philippine Studies* 53 (2005) 1: 32–58, and Robert C. Mings, "Puerto Rico and Tourism: The Struggle for Cultural Autonomy among Developing Nations; The Case of Puerto Rico and Its Tourist Industry," *Caribbean Quarterly* 14 (1968) 3: 7–21. See also Michael Berkowitz, "A 'New Deal' for Leisure: Making Mass Tourism during the Great Depression," in *Being Elsewhere: Tourism, Consumer Culture, and Identity in Modern Europe and North America*, ed. Shelley Baranowski and Ellen Furlough (Ann Arbor: University of Michigan Press, 2001), 185–212.

221. Ford A. Garrow, "New Puerto Rico, Caribbean Playground," *Literary Digest* 118 (December 15, 1934): 25, and "Puerto Rico Carnival Returns" *Christian Science Monitor Magazine* (August 12, 1936): 12.

222. T. Roosevelt, "Island of Enchantment," *House & Garden* 73 (March 1938). "Enchanted Isle: Puerto Rico Shows Its Wares at the New York World's Fair," *Newsweek* 14 (August 7, 1939): 14–15. Roosevelt was also the source of the media appraisal of Puerto Rican children as hungry. See "Porto Rico's Hungry Children," *Literary Digest* 103 (December 12, 1929): 11. See senior Roosevelt's, remarks in *Colonial Policies of the United States*, 108, 111–112. On Eleanor, see "Mrs. Roosevelt regresó de las Islas Vígenes a Puerto Rico," *La Prensa*, March 9, 1934, and "Our Island Possessions," *Woman's Home Companion* 61 (October 1934): 4. Thomas, *Puerto Rican Citizen*, 113–115. On the "state" quarter, see: http://www.statequarterguide.com/2009-puerto-rico-quarter/ (viewed December 29, 2009).

223. Géigel quoted in *Brooklyn Daily Eagle*, November 18, 1937, clipping in Box 1642, folder 2, NYWFP.

224. "Employees of the Department of Agriculture and Commerce," New York Office, n.d., Box 1526, folder 6, NYWFP.

225. *"Palabras Pronunciadas por el Comisionado Residente de Puerto Rico en Washington, Hon. Santiago Iglesias, el día 25 de Julio de 1939, en comemoración del día de Puerto Rico en la Feria Mundial de Nueva York,"* in Box 2155, folder 29, NYWFP. "Puerto Ricans Hold State Claim Timely, See Advantage in Federal Plans to Make Island Base," *New York Times*, May 22, 1939.

226. "Three-Hour 'Preview' Motorcade Gives City Glimpse of 1939 Fair," *New York Times*, May 1, 1938. Two women were reportedly "so chilled" at the end of the festivities that they "required a doctor's care."

227. "World's Fair Girls Fairest in the World," *Daily News*, April 21, 1938; *New York Journal*, April 8, 1938, referred to the event as an "old-time circus parade" in NYWFP Box 1966, folder 1. Christina Cogdell, "The Futurama Recontextualized: Normal Bel Geddes's Eugenic 'World of Tomorrow,'" *American Quarterly* 52 (2000)2: 193–245, and Cogdell, "Biological Efficiency and Streamline Design," chapter 9, in *Popular Eugenics*. See also David E. Nye, "Ritual Tomorrows: The New York World's Fair of 1939," *History & Anthropology* 6 (1992) 1: 1–21, and Nye, *American Technological Sublime* (Cambridge, MA MIT Press, 1994), chapter 8.

228. "*Carroza de Puerto Rico en el desfile de la Feria Mundial motiva investigación,*" *La Prensa*, May 13, 1938. See also "*Al Comisionado de Agricultura y Comercio de Puerto Rico,*" *AL* (May 1938): 16. In *La Prensa's* coverage of the actual parade, no mention of the cart was made. "*2,000,000 vieron el desfile de ensayo para la Feria Mundial el sabado aqui,*" May 2, 1938. The only concrete reference I found is a clipping in the New York World's Fair papers: "Motorcade Lineup," *NY World Telegram*, April 30, 1938, which refers to a "Puerto Rico Band and Group" in the "Tenth Division" of the parade under the "Transportation" theme, Box 1966, folder 3, NYWFP. For related clippings of parade's lineup that make no mention of Puerto Rico, see *Herald Tribune*, March 28, 1938; *New York Times,* April 27, 1938 and May 1, 1938; *New York Post*, April 29, 1938, all in NYWFP.

229. I found no complaints concerning the "cart" in the World's Fair papers. Most of the material under "parade protests" in the World's Fair papers concern controversy over the timing and siting of the preview parade, rather than its content, though a few letters complained about Germany and Japan's presence in Box 1967, folder 6. The preview parade date also conflicted with May Day. For coverage in *La Prensa* see "*En el desfile obrero de hoy participaran unas 20 organizaciones hispanas,*" April 30, 1938.

230. "*La carroza de Puerto Rico,*" *AL* (June 1938): 4.

231. "*Protesta y Contestación,*" *AL* (June 1938): 7; "No critiqué a los puertorriqueos'— contestó Tydings a O. Garcia Rivera," May 12, 1938; "*Padres Hispanos piden a Tydings que rectifique para el publico americano,*" May 13, 1938; "*La Sr. R.C. de Roman protesta ante el senador Tydings por sus declaraciones,*" May 19, 1938, all in *La Prensa.*

232. J. M. Killeen to Mr. Roosevelt, January 18, 1939 with Silva de Cintron's card attached. Silva de Cintrón dropped her *Artes y Letras* business card at the foreign participation office, which Roosevelt headed, Box 1488, folder 13, NYWFP. Whalen letter of August 14, 1939 reprinted and translated in *AL* (October 1939): 9.

233. "*Puerto Rico en La Feria de New York,*" *AL* (June 1939): 13. Jorge Duany, *The Puerto Rican Nation on the Move: Identities on the Island & in the United States* (Chapel Hill: University of North Carolina Press, 2002), 47 and chapter 2.

234. "Report Given to General Nolan by Mr. Gonzalez in re Puerto Rico's Participation in the Fair," January 19, 1940, and "General Nolan's Conference with Mr. Roosevelt," February12 [1940], Box 1526, folder 6, NYWFP.

235. Carmen Luisa Morales, "*Fundando el Mundo de Mañana,*" *AL* (September 1938): 8–9.

236. L. S. Rowe to my dear Mr. Roosevelt, January 13, 1939, Box 1404, folder 13; James J. Carson to Leo S. Rowe, January 25, 1938, Box 315, folder 7; memorandum from Mr. Holmes, May 2, 1940, Box 315, folder 6, NYWFP.

237. "21 Fair Advisors on Consumer Quit," *New York Times,* February 28, 1939.

238. "We are looking to the women leaders of America to carry the ideals and plans of the Fair to every hamlet in the United States," wrote Monica Barry Walsh, director,

as an "*active* Ambassador of Goodwill for the Fair." See *Cultural and Social Aspects of the New York World's Fair, 1939* ([New York, N.Y.]: the Committee, 1939), 12.

239. Meeting minutes, March 10, 1938, Executive Committee of the National Advisory Committee of Women's Participation, Box 1067, folder 13, NYWFP. Related material found in folders 8, 9, 10, 11, and 12 of this box. Letters from Addie Hunton concerning the International Council of Women of the Darker Races of the World and the National Council of Negro Women are in Box 9. On the "Woman's Building" at the Columbia World's Exposition in Chicago (1893), see Jeanne Weimann, *The Fair Women* (Chicago, IL: Academy Chicago, 1981).

240. Meeting minutes, December 23–29, 1937, National Advisory Committee on Women's Participation, Box 115, folder 19, NYWFP.

241. Mrs. Astor's open letter "To Hispanic America" appeared in *Artes y Letras* in Spanish and English with some telling differences in translation. The English version welcomed visitors from Central and South America, admitting that "North Americans are not as familiar" with those regions "as we would like to be" and highlighting the Fair's potential to give "all of us a unique opportunity to study contemporary life." The Spanish-language version, appearing alongside, was pitched at a slightly different register, both friendlier tone to "our neighbors" (*nuestros vecinos*) and pointedly referred to the Fair's location in "our New York metropolis" (*nuestra metropolis Neuyorquiña*). "*A Hispano America,*" *AL* (October 1939), 11.

242. Memorandum "Set up of National Advisory Committee on Women's Participation," December 24, 1938, in Box 1067, folder 17, NYWFP. See also "Function of the Women's Committee on Participation," May 21, 1938, in Box 1067, folder 17, NYWFP. "*El Comite Consultivo de Mujeres en la Feria Mundial de New York*" *AL* (June 1939): 15.

243. "Fair to Have Aid of 1,000 hostesses," *New York Times*, February 7, 1939. "Pan American Women's Association," *AL* (October–November 1938): 9, describes an opening reception attended by UMA and PAWA women at Rockefeller Center.

244. I infer Rowe from language in the source indicating that UMA had been "endorsed by the Pan American Union" via anonymous quotation. See letter from James S. Carson to Miss M. B. Walsh, August 31, 1939, Box 630, folder 3, NYWFP. Not surprisingly, Walsh stated in response: "I know Miss Grant, of course, and I am familiar with the work of 'UMA' but I do not know Sra. de Vaughan [current UMA president] personally," Walsh to Carson, September 1, 1939, in Box 630, folder 3, NYWFP.

245. Z. Evangelina de Vaughan to Edward Roosevelt, April 25, 1939 [on UMA stationery] and response April 27, 1939 in Box 1488, folder 13, NYWFP. See also "Pan American Women's Association," *AL* (October–November 1938): 9.

246. The expressly written anthem, for example, proclaimed: "In America we have no need for conquest. Neighbors' borders don't incite our greed." "Fair's Theme Song Has Its Premier," *New York Times,* February 3, 1940. The Haskell honor guard had also performed in Paris in 1931. See Rydell, *World of Fairs*, chapter 3.

247. "*Espectacular Inauguración de la Feria Mundial de Nueva York*" and "*Servicio de Guias Privados para La Feria Mundial,*" *AL* (June 1939): 7, 15. *La Prensa* performed similar work, offering a "*Guia de Touristas*" and "*Hoy en La Feria*" column to Spanish-language readers and keeping careful track of hispanic activities at the fair. See also "*El Turista Hispano en Nueva York,*" April 28, 1939; "*Consules hispano-americans asistiran hoy al ensayo de la Exposicion Mundial,*" April 30, 1938.

248. Conrado Asenjo, "*Notas de la Feria Mundial,*" *Puerto Rico Illustrado* (July 1939): 3.

249. "*Espectacular,*" and "*Miss Puerto Rico,*" *AL* (October 1939): 35.

250. "*Cartas a Nuestra Directora,*" *AL* (October 1939): 19.

251. Two documents contain flag details: "Radio Program" stamped Edward F. Hickey with two dates, July 23 and July 25, 1940, and "Program for Puerto Rico Day— Thursday—July 25, 1940" both in Box 1526, folder 6, NYWFP.

252. *"El Problema actual de La Nación," AL* (March 1937): 1. On anti-American deployments of cosmopolitanism, see Camilla Fojas, *Cosmopolitanism in the Americas* (West Lafayette, IN: Purdue University Press, 2005).

253. Santiago-Valles, "The Imagined Republic of Puerto Rican Populism," 78–79.

254. Luz de Selenia, *"Prejudicio Racial," AL* (August 1938): 11.

255. Frank Martínez, *The Tragedy of the Puerto Ricans and the Colored Americans: A Summary of the Political Situation in the 17th A.D., Manhattan,* ([New York: n.p., 1935), 10.

256. *"'Artes y Letras' Recibe un Honor," AL* (January 1938): 5.

257. Roberto Cintrón, April 16, 2009. The 1930 census lists, in addition to Felipe, Josefina, and Roberto Cintrón at 101 W. 121st Street in Manhattan, four "roomers" an adult male and three members of the Gritiena family, including 11-year-old Fernando, who was the same age as Roberto. Ancestry.com, *1930 United States Federal Census* [database online]. Provo, UT, USA: The Generations Network, Inc., 2005 (viewed May 4, 2009).

258. Evans Clark to Edward F. Roosevelt, November 19, 1939, telegram in Box 1488, folder 13, NYWFP.

259. Such a lecture is, in fact, the culminating chapter of Labarthe's memoir *Son of Two Nations*. On music see Louise K. Stein, "Before the Latin Tinge: Spanish Music and the 'Spanish Idiom' in the United States, 1178–1940," in *Spain in America: The Origins of Hispanism in the United States*, ed. Richard Kagen (Urbana: University of Illinois Press, 2002), 193–245, and Carl Van Vechten, *The Dance Writings of Carl Van Vechten* (New York: Dance Horizons, 1974), part IV.

4   Becoming Mama Maida

1. Carol Bowen Johnson, "World's Fair Letter," *The Independent* (July 20, 1893): 977. *Exhibition of Objects Illustrating the History and Condition of the Republic of Liberia*, exhibition catalogue March 23 to April 4, 1914 (Chicago: Chicago Historical Society, 1914).

2. Memo of W. H. Standley of telephone conversation with Mr. Firestone, June 29, 1938, folder 7, Box 1497, New York World's Fair 1930 and 1940 Incorporated Records, Manuscripts and Archives Division, The New York Public Library, hereafter NYWFP. See also, Walter F. Walker [U.S. consul to Liberia] to W. H. Standley, February 5, 1938, folder 4, Box 698, and Walker to Standley, July 19, 1938, folder 16, Box 1154, 16, NYWFP.

3. Business had "doubled" in the latter 1930s and would explode during World War II, with Liberia by far the largest of the producers of natural rubber. "Firestone Profit $5,258,041 in Year...Optimistic Note Sounded" (December 21, 1938), and "Big Rubber Output Seen by Firestone" (June 22, 1943), and "Firestone Earns Net of $16,310,845," all in *New York Times*. Synthetic rubber counted for a significant increase in production potentially undermining the natural rubber sector.

4. "Exhibits: A World of Wonders," *New York Times*, May 5, 1940. For a similar display at Chicago, see "How Firestone High Speed Tires Are Made," (n.p.: World's Fair Chicago, 1934).

5. Yevette Richards, "African and African-American Labor Leaders in the Struggle over International Affiliation," *The International Journal of African Historical Studies* 31 (1998) 2: 301–334; Yevette Richards, "Race, Gender, and Anticommunism in the International Labor Movement: The Pan-African Connections of Maida Springer," *Journal of Women's History* 11 (1999): 35–36; Yevette Richards, *Maida Springer: Pan-Africanist and International Labor Leader* (Pittsburgh, PA: University of Pittsburgh Press, 2000); Brigid O'Farrell and Joyce L. Kornbluh, "We Did Change Some Attitudes: Maida Springer-Kemp and the International Ladies' Garment

Workers Union," *Women's Studies Quarterly* 23 (Spring–Summer 1995)1: 41–70; John Charles Stoner, "Anti-Communism, Anti-Colonialism, and African Labor: the AFL-CIO in Africa, 1955–1975," PhD diss., Columbia University, 2001.

6. Penny M. Von Eschen, *Race against Empire: Black Americans and Anticolonialism, 1937–1957* (Ithaca, NY: Cornell University Press, 1997), 78–79. See also Leila J. Rupp, "Challenging Imperialism in International Women's Organizations, 1888–1945," *NWSA Journal* 8 (Spring 1996) 1: 8–27. Rupp notes that World War II almost completely severed interwar feminist connections. Lisa G. Materson, "African American Women's Global Journeys and the Construction of Cross-Ethnic Racial Identity," *Women's Studies International Forum* 32 (January 2009)1: 35–42.

7. Robert Shaffer, "Multicultural Education in New York City during World War II," *New York History* 77 (July 1996)3: 301–332. See also Charles Dorn, "'I Had All Kinds of Kids in My Classes, and It Was Fine': Public Schooling in Richmond, California, During World War II," *History of Education Quarterly* 45 (2006) 4: 538–564, and Benjamin L. Alpers, "This Is the Army: Imagining a Democratic Military in World War II," *Journal of American History* 85 (June 1998) 1: 129–163. On racial assumptions in the founding of the United Nations (on the British side) see Mark Mazower, *No Enchanted Palace: The End of Empire and the Ideological Origins of the United Nations* (Princeton, NJ: Princeton University Press, 2009). In general see Everett Helmut Akam, *Transnational America: Cultural Pluralist Thought in the Twentieth Century* (Lanham, MD: Littleman Rowfield, 2002), 102–108 and 162–164.

8. Most influential in my thinking have been essays in Catherine M. Cole, Takyiwaa Manuh, and Stephen Miescher, eds., *Africa after Gender?* (Bloomington: Indiana University Press, 2007), and Rosalyn Terborg-Penn and Andrea Benton Rushing, eds., *Women in Africa and the African Diaspora: A Reader* (Washington, DC: Howard University Press, 1996).

9. Richard Wright, "Forward," in George Padmore, *Pan-Africanism or Communism? The Coming Struggle for Africa* ([1956] Garden City, NY: Anchor Books, 1972), xxii.

10. The ICFTU was founded in 1949. Patrick Pasture, "A Century of International Trade Unionism," *International Review of Social History* 47 (August 2002) 2: 277–289; Peter Waterman, "The Problematic Past and Uncertain Future of the International Confederation of Free Trade Unions," *International Labor and Working-Class History* 59 (April 1, 2001) 1: 125–132.

11. For similar experience, see Maureen Mahon, "Eslanda Goode Robeson's African Journey: The Politics of Identification and Representation in the Diaspora," in *Transnational Blackness: Navigating the Color Line*, ed. Manning Marable and Vanessa Agard-Jones (New York: Palgrave Macmillan: 2008), 115–134.

12. "Remarks by Maida Springer," African Historical Society Dinner, [1959], 2, Maida Springer Kemp Papers, Schlesinger Library, Radcliffe Institute, Harvard University (hereafter MSKP).

13. Yevette Richards, *Conversations with Maida Springer: A Personal History of Labor, Race, and International Relations* (Pittsburgh, PA: University of Pittsburgh Press, 2004), 164, 151. All future references to this text will be to this edition, cited parenthetically.

14. Nyerere to Randolph, December 7, 1957, quoted in Stoner, "Anti-Communism, Anti-Colonialism, and African Labor," n. 21, p. 115. See also Joseph Thu to Springer, December 6, 1957, and Wiayaki Wambae to Springer, November 8, 1959 in Papers of Maida Springer, Amistad Research Center, Tulane University (hereafter PMS). See also James E. Bass to Maida Springer, December 22, 1963; Maida Springer to James E. Bass January 4, 1965, MSKP.

15. Imanuel Geiss, *The Pan-African Movement: A History of Pan-Africanism in America, Europe, and Africa* (New York: Africana Pub. Co., 1974); Ronald Walters, *Pan Africanism in the African Diaspora: An Analysis of Modern Afrocentric Political Movements* (Detroit,

MI: Wayne State University Press, 1993); James Hunter Meriwether, *Proudly We Can Be Africans: Black Americans and Africa, 1935–1961* (Chapel Hill: University of North Carolina Press, 2002).

16. Springer to Zimmerman, November 10, 1953, Charles Zimmerman Papers, Kheel Center Archives, Cornell University (hereafter CZP).
17. Richards, *Conversations*, 45.
18. "Talk by Maida Springer," Freedom House, March 1949, MSKP.
19. Ula Y. Taylor, "'Negro Women Are Great Thinkers as Well as Doers': Amy Jacques-Garvey and Community Feminism in the United States, 1924–1927," *Journal of Women's History* 12 (2000) 2: 104–126, and Taylor, *The Veiled Garvey: The Life & Times of Amy Jacques Garvey* (Chapel Hill: University of North Carolina Press, 2002). See also Barbara Bair, "True Women, Real Men: Gender Ideology and Social Roles in the Garvey Movement," in *Gendered Domains: Rethinking Public and Private in Women's History*, ed. Dorothy O. Helly (Ithaca, NY: Cornell University Press, 1992), 154–166.
20. Kevin K. Gaines, *American Africans in Ghana: Black Expatriates and the Civil Rights Era* (Chapel Hill: University of North Carolina Press, 2006), 24.
21. Richards acknowledges that Springer reported to Jay Lovestone, head of the Free Trade Union Committee (1942) of the AFL, not the CIA (*Maida Springer*, p. 8). Ted Morgan, *A Covert Life: Jay Lovestone, Communist, Anti-Communist, and Spymaster* (New York: Random House, 1999), names Springer, a bit sensationally, as an "agent" of Lovestone's (304–305). On CIA funding of the FTUC see Beth Sims, *Workers of the World Undermined: American Labor's Role in U.S. Foreign Policy* (Boston, MA: South End Press, 1992), chapter 1, and Anthony Carew, "The American Labor Movement in Fizzland: The Free Trade Union Committee and the CIA," *Labor History* 39 (February 1998) 1: 25–53.

In the Lovestone papers, there are a few documents labeled "TOP SECRET" from Springer in Dar-es-Salaam dated January 13, 1958; see also Springer to Lovestone March 24, 1957; Julius Nyerere to Springer, February 22, 1959, and R. M. Kawawa to Maida Springer, January 31, 1958 in Jay Lovestone Papers, Hoover Institute, Stanford University. These files also contain reports by Springer about phone calls and interviews with various colonial officials in Tanganyika, and summative memoranda of her observations at meetings and other events. Lovestone's so-called JX files sent to James Jesus Angelton at the CIA were deemed mostly useless and ignored. Tom Mangold, *Cold Warrior: James Jesus Angleton: The CIA's Master Spy Hunter* (New York: Simon & Schuster, 1991), 315.
22. Paul Gilroy, *The Black Atlantic: Modernity and Double Consciousness* (Cambridge: Harvard University Press, 1993); Nikhil Pal Singh, *Black Is a Country: Race and the Unfinished Struggle For Democracy* (Cambridge: Harvard University Press, 2004); Brent Hayes Edwards, *The Practice of Diaspora: Literature, Translation, and the Rise of Black Internationalism* (Cambridge: Harvard University Press, 2003). Kinship and family are more prominent in Deborah Gray White, "'YES,' There Is a Black Atlantic," *Itinerario* 23 (1999) 2: 127–140 as isgender in Michelle Ann Stephens, *Black Empire: The Masculine Global Imaginary of Caribbean Intellectuals in the United States, 1914–1962* (Durham, NC: Duke University Press, 2005).
23. "Women Labor Leaders Are Going to England in Good-Will Exchange with Four from There," *New York Times,* January 10, 1945.
24. *Conversations*, 37. Lisa D McGill, *Constructing Black Selves: Caribbean American Narratives and the Second Generation* (New York: New York University Press, 2005); Jerome Krase and Ray Hutchison, eds., *Race and Ethnicity in New York City* (Amsterdam: Elsevier, 2004); Irma Watkins-Owens, *Blood Relations: Caribbean Immigrants and the Harlem Community, 1900–1930* (Bloomington: Indiana University Press, 1996).
25. Murray, *Pauli Murray*, 278–279.
26. *Conversations*, 38–41; Richards, *Maida Springer*, 20–22.

27. Marcus Garvey, "The Negro, Communism, Trade Unionism and His (?) Friend," [1925] in *The Marcus Garvey and Universal Negro Improvement Association Papers*, ed. Robert A Hill (Berkeley: University of California Press, 1990), vol. 6, 214–216; Padmore, *Pan-Africanism or Communism?* 283. William Seraile, "Henrietta Vinton Davis and the Garvey Movement," *Afro-Americans in New York Life & History* 7 (1983) 2: 7–24.

28. *Conversations*, 39. Ira De Augustine Reid, *The Negro Immigrant, His Background, Characteristics, and Social Adjustment, 1899–1937* (New York: Columbia University Press, 1939), and Sherri-Ann Butterfield, "Being Racialized Ethnics: Second Generation West Indian Immigrants in New York City" in *Race and Ethnicity in New York City*, 107–136. Michael L. Conniff, *Black Labor on a White Canal: Panama, 1904–1981* (Pittsburgh, PA: University of Pittsburgh Press, 1985).

29. *Conversations*, 34–35; 54. Census materials confirm these details. Ancestry.com, *1930 United States Federal Census* [database online], (Provo, UT, USA: Ancestry.com Operations, Inc., 2002). (viewed August 15, 2009).

30. Pauli Murray, *Pauli Murray: The Autobiography of a Black Activist, Feminist, Lawyer, Priest and Poet* (Knoxville: University of Tennessee Press, 1989), 279.

31. Delia Jarrett-Macauley, *The Life of Una Marson, 1905–65* (Manchester, UK: Manchester University Press, 1998), chapters 6 and 7.

32. Richards, *Maida Springer*, 25–30; "'The Tuskegee of the North' To expand Technical Training," *New York Times*, December 21, 1930.

33. Petition number 301124, dated December 21, 1937 in Ancestry.com, *U.S. Naturalization Records Indexes, 1794–1995* [database online] (Provo, UT: USA: The generations Network, Inc., 2007). (viewed June 29, 2009). Kevin Gaines made the Garveyite consciousness point to me in personal email communication, June 13, 2010.

34. Nell Irvin Painter, *The Narrative of Hosea Hudson: The Life and Times of a Black Radical* (New York: Norton, 1994), 19–22.

35. Memorandum "To Sasha from Maida," March 15, 1959, MSKP.

36. Zimmerman in *Justice*, quoted in Daniel Katz, "Race, Gender, and Labor Education: ILGWU Locals 22 AND 91, 1933–1937," *Labor's Heritage* 11 (2000)1: 9–10. "Politics Is Your Job!" *Justice* (October 1, 1954): 6, 7. See also "Pledging Themselves to Political Action," in *Justice* (September 15, 1947): 4.

37. "More than a Union—A Way of Life," *Justice* (June 1, 1947): 10. For a full statement see Alice Kessler-Harris, "Organizing the Unorganizable: Three Jewish Women and Their Union," *Labor History* 17 (1976)1: 10, and Annelise Orleck, *Common Sense & a Little Fire: Women and Working-Class Politics in the United States, 1900–1965* (Chapel Hill: University of North Carolina Press, 1995), 177.

38. Dubinsky quoted in Nancy L. Green, *Ready-to-Wear and Ready-to-Work: A Century of Industry and Immigrants in Paris and New York* (Durham, NC: Duke University Press, 1997), 238.

39. Dubinsky's biographer falls right in line with these homilies to family, concluding matter-of-factly that Dubinsky saw "the ILGWU as his family, which it was in a very real sense." Robert D Parmet, *The Master of Seventh Avenue: David Dubinsky and the American Labor Movement* (New York: New York University Press, 2005), 312.

40. "Melting Pot Spirit," *Justice* (May 1, 1947): 4.

41. Israel Zangwill, *From the Ghetto to the Melting Pot: Israel Zangwill's Jewish plays* (Detroit, MI: Wayne State University Press, 2006); Randolph Bourne, "Trans-National America," *Atlantic Monthly* 118 (July 1916): 86–97.

42. E. Iglauer, "Housekeeping for the Family of Nations," *Harper's Magazine* 194 (April 1947): 295–306; Adelai E. Stevenson, "United Nations: Capital of the Family of Man," *National Geographic* 120 (September 1961): 297–303; P. G. Beltran, "American Family of Nations," *Vital Speeches of the Day* 25 (November 1, 1958):

42–45; "U.N. A Family of Nations," *Department of State Bulletin* 29 (November 9, 1953): 628–629; and Dag Hammarskjold, "Vast Pattern of Activity in the Congo, True Cooperation of United Nations Family," *United Nations Review* 7 (November 1960): 13–14.

43. "ILG A 'United Nations'" (October 1, 1960): 12; "The U.N.-Union Style" (January 15, 1961): 5, in *Justice*.
44. "Birthday Salute," *Justice* (July 15, 1955): 10.
45. Herbert H. Lehman, "ILG-A 'United Nations'" *Justice* (October 1, 1960): 12.
46. Green, *Ready-to-Work*, 202–205; Parmet, *Master of Seventh Avenue*, 25, 101–102.
47. Bernardo Vega, *Memoirs of Bernardo Vega: A Contribution to the History of the Puerto Rican Community in New York* (New York: Monthly Review Press, 1984), 179.
48. Minutes of the Meeting of the Education Committee of the General Executive Board, March 9, 1948, CZP.
49. "Ratification of Pact," *Justice* (March 15, 1958): 12.
50. For a useful distinction between pluralism and assimilation focused on New York City, see Daryl Michael Scott, "Postwar Pluralism, *Brown v. Board of Education*, the Origins of Multicultural Education," *Journal of American History* 91 (2004) 1: 69–82. Jennifer Guglielmo, "Transnational Feminism's Radical Past: Lessons from Italian Immigrant Women Anarchists in Industrializing America," *Journal of Women's History* 22 (2010) 1: 10–33.
51. "Pres. Dubinsky Defines ILG Service to Nation" *Justice* (July 15, 1947): 2.
52. "Zimmerman Pictures 10-week Europe Trip," (February 1, 1946): 5. "Feinberg Urges Full Aid On United Jewish Appeal" (May 15, 1945): 12; "$17,000 Relief Given by '22'" (November 1, 1945): 5; "Seven War Orphans Adopted" (December 15, 1947): 11; "N.Y. ILG Gives $100,000 to Stricken Polish Jews" (September 15, 1945): 3; "Local 62 Measures Up—Adopts 62 War Orphans" (January 1, 1948): 1; "21 More Orphans Are 'Adopted' by N.Y. Dressmakers" (April 15, 1948): 3, 4; "Cloak Out-of-Town Marks 'Adoption' of 100 War Orphans" (July 1, 48): 3; "535 Children from All races 'Adopted' by ILG Shop Groups" (July 15, 1948): 3, in *Justice*.
53. "Fighters for Italian Democracy," "Palestine Trade School Soon Ready on ILG's $100,000 Gift" (November 1, 1946): 11, 3; "Cloakmakers' Cable Bids British Labor Open Up Palestine" (November 1, 1945): 3, and "Open Palestine Gates to Ease Jews' Plight, ILG Convention Asks" (July 15, 1947): 10, in *Justice*.
54. "British Labor Is Victor," *Justice* (August 1, 1945): 1.
55. "Mind If We Watch?" *Justice* (April 15, 1945): 8.
56. "Dixie News and Views" (December 15, 1945): 4; "Dixie News and Views" (May 15, 1945): 4; "Dixie News and Views" (May 15, 1946): 15; "Upper South" (April 15, 1947): 2. See also Mark Starr, "Dixie Unions on the March" (March 1, 1946): 13; "Economics-Southern Style" (October 1, 1948): 8; "Stars Fell on Cullman [Alabama] When ILG Organized" (November 1, 1948): 5, in *Justice*.
57. "Pride of the Old Dominion," (September 1, 1946): 4; "Virginia's Advancing Garment Workers" (August 15, 1947): 3; "'My Old Kentucky' Gets New ILG Local" (December 15, 1947): 2, in *Justice*.
58. "Upper South Department Conference" (April 15, 1947): 2; "Dixie News and Views" (August 1, 1947): 4; "The Package" (January 1, 1955): 11; "Upper South Marks Decade of Progress" (May 15, 1952): 1 and 2, in *Justice*.
59. "The Only Way" (May 15, 1952): 1. "Bilbo 'Morally Bankrupt' Says Italian-American Council," (August 15, 1945): 6; "Miss. Fortune"(July 15, 1946): 8; "Listen You Damyankee Red…!" (December 1, 1946): 7; "An Insult to Southern Womanhood, Suh!" (February 15, 1948): 7, in *Justice*.
60. "ILGWU Organizer Jailed in Mississippi on Fake Charge" (June 15, 1953): 2, 10; "NLRB Denies Back Pay to Mississippi Strikers" (January 1, 1955): 3; "Strikers at Atlanta Bell Co. Beat Back Injunction, Arrests" (February 1, 1955): 8; "Mob Attacks

ILG Organizers in Miss." (June 1, 1957): 2; "Serbin Strikers Convicted by 'Iron Curtain' Writ" (June 1, 1955): 3, 6; "Iron Curtain Injunction" (June 15, 1955): 6; "Serbin Strikers File Suits after Illegal Arrests" (July 1, 1955): 2; "Judge Bans All Serbin Picketing in Tennessee" (August 1, 1955): 1, 3; "Strikers Solid at Serbin Despite New Arrests" (August 15, 1955): 8, in *Justice.*

61. "Slurs on ILG Americanism," *Justice* (July 1, 1947): 10. David Witwer, "Westbrook Pegler and the Anti-Union Movement," *Journal of American History* 92 (2005) 2: 527–552

62. Ann K. Ziker, "Containing Democracy: Race, Conservative Politics, and U.S. Foreign Policy in the Postcolonial World, 1948–1968," PhD diss., Rice University, 2008; Carol Anderson, *Eyes off the Prize: The United Nations and the African American Struggle for Human Rights, 1944–1955* (New York: Cambridge University Press, 2003), chapter 5; Thomas Noer, "Segregationists and the World: The Foreign Policy of the White Resistance" in *Window on Freedom: Race, Rights, and Foreign Affairs, 1945–1988*, ed. Brenda Gayle Plummer (Chapel Hill: University of North Carolina Press, 2003), 141–162.

63. Squib in *Justice* (January 15, 1945): 13.

64. "Kentucky's Inland Mermaids" (October 1, 1945): 10; "Good Looking Guardians of the ILG" (August 1, 1946): 4; "Three Little Maids from School" (August 15, 1946): 10; "ILGWU Labor Day Queens Hold Court" (October 15, 1946): 10; "Lovely Line of Cloak Divisions' Pinkers" (November 15, 1946): 7; "Three Gorgeous Garment Girls" (December 15, 1946): 11; "How Girl Meets Boy—and Hangs On" (December 15, 1945): 13; "Who Wouldn't Whistle at Wanda?" (January 1, 1948): 8; "ILGWU Miami Maids" (February 1, 1955): 9, in *Justice.*

65. "Here's How to Highlight Hair," *Justice* (December 1, 1945): 13.

66. "How Labor Betters Race Relations" (January 15, 1947): 4, and "'Justice' Pix Parade" (March 1, 1948): 3, in *Justice.* After the IILG gave up on "Dixie," *Justice* reported more generously on African American women members. "New ILG Bowling Enthusiasts" (December 15, 1948): 8; "All Together for a Nifty 1950!" (January 15, 1950): 11; "Mother's Day in August" (September 1, 1951): 3; "Mother and Child" (July 15, 1952): 1; "Chicago ILG Wins Rehiring of Four" (September 1, 1952): 3; "Monarch Fire Survivors" (April 1, 1958): 9; "For Real" (March 16, 1960): 9, in *Justice.*

67. "'Like Father, Like Son' in '10' As Sons Join Cutters' Ranks," *Justice* (October 15, 1955): 1, 11. "To Thousands, They Are 'The Union'" (April 15, 1961): 8. Pictured were Charles S. Zimmerman, Meyer Krawatz, Israel Breslaw, Jacob Ushelevsky, Harry Rabinowitz, and Meyer Terry.

68. Orleck, *Common Sense & a Little Fire*, chapter 5, has a sunnier appraisal than my research suggests.

69. Parmet, *Master of Seventh Avenue*, 21.

70. "San Antonio Rose" (January 15, 1948): 8; "San Antonio Gals Prepare Broadcasts" (October 15, 1948): 8, in *Justice.* Vicki L. Ruiz, "'Star Struck': Acculturation, Adolescence, and Mexican American Women, 1920–1950" in *Unequal Sisters: An Inclusive Reader in U.S. Women's History*, ed. Vicki L. Ruiz with Ellen Carol DuBois (New York: Routledge, 2008), 363–378.

71. "'22' Spanish Club to Salute Spring with Grand Dance" (March 15, 1948): 4, and "Local 22 Spaniards All Set for Picnic" (March 15, 1948): 4, in *Justice.*

72. "The Dressmakers Have No Minorities" [Local 22] and "Members Angered by Commie Race Slurs at Local 22 Meet" (February 1, 1950): 4 in *Justice.* "14 Negroes Jailed in Altanta Sit-ins," *New York Times*, October 20, 1960.

73. "Aid to Rural [South] Schools," *Justice* (December 1, 1951): 10. Springer to Charles Zimmerman, November 12, 1948, and related communications about fundraising for southern schools from Charles Johnson, B. F. McLaurin, Rae Brandstein, 1948–1956, in CZP.

74. "Dressmakers' Letters, Visits, Spur Puerto Rico Organizing" (December 1, 1955): 2. "ILG 'Goodwill Ambassadors' Go to Puerto Rico" (December 15, 1955): 3; "Local 22 Members on Puerto Rico Trip Have Varied Agenda" (February 1, 1960): 11, in *Justice*.

75. "Island (Sweatshop) Paradise," *Justice* (July 15, 1955): 12.

76. "Dubinsky Appointed Committee Member on Puerto Rican Pay" and "Good Neighbor Policy: Join the Union," *Justice* (December 15, 1955): 3.

77. *New York Times* "Wage Scale in Puerto Rico" [from Dubinsky] and "Wages in Puerto Rico" [from Berdicia] (July 2 and 13, 1955). "Pyrric Victory" (August 1, 1955): 12. "Dubinsky Asks Same Rises in U.S., Puerto Rico" (February 1, 1955): 5; "Ask Same Rise in U.S., Puerto Rico Minimums" (April 15, 1955): 3; "The Puerto Rican Minimum Wage" (May 15, 1955): 2, 10; "Dubinsky Refutes 'Times' on Puerto Rico Minimum," "Urge N.Y. Mayor Repudiate Aide Opposing P.R. Pay Rise," "N.Y. Puerto Ricans Fight Island Sweatshops; Urge Same Rise in Minimums as on Mainland" (July 15, 1955): 2 and 3, in *Justice*. See advertisement"Why 371 U.S. Manufacturers in Puerto Rico Now Enjoy 100% Tax Freedom,"[advt.] *New York Times,* April 15, 1956.

78. Cesar J. Ayala and Raphael Bernabe, *Puerto Rico in the American Century: A History since 1898,* (Chapel Hill: University of North Carolina Press, 2007), 232. See also David Dubinsky, "Turning Point for Puerto Rico," *Free Trade Union News* (April 1956): 3. On union social welfare on the island, see "P.R. Hurricane Aid" (October 1, 1960): 5; "Puerto Rican First," *Justice* (January 15, 1957): 10; "ILGWU Housing Funds for Puerto Rico," and "Lauds Union's Investment in Puerto Rican Homes"(June 1, 1957): 1, 3; "Bra Workers in Puerto Rico Win Rise, Welfare 'Package'" (June 1, 1957): 4; "Puerto Rico Workers Throng to Get ILG-Sponsored Homes" (June 1, 1857): 4, in *Justice*.

79. "Reina de La Aguja," *Justice* (September 1, 1960): 11.

80. Ellen Israel Rosen, *Making Sweatshops: The Globalization of the U.S. Apparel Industry* (Berkeley: University of California Press, 2002), especially chapter 3.

81. "ILG's Intercultural Workshop Reveals Kinship of Peoples," *Justice* (December 15, 1946): 3.

82. "Talk by Dr. Henry David of Queens College," *Justice* (May 5, 1948): 10.

83. "ILG's Race Harmony Efforts Are Fundamental" *Justice* (January 15, 1947): 8.

84. "Labor Spurs Equality of Races," *Justice* (August 15, 1946): 13.

85. "Local 22's Race Equality Seen as FEPC Laboratory" (August 1, 1945): 5; "How ILG Builds Race Amity" (February 1, 1946): 13; " FEPC Law 'Crucial' Says Local 22 Head" (July 1, 1946): 6, in *Justice*.

86. "Union Locals Sing 'Little Songs' to Further Tolerance," *Justice* (May 1, 1948): 10.

87. Katz, "Race, Gender, and Labor Education."

88. Richards, *Maida Springer,* 73–74. Anna Hedgeman, *The Trumpet Sounds: A Memoir of Negro Leadership* (New York: Holt, Rinehart and Winston, 1964), 80–83; Thomas A. Guglielmo, "'Red Cross, Double Cross': Race and America's World War II–Era Blood Donor Service," *Journal of American History* 97 (June 2010) 1: 63–90.

89. Richards, *Maida Springer,* 71; *Conversations,* 129, 131.

90. Murray, *Pauli Murray,* 280.

91. Betty Balanoff, "Interview with Maida Springer Kemp," 1970, 17–18. Full text online at http://www2.roosevelt.edu/library/oralhistory/oralhistory.htm. (viewed September 1, 2008).

92. "Madia Springer Represents AFL in Britain Tour," *Justice* (January 15, 1945): 2.

93. "Maida Springer to Represent American Labor in England," *Labor Vanguard* (February 1945), clipping in CZP. John Walter, "Frank R. Crosswaith and Labor Unionization in Harlem, 1939–1945," *Afro-Americans in New York Life and History* 7 (July 1983) 2: 47–58.

94. "British Shops Seen by Maida Springer," *Justice* (March 1, 1945): 2. Photo in February 1 and 15, 1945, of *Justice*, 3 and 13, respectively.
95. "Maida Springer Touring England's Labor Centers," *Justice* (March 15, 1945): 3. Ruth Milkman, *Gender at Work: The Dynamics of Job Segregation by Sex during World War II* (Urbana: University of Illinois Press, 1987), chapters 4 and 5.
96. "Four Labor Women Coming Home with Gt. Britain Sisters" (April 15, 1945): 3; "All-Day Tour of Garment Center Dazzles British, American Girl Labor Delegates" (May 1, 1945): 6; "Garment Workers of U.S. Urged as Model for British" (August 15, 1945): 13; "U.S. Women Workers Not On Par with British Sisters" (November 15, 1945): 14, in *Justice*.
97. Maida S. Springer, "What I Saw in Britain" (May 15, 1945): 6, and (June 1, 1945): 6, *Justice*.
98. *Conversations*, 142–144; "Maida Springer Kemp on Dr. Caroline F. Ware," 5, MSKP.
99. "Maida Springer Put among Outstanding Women of the Year," *Justice* (April 15, 1946): 6.
100. Jarrett-Macaley, *Una Marson*, 68–70.
101. "Views on the Cuban Negro" (February 1942); "Africa Speaks" (July 1942); "The Isthmian Negro" (August 1942); "Africa in the War of Destiny" (September and October 1942); "Haiti's Voice" and "Poems of Africa" (October 1943); and especially L. D. Reddick, "The Battle of Africa and the African People" (December 1942), all in *Opportunity*.
102. Maida Steward Springer, "Toward a New Job Outlook," *Opportunity* (April 1946): 82–83.
103. Ibid., 83.
104. Ibid.
105. Nancy L. Green, "Blacks, Jews, and the 'Natural Alliance': Labor Cohabitation and the ILGWU," *Jewish Social Studies* 4 (1997) 1: 79–104. A more critical look is Alan Wald, "Narrating Nationalisms: Black Marxism and Jewish Communists through the Eyes of Harold Cruse," in *Left of the Color Line: Race, Radicalism, and Twentieth Century Literature of the United States*, ed. Bill V. Mullen and James Smethurst (Chapel Hill: University of North Carolina Press, 2003), 140–162. See also Jesse Thomas Moore Jr., *A Search for Equality: The National Urban League, 1910–1961* (University Park: The Pennsylvania State University Press, 1981), 94–105.
106. "1946–47 ILGWU Education Schedule in New York," *Justice* (September 1, 1946): 13. "Third ILG Institute Labor Day Weekend" (August 15, 1946): 13, both in *Justice*. "Report of ILGWU Educational Director," March 9, 1948. Schedule "A" of this report listed multiple offerings at the central location for art, English, social dancing, bowling, esperanto, public speaking, glee club, dance, gym and swimming, music appreciation, handcrafts, dramatics, indoor tennis, and only one class called "Current Events." Abstract of Minutes of Meeting of Education Committee of General Executive Board, May 20, 1948, noted competition from the movies for workers' attention and the migration of labor relations curricula to the colleges and universities, notably Harvard. Both reports in CZP.
107. "Stop It!—You War-Mongering Imperialist" (June 1, 1946): 9; "Members Angered by Commie Race Slurs at Local 22 Meet" (February 1, 1950): 4, in *Justice*.
108. "Starr Teaches Jap Unions Democracy" (October 1, 1946): 13; "Latin America's Organized Labor Honors Haymarket Martyrs" (November 1, 1946): 11; "Free Trade Unions Form Labor Center for the Americas" (February 1, 1948): 1; "Program for a Free Latin America" (October 15, 1952): 7; Mark Starr Adviser [sic] at London Education Parleys" (November 1, 1945): 4; "Starr Returns from Britain Trip" (December 1, 1945): 13, in *Justice*.
109. Sims, *Workers of the World Undermined*, chapter 1. See also Nathan Godfried, "Spreading American Corporatism: Trade Union Education for Third World Labour," *Review of African Political Economy* 39 (September 1987): 51–63.

110. "Maida Springer Broadcasts on U.S. Women in Industry," *Justice* (January 1, 1948): 10.
111. "'Equal Rights' Bill A Threat to Women—Pauline Newman" (March 15, 1948): 2, and "'Equal Rights' Anti-Women" (October 1, 1945): 6, in *Justice*.
112. "Maida Springer Is Named Bus. Agent by N.Y. Dress Bd.," *Justice* (March 15, 1948): 4.
113. *Conversations*, 154. "A Productive League Activity: Summary Record of Urban League Fellowships," *Opportunity* (Fall 1944): 166–168.
114. "Report to the Urban League on 1951–1952 Study Abroad," 10–11, MSKP.
115. Maida Springer to Charles Zimmerman, March 17, 1952, CZP. Maida Springer to Pauli Murray, October 8, 1951, postcard in Pauli Murray Papers, Schlesinger Library, Radcliffe Institute, Harvard University.
116. James R. Hooker, *Black Revolutionary: George Padmore's Path from Communism to Pan-Africanism* (New York: Praeger, 1967), 140.
117. Isadore Schneider, "A Negro Citizen of Soviet Georgia," *Opportunity* (May 1942): 148–149, 157. Erik S. McDuffie, "'[She] Devoted Twenty Minutes Condemning All Other Forms of Government but the Soviet': Black Women Radicals in the Garvey Movement and in the Left during the 1920s" in *Diasporic Africa: A Reader*, ed. Michael Gomez (New York: New York University Press, 2006), 219–250.
118. George Padmore, *How Russia Transformed Her Colonial Empire: A Challenge to the Imperialist Powers* (London: Dennis Dobson Limited, 1946), xi, 136.
119. Hooker, *Black Revolutionary*, chapters 1–4; Gaines, *American Africans in Ghana*, 34–39; "George Padmore," in *Pan-African History: Political Figures from Africa and the Diaspora since 1787*, ed. Hakim Adi and Marika Sherwood (London: Routledge, 2003), 152–158.
120. Schuyler broke the story in the *New York Post* in June 1931. Ibrahim Sundiata, *Black Scandal, America and the Liberian Labor Crisis, 1929–1936* (Philadelphia, PA: Institute for the Study of Human Issues, 1980), 151–153. Raymond Leslie Buell, *The Native Problem in Africa* (New York: MacMillan, 1928); Buell, "Slavery and Forced Labor," *The Nation* 131 (December 24, 1930): 699–701.
121. Sundiata, *Black Scandal*, 67–69, 73–74, 88; Elizabeth Normandy, "African-Americans and U.S. Policy Towards Liberia, 1929–1935," *Liberian Studies Journal* 18 (1993) 2: 203–230; Baljit Singh, "The Survival of the Weakest: A Case History of the Liberian Crisis of the 1930's," *Journal of Human Relations* 14 (1966) 2: 242–260.
122. George Padmore, *American Imperialism Enslaves Liberia* (Moscow: Centrizdat, 1931), 45.
123. Ibid., 20.
124. Tamba E. M'Bayo, "W. E. B. Du Bois, Marcus Garvey, and Pan-Africanism in Liberia, 1919–1924," *Historian* 66 (2004)1: 19–44; Emily S. Rosenberg, "The Invisible Protectorate: The United States, Liberia, and the Evolution of Neocolonialism, 1909–40," *Diplomatic History* 9 (1985)3: 191–214. On Du Bois in Liberia, see "Liberia: Progress" (March 31, 1924), and "Liberia: Envoy Extraordinary" (February 18, 1924), both in *Time* at http://www.time.com/time/magazine/article/0,9171,717749,00.html and http://www.time.com/time/magazine/article/0,9171,718094,00.html viewed July 14, 2010. See also James T. Campbell, *Middle Passages: African American Journeys to Africa, 1787–2005*, (New York: Penguin Press, 2006), chapter 6.
125. Balanoff, "Interview with Maida Springer Kemp," 43; *Conversations*, 156.
126. George Padmore, *Africa: Britain's Third Empire* (New York: Negro Universities Press, 1969), 9.
127. Ibid., 218.
128. Ibid., 216.
129. Sundiata, *Black Scandal*, 123. Padmore (and Nancy Cundard), *The White Man's Duty* (London: W. H. Allen, 1942), 48. Bernard I. Swift, "The Negro Plays an Important

Role in British Empire War Effort," *Opportunity* (August 1942), and Henri Fast, "The Belgian Congo Fights the Axis," *Opportunity* (September 1942). On the tensions around international lawbetween the Atlantic Charter and United Nations, see Elizabeth Borgwardt, *A New Deal for the World; America's Vision for Human Rights* (Cambridge: Harvard University Press, 2005), chapter 9.

130. Springer, "Report to the Urban League," 13, MSKP.
131. Ibid.,18.
132. Springer, "Urban League Fellowship—Oxford, England, 1952–1953," 7, MSKP.
133. Ibid., 19.
134. For context, see Brenda Gayle Plummer, *Rising Wind: Black Americans and U.S. Foreign Affairs, 1935–1960* (Chapel Hill: University of North Carolina Press, 1996), especially chapters 4 and 5.
135. Padmore, *Pan-Africanism or Communism*, xvii, xv.
136. Du Bois, "What Is Africa to Me?" [1940], and also "The Negro's Fatherland" [1917], both in David Levering Lewis, *W. E. B. Du Bois: A Reader* (New York: Holt Paperbacks, 1995), 652–659. Interestingly, the later article calls Africa "perhaps better, motherland."
137. Padmore, *Pan-Africanism or Communism*, 43–44 For the Liberia loan, see *Congressional Record: Proceedings and Debates of the Second Session of the Sixty-Seventh Congress of the United States of America*, vol. LXII-Part 7 (May 9–24, 1922), and Part 12 (August 29 to September 22, 1922).
138. Padmore, *Pan-Africanism or Communism*, 51–52.
139. Ibid., 49. Garvey's rehabilitation began in "How Russia Reformed her Colonial Empire," 83–85.
140. Padmore, *Pan Africanism or Communism*, 150.
141. Quoted in Hooker, *Black Revolutionary*, 126.
142. Maida Springer to Jay Lovestone, March 24, 1957, Lovestone Papers.
143. Padmore, "How Russia Transformed Her Colonial Empire," 91.
144. Springer, "The International Trade Unions and the African Labor Movement" [ca. 1960], 4, MSKP.
145. Padmore, "How Russia Transformed her Colonial Empire," 165–170.
146. Editorial, "Politics and the Negro," *International African Opinion* (November 1938): 3.
147. Padmore, *Pan Africanism or Communism*, 320, xvi.
148. Editorial, *International African Opinion* (July 1938): 2.
149. Padmore and Cunard, "The White Man's Duty," 43.
150. Padmore, "How Russia Transformed Her Colonial Empire," 82.
151. "American Notes," *International African Opinion* (July 1938): 12.
152. Quoted in Hooker, *Black Revolutionary*, 126.
153. Padmore, "How Russia Transformed Her Colonial Empire," 79–83. He defined Pan-Africanism's "fundamental principles" to be nationalism, political democracy, and socialism in *Pan-Africanism or Communism*, 159.
154. Padmore, "How Russia Transformed Her Colonial Empire," 151.
155. Mrs. Stanley Pargellis to Charles S. Zimmerman, March 28, 1955; Mattie Brown to Charles S. Zimmerman, May 6, 1955, CZP; Maida Springer to Shelley Appleton, April 18, 1959, and other invitations, PMS; *Conversations*, 43, 172.
156. Maida to Sasha, Memorandum, February 6, 1955, CZP. Maida Springer to Dearest Pawnee, April 5, 1954, Pauli Murray Papers, Schlesinger Library.
157. Maida to Sasha, September 24, 1955, CZP.
158. F. E. Tachie-Menson to J. H. Oldenbrook, September 2, 1955, CZP.
159. "Passport" phrase found in Maida Springer to William Schnitzler, December 5, 1959, PMS.
160. "Thumbnail Sketch of my African Journey [1956]," in PMS. Zimmerman to Springer, March 8, 1957, CZP.

161. Maida Springer, "Progress and Problems of Gold Coast Unions," *Free Trade Union News* (June 1956): 6, 7; and Springer, "West Africa in Transition," *Free Trade Union News* (April 1956): 8.
162. Colin Legum, *Bandung, Cairo and Accra: A report on the First Conference of Independent African States* ([London]: Africa Bureau, 1958); Matthew Jones, "A 'Segregated' Asia? Race, The Bandung Conference, and Pan-Asianist Fears in American Thought and Policy, 1954–1955," *Diplomatic History* 29 (2005)5: 841–868; Jason Parker, "Cold War II: The Eisenhower Administration, the Bandung Conference, and the Reperiodization of the Postwar Era," *Diplomatic History* 30 (2006)5: 867–892; Cary Fraser, "An American Dilemma: Race and Real Politik in the American Response to the Bandung Conference, 1955," in *Window on Freedom*, 115-140.
163. Maida Springer to Jay Lovestone, January 17, 1956, Lovestone Papers.
164. Bernard Weissman to Zimmerman, December 12, 1956, CZP.
165. Gaines, *American Africans in Ghana*, 1–26.
166. Maida Springer, "West Africa's Fight for Freedom Should Inspire U.S. Negroes," *Pittsburgh Courier* April 13, 1957, clipping in CZP. "Counts, Springer Scan Russia, Africa via Series at 'Unity,' *Justice* (May 15, 1957): 10.
167. To the Editor, September 6, 1957, typescript copy in CZP. Springer referred to Elspeth Huxley, "Clouds over the Black Continent: Are the White Man's Days in Africa Numbered?" *New York Times,* September 1, 1957, 123 (magazine).
168. Maida Springer to Ted Brown, January 16, 1958, PMS.
169. *Conversations*, 218; Springer asked the treasurer of the AFL-CIO for $5,000. See Maida Springer to Mr. William Schnitzler, November 28, 1958, PMS. Richards, *Maida Springer*, 179, and n. 11 and 12 on p. 321. George McCray to Jay Lovestone, May 31, 1958, Lovestone Papers; McCray to Randolph, July 21, 1958, The Papers of A. Philip Randolph (Bethesda: University Publications of America, 1990), reel #2.
170. A. Philip Randolph to George F. McCray, July 10, 1958, Randolph Papers. Springer and Randolph to Zimmerman, May 7, 1958, CZP.
171. Springer to Lovestone, December 14, 1958, Lovestone Papers. See Darlene Clark Hine, "Rape and the Inner Lives of Black Women in the Middle West: Preliminary Notes on the Culture of Dissemblance," *Signs* 14 (Summer 1989) 4: 912–920. Kevin Gaines brought this dimension to my attention.
172. Springer, "Observations on the All-African People's Conference Held in Accra, Ghana, December 5–13, and Its Trade Union Implications," CZP.
173. Karen B. Bell, "Developing a 'Sense of Community': U.S Cultural Diplomacy and the Place of Africa during the Early Cold War," in *The United States and West Africa: Interactions and Relations*, ed. Allosine Jalloh and Toyin Falola (New York: Routledge, 2008), 131.
174. "AFL-CIO Convention Declaration" in *Free Trade Union News* (January 1958): 2–3.
175. George McCray to Brother Lovestone, April 6, 1959, Lovestone papers.
176. "Vocational School for African Women," CZP. Zimmerman to Miss Yvonne O. Walker, June 5, 1958, CZP, and a dozen related communications. Von Eschen, *Race against Empire*, 143–144; Nathan Godfried, "Revising Labor History for the Cold War: The ILGWU and the Film, *With These Hands*," *Historical Journal of Film, Radio & Television* 28 (2008)3: 311–333, and Parmet, *Master of Seventh Avenue*, chapter 15.
177. "Speech by the Prime Minister of Ghana at the Opening Session of the All-African People's Conference on Monday, 8th December, 1958," and his "Speech at Close of All-African People'sConference 13th December, 1958" in *All-Africa People's Conference News Bulletin*, vol. 1, no. 1.
178. Ayala and Bernabe, *Puerto Rico in the American Century*, 232. "ILG 'Goodwill Ambassadors' Go to Puerto Rico" (December 15, 1955): 3; "Local 22 Members on Puerto Rico Trip Have varied Agenda" (February 1, 1960): 11; "P.R. Hurricane Aid,"

(October 1, 1960): 5; "Another Puerto Rican 'First'" (January 15, 1957): 10; "ILGWU Housing Funds for Puerto Rico" (May 15, 1957): 3, in *Justice*.

179. Susan Geiger, "Women in Nationalist Struggle: Tanu Activists in Dar es Salaam," *The International Journal of African Historical Studies* 20 (1987) 1: 1–26. See also *Conversations*, 191.

180. Granger to Doctor Azikiwe, July 17, 1958; Azikiwe to Lester Granger, August 23, 1958; Granger to Azikiwe, September 15, 1958; Springer to Azikiwe, October 16, 1958, all in PMS. Andrew Zimmerman, "Booker T. Washington, Tuskegee Institute, and the German Empire: Race and Cotton in Black Atlantic," *GHI Bulletin* 43 (Fall 2008): 9–20.

181. Jay Lovestone to Miss Maida Springer, May 12, 1958, Lovestone Papers.

182. To Sasha from Maida, March 15, 1959, MSKP.

183. Maida Springer to Israel Breslaw, March 22, 1959, CZP.

184. Lisa Lindsay, "Working with Gender: The Emergence of the "Male Breadwinner" in Colonial Southwestern Nigeria," in *Africa after Gender?* 241–252.

185. "Vocational School for African Women," CZP.

186. Springer to Granger, July 4, 1959, PMS. E. Franklin Frazier, "What Can the American Negro Contribute to the Social Development of Africa?" in *Africa from the point of view of American Negro Scholars* (Paris: Présence Africaine, 1958), 264–266.

187. Maida to Sasha, March 15, 1959, CZP.

188. Maida Springer to Saul Miller, February 8, 1965, MSKP.

189. Dew Tuan-Wleh Mayson and Amos Sawyer, "Labour in Liberia," *Review of African Political Economy*, 14 (April 1979): 3–4. Barbara Wagner, "Labor Unions in the Liberian State and Politics," *Liberia-Forum* 4 (1988)6: 33–44. "Fourth Strike Hits Rubber Plantation," September 29, 1961; "Serious Talks to Be Held Soon," September 27, 1961; "Tubman Names Special Body to Probe Labor Grievances," September 1961, untitled clippings, possibly the Monrovia *Listener*, in Claude Barnett Research Collection, Africana Collection, Melville J. Herskovits Library, Northwestern University.

190. Russell U. McLaughlin, *Foreign Investment and Development in Liberia* (New York: Praeger, 1966), 105. U.S. Department of Labor, *Labor in Liberia* (May 1960): 15, asserted: "No active trade unions are in existence in Liberia." U.S. Department of Commerce, *Establishing a Business in Liberia* (vol. 62–53, part 1, 1962):14, noted: "Two unions are operating in Liberia" (CIO and LCL). The American Embassy in Monrovia finally acknowledged, "Confrontation between management and labor, and sometimes government, in response to specific labor demands occurs with increasing frequency," Nancy Rawls, *Establishing a Business in Liberia* (Washington, DC: Department of Commerce Bureau of International Commerce, 1966): 9.

191. Liberia, *Study of the Firestone Strike: Progress Report* (Monrovia: Office of National Planning, 1964), 12. Copy in Library of Congress.

192. Arthur J. Knoll, "Firestone's Labor Policy, 1924–1939," *Liberian Studies Journal* 16 (1991)2: 49–75.

193. Alfred Lief, *The Firestone Story: A History of the Firestone Tire & Rubber Company* (New York: Whittlesey House, 1951), 253–254, quote on 327. George A. Padmore [no relation], *The Memoirs of a Liberian Ambassador: George Arthur Padmore* (Lewiston, ME: The Edwin Mellen Press, 1996), 152; Bell, "Developing 'A Sense of Community,'" 133.

194. "Liberia: Uncle Shad Forever?" *Time* 82 (October 25, 1963): 99 http://www.time.com/time/magazine/article/0,9171,875582,00.html, and "Resilient Uncle," *Time* 91 (January 5, 1968): 35 http://www.time.com/time/magazine/article/0,9171,712070,00.html; (viewed July 14, 2010). "Landscape of Ore," *Fortune* 64 (December 1961): 65–66.

195. "Liberia Reports to Business" (January 25, 1965); "Free Port of Monrovia" (January 31, 1966 and November 27, 1966) in *New York Times*.

196. Hooker, *Black Revolutionary*, 12. "Opening Speech at the First West African Summit Conference, July 16, 1959 in William Tubman, *The Official Papers of William V. S. Tubman*, (London: Longmans, 1968), 671–674. "News Release— African Summit Conference," July 14, 1959, fragment in Claude Barnett Research Collection.

197. Sundiata, *Black Scandal*, 112–115. D. Ellwood Dunn, "Anti-Colonialism in Liberian Foreign Policy: A Case Study," *Liberian Studies Journal* 5 (1972–74)1: 47–66; C. O. C. Amate, "The OAU and the Conflicts in Africa," *Africa Quarterly* 33 (1993): 59–75; Kwamina Panford, "Pan-Africanism and Africans in the Diaspora and the OAU," *Western Journal of Black Studies* 20(Fall 1996)3: 140–151.

198. Liberia seems to have only asserted itself in the roll call of those meetings on April 11, 1919. See James Shotwell and Carnegie Endowment for International Peace, *The Origins of the International Labor Organization, vol. II* (New York: Columbia University Press, 1934), 389.

199. Tubman, "Address at Dinner in His Honour tendered by the American Business Leaders," New York City, October 18, 1962, in *Official Papers*, 336.

200. "Remarks at Luncheon in His Honour before the Washington Press, Club, Ibid., 339, 354–361.

201. Tubman, "Radio Broadcast to the Nation on Austerity Measures," Monrovia, April 15, 1963, *Official Papers*, 341.

202. "Strike Settled in Liberia" *New York Times* (July 16, 1963). McLaughlin, *Foreign Investment and Development in Liberia*, 98–99; *Study of the Strike*, Appendix D; "Statement Concerning Labor Problems in Liberia," Lovestone Papers.

203. *Study of the Strike*, 4.

204. Tubman, "To the International Labour Conference," June 26, 1964, *Official Papers*, 349–350.

205. Maida Springer to Saul Miller, February 8, 1965, MSKP.

206. Springer to Lovestone, February 20, 1965,Lovestone Papers. Granger to Springer, February 24, 1963, PMS.

207. United States Bureau of Labor Statistics Office of Labor Affairs, *Summary of the Labor Situation in Liberia* ([Washington, D.C.]: U.S. International Cooperation Administration, Office of Labor Affairs, 1959), copy in PMS.

208. "Proposed Working Paper to be presented by the CONGRESS OF INDUSTRIAL ORGANIZATIONS OF LIBERIA" [January 1965], 3. Springer to "Dear brother Bass," January 4, 1965, both in MSKP. See also "C.I.O. Wants Minimum Wages of All Unskilled Workers Raised," Monrovia [*Listener*?] January 4, 1963, Claude Barnett Research Collection.

209. Memorandum, "Labour's Role in the Post-National Industrial Relations Conference for the Implementation of Its Apparent Gains," February 1, 1965, signed by J. B. McGill and Amos N. Gray [for James E. Bass, Secretary General], MSKP.

210. *Study of the Firestone Strike*, 20–21.

211. Ibid., Appendix D.

212. J. Gus Liebenow, *Liberia: The Evolution of Privilege* (Ithaca, NY: Cornell University Press, 1969), 88. Untitled clippings: "Statement Just Issued Says Union Sticks to No Ideology," October 7, 1961, and "CIO Will No Longer Participate in Violent Strikes in Liberia," same date, in Claude Barnett Research Collection.

213. Heather J. Stecklein, "Workers' Control and Militancy in an Iowa Labor Movement: The Use of Wildcat Strikes at the Des Moines Firestone Tire and Rubber Company, 1950–1959," *Annals of Iowa* 64 (2005) 3: 246–265.

214. "The President's Message," in *Partners in Production: Labour-Management-Government: Liberia First National Industrial Relations Conference* (Monrovia, Liberia: Republic Press, 1965), 2, in *William V. S. Tubman Papers* (Bloomington: Liberian Collections Project, Indiana University Archives of Traditional Music, 2008), microform edition,

reel #4, frame 687+. The version of his speech printed in Tubman's published official papers deleted all references to legislation, giving the statement a surreal dimension. See "At the Opening of the National Industrial Relations Conference," Monrovia, January 27, 1965, *Official Papers*, 358.

215. From yet another version of the speech. See "Address Delivered by Dr. William V.S. Tubman at the opening of the National Industrial Relations Conference," January 27, 1965," typescript copy in MSKP.

216. Springer to Saul Miller, February 8, 1965, MSKP.

217. A. Romeo Horton, "Response by Chairman of the Conference." See also "The Rules of the National Industrial Relations Conference," both in PMS. Both documents were marked "J.L." in Springer's hand writing, suggesting copies were sent or intended to be sent to him.

218. Springer to Miller, February 8, 1965, MSKP.

219. Handwritten Notes to "J.L." on "Report of the Committee on Productivity of First National Industrial relations Conference" in MSKP. See also "Provisional Record No. III," National Industrial Relations Conference, List of Participants, in same.

220. "Venerable Order of Human Rights," MSKP. Stephen Hlophe, *Class, Ethnicity, and Politics in Liberia: A Class Analysis of Power Struggles in the Tubman and Tolbert administrations, 1944–1975* (Washington, DC: University Press of America, 1979), chapter 5.

221. Carl E. Meacham, "Peace Corps Service in Liberia, 1965–66: Reflections of an African American Volunteer," *Liberian Studies Journal* 15 (1990) 1: 94. Bayo Lawal, "Double-Consciousness and the Homecoming of African Americans: Building Cultural Bridges in West Africa," in *The United States and West Africa*.

222. Springer to "Dear Shad," February 15, 1965, MSKP.

223. Springer to Jay Lovestone, February 9, 1965, and attached memorandum; Springer to James E. Bass, April 1, 1965. "Labour's Role in the Post-National Industrial Relations Conference for the Implementation of Its Apparent Gains," February 1, 1965, all in MSKP. Richards, *Maida Springer*, 248.

224. "Liberian Troops Act in Strike," February 4, 1966; "10,000 Rubber Workers End 5-Day Walkout in Liberia," February 8, 1966, both in *New York Times*.

225. William V. S. Tubman, "A Nation-Wide Broadcast on the Firestone Strike," Monrovia, February 12, 1966, in *Official Papers*, 375–378. Emphasis added.

226. "Brief Account of the Discussion Held between the Liberian Government Delegation and Representatives of the International Free Labour Movement," February 1967, Lovestone Papers. "Jailed CIO Men Are to Be Tried," September 1961, clippings in Claude Barnett Research Collection.

227. Tubman, "A Nation-Wide Broadcast," in *Official Papers*, 378.

228. "Brief Account of the Discussion Held between the Liberian Government Delegation and the Representatives of the International Free Labour Movement."

229. Tubman, "A Nation-Wide Broadcast," in *Official Papers*, 378.

230. "Statement Concerning Labor Problems in Liberia," Lovestone Papers.

231. Jay Lovestone to Maida Springer, March 4, 1965, Lovestone Papers.

232. Richards, *Maida Springer*, 254.

233. Frazier, "What Can the American Negro Contribute to African Social Development?" 277.

234. Murray identified publicly as a "Negro woman," but privately gave voice to her more complex heritage, which included Native American ancestors. Springer referred to her as "Dearest Pawnee" (see note 156). Anne Rapp, "Black Liberation Is an International Cause: Charlotta Bass's Transnational Politics, 1914–1952," in *Women and Transnational Activism in Historical Perspective*, ed. Kimberly Jensen and Erika Kuhlman (Dordrecht, Netherlands: Republic of Letters Publishing, 2010), 89–116.

235. Pauli Murray to Spingarn Award Committee, April 7, 1959 in CZP.
236. Richards, *Maida Springer*, chapter 9; "Maida Springer Is on AFL-CIO Staff" (May 15, 1960): 10, and "6 African Unionists Finish Training at ILG Hq." (December 1, 1961): 8, in *Justice*. Springer "Africa Programs and Activities of the Department of International Affairs, AFL-CIO, 1961–63," in MSKP. "African Students Start ILG Training Course" (July 1, 1961): 3, and "Curriculum for Progress" (August 15, 1961): 6–7, in *Justice*.
237. Granger to Springer, February 24, 1963, PMS.
238. Richards, *Maida Springer*, chapter 6.
239. Maida Springer, "Africans War on Poverty, Ignorance, Prejudice," *Free Trade Union News* (July 1957): 7.
240. Maida Springer to William Schnitzler, December 5, 1959, PMS.
241. Maida Springer to Skipper [Caroline Ware], December 18, 1957, PMS.

Conclusion

1. Ann Laura Stoler, "Tense and Tender Ties: The Politics of Comparison in North American History and (Post) Colonial Studies" in *Haunted by Empire: Geographies of Intimacy in North American History*, ed. Ann Laura Stoler (Durham, NC: Duke University Press, 2006), 23–70.
2. For a survey of related issues touching on teaching US history outside of the United States, see "Teaching U.S. History Abroad," *Journal of American History* 96 (2010) 4: 1085–1144.
3. Ann Laura Stoler, *Along the Archival Grain: Epistemic Anxieties and Colonial Common Sense* (Princeton, NJ: Princeton University Press, 2009). Antoinette Burton, *Dwelling in the Archive: Women Writing House, Home, and History in Late Colonial India* (Oxford: Oxford University Press, 2003). Carolyn Steedman, *Dust: The Archive and Cultural History* (New Brunswick, NJ: Rugters University Press, 2002).
4. Chicago Historical Society has two entries for the Claude A Barnett Papers, the original manuscript materials and the UPA microfilm. http://www.chsmedia. org:8081/ipac20/ipac.jsp?session=E27R7E0406352.705&profile=public&source=~! horizon&view=subscriptionsummary&uri=full=3100046~!65199~!5&ri=1&aspect =subtab112&menu=search&ipp=20&spp=20&staffonly=&term=associated+negro +press&index=.GW&uindex=&aspect=subtab112&menu=search&ri=1. Viewed on June 17, 2010.
5. "On Transnational History," *The American Historical Review* 111 (2006) 5: 1447; Laura Briggs, "Gender and Imperialism in U.S. Women's History," in *The Practice of U.S. Women's History: Narratives, Intersections and Dialogues*, ed. S. J. Kleinberg, Eileen Boris, and Vicki Ruíz (New Brunswick, NJ: Rutgers University Press, 2007), 153.
6. According to Dr. Verlon Stone at Indiana University, The National Archives Records Administration of the United States holds approximately a 1,000 linear feet, the Liberia Collection at the University of Indiana holds about 500 feet, and the Schomburg Center for Research in Black Culture holds slightly less. For details about the restoration of the William V. S. Tubman Papers and the new microform edition, see: http://www.onliberia.org/index_tubman.htm. The Executive Mansion Presidential Archives in Monrovia has the most material (approximately 5,000), but it is currently not open to users. Email from Verlon Stone to author, July 21, 2010.

Bibliography

Primary Sources—Manuscript Archives

Annapolis, Maryland
Maryland State Archives
    Maryland Clubwoman Papers

Baltimore, Maryland
Baltimore Museum of Art
    Dr. Claribel and Miss Etta Cone Papers

Bloomington, Indiana
University of Indiana
    Liberia Collection

Cambridge, Massachusetts
Schlesinger Library, Radcliffe Institute, Harvard University
    Maida Springer Kemp Papers
    Pauli Murray Papers

College Park, Maryland
National Archives and Records Administration
    RG 350 Records of the Bureau of Insular Affairs
    RG 59 Records of the U.S. Department of State, Passports, Great Britain

Evanston, Illinois
Melville J. Herskovits Library of African Studies, Northwestern University
    Claude A. Barnett Research Collection

Ithaca, New York
Kheel Center for Labor-Management Documentation & Archives, Cornell University
    Charles Zimmerman Papers

London, England
British Library
    John Lane Papers

New Brunswick, New Jersey

Rutgers University Library Special Collections, Rutgers University
Frances R. Grant Papers

New Haven, Connecticut

Beinecke Rare Book and Manuscript Library, Yale University
Stein-Toklas Papers

New Orleans, Louisiana

Amistad Research Center, Tulane University
Papers of Maida Springer

New York City, New York

Rare Book and Manuscript Library, Columbia University
Bennett Cerf Papers
Centro de Estudios Puertorriqueños, Hunter College
Josefina Silva de Cintrón (vertical file)
Municipal Archives, New York City Department of Records
Marriage Records
Manuscripts and Archives Division, New York Public Library
New York World's Fair 1939 and 1940 Incorporated Records

Palo Alto, California

Hoover Institute Archives, Stanford University
Jay Lovestone Papers

Primary Sources—microform/electronic editions

Ancestry.com (online database)
Calvin Coolidge Papers (Library of Congress)
Despatches from the US Ministers to Liberia, 1863–1906 (Schomburg Center for Research in Black Culture)
Documenting the American South (University of North Carolina, Chapel Hill)
New York Times Historical File, 1851–2001 (online database)
Papers of A. Philip Randolph (University Publications of America)
Records of the American Colonization Society (Library of Congress)
William V. S. Tubman Papers (Indiana University Archives of Traditional Music)

Primary Sources—major newspapers and periodicals (selected)

Artes y Letras, New York, NY
African Repository and Colonial Journal, Washington, DC
Atlantic Monthly, Boston, MA
Bulletin of the Pan American Union, Washington, DC
Christian Standard, Cincinnati, OH
Free Trade Union News, Washington, DC
International African Opinion, London, England

Justice: International Ladies' Garment Workers' Union, New York, NY
North American Review, Boston, MA
Opportunity Magazine, New York, NY
Prensa, New York, NY
Psychological Review, Washington, DC

Primary Sources (selected)

American Society of African Culture. *Africa from the Point of View of American Negro scholars*. Paris: Présence Africaine, 1958.

Balanoff, Betty. "Interview with Maida Springer Kemp," 1970. http://www2.roosevelt .edu/library/oralhistory/oralhistory.htm.

Barlow, Judith E. *Plays by American Women, 1930–1960*. New York: Applause, 1994.

Blyden, Edward. *Black Spokesman: Selected Published Writings of Edward Wilmot Blyden*. Edited by Hollis R. Lynch. New York: Humanities Press, 1971.

———. *Christianity, Islam and the Negro Race*. Edinburgh: University Press, 1967.

———. *Liberia's Offering: Being Addresses, Sermons, etc.* New York: J. A. Gray, 1862.

Brown, Hallie Q. *Homespun Heroines and Other Women of Distinction*. New York: Oxford University Press, 1988.

Buell, Raymond. *The Native Problem in Africa*. New York: The Macmillan Company, 1928.

Camblor, Angel. *La Bandera De La Raza: Símbolo De Las Américas En El Cielo De Buenos Aires; Breve Exposición Por El Creador De La Bandera Y Notas De La Prensa Argentina Con Motivo Del Izamiento De La Enseña Común, En La Rural De Palermo, El Día 12 De Octubre De 1933. Contribución a La Historia Y a La Propagación Del Ideal*. Montevideo: Editorial Unión Hispanamericana, 1935.

Cerf, Bennett. *At Random: The Reminiscences of Bennett Cerf*. New York: Random House, 1977.

Chenault, Lawrence Royce. *The Puerto Rican Migrant in New York City*. New York: Russell & Russell, 1970.

Clark, Victor and Brookings Institution. *Porto Rico and Its Problems*. Washington, DC: Brookings Institution, 1930.

Colón, Jesús. *A Puerto Rican in New York, and Other Sketches*. New York: International Publishers, 1982.

Cunard, Nancy and George Padmore. *The White Man's Duty: An Analysis of the Colonial Question in the Light of the Atlantic Charter*. London: W. H. Allen, 1942.

Delany, Martin R. *Principia of Ethnology: The Origin of Races and Color, with an Archeological Compendium of Ethiopian and Egyptian Civilization, from Years of Careful Examination and Enquiry*. Philadelphia, PA: Harper & Brothers, 1879.

Du Bois, W. E. B. *The College-Bred Negro Report of a Social Study Made under the Direction of Atlanta University; Together with the Proceedings of the Fifth Conference for the Study of the Negro Problems, Held at Atlanta University, May 29–30, 1900*. Atlanta University publications, no. 5. Atlanta, GA: Atlanta University Press, 1900.

Duster, Alfreda M. ed. *Crusade for Justice: The Autobiography of Ida B. Wells*. Chicago, IL: University of Chicago Press, 1970.

Emerson, Ralph Waldo. *The Complete Essays and Other Writings of Ralph Waldo Emerson*. New York: Random House, 1950.

Gallup, Donald Clifford. *The Flowers of Friendship: Letters Written to Gertrude Stein*. New York: Octagon Books, 1979.

Gilman, Charlotte Perkins. *Women and Economics: A Study of the Economic Relation between Men and Women as a Factor in Social Evolution*. New York: Harper & Row, 1966.

Hedgeman, Anna Arnold. *The Trumpet Sounds: A Memoir of Negro Leadership.* New York: Holt, Rinehart and Winston, 1964.

Inter-American Commission of Women. *A Summary of the Activities of the Inter-American Commission of Women, 1928–1947.* Washington, DC: Pan American Union, 1947.

James, William. *The Principles of Psychology.* New York: Dover Publications, 1950.

———. *The Writings of William James: A Comprehensive Edition, Including an Annotated Bibliography Updated through 1977.* Chicago, IL: University of Chicago Press, 1977.

Labarthe, Pedro Juan. *The Son of Two Nations: The Private Life of a Columbia Student.* New York: Carranza & Co., 1931.

Lewis, David Levering, ed. *W. E. B. Du Bois: A Reader.* New York: Holt Paperbacks, 1995.

Liberia. Office of National Planning. *Study of the Firestone Strike: Progress Report.* [Monrovia, 1964].

Lutz, Bertha. *Nationality of Married Women in the American Republics.* Washington, DC: Pan American Union, 1926.

Martí, José. *José Martí: Selected Writings.* Ed. Esther Allen and Roberto González Echevarriía. New York: Penguin Books, 2002.

Martínez, Frank. *The Tragedy of the Puerto Ricans and the Colored Americans: A Summary of the Political Situation in the 17th A.D., Manhattan.* New York: n.p. 1935.

Murray, Pauli. *Pauli Murray: The Autobiography of a Black Activist, Feminist, Lawyer, Priest and Poet.* Knoxville: University of Tennessee Press, 1989.

Nelson, Carolyn Christensen. *A New Woman Reader: Fiction, Articles, and Drama of the 1890s.* Peterborough, ON: Broadview Press, 2001.

Nordau, Max Simon. *Degeneration.* London: W. Heinemann, 1895.

Padmore, George. *Africa: Britain's Third Empire.* New York: Negro Universities Press, 1969.

———. *American Imperialism Enslaves Liberia.* Moscow: Centrizdat, 1931.

———. *How Russia Transformed Her Colonial Empire: A Challenge to the Imperialist Powers.* London: Dennis Dobson, 1946.

———. *Pan-Africanism or Communism? The Coming Struggle for Africa.* Garden City, NJ: Anchor Books, 1972.

Padmore, George A. *The Memoirs of a Liberian Ambassador, George Arthur Padmore.* Lewiston, NY: E. Mellen Press, 1996.

Parkhurst, G. "Is Feminism Dead?" *Harper's Magazine* 170 (May 1935): 735–745.

Reed. Myrtle. *Lavender and Old Lace.* New York, London, G. P. Putnam's sons, 1908.

Reid, Ira De Augustine. *The Negro Immigrant, His Background, Characteristics, and Social Adjustment, 1899–1937.* New York: Columbia University Press, 1939.

Richards, Yevette. *Conversations with Maida Springer: A Personal History of Labor, Race, and International Relations.* Pittsburgh, PA: University of Pittsburgh Press, 2004.

Robles de Mendoza, Margarita. *Ciudadanía De La Mujer Mexicana.* Morelia, MI: A. Obregon, 1932.

———. *La Evolución De La Mujer En México.* México: Imp. Galas, 1931.

Roosevelt, Theodore. *Colonial Policies of the United States.* New York: Arno Press, 1970.

Rowe, Leo S. *The United States and Porto Rico.* New York: Arno Press, 1975.

Schuyler, George. *Slaves Today: A Story of Liberia.* College Park: McGrath Pub. Co., 1969.

Smith, Amanda. *An Autobiography: The Story of the Lord's Dealings with Mrs. Amanda Smith, the Colored Evangelist.* New York: Oxford University Press, 1988.

Smith, C. S. and University of North Carolina at Chapel Hill. *A History of the African Methodist Episcopal Church Being a Volume Supplemental to A History of the African Methodist Episcopal Church, by Daniel Alexander Payne, D.D., LL. D., Late One of its*

Bishops. Chapel Hill: Academic Affairs Library, University of North Carolina at Chapel Hill, 2001.

Solá, Mercedes. *Feminismo: Estudio Sobre Su Aspecto Social, Económico Y Político*. San Juan, P.R: Cantero, Fernández & Co, 1922.

Springer, Maida. "Toward a New Job Outlook." *Opportunity* 24 (April 1946): 82–83.

Stein, Gertrude. *Everybody's Autobiography*. New York: Vintage Books, 1973.

———. *Fernhurst, Q.E.D., and Other Early Writings*. New York: Liveright, 1971.

———. *Four in America*. New Haven, CT: Yale University Press, 1947.

———. *Lectures in America*. Boston, MA: Beacon Press, 1985.

———. *PICASSO The Complete Writings*. Boston, MA: Beacon Press, 1985.

———. *Matisse Picasso and Gertrude Stein: With Two Shorter Stories*. Mineola, NY: Dover Publications, 2000.

———. *Tender Buttons: Objects, Food, Rooms*. Los Angeles, CA: Sun & Moon Press, 1991.

———. *The Autobiography of Alice B. Toklas*. New York: Vintage Books, 1960.

———. *The Geographical History of America, or, the Relation of Human Nature to the Human Mind*. Baltimore, MD: Johns Hopkins University Press, 1995.

———. *The Letters of Gertrude Stein and Carl Van Vechten, 1913–1946*. New York: Columbia University Press, 1986.

———. *The Making of Americans: Being a History of a Family's Progress*. Normal, IL: Dalkey Archive Press, 1995.

———. *Wars I Have Seen*. New York: Random House, 1945.

Stewart, T. *Liberia: The Americo-African Republic: Being Some Impressions of the Climate, Resources, and People, Resulting from Personal Observations and Experiences in West Africa*. New York: E. O. Jenkins' Sons, 1886.

Taylor, Marshall. *The Life, Travels, Labors, and Helpers of Mrs. Amanda Smith the Famous Negro Missionary Evangelist*. Cincinnati, OH: Printed by Cranston & Stowe for the author, 1886.

Taylor, Wayne Chatfield and National Planning Association. *The Firestone Operations in Liberia*. Washington, DC: National Planning Association, 1956.

Taylor, William. *Story of My Life; an Account of What I Have Thought and Said and Done in My Ministry of More Than Fifty-Three Years in Christian Lands and among the Heathen*. New York: Hunt & Eaton, 1895.

———. *The Flaming Torch in Darkest Africa*. New York: Eaton & Mains, 1898.

Tubman, William and Liberia. *The Official papers of William V. S. Tubman, President of the Republic of Liberia: Covering Addresses, Messages, Speeches and Statements 1960– 1967*. London: published for the Department of Information and Cultural Affairs Monrovia, Liberia, by Longmans, 1968.

Van Vechten, Carl. *Selected Writings of Gertrude Stein*. New York: Vintage, 1972.

Vasconcelos, José. *The Cosmic Race: A Bilingual Edition*. Baltimore, MD: Johns Hopkins University Press, 1997.

Vega, Bernardo. *Memoirs of Bernardo Vega: A Contribution to the History of the Puerto Rican Community in New York*. New York: Monthly Review Press, 1984.

Young, Rose and National Committee on the Cause and Cure of War (US). *Why Wars Must Cease*. New York: The Macmillan Co., 1935.

Secondary Sources (selected)

"AHR Conversation: On Transnational History." *American Historical Review*. 111 (2006) 5: 1440–1464.

Acosta-Belén, Edna. *The Puerto Rican Woman: Perspectives on Culture, History and Society*. New York: Praeger, 1986.

Alonso, Harriet Hyman. *Peace as a Women's Issue: A History of the U.S. Movement for World Peace and Women's Rights*. Syracuse, NY: Syracuse University Press, 1993.

Anderson, Carol. *Eyes off the Prize: The United Nations and the African American Struggle for Human Rights, 1944–1955*. New York: Cambridge University Press, 2003.

Ashton, Jennifer. *From Modernism to Postmodernism: American Poetry and Theory in the Twentieth Century*. Cambridge, UK: Cambridge University Press, 2008.

Ayala, Cesar J. and Rafael Bernabe. *Puerto Rico in the American Century: A History since 1898*. Chapel Hill: The University of North Carolina Press, 2007.

Ballantyne, Tony and Antoinette Burton, eds. *Bodies in Contact: Rethinking Colonial Encounters in World History*. Durham, NC: Duke University Press, 2005.

――――. *Moving Subjects: Gender, Mobility and Intimacy in an Age of Global Empire*. Urbana: University of Illinois Press, 2009.

Baum, Bruce and Duchess Harris, eds. *Racially Writing the Republic: Racists, Race Rebels, and Transformations of American Identity*. Durham, NC: Duke University Press, 2009.

Bay, Mia. *The White Image in the Black Mind: African-American Ideas about White People, 1830–1925*. New York: Oxford University Press, 2000.

Beckson, Karl E. *London in the 1890s: A Cultural History*. New York: W. W. Norton, 1992.

Bederman, Gail. *Manliness & Civilization: A Cultural History of Gender and Race in the United States, 1880–1917*. Chicago, IL: University of Chicago Press, 1995.

Bender, Thomas, ed. *Rethinking American History in a Global Age*. Berkeley: University of California Press, 2002.

Bergmann, Emilie L., ed. *Women, Culture, and Politics in Latin America*. Berkeley: University of California Press, 1990.

Branche, Jerome, ed. *Race, Colonialism, and Social Transformation in Latin America and the Caribbean*. Gainesville: University Press of Florida, 2008.

Bredbenner, Candice Lewis. *A Nationality of Her Own Women, Marriage, and the Law of Citizenship*. Berkeley: University of California Press, 1998.

Briggs, Laura. "The Race of Hysteria: 'Overcivilization and the 'Savage' Woman in Late Nineteenth-Century Obstetrics and Gynecology." *American Quarterly* 52 (2000) 2: 246–273.

――――. *Reproducing Empire: Race, Sex, Science, and U.S. Imperialism in Puerto Rico*. Berkeley: University of California Press, 2002.

Briggs, Laura, Gladys McCormick, and J. T. Way. "Transnationalism: A Category of Analysis." *American Quarterly* 60 (2008) 3: 625–648.

Burnett, Christina Duffy and Burke Marshall, eds. *Foreign in a Domestic Sense: Puerto Rico, American Expansion, and the Constitution*. Durham, NC: Duke University Press, 2001.

Campbell, James T. *Middle Passages: African American Journeys to Africa, 1787–2005*. New York: Penguin Press, 2006.

――――. *Songs of Zion: The African Methodist Episcopal Church in the United States and South Africa*. New York: Oxford University Press, 1995.

Canaday, Margot. *The Straight State: Sexuality and Citizenship in Twentieth-Century America*. Princeton, N.J.: Princeton University Press, 2009.

Carew, Anthony. "The American Labor Movement in Fizzland: The Free Trade Union Committee and the C.I.A." *Labor History* 39 (1998) 1: 25–42.

Carrasquillo, Rosa. *Our Landless Patria: Marginal Citizenship and Race in Caguas, Puerto Rico, 1880–1910*. Lincoln: University of Nebraska Press, 2006.

Choy, Catherine Ceniza. *Empire of Care: Nursing and Migration in Filipino American History*. Durham, NC: Duke University Press, 2003.

Clegg, Claude Andrew. *The Price of Liberty: African Americans and the Making of Liberia*. Chapel Hill: University of North Carolina Press, 2004.

Cole, Catherine M., Takyiwaa Manuh, and Stephen Miescher, eds. *Africa After Gender?* Bloomington: Indiana University Press, 2007.

Cope, Karin. *Passionate Collaborations: Learning to Live with Gertrude Stein*. Victoria, BC: ELS Editions, 2005.

Crunden, Robert Morse. *American Salons: Encounters with European Modernism, 1885–1917*. New York: Oxford University Press, 1993.
———. *Body & Soul: The Making of American Modernism*. New York: Basic Books, 2000.
Curnutt, Kirk, ed. *The Critical Response to Gertrude Stein*. Westport, CT: Greenwood Press, 2000.
Currell, Susan and Christina Cogdell, eds. *Popular Eugenics: National Efficiency and American Mass Culture in the 1930s*. Athens: Ohio University Press, 2006.
Curthoys, Ann and Marilyn Lake, eds. *Connected Worlds: History in Transnational Perspective*. Canberra: Australian National University, 2004.
Damon, Maria. "Gertrude Stein's Jewishness, Jewish Social Scientists, and the 'Jewish Question.'" *Modern Fiction Studies* 42 (1996)3: 489–506.
DeGuzmán, María. *Spain's Long Shadow: The Black Legend, Off-Whiteness, and Anglo-American Empire*. Minneapolis: University of Minnesota Press, 2005.
Doane, Janice L. *Silence and Narrative: The Early Novels of Gertrude Stein*. Westport, CT: Greenwood Press, 1986.
Dorr, Rheta Childe. *Susan B. Anthony, the Woman Who Changed the Mind of a Nation*. New York: Frederick A. Stokes, 1928.
Duany, Jorge. *The Puerto Rican Nation on the Move: Identities on the Island & in the United States*. Chapel Hill: University of North Carolina Press, 2002.
———. "The Rough Edges of Puerto Rican Identities: Race, Gender, and Transnationalism." *Latin American Research Review* 40 (2005) 3: 177–190.
Dudziak, Mary. *Cold War Civil Rights: Race and the Image of American Democracy*. Princeton NJ: Princeton University Press, 2000.
Fahs, Alice. "The Feminized Civil War: Gender, Northern Popular Literature, and the Memory of the War, 1861–1900." *Journal of American History* 85 (1999) 4: 1461.
Farland, Maria. "Gertrude Stein's Brain Work." *American Literature* 76 (2005) 1: 117–148.
Fernandez, Ronald. *The Disenchanted Island: Puerto Rico and the United States in the Twentieth Century*. New York: Praeger, 1992.
Findlay, Eileen. *Imposing Decency: The Politics of Sexuality and Race in Puerto Rico, 1870–1920*. Durham, NC: Duke University Press, 1999.
Flores, Juan. *Divided Borders: Essays on Puerto Rican Identity*. Houston, TX: Arte Público Press, 1993.
Fredrickson, George M. *The Black Image in the White Mind: The Debate on Afro-American Character and Destiny, 1817–1914*. New York: Harper & Row, 1971.
Gaines, Kevin Kelly. *American Africans in Ghana: Black Expatriates and the Civil Rights Era*. Chapel Hill: University of North Carolina Press, 2006.
Galvin, Miles. *The Organized Labor Movement in Puerto Rico*. Cranbury, NJ: Associated University Presses, 1979.
Geiger, Susan. "Women in Nationalist Struggle: Tanu Activists in Dar es Salaam." *International Journal of African Historical Studies* 20 (1987)1: 1–26.
Geiss, Imanuel. *The Pan-African Movement: A History of Pan-Africanism in America, Europe, and Africa*. New York: Africana Pub. Co., 1974.
Gilkes, Cheryl. *If It Wasn't for the Women: Black Women's Experience and Womanist Culture in Church and Community*. Maryknoll, NY: Orbis Books, 2001.
Go, Julian. *American Empire and the Politics of Meaning: Elite Political Cultures in the Philippines and Puerto Rico during U.S. Colonialism*. Durham, NC: Duke University Press, 2008.
Goldstein, Eric L. "The Unstable Other: Locating the Jew in Progressive-Era American Racial Discourse." *American Jewish History* 89 (2001) 4: 383–409.
Graham, Richard. *The Idea of Race in Latin America, 1870–1940*. Austin: University of Texas Press, 1990.
Green, Nancy L. "Blacks, Jews, and the 'Natural Alliance' Labor Cohabitation and the ILGWU." *Jewish Social Studies* 4 (1997) 1: 79–104.

Green, Nancy L. *Ready-to-Wear and Ready-to-Work: A Century of Industry and Immigrants in Paris and New York*. Durham, NC: Duke University Press, 1997.

Grewal, Inderpal. *Transnational America: Feminisms, Diasporas, Neoliberalisms*. Durham, NC: Duke University Press, 2005.

Guglielmo, Jennifer. "Transnational Feminism's Radical Past: Lessons from Italian Immigrant Women Anarchists in Industrializing America." *Journal of Women's History* 22 (2010) 1: 10–33.

Guglielmo, Jennifer and Salvatore Salerno, eds. *Are Italians White? How Race Is Made in America*. New York: Routledge, 2003.

Guglielmo, Thomas A. "'Red Cross, Double Cross': Race and America's World War II—Era Blood Donor Service." *Journal of American History* 97 (2010) 1: 63–90.

Guy, Donna J. "The Politics of Pan-American Cooperation: Maternalist Feminism and the Child Rights Movement, 1913–1960." *Gender & History* 10 (1998) 3: 449–469.

Hall, Catherine and Keith McClelland, eds. *Race, Nation and Empire: Making Histories, 1750 to the Present*. Manchester: University of Manchester Press, 2010.

Hansen, Karen. *African Encounters with Domesticity*. New Brunswick, NJ: Rutgers University Press, 1992.

Harmon, Robert B. *The First Editions of Gertrude Stein*. Los Altos, CA: Hermes Publications, 1978.

Harrowitz, Nancy and Barbara Hyams, eds. *Jews & Gender: Responses to Otto Weininger*. Philadelphia, PA: Temple University Press, 1995.

Harper, Ida Husted. *Life and Work of Susan B. Anthony*. Salem, NH: Ayer Co., 1983.

Hawkins, Stephanie L. "The Science of Superstition: Gertrude Stein, William James, and the Formation of Belief." *Modern Fiction Studies* 51 (2005) 1: 60–87.

Heilmann, Ann. *New Woman Fiction: Women Writing First-Wave Feminism*. Houndmills, Basingstoke, Hampshire: Macmillan Press, 2000.

Heiss, M. A. "The Evolution of the Imperial Idea and U.S. National Identity." *Diplomatic History* 26 (2002) 4: 511–540.

Hoffman, Michael, ed. *Critical Essays on Gertrude Stein*. Boston, MA: G. K. Hall, 1986.

Hoganson, Kristin L. "'As Badly off as the Filipinos': U.S. Women's Suffragists and the Imperial Issue at the Turn of the Twentieth Century." *Journal of Women's History* 13 (2001) 2: 9–33.

———. *Consumers' Imperium: The Global Production of American Domesticity, 1865–1920*. Chapel Hill: University of North Carolina Press, 2007.

Horsman, Reginald. *Race and Manifest Destiny: The Origins of American Racial Anglo-Saxonism*. Cambridge: Harvard University Press, 1981.

Hunter, Jane. *The Gospel of Gentility: American Women Missionaries in Turn-of-the-Century China*. New Haven, CT: Yale University Press, 1984.

Iriye, Akira. *Cultural Internationalism and World Order*. Baltimore, MD: Johns Hopkins University Press, 1997.

Israel, Adrienne. *Amanda Berry Smith: From Washerwoman to Evangelist*. Lanham, MD: Scarecrow Press, 1998.

Jacobs, Sylvia. *Black Americans and the Missionary Movement in Africa*. Westport, CT: Greenwood Press, 1982.

Jacobson, Matthew. *Barbarian Virtues: The United States Encounters Foreign Peoples at Home and Abroad, 1876–1917*. New York: Hill and Wang, 2000.

Jalloh, Alusine and Toyin Falola, eds. *The United States and West Africa: Interactions and Relations*. Rochester, NY: University of Rochester Press, 2008.

Jameson, Elizabeth and Susan Armitage, eds. *Writing the Range: Race, Class, and Culture in the Women's West*. Norman: University of Oklahoma Press, 1997.

Jarrett-Macauley, Delia. *The Life of Una Marson, 1905–65*. Manchester: Manchester University Press, 1998.

Jensen, Kimberly and Erika Kuhlman, eds. *Women and Transnational Activism in Historical Perspective*. Dordrecht: Republic of Letters, 2010.

Jiménez-Munoz, Gladys. "Carmen Maria Colon Pellot: On 'Womanhood' and 'Race' in Puerto Rico during the Interwar Period." *CR: The New Centennial Review* 3 (2003) 3: 71–91.

———. "Deconstructing Colonialist Discourse: Links between the Women's Suffrage Movement in the United States and Puerto Rico." *Phoebe: An International Journal of Feminist Scholarship, Theory, and Aesthetics* 5 (1993): 9–34.

Johnson, Robert David. "Anti-Imperialism and the Good Neighbour Policy: Ernest Gruening and Puerto Rican Affairs, 1934–1939." *Journal of Latin American Studies* 29 (February 1997) 1: 89–110.

Joseph, G. M., Catherine LeGrand, and Ricardo Donato Salvatore, eds. *Close Encounters of Empire: Writing the Cultural History of US-Latin American Relations*. Durham, NC: Duke University Press, 1998.

Journal of American History. Special Issue. *The Nation and Beyond: Transnational Perspectives on United States History* 86 (1999) 3: 965–1307.

Kaplan, Amy. *The Anarchy of Empire in the Making of U.S. Culture*. Cambridge: Harvard University Press, 2002.

Kaplan, Caren, Norma Alarcón, and Minoo Moallem, eds. *Between Woman and Nation: Nationalisms, Transnational Feminisms, and the State*. Durham, NC: Duke University Press, 1999.

Katz, Daniel. "Race, Gender, and Labor Education; ILGWU Locals 22 and 91, 1933–1937." *Labor's Heritage* 11 (2000) 1: 4–19.

Katz, Leon. "The First Making of 'The Making of Americans': A Study Based on Gertrude Stein's Notebooks and Early Versions of Her Novel (1902–1908)." PhD diss., Columbia University, 1963.

Kessler-Harris, Alice. "Organizing the Unorganizable: Three Jewish Women and Their Union." *Labor History* 17 (1976) 1: 5–23.

Kleinberg, S. J., Eileen Boris, and Vicki Ruíz, eds. *The Practice of U.S. Women's History: Narratives, Intersections, and Dialogues*. New Brunswick, NJ: Rutgers University Press, 2007.

Knoll, Arthur J. "Firestone's Labor Policy, 1924–1939." *Liberian Studies Journal* 16 (1991) 2: 49–75.

Krase, Jerome and Ray Hutchison, eds. *Race and Ethnicity in New York City*. Amsterdam: Elsevier, 2004.

Krenn, Michael L. *Black Diplomacy: African Americans and the State Department, 1945–1969*. Armonk, NY: M.E. Sharpe, 1999.

Lake, Marilyn. "Nationalist Historiography, Feminist Scholarship, and the Promise and Problems of New Transnational Histories: The Australian Case." *Journal of Women's History* 19 (Spring 2007) 1: 180–186.

Lake, Marilyn and Henry Reynolds. *Drawing the Global Colour Line: White Men's Countries and the International Challenge of Racial Equality*. Cambridge: Cambridge University Press, 2008.

Lara, Irene. "Goddess of the Americas in the Decolonial Imaginary: Beyond the Virtuous Virgin/Pagan Puta Dichotomy." *Feminist Studies* 34 (2008) 1: 99–127.

Latimer, Tirza. "'In the Jealous Way of Pictures': Gertrude Stein's Collections." *Women's Studies* 39 (2010) 6: 562–584.

Lavrin, Asunción. *Women, Feminism, and Social Change in Argentina, Chile, and Uruguay, 1890–1940*. Lincoln: University of Nebraska Press, 1995.

Ledger, Sally. *The New Woman: Fiction and Feminism at the Fin de Siècle*. Manchester: Manchester University Press, 1997.

Levander, Caroline F. and Robert S. Levine, eds. *Hemispheric American Studies*. New Brunswick NJ: Rutgers University Press, 2008.

Liebenow, J. Gus. *Liberia: The Evolution of Privilege*. Ithaca, NY: Cornell University Press, 1969.

_____. *Liberia: The Quest for Democracy*. Bloomington: Indiana University Press, 1987.

Lief, Alfred. *The Firestone Story: A History of the Firestone Tire & Rubber Company*. New York: Whittlesey House, 1951.

Little, Lawrence S. "AME Responses to Events and Issues in Asia in the Age of Imperialism, 1880–1916." *Journal of Asian & African Studies* 33 (November 1998) 4: 317–331.

Lomas, Laura. *Translating Empire: José Martí, Migrant Latino Subjects, and American Modernities*. Durham, NC: Duke University Press, 2008.

Love, Eric Tyrone Lowery. *Race over Empire: Racism and U.S. Imperialism, 1865–1900*. Chapel Hill: University of North Carolina Press, 2004.

Lutz, Alma. *Susan B. Anthony: Rebel, Crusader, Humanitarian*. Boston, MA: Beacon Press, 1959.

Lynch, Hollis Ralph. *Edward Wilmot Blyden: Pan-Negro Patriot 1832–1912*. London: Oxford University Press, 1967.

Lynch, John. *Simón Bolívar: A Life*. New Haven, CT: Yale University Press, 2006.

Lynd, G. E. *The Politics of African Trade Unionism*. New York: Praeger, 1968.

Macías, Anna. *Against All Odds: The Feminist Movement in Mexico to 1940*. Westport, CT: Greenwood Press, 1982.

Mangold, Tom. *Cold Warrior: James Jesus Angleton: The CIA's Master Spy Hunter*. New York: Simon & Schuster, 1991.

Marrable, Manning and Vanessa Agard-Jones, eds. *Transnational Blackness: Navigating the Color Line*. New York: Palgrave Macmillan, 2008.

Masters, Paul E. "The International Labor Organization: America's Withdrawal and Reentry." *International Social Science Review* 71 (1996) 3: 14–26.

Materson, Lisa G. "African American Women's Global Journeys and the Construction of Cross-Ethnic Racial Identity." *Women's Studies International Forum* 32 (January 2009) 1: 35–42.

Mathews, Thomas G. *Puerto Rican Politics and the New Deal*. Gainesville: University of Florida Press, 1960.

May, J. Lewis. *John Lane and the Nineties*. London: John Lane, 1936.

Mayson, Dew Tuan-Wleh and Amos Sawyer. "Labour in Liberia." *Review of African Political Economy*, 14 (April 1979) : 3–15.

M'Bayo, Tamba E. "W. E. B. Du Bois, Marcus Garvey and Pan-Africanism in Liberia, 1919–1924." *Historian* 66 (2004) 1: 19–44.

McCoy, Alfred W. and Francisco A. Scarano, eds. *Colonial Crucible: Empire in the Making of the Modern American State*. Madison: University of Wisconsin Press, 2009.

McLaughlin, Russell U. *Foreign Investment and Development in Liberia*. New York: Praeger, 1966.

Meacham, Carl E. "Peace Corps Service in Liberia, 1965–1966: Reflections of an African-American Volunteer." *Liberian Studies Journal* 15 (1990) 1: 85–107.

Mendoza, Breny, ed. *Rethinking Feminisms in the Americas*. Ithaca, NY: Latin American Studies Program, Cornell University, 2000.

Meriwether, James Hunter. *Proudly We Can Be Africans: Black Americans and Africa, 1935–1961*. Chapel Hill: University of North Carolina Press, 2002.

Meyer, Steven. *Irresistible Dictation: Gertrude Stein and the Correlations of Writing and Science*. Stanford, CA: Stanford University Press, 2001.

Mignolo, Walter D. "Citizenship, Knowledge, and the Limits of Humanity." *American Literary History* 18 (2006) 2: 312–331.

Miller, Marilyn Grace. *Rise and Fall of the Cosmic Race: The Cult of Mestizaje in Latin America*. Austin: University of Texas Press, 2004.

Miller, Rosalind S. *Gertrude Stein: Form and Intelligibility; Containing the Radcliffe Themes*. New York: Exposition Press, 1949.

Mitchell, S. E. *The Women's Revolution in Mexico, 1910–1953.* Lanham, MD: Rowman & Littlefield, 2007.

Moore, Jesse Thomas. *A Search for Equality: The National Urban League, 1910–1961.* University Park: Pennsylvania State University Press, 1981.

Moran, Mary H. *Civilized Women: Gender and Prestige in Southeastern Liberia.* Ithaca, NY: Cornell University Press, 1990.

Morgan, Ted. *A Covert Life: Jay Lovestone, Communist, Anti-communist, and Spymaster.* New York: Random House, 1999.

Moses, Wilson. *Alexander Crummell: A Study of Civilization and Discontent.* New York: Oxford University Press, 1989.

———. *The Golden Age of Black Nationalism, 1850–1925.* New York: Oxford University Press, 1988.

———. *Liberian Dreams: Back-to-Africa Narratives from the 1850s.* University Park: Pennsylvania State University Press, 1998.

Newman, Louise. *White Women's Rights: The Racial Origins of Feminism in the United States.* New York: Oxford University Press, 1999.

Newman, Debra Lynn. "The Emergence of Liberian Women in the Nineteenth Century." PhD diss., Howard University, 1984.

Normandy, Elizabeth L. "African-Americans and U.S. Policy Towards Liberia 1929–35." *Liberian Studies Journal* 18 (1993) 2: 203–230.

Nye, David E. "Ritual Tomorrows: The New York World's Fair of 1939." *History & Anthropology* 6 (1992) 1: 1–21.

O'Farrell, Brigid and Joyce L. Kornbluh. "We Did Change Some Attitudes: Maida Springer-Kemp and the International Ladies' Garment Workers Union." *Women's Studies Quarterly* 23 (Spring–Summer 1995) 1: 41–70.

Oldfield, J. R. "The Protestant Episcopal Church, Black Nationalists, and the Expansion of the West African Missionary Field, 1851–1871." *Church History* 57 (1988) 1: 31–35.

Opie, Frederick Douglass. "Eating, Dancing, and Courting in New York Black and Latino Relations, 1930–1970." *Journal of Social History* 42 (2008) 1: 79–109.

Orleck, Annelise. *Common Sense and a Little Fire: Women and Working-Class Politics in the United States, 1900–1965.* Chapel Hill: University of North Carolina Press, 1995.

Painter, Nell Irvin. *Exodusters: Black Migration to Kansas after Reconstruction.* New York: Knopf, 1977.

———. *The History of White People.* New York: W. W. Norton, 2010.

———. *The Narrative of Hosea Hudson, His Life as a Negro Communist in the South.* Cambridge, MA: Harvard University Press, 1979.

———. "Representing Truth: Sojourner Truth's Knowing and Becoming Known." *Journal of American History* 81 (1994) 2: 461–492.

———. *Sojourner Truth: A Life, A Symbol.* New York: W. W. Norton, 1996.

Panford, Kwamina. "Pan-Africanism, Africans in the Diaspora and the OAU." *Western Journal of Black Studies* 20 (1996) 3: 140–150.

Park, Eunjin. *"White" Americans in "Black" Africa: Black and White American Methodist Missionaries in Liberia, 1820–1875.* New York: Routledge, 2001.

Park, James William. *Latin American Underdevelopment: A History of Perspectives in the United States, 1870–1965.* Baton Rouge: Louisiana State University Press, 1995.

Parmet, Robert D. *The Master of Seventh Avenue: David Dubinsky and the American Labor Movement.* New York: New York University Press, 2005.

Pascoe, Peggy. *What Comes Naturally: Miscegenation Law and the Making of Race in America.* Oxford: Oxford University Press, 2009.

Pasture, Patrick. "A Century of International Trade Unionism." *International Review of Social History* 47 (2002) 2: 277–289.

Patterson, Martha H., ed. *The American New Woman Revisited: A Reader, 1894–1930.* New Brunswick, NJ: Rutgers University Press, 2008.

_____. *Beyond the Gibson Girl: Reimagining the American New Woman, 1895–1915.* Urbana: University of Illinois Press, 2005.

Pernet, Corinne A. "Chilean Feminists, the International Women's Movement and Suffrage, 1915–1950." *Pacific Historical Review* 69 (2000) 4: 663–688.

Pérez, Emma. *The Decolonial Imaginary: Writing Chicanas into History.* Bloomington: Indiana University Press, 1999.

Pierson, Ruth Roach, Nupur Chaudhuri, Beth McAuley, eds. *Nation, Empire, Colony: Historicizing Gender and Race.* Bloomington: Indiana University Press, 1998.

Pike, Fredrick. *FDR's Good Neighbor Policy: Sixty Years of Generally Gentle Chaos.* Austin: University of Texas Press, 1995.

———. *Hispanismo, 1898–1936: Spanish Conservatives and Liberals and their Relations with Spanish America.* Notre Dame, IN: University of Notre Dame Press, 1971.

Plummer, Brenda Gayle. *Rising Wind: Black Americans and U.S. Foreign Affairs, 1935–1960.* Chapel Hill: University of North Carolina Press, 1996.

_____, ed. *Window on Freedom: Race, Civil Rights, and Foreign Affairs, 1945–1988.* Chapel Hill: University of North Carolina Press, 2003.

Pryor, Elizabeth Anne. "'Jim Crow' Cars, Passport Denials and Atlantic Crossings: African-American Travel, Protest, and Citizenship at Home and Abroad, 1827–1865." PhD diss., University of California, Santa Barbara, 2008.

Rado, Lisa, ed. *Rereading Modernism: New Directions in Feminist Criticism.* New York: Garland Publishing, 1994.

Reed, Christopher. *All the World Is Here!: The Black Presence at White City.* Bloomington: Indiana University Press, 2000.

Reef, Catherine. *This Our Dark Country: The American Settlers of Liberia.* New York: Clarion Books, 2002.

Renshaw, Patrick. "Why Shouldn't a Union Man 'Be' a Union Man? The ILGWU and Four." *Journal of American Studies* 29 (1995) 2: 185–198.

Richards, Yevette. *Maida Springer: Pan-Africanist and International Labor Leader.* Pittsburgh, PA: University of Pittsburgh Press, 2000.

———. "Race, Gender, and Anticommunism in the International Labor Movement: The Pan-African Connections of Maida Springer." *Journal of Women's History* 11 (1999) 2: 35–59.

Rodríguez, Félix V. Matos and Linda C. Delgado, eds. *Puerto Rican Women's History: New Perspectives.* Armonk, NY: M.E. Sharpe, 1998.

Rodríguez, Manuel R. "Representing Development: New Perspectives about the New Deal in Puerto Rico, 1933–36." *Centro: Journal of the Center for Puerto Rican Studies* 14 (2002) 2: 148–179.

Rosen, Ellen Israel. *Making Sweatshops: The Globalization of the U.S. Apparel Industry.* Berkeley: University of California Press, 2002.

Rosenberg, Emily S. "The Invisible Protectorate: The United States, Liberia, and the Evolution of Neocolonialism, 1909–40." *Diplomatic History* 9 (1985) 3: 191–214.

Rout, Leslie B. *The Politics of the Chaco Peace Conference, 1935–39.* Austin: University of Texas Press, 1970.

Rowe, John Carlos. *Literary Culture and U.S. Imperialism: From the Revolution to World War II.* Oxford: Oxford University Press, 2000.

Roy-Féquière, Magali. *Women, Creole Identity, and Intellectual Life in Early Twentieth-Century Puerto Rico.* Philadelphia, PA: Temple University Press, 2004.

Ruddick, Lisa Cole. *Reading Gertrude Stein: Body, Text, Gnosis*. Ithaca, NY: Cornell University Press, 1990.

Ruiz, Vicki L. ed., with Ellen Carol DuBois. *Unequal Sisters: An Inclusive Reader in U.S. Women's History*. New York: Routledge, 2008.

Rupp, Leila J. "Challenging Imperialism in International Women's Organizations, 1888–1945." *NWSA Journal* 8 (1996) 1: 8–27.

———. "Constructing Internationalism: The Case of Transnational Women's Organizations, 1888–1945." *American Historical Review* 99 (December 1994) 5: 1571–1600.

Rydell, Robert W. *All the World's a Fair: Visions of Empire at American International Expositions, 1876–1916*. Chicago, IL: University of Chicago Press, 1984.

———. *Fair America: World's Fairs in the United States*. Washington, DC: Smithsonian Institution Press, 2000.

———. *World of Fairs: The Century-of-Progress Expositions*. Chicago, IL: University of Chicago Press, 1993.

Said, Edward. *Orientalism*. New York: Vintage, 1979.

Sánchez Korrol, Virginia. *From Colonia to Community: The History of Puerto Ricans in New York City*. Berkeley: University of California Press, 1994.

———. "In Search of Unconventional Women: Histories of Puerto Rican Women in Religious Vocations before Mid-Century." *Oral History Review* 16 (1988) 2: 47.

Santiago-Valles, Kelvin A. "'Higher Womanhood' Among the 'Lower Races': Julia McNair Henry in Puerto Rico and the 'Burdens' of 1898." *Radical History Review* 73 (1999): 47–74.

Schraeder, Peter J. *United States Foreign Policy toward Africa: Incrementalism, Crisis, and Change*. Cambridge: Cambridge University Press, 1994.

Scott, Bonnie K., ed. *Gender in Modernism: New Geographies, Complex Intersections*. Urbana: University of Illinois Press, 2007.

Scott, Daryl Michael. "Postwar Pluralism, *Brown v. Board of Education*, and the Origins of Multicultural Education." *Journal of American History* 91(2004) 1: 69–82.

Seminar on Feminism and Culture in Latin America. *Women, Culture, and Politics in Latin America*. Berkeley: University of California Press, 1990.

Sengoopta, Chandak. *Otto Weininger: Sex, Science, and Self in Imperial Vienna*. Chicago, IL: University of Chicago Press, 2000.

Sheinin, David, ed. *Beyond the Ideal: Pan Americanism in Inter-American Affairs*. Westport, CT: Greenwood Press, 2000.

Shick, Tom W. *Behold the Promised Land: A History of Afro-American Settler Society in Nineteenth-Century Liberia*. Baltimore, MD: Johns Hopkins University Press, 1980.

Silvestrini, Blanca G. *Historia De Puerto Rico: Trayectoria De Un Pueblo / Luque De Sánchez, María Dolores*. San Juan, P.R.: Ediciones Cultural Panamericana, Rotedic, S. A. Grupo Novograph, 1992.

Sims, Beth. *Workers of the World Undermined: American Labor's Role in U.S. Foreign Policy*. Boston, MA: South End Press, 1992.

Sinha, Manisha and Penny Von Eschen, eds. *Contested Democracy: Freedom, Race, and Power in American History*. New York: Columbia University Press, 2007.

Sinha, Mrinalini. "Mapping the Imperial Social Formation: A Modest Proposal for Feminist History." *Signs* 25 (2000) 4: 1077–1082.

Sneider, Allison. *Suffragists in an Imperial Age: U.S. Expansion and the Woman Question, 1870–1929*. New York: Oxford University Press, 2008.

Soto, Shirlene. *Emergence of the Modern Mexican Woman: Her Participation in Revolution and Struggle for Equality, 1910–1940*. Denver, CO: Arden Press, 1990.

Stanley, Susie. *Holy Boldness: Women Preachers' Autobiographies and the Sanctified Self*. Knoxville: University of Tennessee Press, 2002.

Stecklein, Heather J. "Workers' Control and Militancy in an Iowa Labor Movement: The Use of Wildcat Strikes at the Des Moines Firestone Tire and Rubber Company, 1950–1959." *Annals of Iowa* 64 (2005) 3: 246–265.

Stepan, Nancy. *The Hour of Eugenics: Race, Gender, and Nation in Latin America*. Ithaca, NY: Cornell University Press, 1991.

Stephens, Michelle Ann. *Black Empire: The Masculine Global Imaginary of Caribbean Intellectuals in the United States, 1914–1962*. Durham, NC: Duke University Press, 2005.

Stewart, Allegra. *Gertrude Stein and the Present*. Cambridge: Harvard University Press, 1967.

Stimpson, Catharine R. "Gertrude Stein: Humanism and Its Freaks." *Boundary 2* 12 (1984) 3: 301–319.

Stoler, Ann Laura. *Carnal Knowledge and Imperial Power: Race and the Intimate in Colonial Rule*. Berkeley: University of California Press, 2002.

———, ed. *Haunted by Empire: Geographies of Intimacy in North American History*. Durham, NC: Duke University Press, 2006.

Stoner, John Charles. "Anti-Communism, Anti-Colonialism, and African Labor: The AFL-CIO in Africa, 1955–1975." PhD diss., Columbia University, 2001.

Stoner, K. Lynn. *From the House to the Streets: The Cuban Woman's Movement for Legal Reform, 1898–1940*. Durham, NC: Duke University Press, 1991.

Strout, Cushing. "The Unfinished Arch: William James and the Idea of History." *American Quarterly* 13 (Winter 1961) 4: 505–515.

Sundiata, Ibrahim. *Black Scandal: America and the Liberian Labor Crisis, 1929–1936*. Philadelphia, PA: Institute for the Study of Human Issues, 1980.

Taylor, Melanie. "A Poetics of Difference: *The Making of Americans* and Unreadable Subjects." *NWSA Journal* 15 (2003) 3: 26–42.

Taylor, Ula Y. "'Negro Women Are Great Thinkers as Well as Doers': Amy Jacques-Garvey and Community Feminism in the United States, 1924–1927." *Journal of Women's History* 12 (2000) 2: 104–126.

Terborg-Penn, Rosalyn and Andrea Benton Rushing, eds. *Women in Africa and the African Diaspora: A Reader*. 2nd ed. Washington, DC: Howard University Press, 1996.

Thomas, Lorrin. *Puerto Rican Citizen: History and Political Identity in Twentieth-Century New York City*. Chicago, IL: University of Chicago Press, 2010.

Torpey, John. *The Invention of the Passport: Surveillance, Citizenship, and the State*. New York: Cambridge University Press, 2000.

Tyler-McGraw, Marie. *An African Republic: Black & White Virginians in the Making of Liberia*. Chapel Hill: University of North Carolina Press, 2007.

Tyrrell, Ian. *Reforming the World: The Creation of America's Moral Empire*. Princeton, NJ: Princeton University Press, 2010.

———. *Transnational Nation: United States History in Global Perspective since 1789*. Basingstoke: Palgrave Macmillan, 2007.

———. *Woman's World/Woman's Empire: The Woman's Christian Temperance Union in International Perspective*. Chapel Hill: University of North Carolina Press, 1991.

Von Eschen, Penny M. *Race against Empire: Black Americans and Anticolonialism, 1937–1957*. Ithaca, NY: Cornell University Press, 1997.

Wagers, Kelley. "Gertrude Stein's 'Historical' Living." *Journal of Modern Literature* 31(2008) 3: 22–43.

Wald, Priscilla. *Constituting Americans: Cultural Anxiety and Narrative Form*. Durham, NC: Duke University Press, 1995.

Walker, Jayne L. *The Making of a Modernist: Gertrude Stein from Three Lives to Tender Buttons*. Amherst: University of Massachusetts Press, 1984.

Walters, Ronald. *Pan Africanism in the African Diaspora: An Analysis of Modern Afrocentric Political Movements*. Detroit, MI: Wayne State University Press, 1993.

Wamsley, Esther Sue. "'A Hemisphere of Women': Latin American and U.S. Feminists in the IACW, 1915–1939. PhD diss., Ohio State University, 1998.

Ward, Andrew. *Dark Midnight When I Rise: The Story of the Jubilee Singers, Who Introduced the World to the Music of Black America*. New York: Farrar, Straus, and Giroux, 2000.

Wasserstrom, William. "The Sursymamericubealism of Gertrude Stein." *Twentieth Century Literature: A Scholarly and Critical Journal* 21 (February 1975) 1: 90–106.

Webb, Barbara. "The Centrality of Race to the Modernist Aesthetics of Gertrude Stein's Four Saints in Three Acts." *Modernism/modernity* 7 (2000) 3: 447–469.

Weisenfeld, Judith. *This Far by Faith: Readings in African-American Women's Religious Biography*. New York: Routledge, 1996.

Weiss, M. Lynn. *Gertrude Stein and Richard Wright: The Poetics and Politics of Modernism*. Jackson: University Press of Mississippi, 1998.

Wells, Henry. *The Modernization of Puerto Rico: A Political Study of Changing Values and Institutions*. Cambridge, MA: Harvard University Press, 1969.

Whalen, Carmen Teresa. "Sweatshops Here and There: The Garment Industry, Latinas, and Labor Migrations." *International Labor & Working-Class History* 61 (2002): 45–68.

Whitaker, William G. "The Santiago Iglesias Case, 1901–1902: Origins of American Trade Union Movement in Puerto Rico." *Americas* 24 (1968) 4: 378–393.

White, Deborah Gray. "'YES,' There Is a Black Atlantic." *Itinerario* 23 (1999) 2: 127–140.

Will, Barbara. "Lost in Translation: Stein's Vichy Collaboration." *Modernism/modernity* 11 (2004) 4: 651–668.

Williams, Walter. *Black Americans and the Evangelization of Africa, 1877–1900*. Madison: University of Wisconsin Press, 1982.

Wimberly, Anne Streaty. "Called to Witness, Called to Serve: African American Methodist Women in Liberian Missions 1834–1934." *Methodist History* 34 (1996) 2: 67–77.

Wineapple, Brenda. *Sister Brother: Gertrude and Leo Stein*. New York: G. P. Putnam's Sons, 1996.

Witwer, David. "Westbrook Pegler and the Anti-union Movement." *Journal of American History* 92 (2005) 2: 527–552.

Wolensky, Kenneth C. *Fighting for the Union Label: The Women's Garment Industry and the ILGWU in Pennsylvania*. University Park: Pennsylvania State University Press, 2002.

Zangrando, Robert L. "The NAACP and a Federal Antilynching Bill, 1934–1940." *Journal of Negro History* 50 (1965) 2: 106–117.

Ziker, A. "Containing Democracy: Race, Conservative Politics, and U.S. Foreign Policy in the Postcolonial World, 1948–1968." PhD diss., Rice University, 2008.

Zimmerman, Andrew. "Booker T. Washington, Tuskegee Institute, and the German Empire: Race and Cotton in the Black Atlantic." *German Historical Institute Bulletin* 43 (Fall 2008): 9–20.

Index

Page numbers in italic refer to illustrations

251

Reconciliation Trips, Inc., 109
Reconstruction
  imperialism and, 169
  Smith and, 2, 13, 20, 46
  Stein and, 2, 6, 7, 61, 76, 83
Reconstruction Amendments, 18, 79,
  84, 85
Red Cross, 141
redemptionism, 25, 26, 28, 42–3, 44
Redfern, Philip (character), 65,
  66, 71
Reed, Myrtle, 96, 109
religion
  African, 15, 36
  transnationalism and, 15, 46
  women's authority in, 13–14, 15,
  20, 48
Republican party, 94, 95, 97, 142
Rhodes, Cecil, 150
Richards, Mary Jane, 20
Richards, Yevette, 131, 151, 167
Ricks, Martha, 39
Riggs, Francis E., 117, 118
rights, *see* civil rights
Rivera, Arcadio, 93–4
Roberts, John, 21, 22
Robertsfield, 160–1
Robeson, Paul, 132, 134, 155
Robles, Salazar, 106
Robles de Mendoza, Margarita, 92, 100,
  106, 112, 113, 114
Rockefeller Center, 124–5
Rodriguez, Carlotta, 139–40
Roerich, Nicolay, 107–8, 112
Roerich Museum, 100, 103, 107, 112, 119
Román, Remedios Cruz de, 99, 108,
  122, 123
Romo y Silva, Pura, 99, 107
Roosevelt, Eleanor, 119
Roosevelt, Franklin Delano, 92, 95, 97,
  107, 120, 140
Roosevelt, Theodore, Jr., 94, 121
Root, Elihu, 120
Rowe, Leo S., 110–11, 124
Roy-Féquière, Magali, 99, 103, 115
rubber industry, 8, 21, 129,
  159, 160–3
Ruskin Labor College, 147, 150
Russell, Bertrand, 53

Said, Edward, 9
sainthood, 13, 15, 36, 169
salons, 6, 7, 100
Sánchez Korrol, Virginia, 9

sanctification, *see* holiness
San Juan, Puerto Rico, 95, 99
Santiago-Valles, Kelvin, 105, 126
Sarah (wife of Blyden), 29
schools, *see* education; *individual schools*
Schuyler, George, 148
"scientific" views of race, 7, 24, 25, 57,
  93, 102, 120, 126
Scott, Dred, 16, 18
Scott, Emmet J., 8
Second Conference of African States, 161
Sedgwick, Ellery, 73, 88
Selenia, Luz de, 126
Sex and Character (Weininger), 53, 54
sexism, 29–30, 52, 123–5, 130, 170
sexual politics, 27–8, 29–30, 62
Shad, William, Jr., 160, 162, 163
Sharpe, Mary L., 27
Sheppard, William, 21, 35
Sierra Leone, 30, 32
Silva de Cintrón, Josefina, 2, 7, 9,
  91–127, *98*,170
  early life, 93
  education, 93
  employment, 94, 97, 126–7
  family members, 93–4, 97, 101, 126
  migration, 7, 97, 98
  writings, 100, 101, 111
Silva y Acuñoz, Maria, 93
Silva y Yasta, Josefa, 93, 94, 101
Sinoe County, Liberia, 34
skin
  skin color, 16, 19, 27, 83, 132, 154
  in Stein's work, 70, 83
slavery, 15–16, 20, 23, 26, 38–9,
  42–3, 83
Smith, Al, 95
Smith, Amanda Berry, 2, 5–6, 9, 11–48,
  14, 169–70
  early life, 5–6
  employment, 16, 17–18
  family members, 5–6, 15, 16, 18–19,
  38–9, 44
  travel, 6, 16, 20, 23, 33–5,
  40–4, 169–70
  writings, 12–13, 32, 34, 35–40, 47
Smith, Charles S., 23, 47
"social unionism," 131–2, 136, 157
Solá, Mercedes, 92, 98, 115–16
The Son of Two Nations (Labarthe), 102
South Africa, 20, 157
Southern US, 138–9, 140
Southwestern US, 139–40
Soviet Union, 145, 147–8